D1046765

THE ADVENTURE ZONE

Murder on the Rockport Limited!

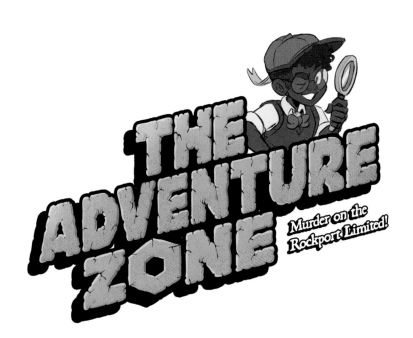

THE ADVENTURE ZONE

Murder on the Rockport Limited!

Based on the podcast by

Griffin McElroy **Clint McElroy**
Travis McElroy **Justin McElroy**

Adaptation by

Clint McElroy **Carey Pietsch**

Art by

Carey Pietsch

First Second
New York

First Second

Text copyright © 2019 by Clint McElroy, Griffin McElroy, Justin McElroy, Travis McElroy
Illustrations copyright © 2019 by Carey Pietsch
Letterer: Tess Stone

Flatters: Megan Brennan, Rachael Cohen, Cassandra Tassoni
Bulletin Board Photo Copyright © 2019 by Megan Brennan and Lisa Aurigemma
Fan Art Gallery Copyright © 2019 by (respectively):
Jay Pirfano
My Murphy
Gene Monteith McKechnie
Galogenida
Jeinu
Starlia Prichard
Pola Kowalewska
Haveafreakday
Nicky Beaton
Phoebe Ayscough
Karoline Stjernfelt
Devon Pasternak

Published by First Second
First Second is an imprint of Roaring Brook Press,
a division of Holtzbrinck Publishing Holdings Limited Partnership
120 Broadway, New York, NY 10271

Don't miss your next favorite book from First Second!
For the latest updates go to firstsecondnewsletter.com and sign up for our newsletter.

All rights reserved

Library of Congress Control Number: 2018953551

ISBN: 978-1-250-15371-5 (Paperback)
ISBN: 978-1-250-22928-1 (Hardcover)
ISBN: 978-1-250-23436-0 (B&N Edition)
ISBN: 978-1-250-24004-0 (Indigo Edition)
ISBN: 978-1-250-25368-2 (BAM Edition)

Our books may be purchased in bulk for promotional, educational, or business use.
Please contact your local bookseller or the Macmillan Corporate and Premium Sales Department
at (800) 221-7945 ext. 5442 or by email at MacmillanSpecialMarkets@macmillan.com.

First edition, 2019
Edited by Calista Brill and Alison Wilgus
Book design by Andrew Arnold and Molly Johanson
Printed in the United States of America

Penciled with a 2B pencil-style tool in Procreate. Inked with a brush-style
digital nib in Clip Studio Paint and colored digitally in Photoshop.

Paperback: 10 9 8 7 6 5 4 3 2 1
Hardcover: 10 9 8 7 6 5 4 3 2 1

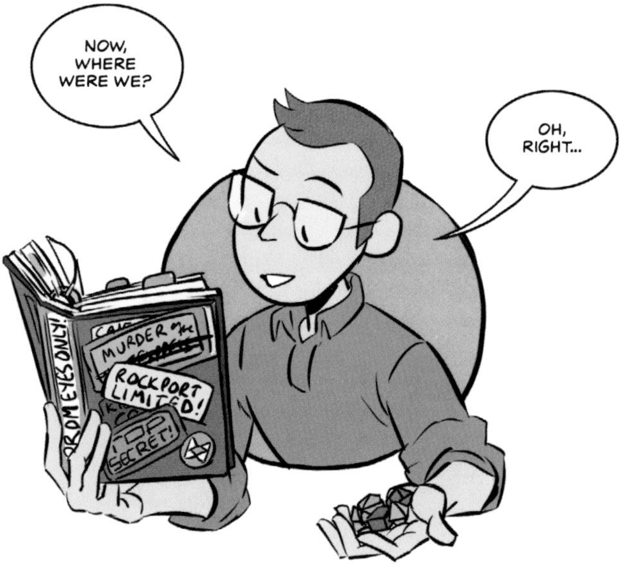
NOW, WHERE WERE WE?
OH, RIGHT...
MURDER on the
ROCKPORT LIMITED!
TOP SECRET!

CAMPAIGN SO FAR:
THE ORIGINAL "CRAIG'S LIST
YOU!
GO ON AN ADVENTU
LOW:
Taako
-Elf mage
- "from TV!"
Merle
-Dwarf Cleric
-#1 Pan Fan!
Magnus
-Human fighter
-Rushing in 24/7!
GERBLINS
RIP...
QUEST BEGIN: SPOOKY CAVE!
HAVERDALE!
Barry
-Human guy
-likes a blue jea
#1 gerblinz boss
G'NASH
(charmed*)
* literally
Merle's cool cousin BOGART

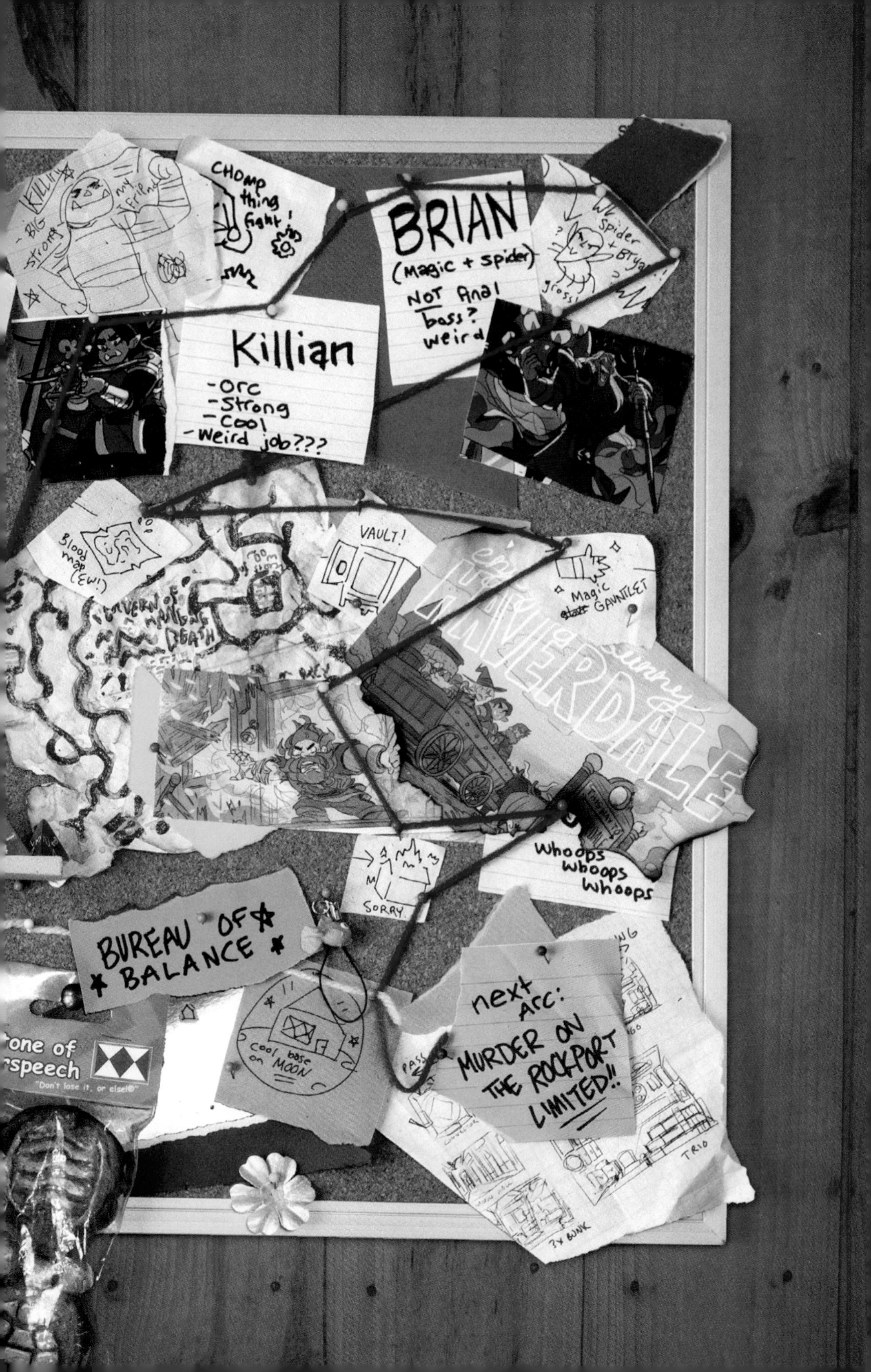

CHOMP thing fight!
BRIAN
(magic + spider)
NOT final boss? weird
gross!
Killian
-Orc
-Strong
-Cool
-weird job???
VAULT!
Magic GAUNTLET
whoops whoops whoops
SORRY
BUREAU OF BALANCE
cool base on MOON
next Arc:
MURDER ON THE ROCKPORT LIMITED!!
TRIO
"Don't lose it, or else!"

Chapter 1

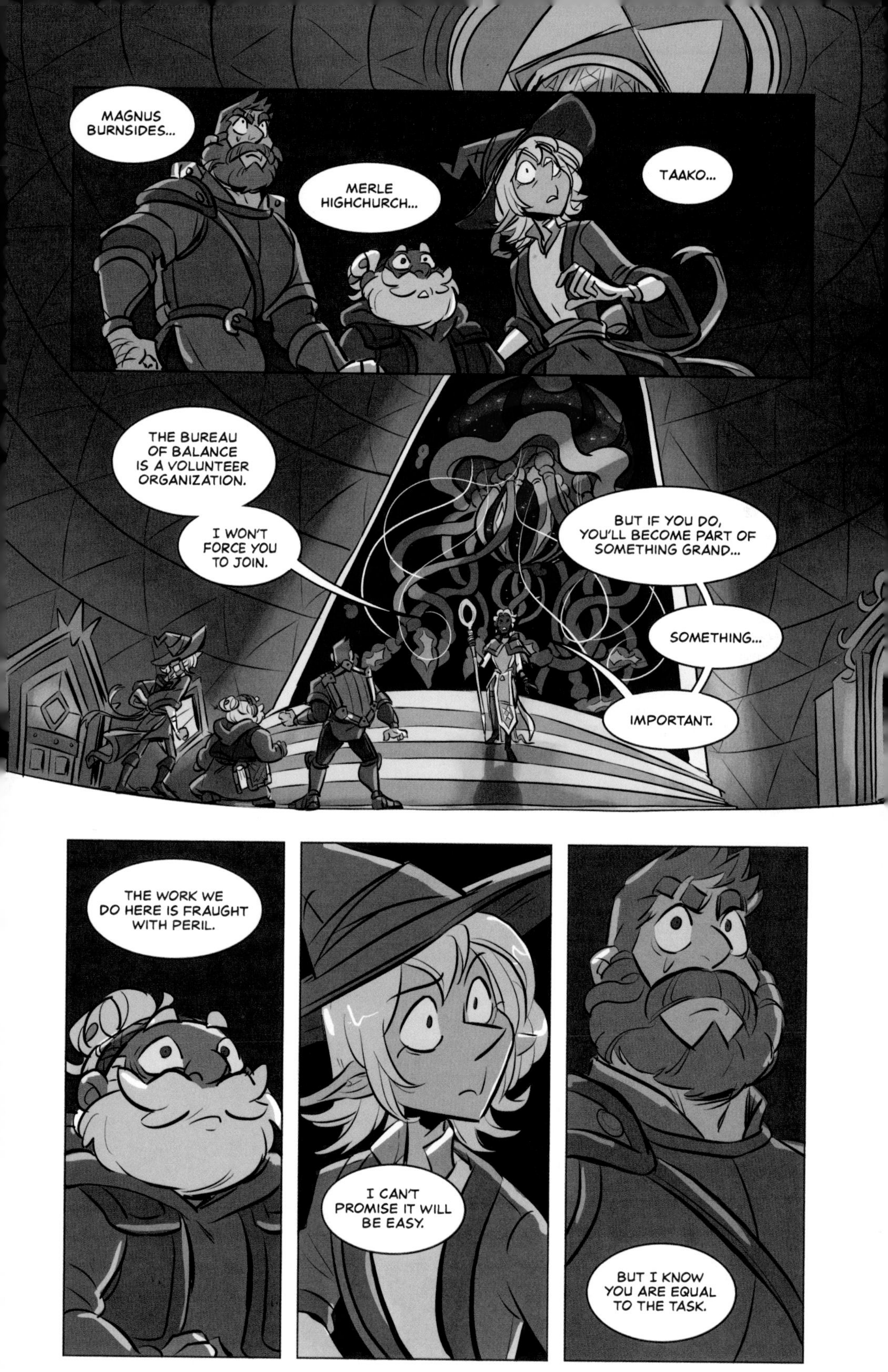
MAGNUS BURNSIDES...
MERLE HIGHCHURCH...
TAAKO...
THE BUREAU OF BALANCE IS A VOLUNTEER ORGANIZATION.
I WON'T FORCE YOU TO JOIN.
BUT IF YOU DO, YOU'LL BECOME PART OF SOMETHING GRAND...
SOMETHING...
IMPORTANT.
THE WORK WE DO HERE IS FRAUGHT WITH PERIL.
I CAN'T PROMISE IT WILL BE EASY.
BUT I KNOW YOU ARE EQUAL TO THE TASK.

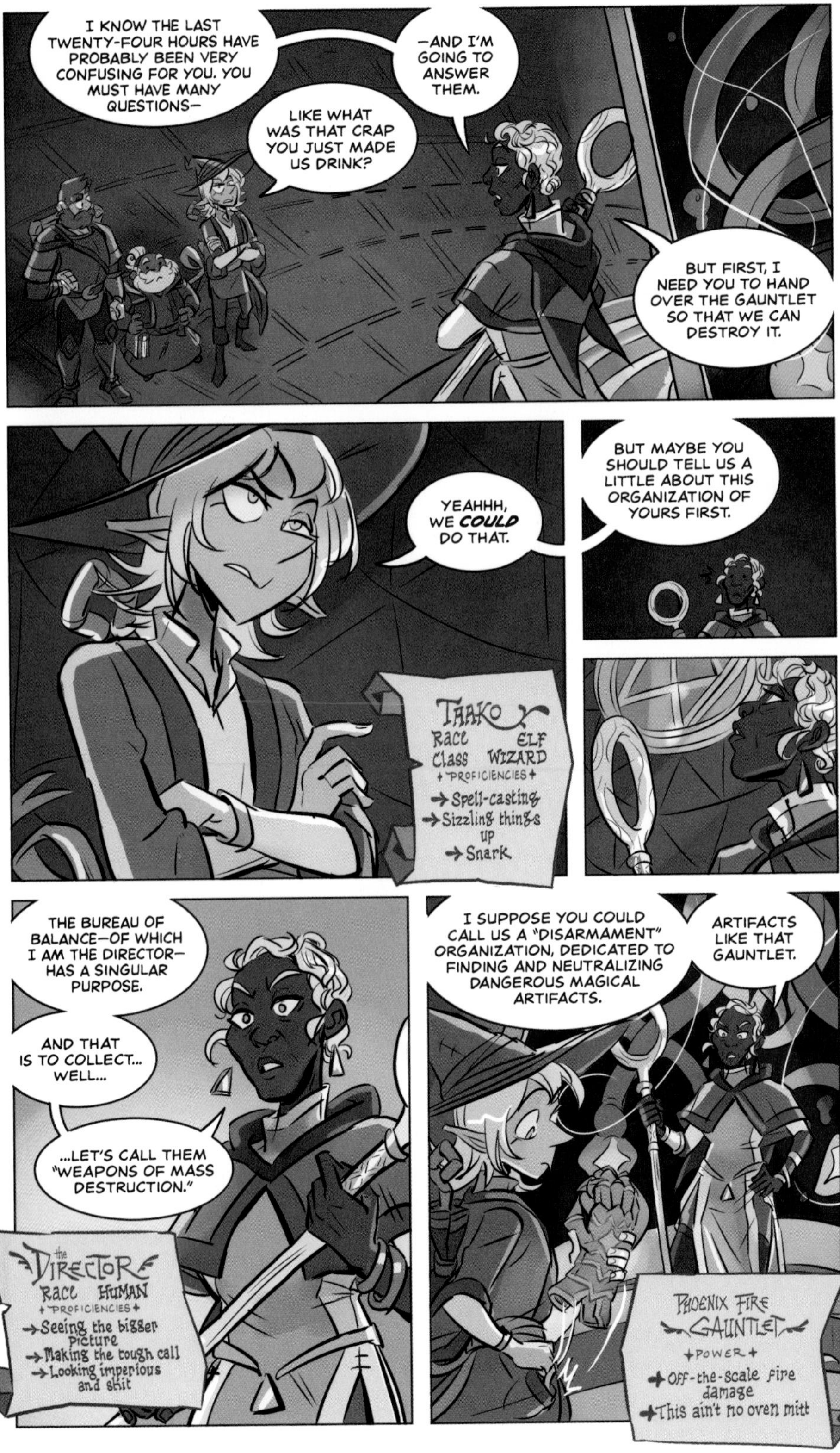
I KNOW THE LAST TWENTY-FOUR HOURS HAVE PROBABLY BEEN VERY CONFUSING FOR YOU. YOU MUST HAVE MANY QUESTIONS—
LIKE WHAT WAS THAT CRAP YOU JUST MADE US DRINK?
—AND I'M GOING TO ANSWER THEM.
BUT FIRST, I NEED YOU TO HAND OVER THE GAUNTLET SO THAT WE CAN DESTROY IT.
YEAHHH, WE COULD DO THAT.
BUT MAYBE YOU SHOULD TELL US A LITTLE ABOUT THIS ORGANIZATION OF YOURS FIRST.
TAAKO
RACE ELF
CLASS WIZARD
PROFICIENCIES
→Spell-casting
→Sizzling things up
→Snark
THE BUREAU OF BALANCE—OF WHICH I AM THE DIRECTOR—HAS A SINGULAR PURPOSE.
AND THAT IS TO COLLECT... WELL...
...LET'S CALL THEM "WEAPONS OF MASS DESTRUCTION."
the DIRECTOR
RACE HUMAN
PROFICIENCIES
→Seeing the bigger picture
→Making the tough call
→Looking imperious and shit
I SUPPOSE YOU COULD CALL US A "DISARMAMENT" ORGANIZATION, DEDICATED TO FINDING AND NEUTRALIZING DANGEROUS MAGICAL ARTIFACTS.
ARTIFACTS LIKE THAT GAUNTLET.
PHOENIX FIRE GAUNTLET
POWER
Off-the-scale fire damage
This ain't no oven mitt

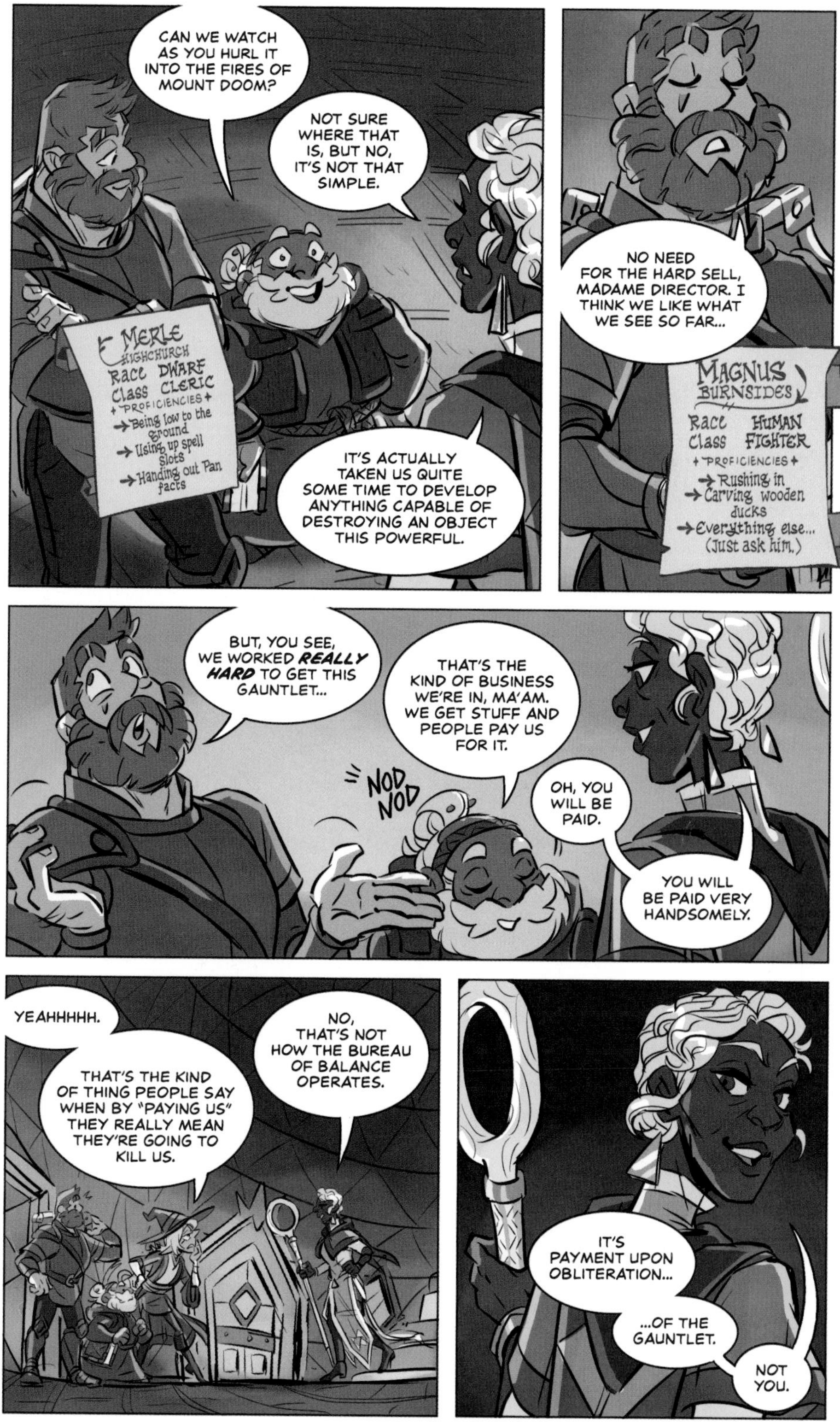
CAN WE WATCH AS YOU HURL IT INTO THE FIRES OF MOUNT DOOM?
NOT SURE WHERE THAT IS, BUT NO, IT'S NOT THAT SIMPLE.
MERLE HIGHCHURCH
RACE DWARF
CLASS CLERIC
PROFICIENCIES
Being low to the ground
Using up spell slots
Handing out Pan facts
IT'S ACTUALLY TAKEN US QUITE SOME TIME TO DEVELOP ANYTHING CAPABLE OF DESTROYING AN OBJECT THIS POWERFUL.
NO NEED FOR THE HARD SELL, MADAME DIRECTOR. I THINK WE LIKE WHAT WE SEE SO FAR...
MAGNUS BURNSIDES
RACE HUMAN
CLASS FIGHTER
PROFICIENCIES
Rushing in
Carving wooden ducks
Everything else... (Just ask him.)
BUT, YOU SEE, WE WORKED ***REALLY HARD*** TO GET THIS GAUNTLET...
THAT'S THE KIND OF BUSINESS WE'RE IN, MA'AM. WE GET STUFF AND PEOPLE PAY US FOR IT.
NOD NOD
OH, YOU WILL BE PAID.
YOU WILL BE PAID VERY HANDSOMELY.
YEAHHHHH.
THAT'S THE KIND OF THING PEOPLE SAY WHEN BY "PAYING US" THEY REALLY MEAN THEY'RE GOING TO KILL US.
NO, THAT'S NOT HOW THE BUREAU OF BALANCE OPERATES.
IT'S PAYMENT UPON OBLITERATION...
...OF THE GAUNTLET.
NOT YOU.

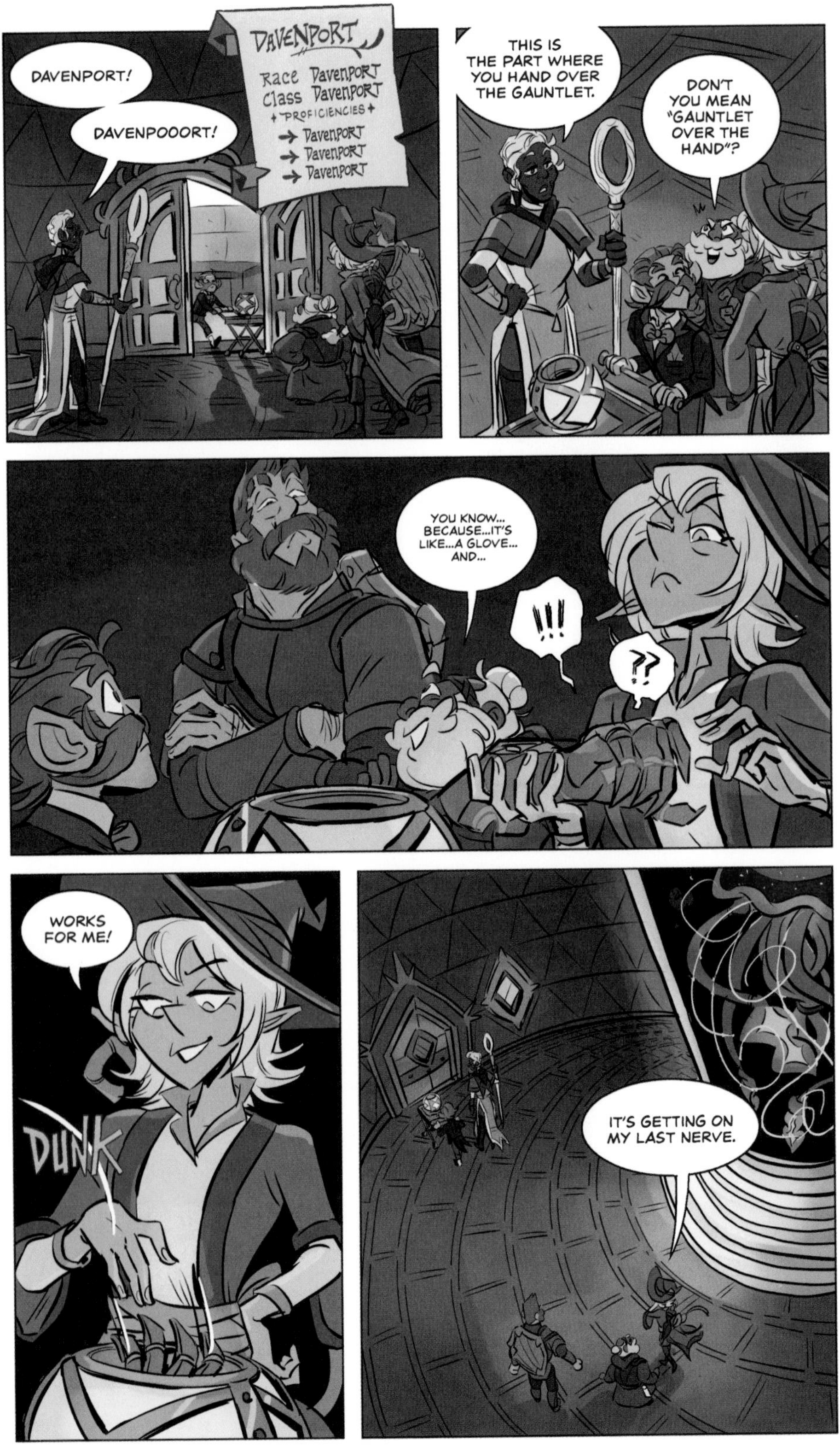
DAVENPORT!
DAVENPOOORT!
DAVENPORT
Race DavenPORT
Class DavenPORT
PROFICIENCIES
DavenPORT
DavenPORT
DavenPORT
THIS IS THE PART WHERE YOU HAND OVER THE GAUNTLET.
DON'T YOU MEAN "GAUNTLET OVER THE HAND"?
YOU KNOW... BECAUSE...IT'S LIKE...A GLOVE... AND...
!!!
??
WORKS FOR ME!
DUNK
IT'S GETTING ON MY LAST NERVE.

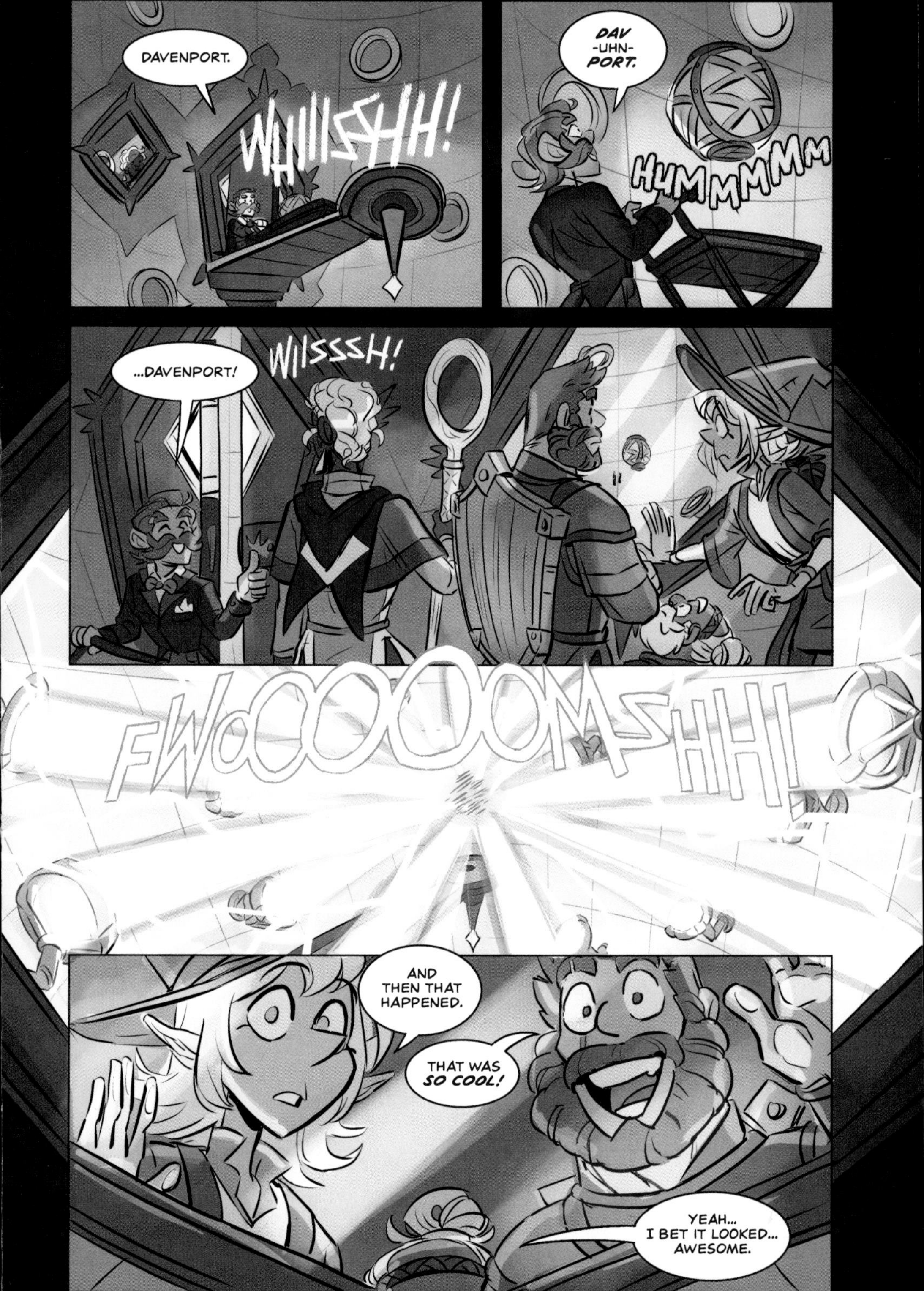
DAVENPORT.
WHIIISSHH!
DAV -UHN- PORT.
HUMMMMMM
...DAVENPORT!
WISSSH!
FWOOOOOMSHH!
AND THEN THAT HAPPENED.
THAT WAS SO COOL!
YEAH... I BET IT LOOKED... AWESOME.

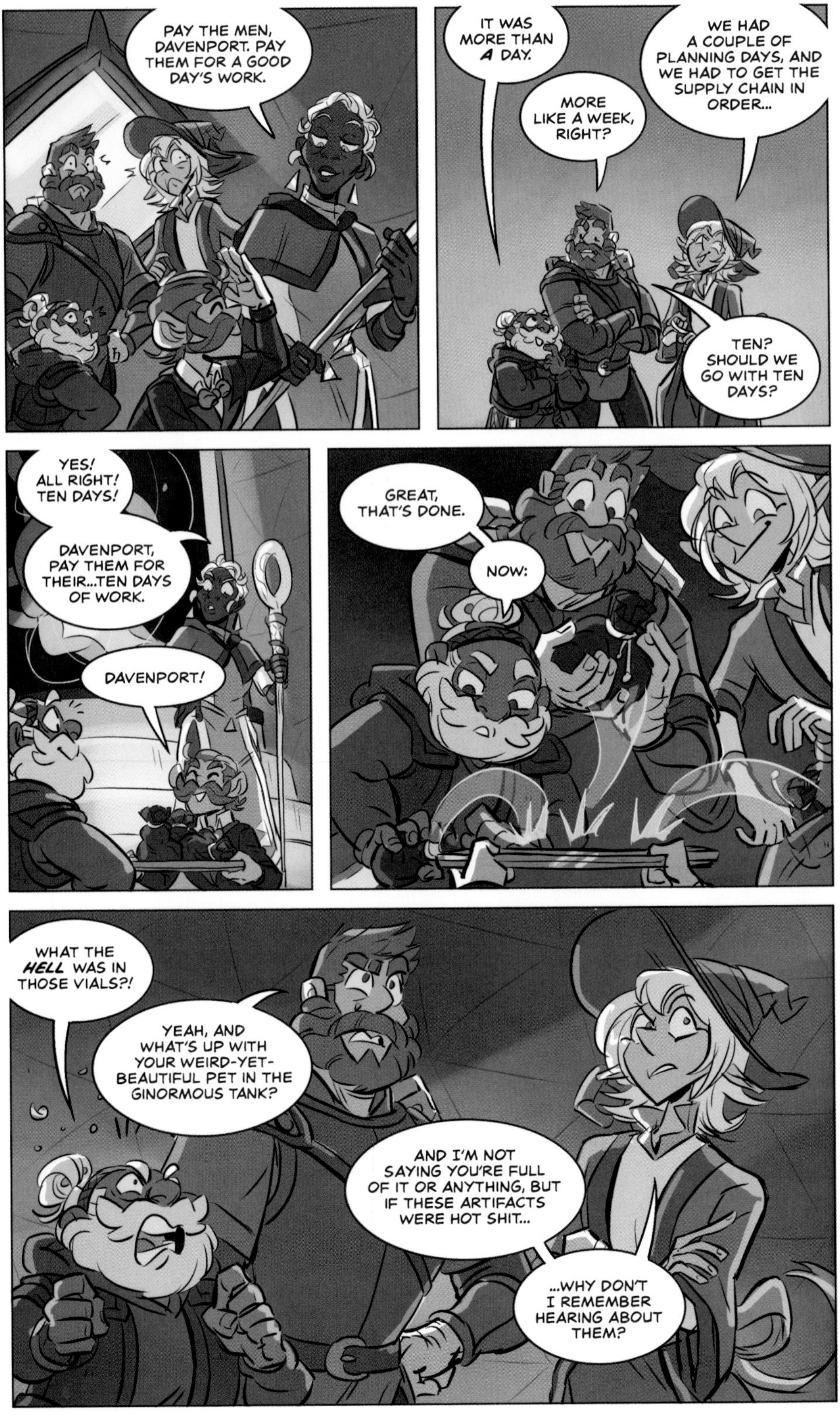
PAY THE MEN, DAVENPORT. PAY THEM FOR A GOOD DAY'S WORK.
IT WAS MORE THAN *A* DAY.
MORE LIKE A WEEK, RIGHT?
WE HAD A COUPLE OF PLANNING DAYS, AND WE HAD TO GET THE SUPPLY CHAIN IN ORDER...
TEN? SHOULD WE GO WITH TEN DAYS?
YES! ALL RIGHT! TEN DAYS!
DAVENPORT, PAY THEM FOR THEIR...TEN DAYS OF WORK.
DAVENPORT!
GREAT, THAT'S DONE.
NOW:
WHAT THE ***HELL*** WAS IN THOSE VIALS?!
YEAH, AND WHAT'S UP WITH YOUR WEIRD-YET-BEAUTIFUL PET IN THE GINORMOUS TANK?
AND I'M NOT SAYING YOU'RE FULL OF IT OR ANYTHING, BUT IF THESE ARTIFACTS WERE HOT SHIT...
...WHY DON'T I REMEMBER HEARING ABOUT THEM?

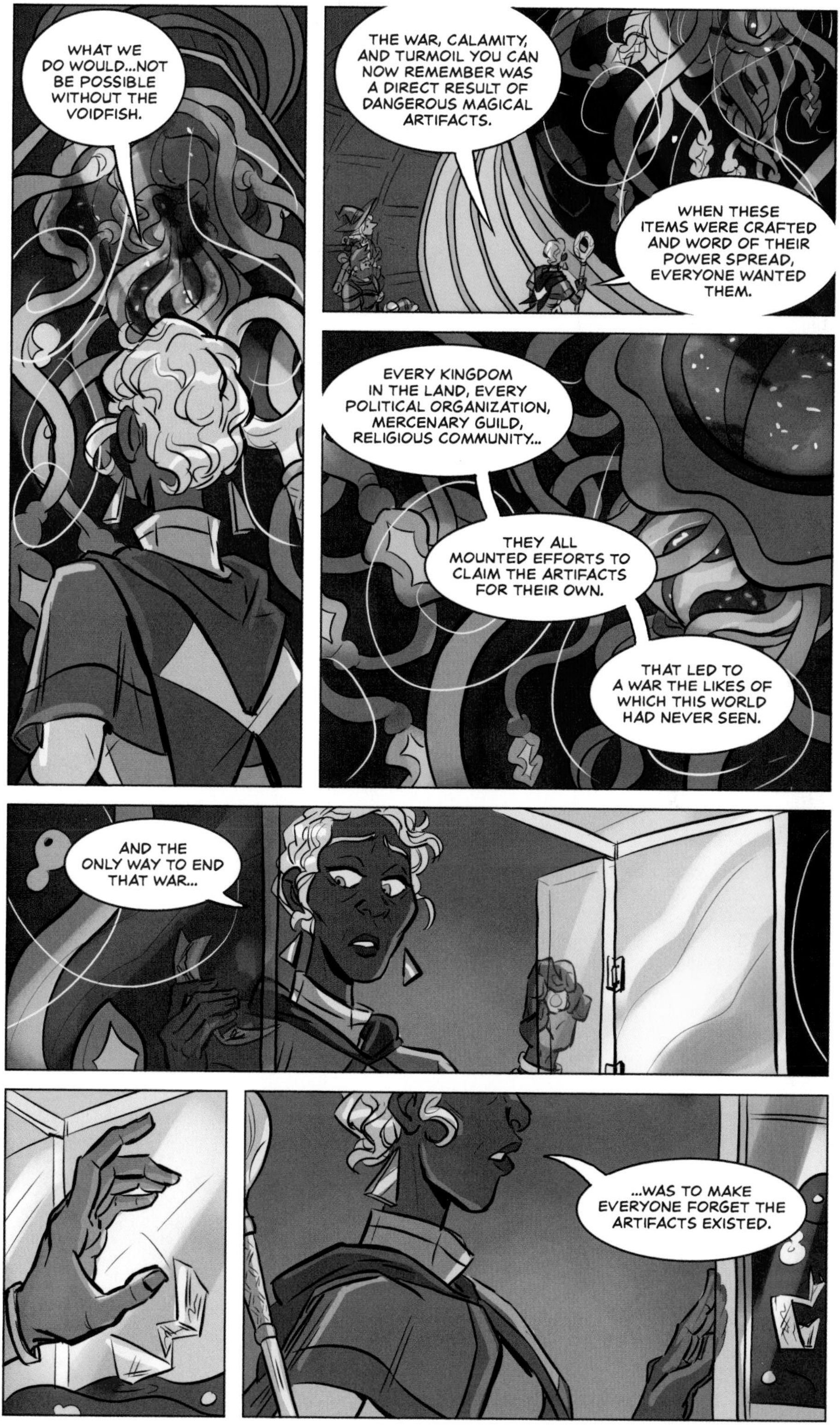
WHAT WE DO WOULD...NOT BE POSSIBLE WITHOUT THE VOIDFISH.
THE WAR, CALAMITY, AND TURMOIL YOU CAN NOW REMEMBER WAS A DIRECT RESULT OF DANGEROUS MAGICAL ARTIFACTS.
WHEN THESE ITEMS WERE CRAFTED AND WORD OF THEIR POWER SPREAD, EVERYONE WANTED THEM.
EVERY KINGDOM IN THE LAND, EVERY POLITICAL ORGANIZATION, MERCENARY GUILD, RELIGIOUS COMMUNITY...
THEY ALL MOUNTED EFFORTS TO CLAIM THE ARTIFACTS FOR THEIR OWN.
THAT LED TO A WAR THE LIKES OF WHICH THIS WORLD HAD NEVER SEEN.
AND THE ONLY WAY TO END THAT WAR...
...WAS TO MAKE EVERYONE FORGET THE ARTIFACTS EXISTED.

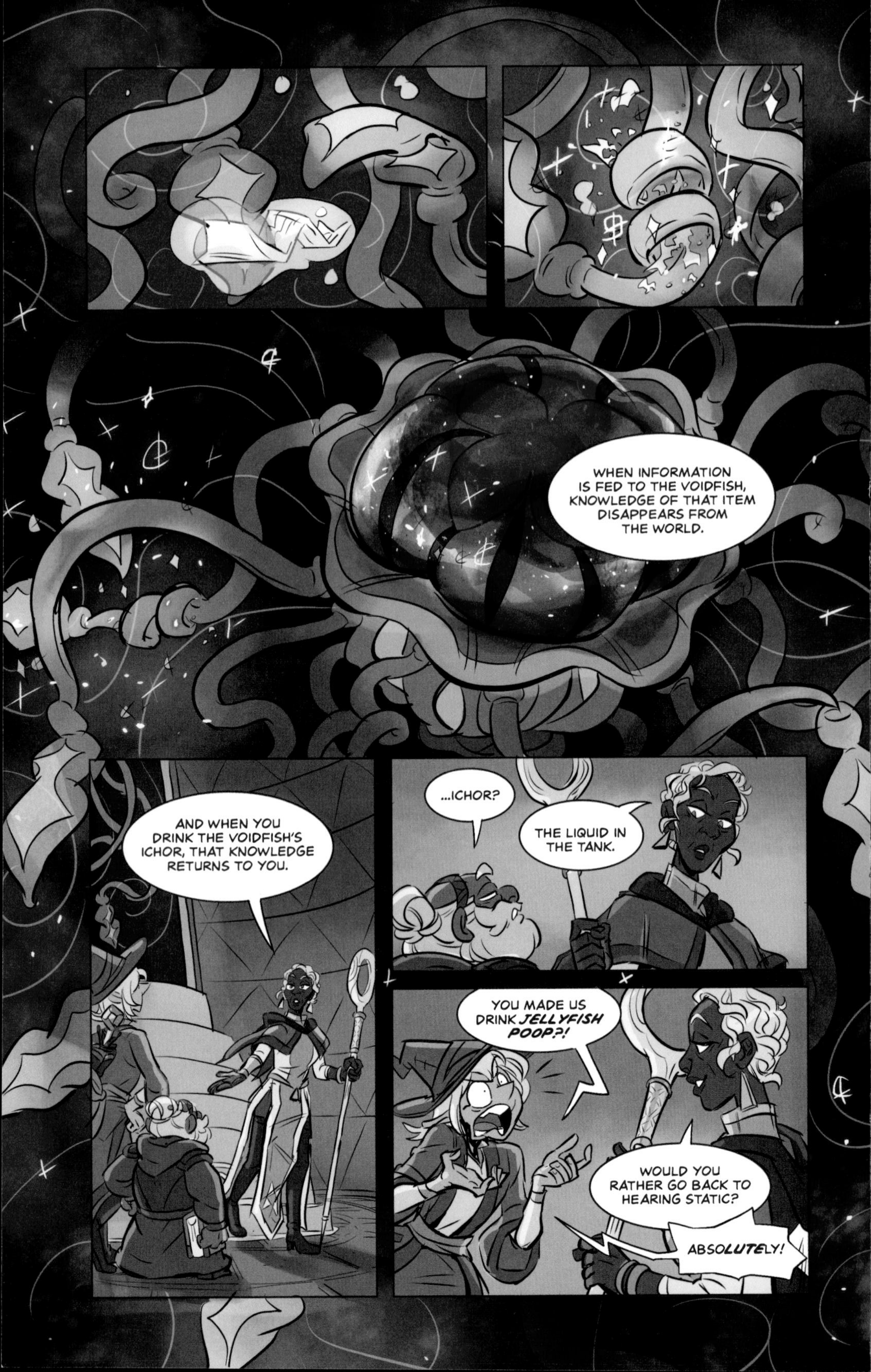
WHEN INFORMATION IS FED TO THE VOIDFISH, KNOWLEDGE OF THAT ITEM DISAPPEARS FROM THE WORLD.
AND WHEN YOU DRINK THE VOIDFISH'S ICHOR, THAT KNOWLEDGE RETURNS TO YOU.
...ICHOR?
THE LIQUID IN THE TANK.
YOU MADE US DRINK *JELLYFISH POOP?!*
WOULD YOU RATHER GO BACK TO HEARING STATIC?
ABSO*LUTE*LY!

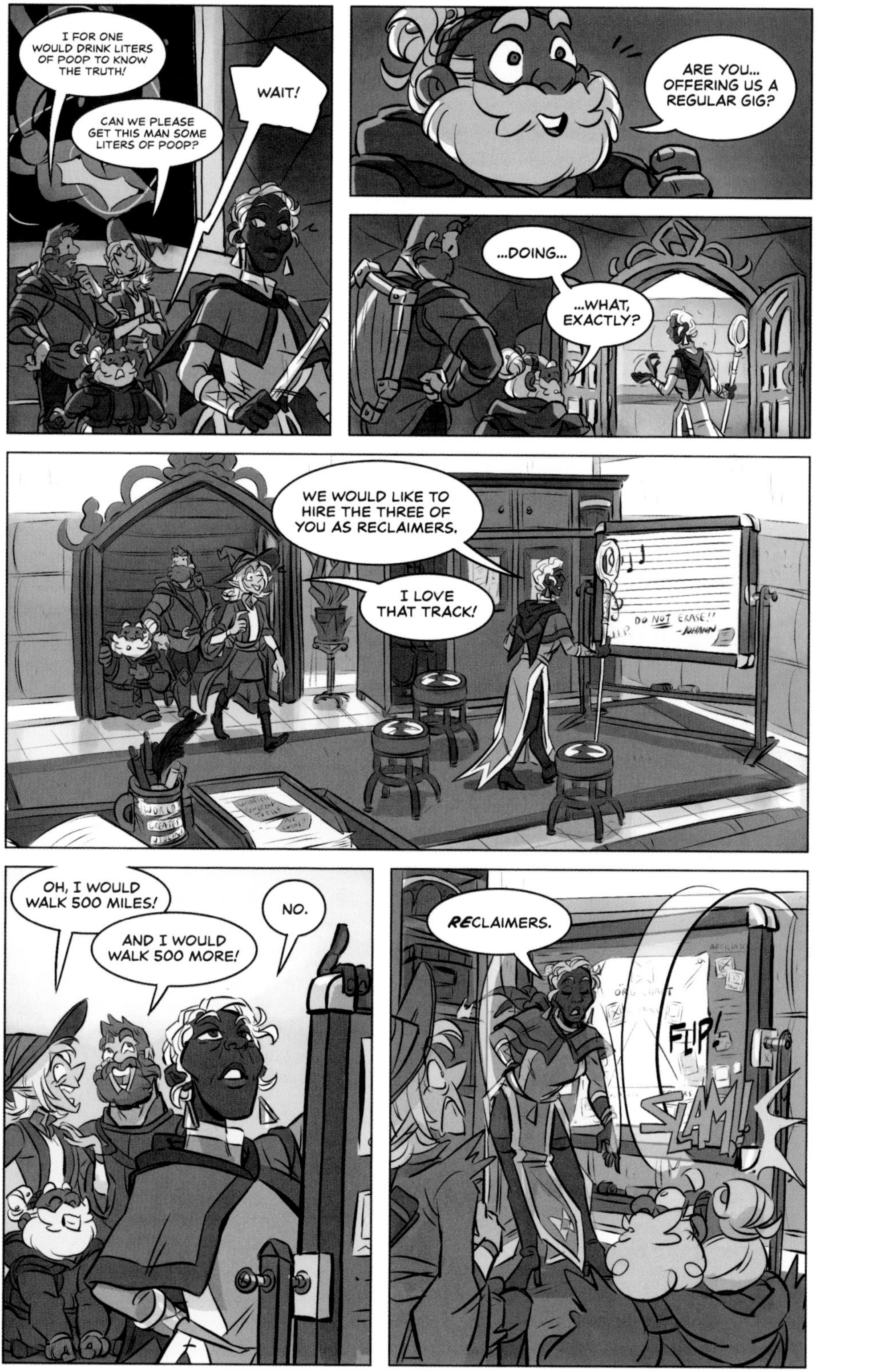
I FOR ONE WOULD DRINK LITERS OF POOP TO KNOW THE TRUTH!
CAN WE PLEASE GET THIS MAN SOME LITERS OF POOP?
WAIT!
ARE YOU... OFFERING US A REGULAR GIG?
...DOING...
...WHAT, EXACTLY?
WE WOULD LIKE TO HIRE THE THREE OF YOU AS RECLAIMERS.
I LOVE THAT TRACK!
DO NOT ERASE!! -JOHANN
OH, I WOULD WALK 500 MILES!
AND I WOULD WALK 500 MORE!
NO.
RECLAIMERS.
FLIP!
SLAM!

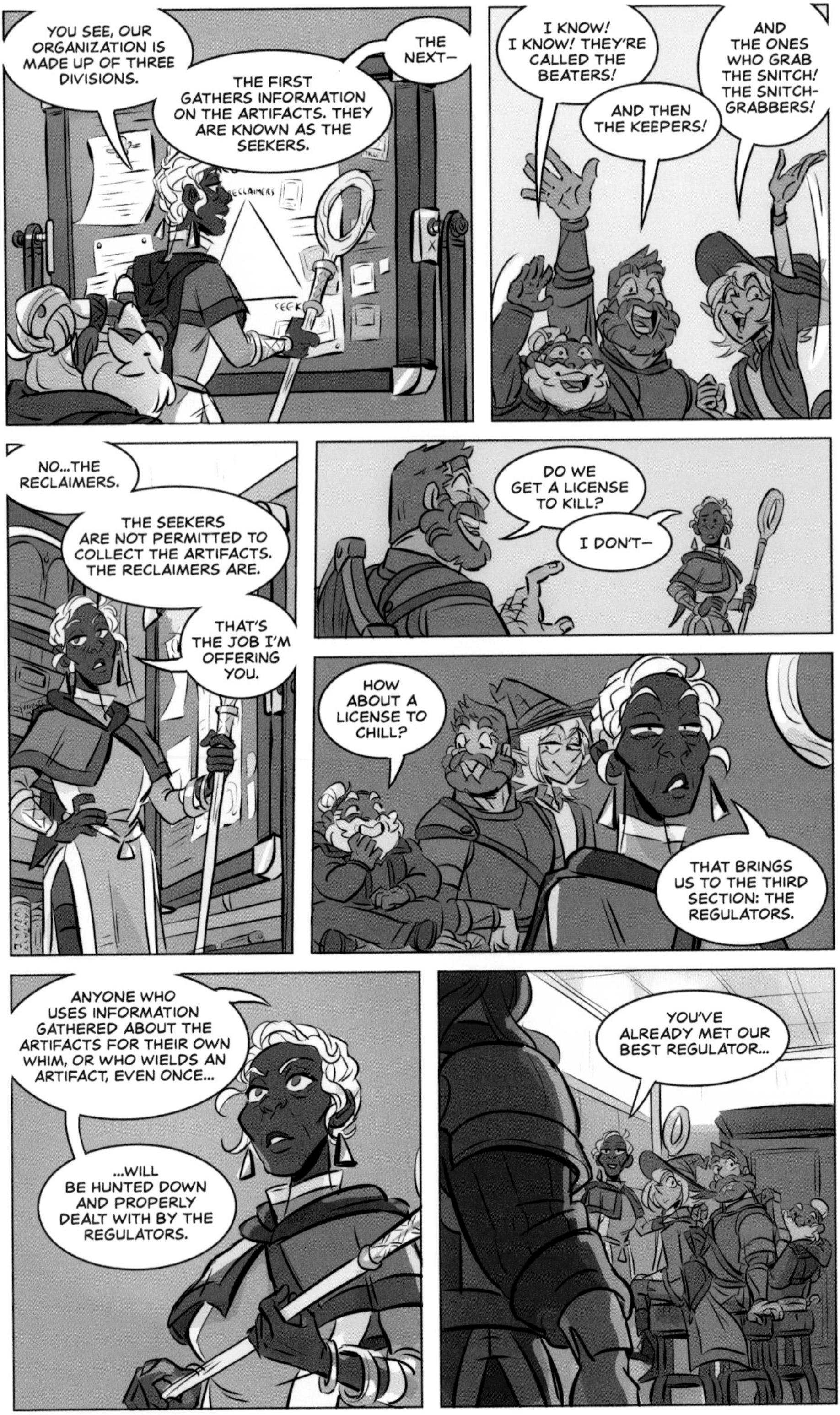
YOU SEE, OUR ORGANIZATION IS MADE UP OF THREE DIVISIONS.
THE FIRST GATHERS INFORMATION ON THE ARTIFACTS. THEY ARE KNOWN AS THE SEEKERS.
THE NEXT—
I KNOW! I KNOW! THEY'RE CALLED THE BEATERS!
AND THEN THE KEEPERS!
AND THE ONES WHO GRAB THE SNITCH! THE SNITCH-GRABBERS!
NO...THE RECLAIMERS.
THE SEEKERS ARE NOT PERMITTED TO COLLECT THE ARTIFACTS. THE RECLAIMERS ARE.
THAT'S THE JOB I'M OFFERING YOU.
DO WE GET A LICENSE TO KILL?
I DON'T—
HOW ABOUT A LICENSE TO CHILL?
THAT BRINGS US TO THE THIRD SECTION: THE REGULATORS.
ANYONE WHO USES INFORMATION GATHERED ABOUT THE ARTIFACTS FOR THEIR OWN WHIM, OR WHO WIELDS AN ARTIFACT, EVEN ONCE...
...WILL BE HUNTED DOWN AND PROPERLY DEALT WITH BY THE REGULATORS.
YOU'VE ALREADY MET OUR BEST REGULATOR...

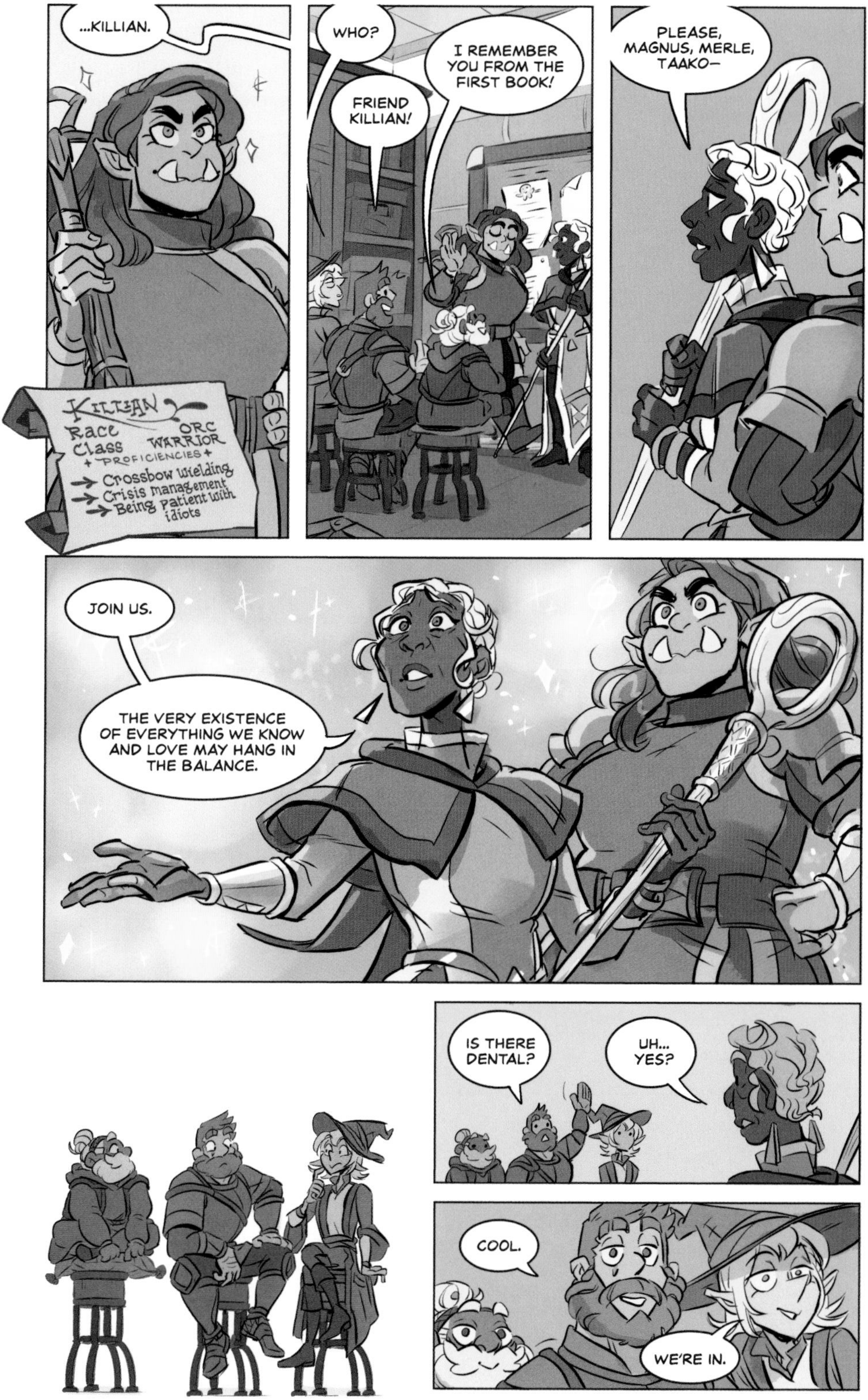
...KILLIAN.
KILLIAN
Race ORC
Class WARRIOR
PROFICIENCIES
Crossbow Wielding
Crisis management
Being patient with idiots
WHO?
FRIEND KILLIAN!
I REMEMBER YOU FROM THE FIRST BOOK!
PLEASE, MAGNUS, MERLE, TAAKO—
JOIN US.
THE VERY EXISTENCE OF EVERYTHING WE KNOW AND LOVE MAY HANG IN THE BALANCE.
IS THERE DENTAL?
UH... YES?
COOL.
WE'RE IN.

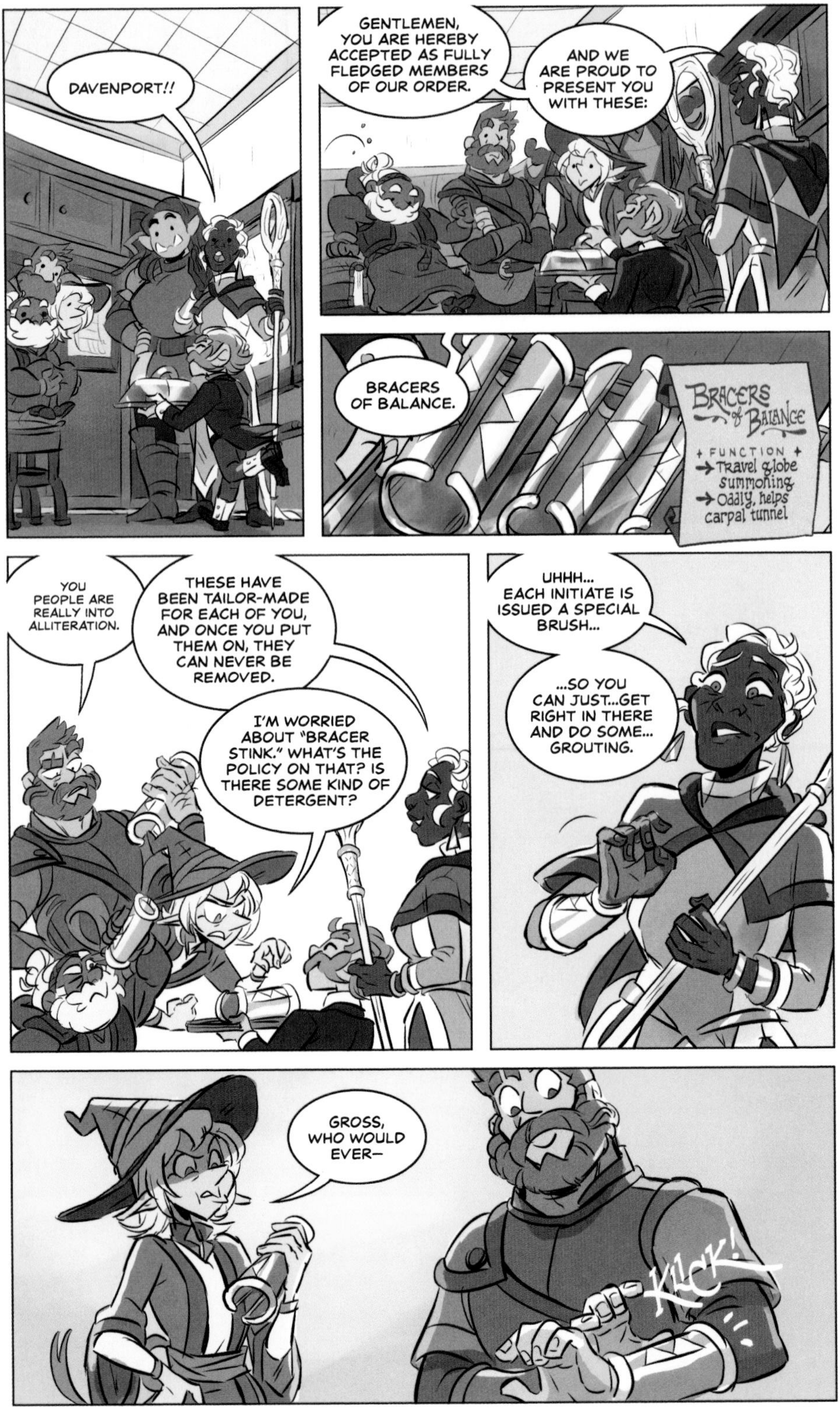
DAVENPORT!!
GENTLEMEN, YOU ARE HEREBY ACCEPTED AS FULLY FLEDGED MEMBERS OF OUR ORDER.
AND WE ARE PROUD TO PRESENT YOU WITH THESE:
BRACERS OF BALANCE.
BRACERS of BALANCE
FUNCTION
→ Travel globe summoning
→ Oddly, helps carpal tunnel
YOU PEOPLE ARE REALLY INTO ALLITERATION.
THESE HAVE BEEN TAILOR-MADE FOR EACH OF YOU, AND ONCE YOU PUT THEM ON, THEY CAN NEVER BE REMOVED.
I'M WORRIED ABOUT "BRACER STINK." WHAT'S THE POLICY ON THAT? IS THERE SOME KIND OF DETERGENT?
UHHH... EACH INITIATE IS ISSUED A SPECIAL BRUSH...
...SO YOU CAN JUST...GET RIGHT IN THERE AND DO SOME... GROUTING.
GROSS, WHO WOULD EVER—
KLICK!

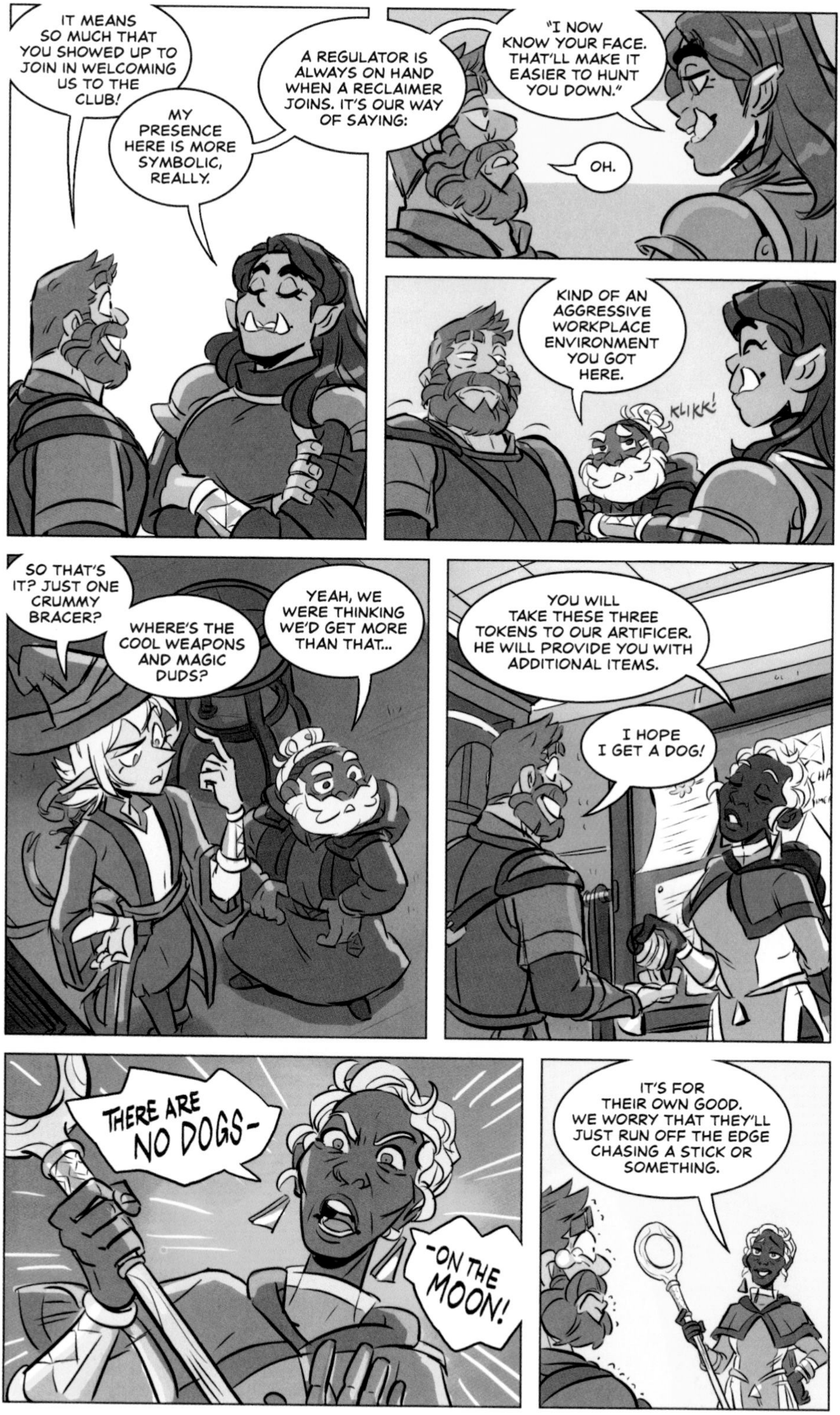
IT MEANS SO MUCH THAT YOU SHOWED UP TO JOIN IN WELCOMING US TO THE CLUB!
MY PRESENCE HERE IS MORE SYMBOLIC, REALLY.
A REGULATOR IS ALWAYS ON HAND WHEN A RECLAIMER JOINS. IT'S OUR WAY OF SAYING:
"I NOW KNOW YOUR FACE. THAT'LL MAKE IT EASIER TO HUNT YOU DOWN."
OH.
KIND OF AN AGGRESSIVE WORKPLACE ENVIRONMENT YOU GOT HERE.
KLIKK!
SO THAT'S IT? JUST ONE CRUMMY BRACER?
WHERE'S THE COOL WEAPONS AND MAGIC DUDS?
YEAH, WE WERE THINKING WE'D GET MORE THAN THAT...
YOU WILL TAKE THESE THREE TOKENS TO OUR ARTIFICER. HE WILL PROVIDE YOU WITH ADDITIONAL ITEMS.
I HOPE I GET A DOG!
THERE ARE NO DOGS-
-ON THE MOON!
IT'S FOR THEIR OWN GOOD. WE WORRY THAT THEY'LL JUST RUN OFF THE EDGE CHASING A STICK OR SOMETHING.

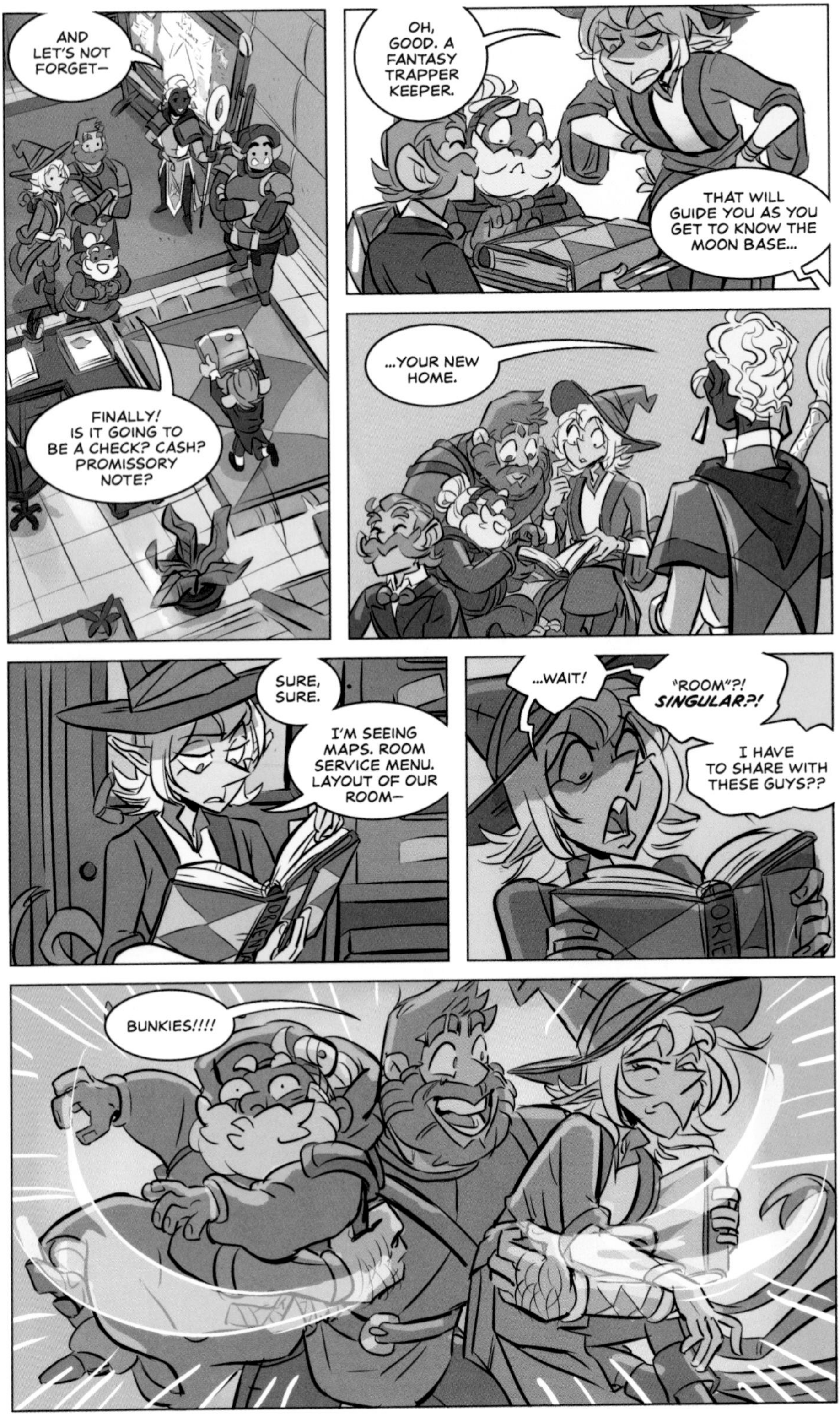
AND LET'S NOT FORGET—
OH, GOOD. A FANTASY TRAPPER KEEPER.
THAT WILL GUIDE YOU AS YOU GET TO KNOW THE MOON BASE...
FINALLY! IS IT GOING TO BE A CHECK? CASH? PROMISSORY NOTE?
...YOUR NEW HOME.
SURE, SURE.
I'M SEEING MAPS. ROOM SERVICE MENU. LAYOUT OF OUR ROOM—
...WAIT!
"ROOM"?! SINGULAR?!
I HAVE TO SHARE WITH THESE GUYS??
BUNKIES!!!!

LOOKS LIKE WE HAVE TO SEE "LEON THE ARTIFICER" FIRST.

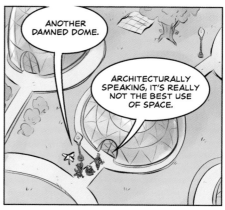

ANOTHER DAMNED DOME.

ARCHITECTURALLY SPEAKING, IT'S REALLY NOT THE BEST USE OF SPACE.

WELCOME!

I AM LEON THE ARTIFICER!

AND THIS IS MY—

LEON
RACE Gnome
CLASS Artificer
+PROFICIENCIES+
→ Artificing
→ Frustration
→ Vending Machine Expertise

I AM REALLY JONESING FOR A GUMBALL!

NO, IT'S—

A GASHAPON MACHINE!

NO. THIS IS MY—

VENDING MACHINE FROM SHENMUE!

NO—

FINE...

IT'S A BIG GASHAPON MACHINE FULL OF MAGICAL ITEMS.

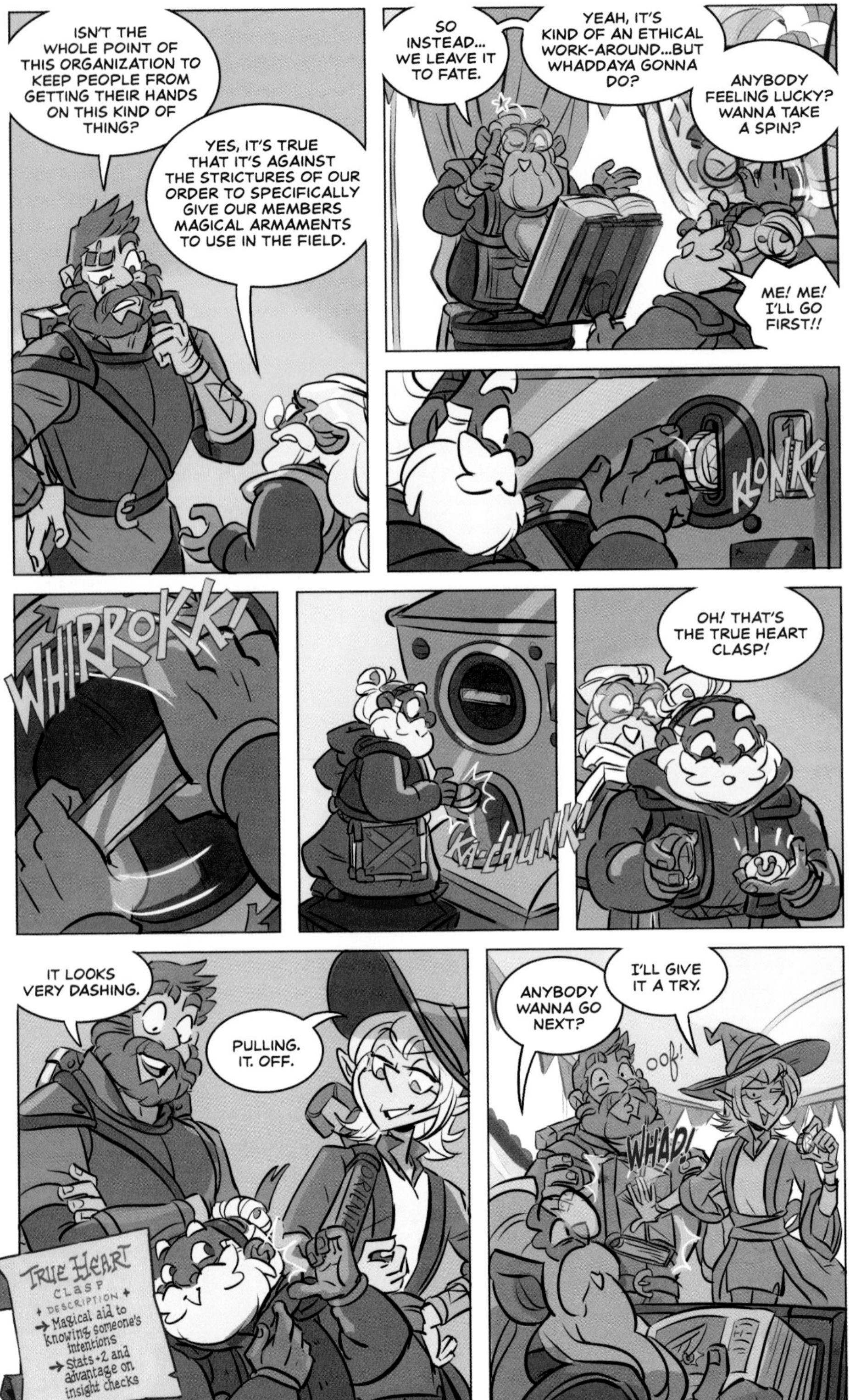
ISN'T THE WHOLE POINT OF THIS ORGANIZATION TO KEEP PEOPLE FROM GETTING THEIR HANDS ON THIS KIND OF THING?
YES, IT'S TRUE THAT IT'S AGAINST THE STRICTURES OF OUR ORDER TO SPECIFICALLY GIVE OUR MEMBERS MAGICAL ARMAMENTS TO USE IN THE FIELD.
SO INSTEAD... WE LEAVE IT TO FATE.
YEAH, IT'S KIND OF AN ETHICAL WORK-AROUND...BUT WHADDAYA GONNA DO?
ANYBODY FEELING LUCKY? WANNA TAKE A SPIN?
ME! ME! I'LL GO FIRST!!
KLONK!
WHIRROKK!
KA-CHUNK!
OH! THAT'S THE TRUE HEART CLASP!
IT LOOKS VERY DASHING.
PULLING. IT. OFF.
TRUE HEART CLASP
DESCRIPTION
→ Magical aid to knowing someone's intentions
→ Stats +2 and advantage on insight checks
I'LL GIVE IT A TRY.
ANYBODY WANNA GO NEXT?
OOF!
WHAP!

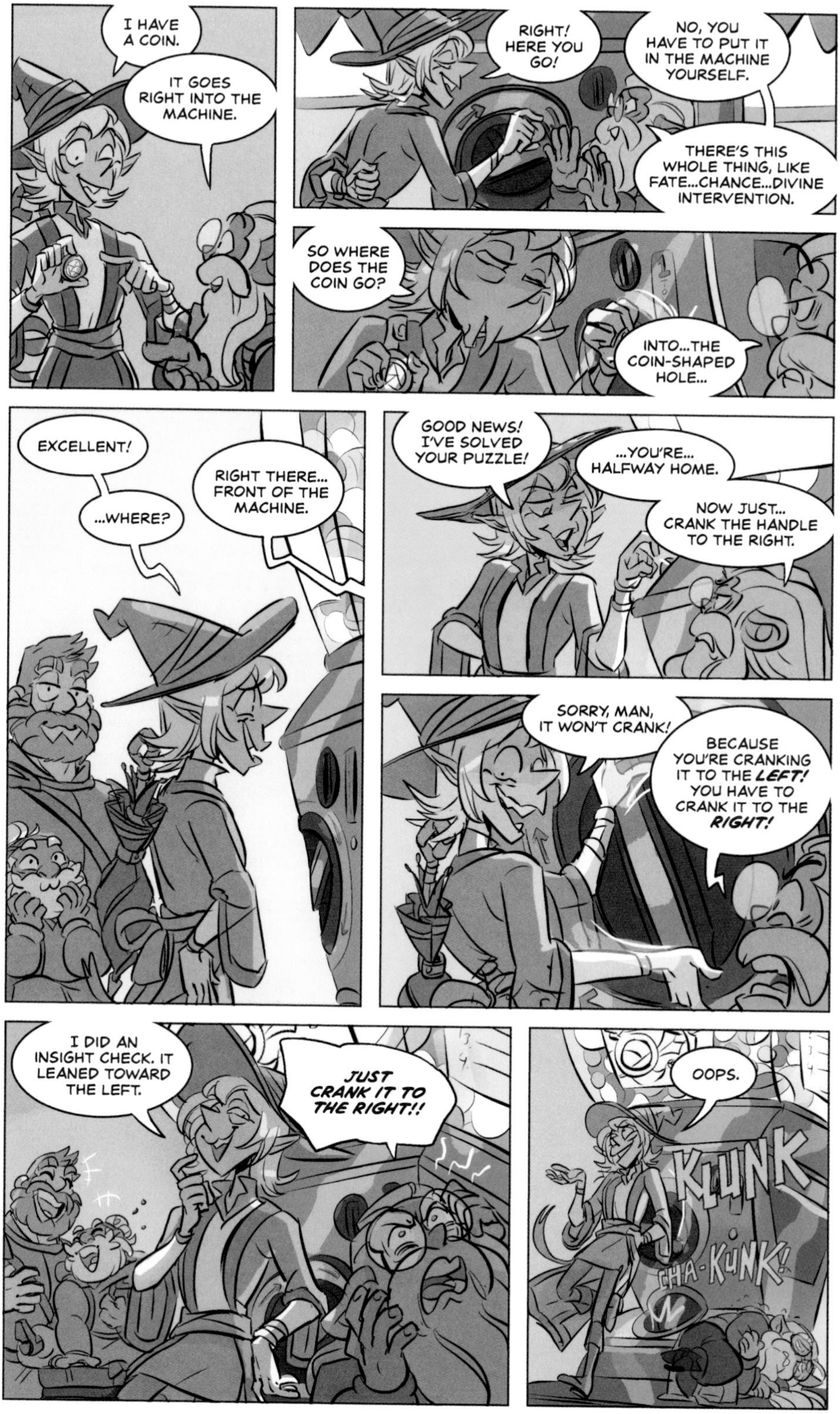
I HAVE A COIN.
IT GOES RIGHT INTO THE MACHINE.
RIGHT! HERE YOU GO!
NO, YOU HAVE TO PUT IT IN THE MACHINE YOURSELF.
THERE'S THIS WHOLE THING, LIKE FATE...CHANCE...DIVINE INTERVENTION.
SO WHERE DOES THE COIN GO?
INTO...THE COIN-SHAPED HOLE...
EXCELLENT!
...WHERE?
RIGHT THERE... FRONT OF THE MACHINE.
GOOD NEWS! I'VE SOLVED YOUR PUZZLE!
...YOU'RE... HALFWAY HOME.
NOW JUST... CRANK THE HANDLE TO THE RIGHT.
SORRY, MAN, IT WON'T CRANK!
BECAUSE YOU'RE CRANKING IT TO THE *LEFT!* YOU HAVE TO CRANK IT TO THE *RIGHT!*
I DID AN INSIGHT CHECK. IT LEANED TOWARD THE LEFT.
JUST CRANK IT TO THE RIGHT!!
OOPS.
KLUNK
CHA-KUNK!

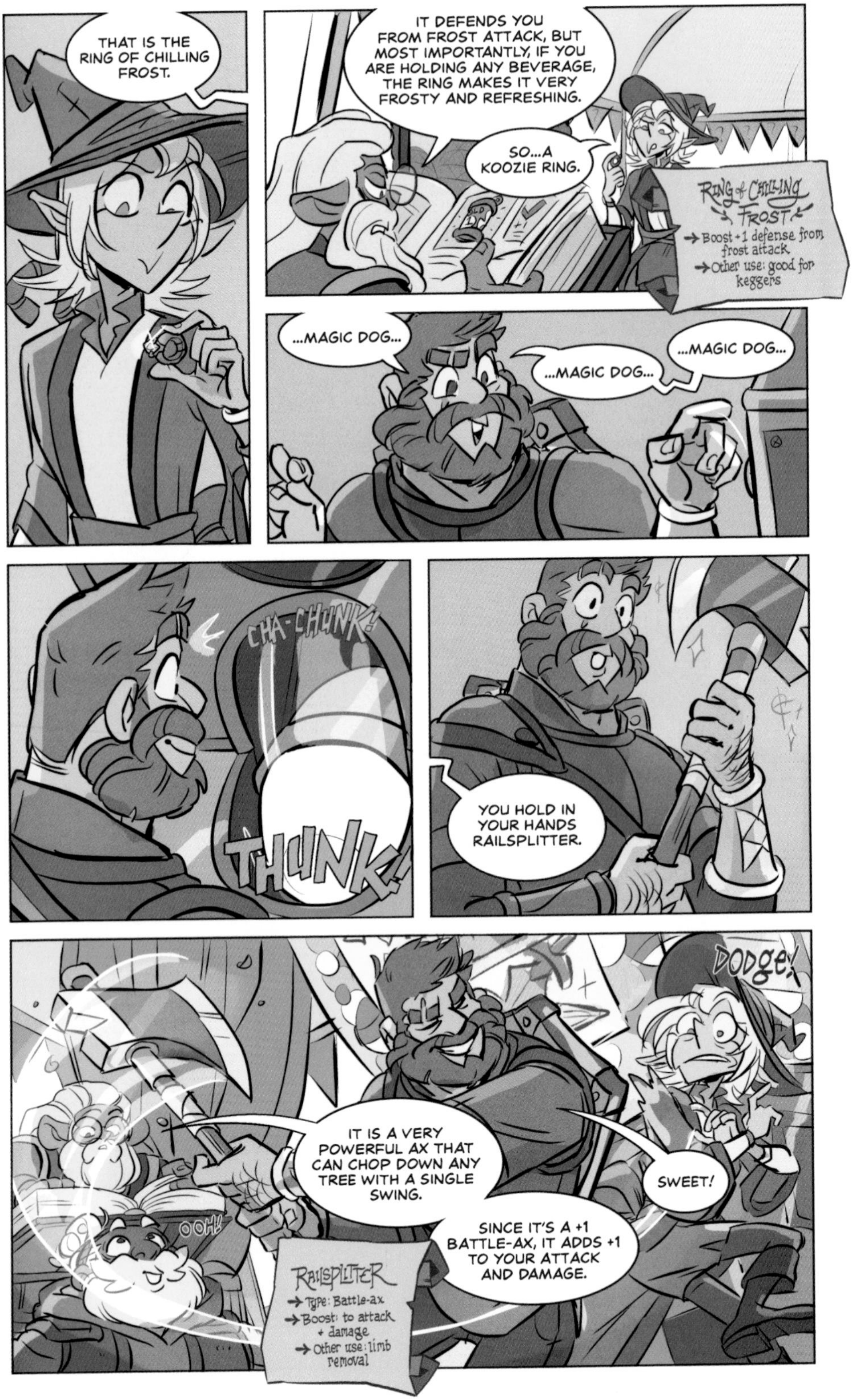
THAT IS THE RING OF CHILLING FROST.
IT DEFENDS YOU FROM FROST ATTACK, BUT MOST IMPORTANTLY, IF YOU ARE HOLDING ANY BEVERAGE, THE RING MAKES IT VERY FROSTY AND REFRESHING.
SO...A KOOZIE RING.
RING of CHILLING FROST
→ Boost +1 defense from frost attack
→ Other use: good for keggers
...MAGIC DOG...
...MAGIC DOG...
...MAGIC DOG...
CHA-CHUNK!
THUNK!
YOU HOLD IN YOUR HANDS RAILSPLITTER.
DODGE!
IT IS A VERY POWERFUL AX THAT CAN CHOP DOWN ANY TREE WITH A SINGLE SWING.
SWEET!
OOH!
SINCE IT'S A +1 BATTLE-AX, IT ADDS +1 TO YOUR ATTACK AND DAMAGE.
RAILSPLITTER
→ Type: Battle-ax
→ Boost: to attack + damage
→ Other use: limb removal

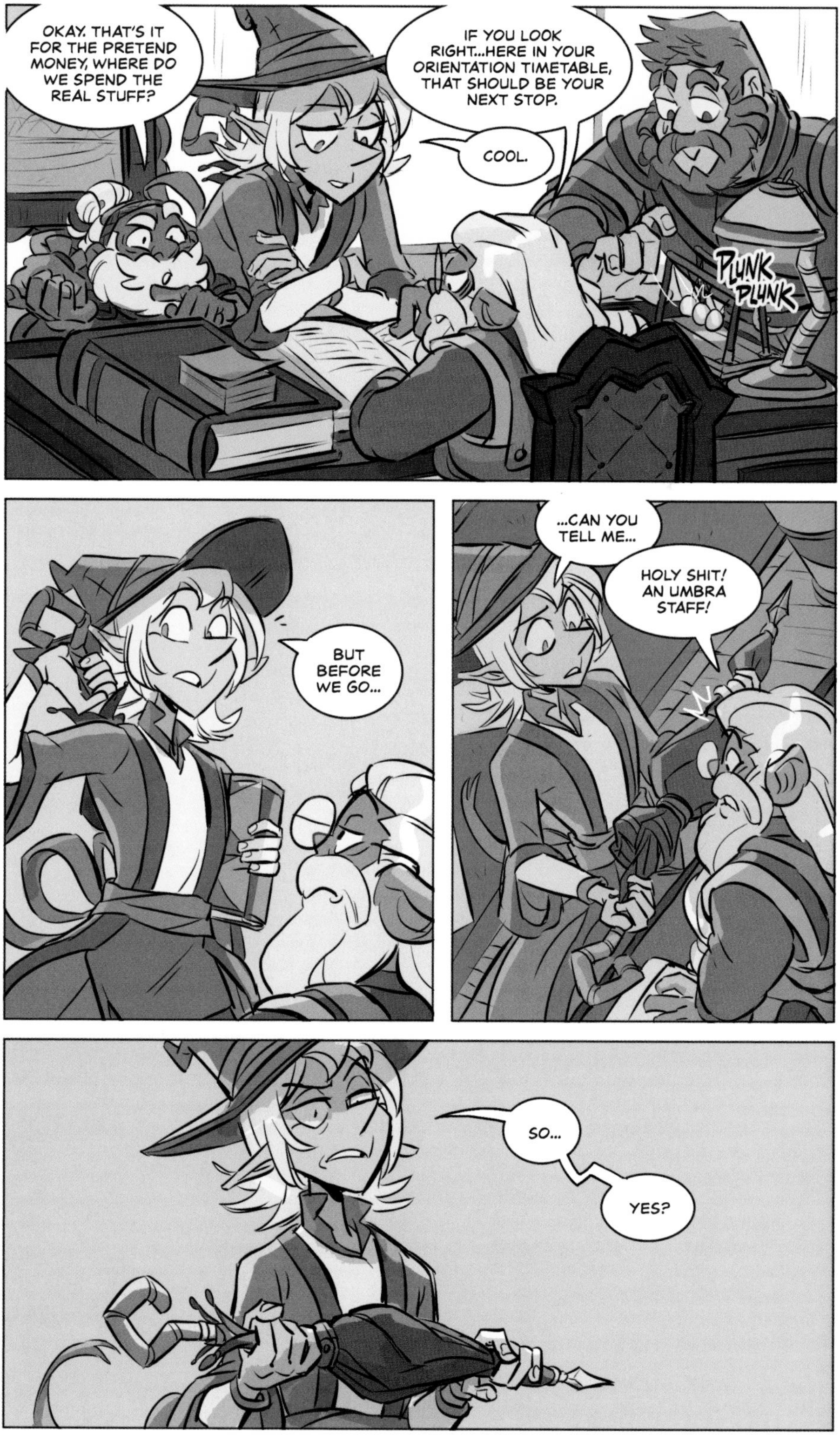
OKAY. THAT'S IT FOR THE PRETEND MONEY, WHERE DO WE SPEND THE REAL STUFF?
IF YOU LOOK RIGHT...HERE IN YOUR ORIENTATION TIMETABLE, THAT SHOULD BE YOUR NEXT STOP.
COOL.
PLUNK PLUNK
BUT BEFORE WE GO...
...CAN YOU TELL ME...
HOLY SHIT! AN UMBRA STAFF!
SO...
YES?

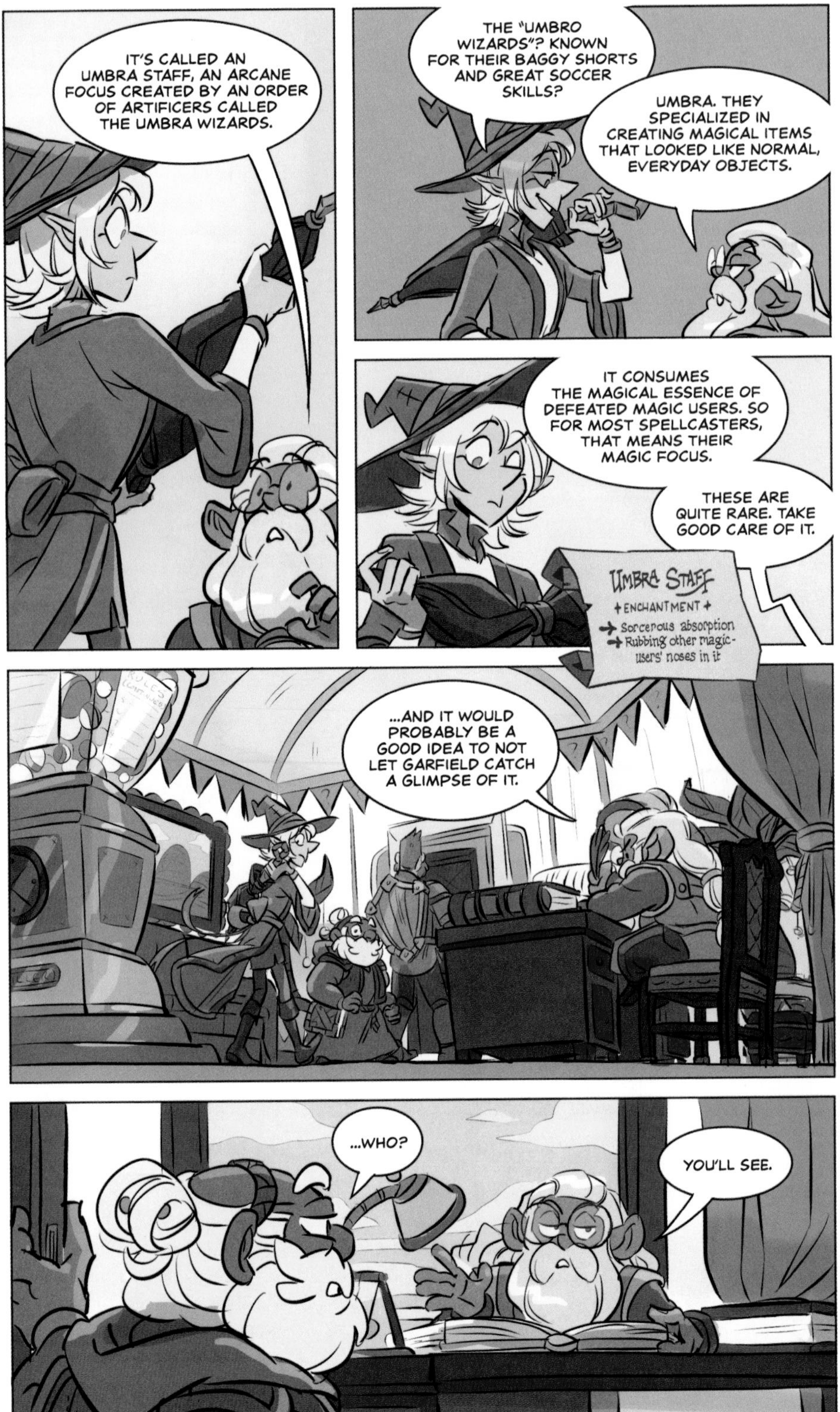

IT'S CALLED AN UMBRA STAFF, AN ARCANE FOCUS CREATED BY AN ORDER OF ARTIFICERS CALLED THE UMBRA WIZARDS.
THE "UMBRO WIZARDS"? KNOWN FOR THEIR BAGGY SHORTS AND GREAT SOCCER SKILLS?
UMBRA. THEY SPECIALIZED IN CREATING MAGICAL ITEMS THAT LOOKED LIKE NORMAL, EVERYDAY OBJECTS.
IT CONSUMES THE MAGICAL ESSENCE OF DEFEATED MAGIC USERS. SO FOR MOST SPELLCASTERS, THAT MEANS THEIR MAGIC FOCUS.
THESE ARE QUITE RARE. TAKE GOOD CARE OF IT.
UMBRA STAFF
✦ENCHANTMENT✦
➔ Sorcerous absorption
➔ Rubbing other magic-users' noses in it
...AND IT WOULD PROBABLY BE A GOOD IDEA TO NOT LET GARFIELD CATCH A GLIMPSE OF IT.
...WHO?
YOU'LL SEE.

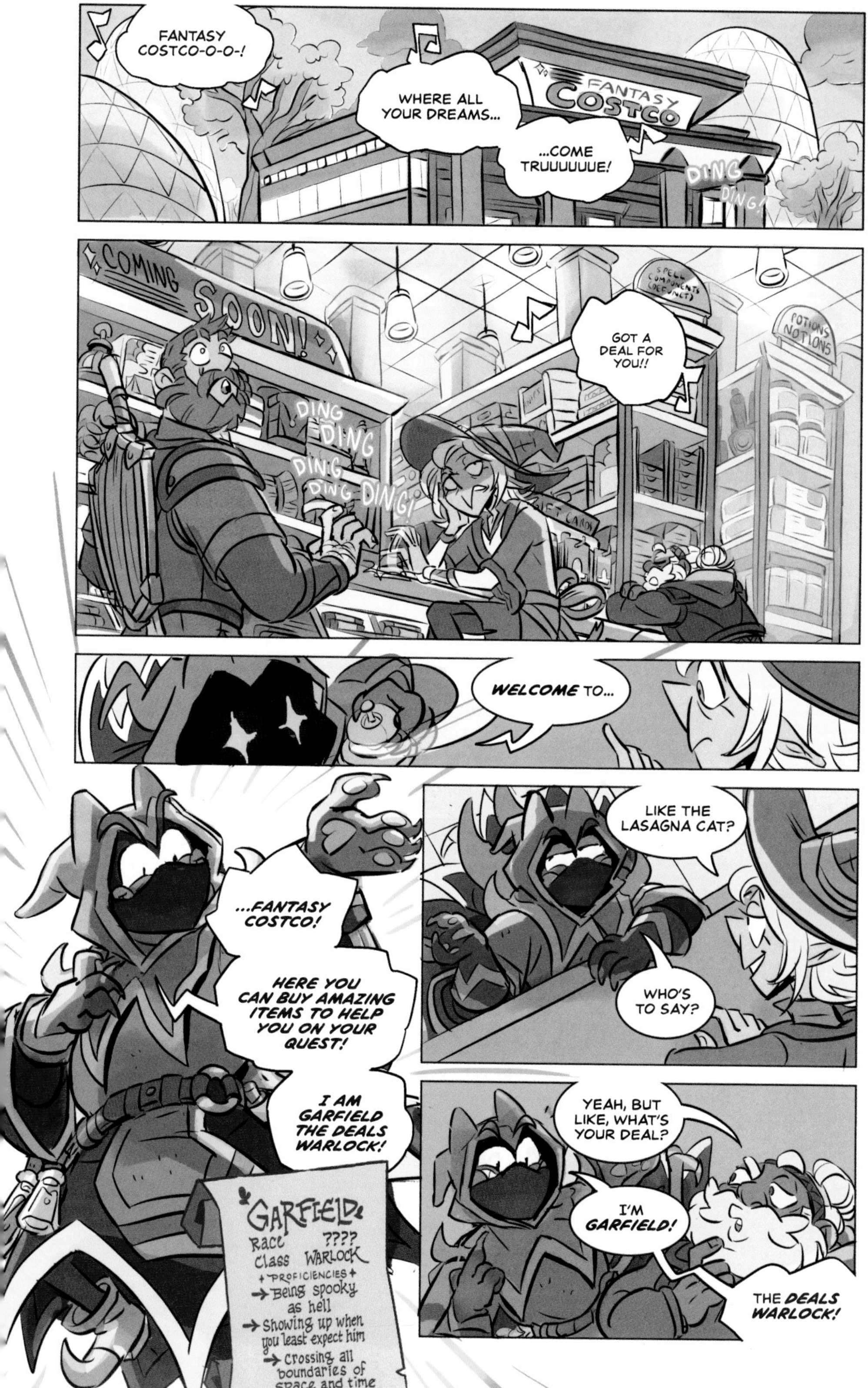
FANTASY COSTCO-O-O-!
WHERE ALL YOUR DREAMS...
...COME TRUUUUUUE!
FANTASY COSTCO
DING DING!
COMING SOON!
SPELL COMPONENTS (DEFUNCT)
POTIONS NOTIONS
GOT A DEAL FOR YOU!!
DING DING DING DING DING!
WELCOME TO...
...FANTASY COSTCO!
HERE YOU CAN BUY AMAZING ITEMS TO HELP YOU ON YOUR QUEST!
I AM GARFIELD THE DEALS WARLOCK!
GARFIELD
Race ????
Class WARLOCK
PROFICIENCIES
Being spooky as hell
Showing up when you least expect him
Crossing all boundaries of space and time
LIKE THE LASAGNA CAT?
WHO'S TO SAY?
YEAH, BUT LIKE, WHAT'S YOUR DEAL?
I'M GARFIELD!
THE DEALS WARLOCK!

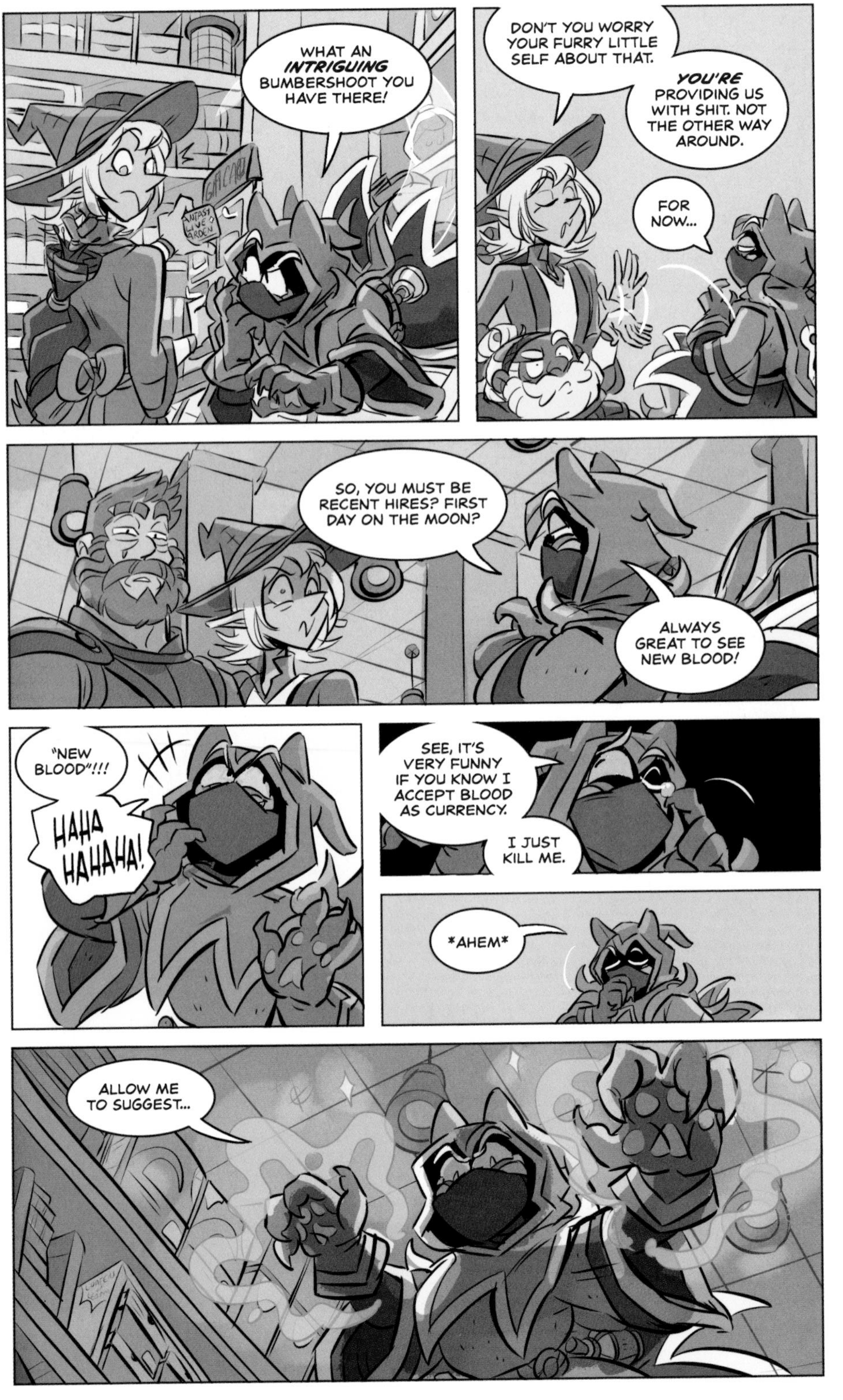
WHAT AN INTRIGUING BUMBERSHOOT YOU HAVE THERE!
DON'T YOU WORRY YOUR FURRY LITTLE SELF ABOUT THAT.
YOU'RE PROVIDING US WITH SHIT. NOT THE OTHER WAY AROUND.
FOR NOW...
SO, YOU MUST BE RECENT HIRES? FIRST DAY ON THE MOON?
ALWAYS GREAT TO SEE NEW BLOOD!
"NEW BLOOD"!!!
HAHA HAHAHA!
SEE, IT'S VERY FUNNY IF YOU KNOW I ACCEPT BLOOD AS CURRENCY.
I JUST KILL ME.
AHEM
ALLOW ME TO SUGGEST...

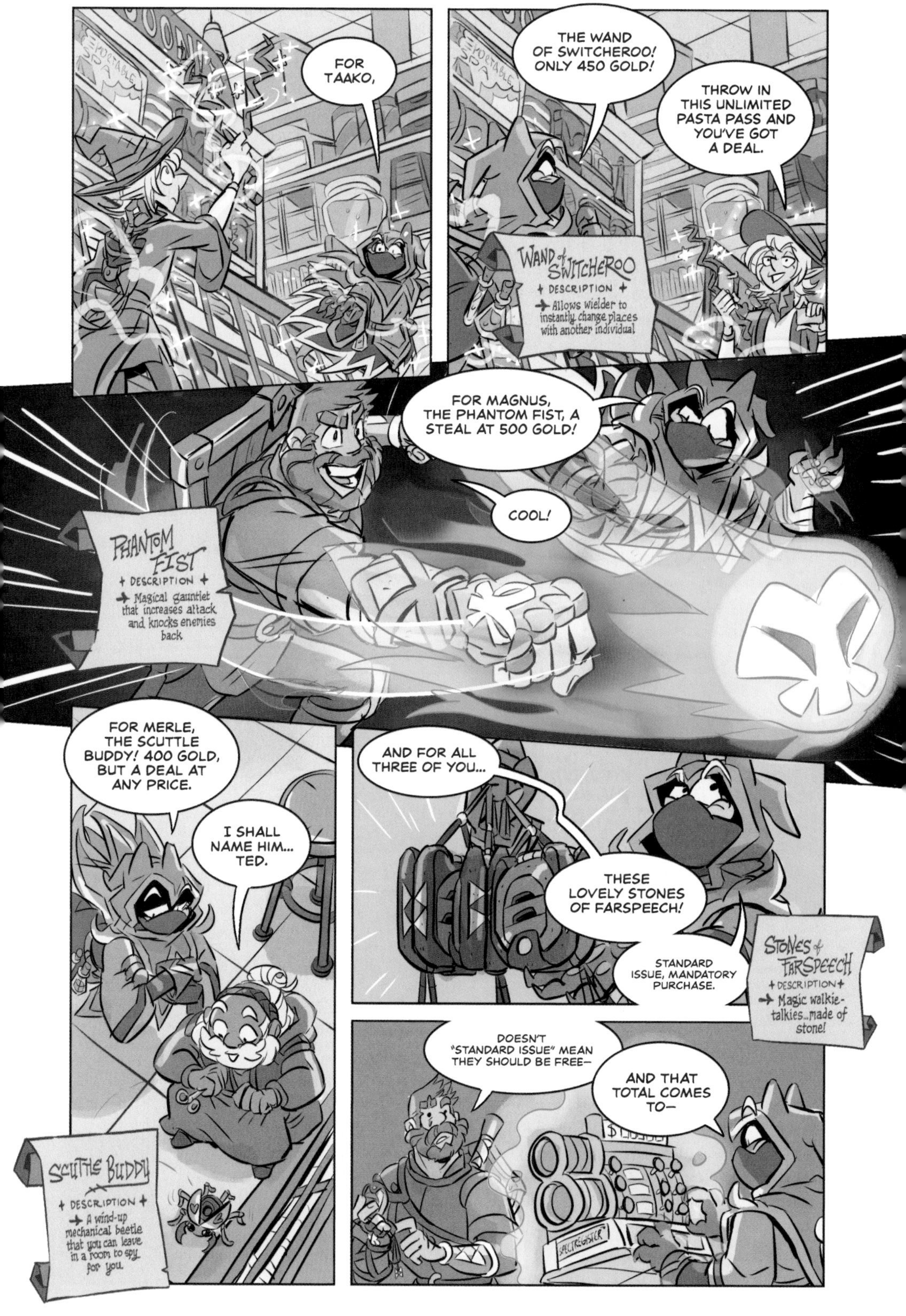
FOR TAAKO,
THE WAND OF SWITCHEROO! ONLY 450 GOLD!
THROW IN THIS UNLIMITED PASTA PASS AND YOU'VE GOT A DEAL.
PORTABLE SPA
WAND of SWITCHEROO
DESCRIPTION
Allows wielder to instantly change places with another individual
FOR MAGNUS, THE PHANTOM FIST, A STEAL AT 500 GOLD!
COOL!
PHANTOM FIST
DESCRIPTION
Magical gauntlet that increases attack and knocks enemies back
FOR MERLE, THE SCUTTLE BUDDY! 400 GOLD, BUT A DEAL AT ANY PRICE.
I SHALL NAME HIM... TED.
SCUTTLE BUDDY
DESCRIPTION
A wind-up mechanical beetle that you can leave in a room to spy for you.
AND FOR ALL THREE OF YOU...
THESE LOVELY STONES OF FARSPEECH!
STANDARD ISSUE, MANDATORY PURCHASE.
STONES of FARSPEECH
DESCRIPTION
Magic walkie-talkies...made of stone!
DOESN'T "STANDARD ISSUE" MEAN THEY SHOULD BE FREE—
AND THAT TOTAL COMES TO—
SPECTREGISTER

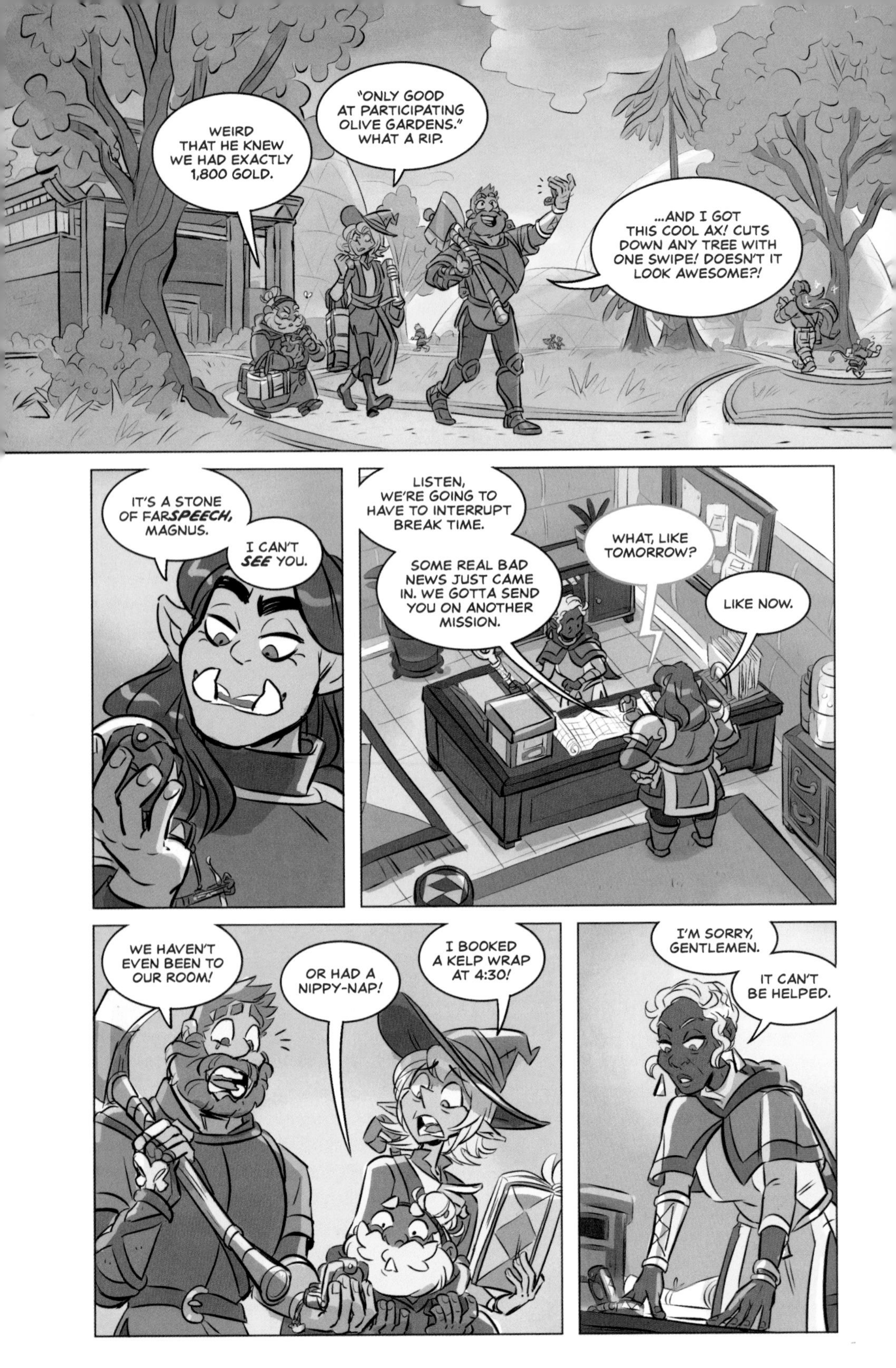
WEIRD THAT HE KNEW WE HAD EXACTLY 1,800 GOLD.
"ONLY GOOD AT PARTICIPATING OLIVE GARDENS." WHAT A RIP.
...AND I GOT THIS COOL AX! CUTS DOWN ANY TREE WITH ONE SWIPE! DOESN'T IT LOOK AWESOME?!
IT'S A STONE OF FAR*SPEECH*, MAGNUS.
I CAN'T *SEE* YOU.
LISTEN, WE'RE GOING TO HAVE TO INTERRUPT BREAK TIME.
SOME REAL BAD NEWS JUST CAME IN. WE GOTTA SEND YOU ON ANOTHER MISSION.
WHAT, LIKE TOMORROW?
LIKE NOW.
WE HAVEN'T EVEN BEEN TO OUR ROOM!
OR HAD A NIPPY-NAP!
I BOOKED A KELP WRAP AT 4:30!
I'M SORRY, GENTLEMEN.
IT CAN'T BE HELPED.

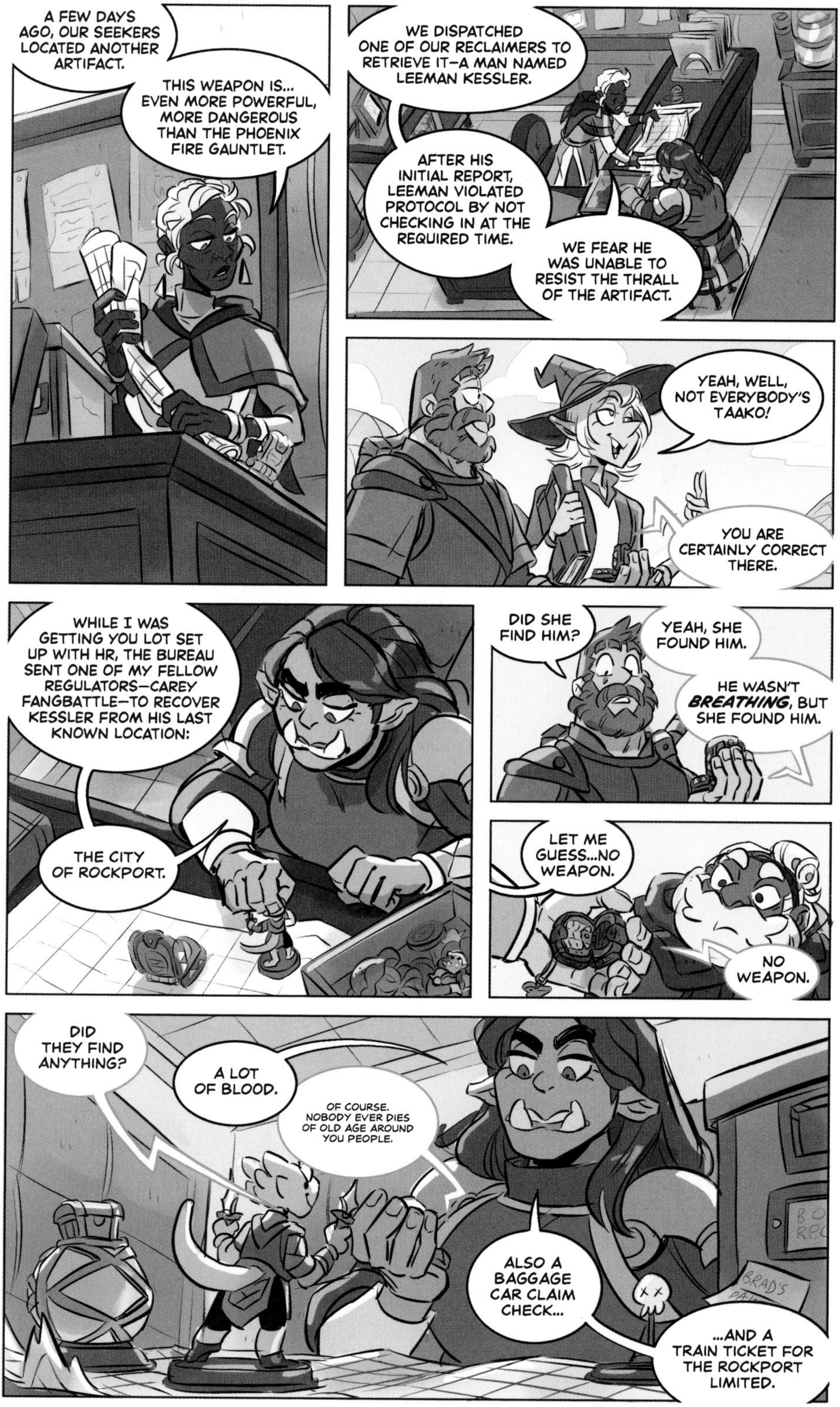

A FEW DAYS AGO, OUR SEEKERS LOCATED ANOTHER ARTIFACT.
THIS WEAPON IS... EVEN MORE POWERFUL, MORE DANGEROUS THAN THE PHOENIX FIRE GAUNTLET.
WE DISPATCHED ONE OF OUR RECLAIMERS TO RETRIEVE IT—A MAN NAMED LEEMAN KESSLER.
AFTER HIS INITIAL REPORT, LEEMAN VIOLATED PROTOCOL BY NOT CHECKING IN AT THE REQUIRED TIME.
WE FEAR HE WAS UNABLE TO RESIST THE THRALL OF THE ARTIFACT.
YEAH, WELL, NOT EVERYBODY'S TAAKO!
YOU ARE CERTAINLY CORRECT THERE.
WHILE I WAS GETTING YOU LOT SET UP WITH HR, THE BUREAU SENT ONE OF MY FELLOW REGULATORS—CAREY FANGBATTLE—TO RECOVER KESSLER FROM HIS LAST KNOWN LOCATION:
THE CITY OF ROCKPORT.
DID SHE FIND HIM?
YEAH, SHE FOUND HIM.
HE WASN'T ***BREATHING***, BUT SHE FOUND HIM.
LET ME GUESS...NO WEAPON.
NO WEAPON.
DID THEY FIND ANYTHING?
A LOT OF BLOOD.
OF COURSE. NOBODY EVER DIES OF OLD AGE AROUND YOU PEOPLE.
ALSO A BAGGAGE CAR CLAIM CHECK...
...AND A TRAIN TICKET FOR THE ROCKPORT LIMITED.

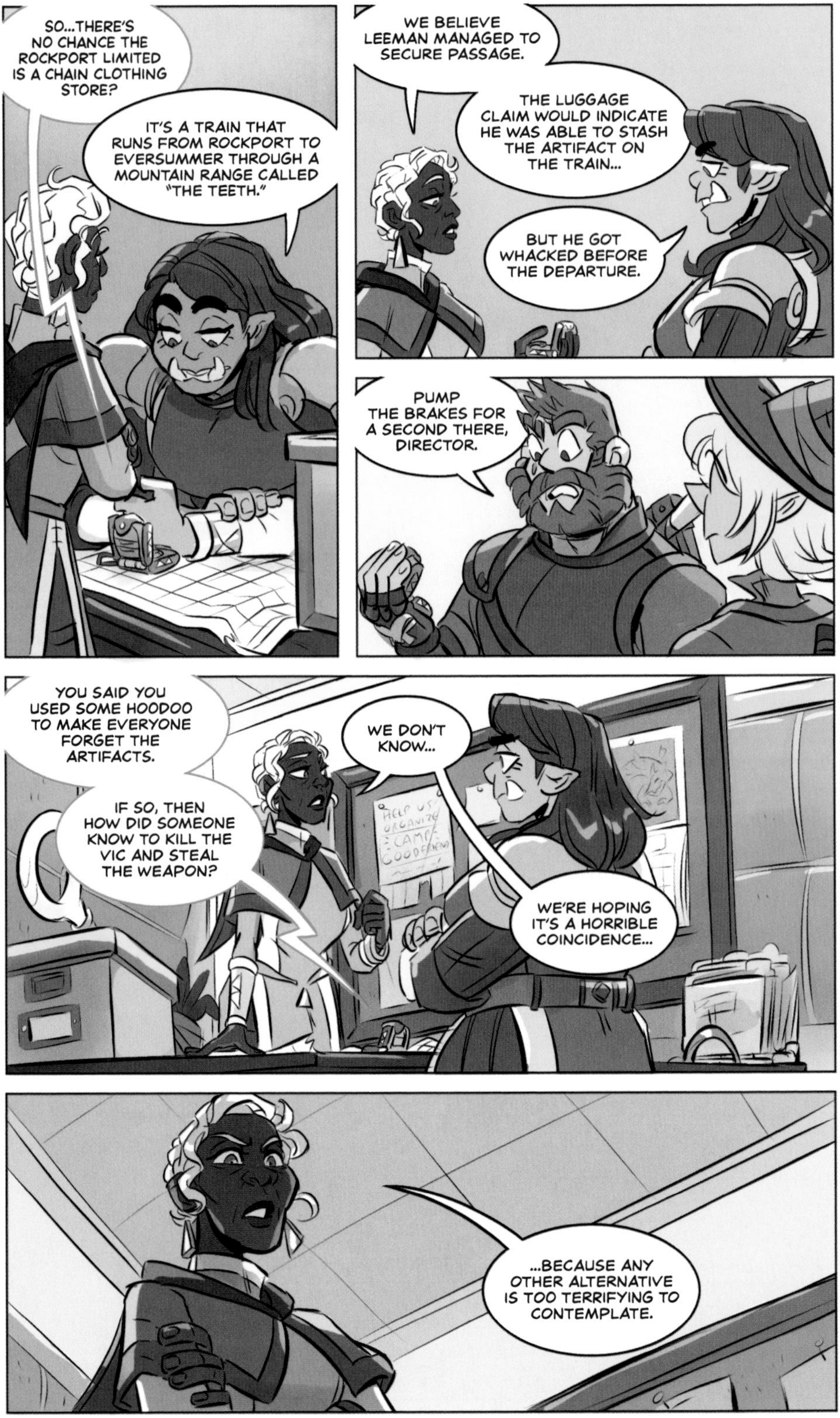
SO...THERE'S NO CHANCE THE ROCKPORT LIMITED IS A CHAIN CLOTHING STORE?
IT'S A TRAIN THAT RUNS FROM ROCKPORT TO EVERSUMMER THROUGH A MOUNTAIN RANGE CALLED "THE TEETH."
WE BELIEVE LEEMAN MANAGED TO SECURE PASSAGE.
THE LUGGAGE CLAIM WOULD INDICATE HE WAS ABLE TO STASH THE ARTIFACT ON THE TRAIN...
BUT HE GOT WHACKED BEFORE THE DEPARTURE.
PUMP THE BRAKES FOR A SECOND THERE, DIRECTOR.
YOU SAID YOU USED SOME HOODOO TO MAKE EVERYONE FORGET THE ARTIFACTS.
IF SO, THEN HOW DID SOMEONE KNOW TO KILL THE VIC AND STEAL THE WEAPON?
WE DON'T KNOW...
WE'RE HOPING IT'S A HORRIBLE COINCIDENCE...
...BECAUSE ANY OTHER ALTERNATIVE IS TOO TERRIFYING TO CONTEMPLATE.

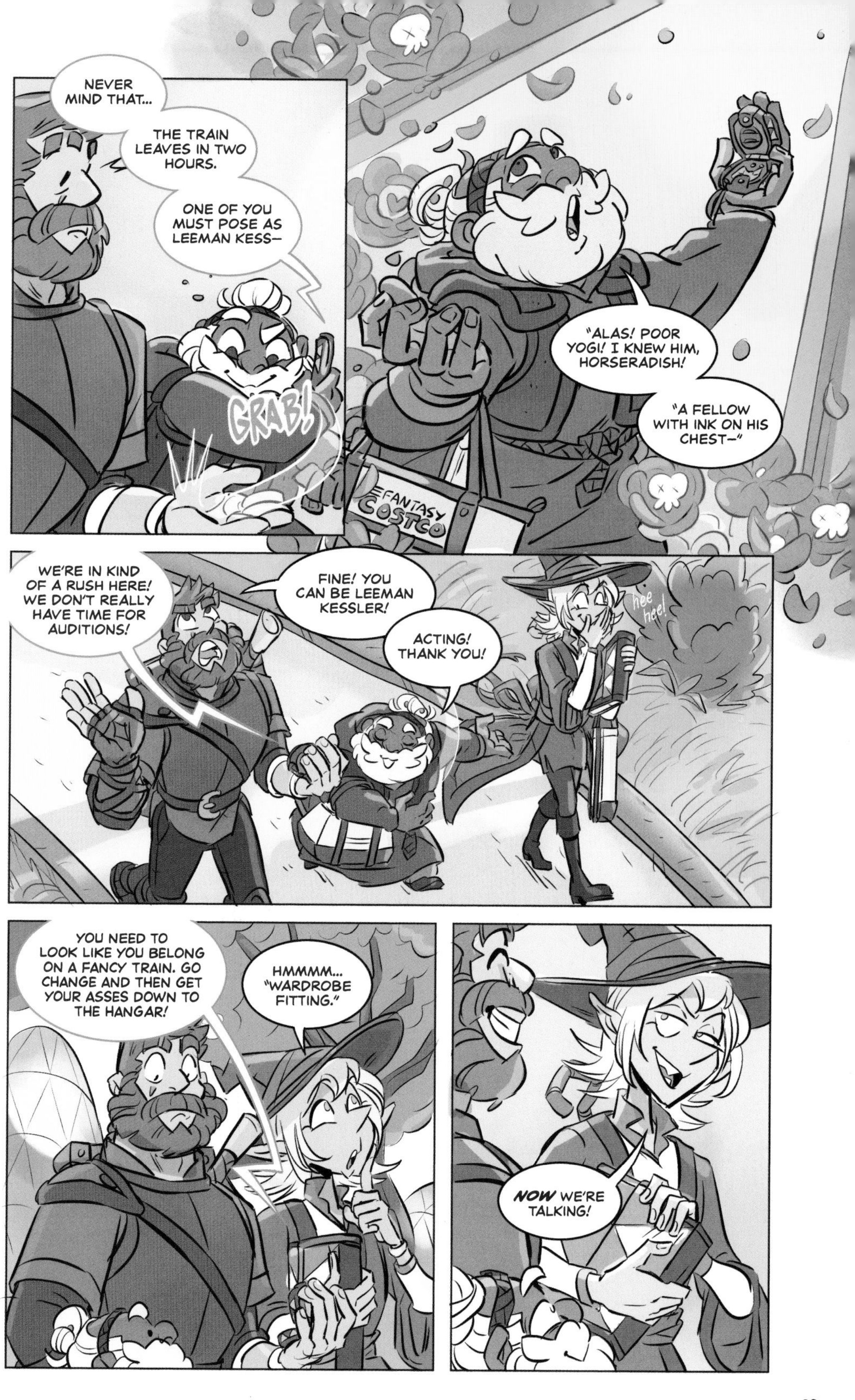
NEVER MIND THAT...
THE TRAIN LEAVES IN TWO HOURS.
ONE OF YOU MUST POSE AS LEEMAN KESS—
GRAB!
FANTASY COSTCO
"ALAS! POOR YOGI! I KNEW HIM, HORSERADISH!
"A FELLOW WITH INK ON HIS CHEST—"
WE'RE IN KIND OF A RUSH HERE! WE DON'T REALLY HAVE TIME FOR AUDITIONS!
FINE! YOU CAN BE LEEMAN KESSLER!
ACTING! THANK YOU!
hee hee!
YOU NEED TO LOOK LIKE YOU BELONG ON A FANCY TRAIN. GO CHANGE AND THEN GET YOUR ASSES DOWN TO THE HANGAR!
HMMMM... "WARDROBE FITTING."
NOW WE'RE TALKING!

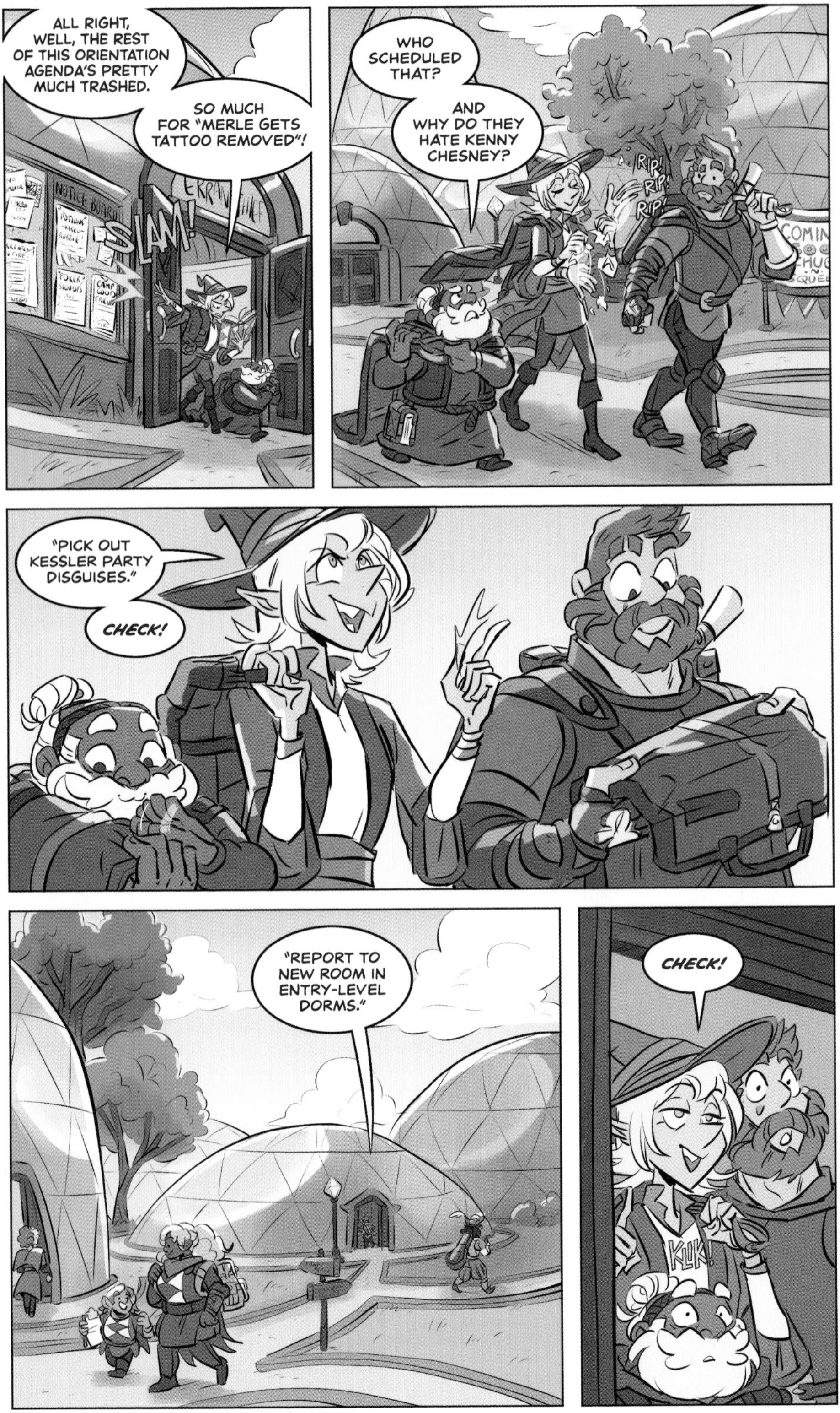
ALL RIGHT, WELL, THE REST OF THIS ORIENTATION AGENDA'S PRETTY MUCH TRASHED.
SO MUCH FOR "MERLE GETS TATTOO REMOVED"!
NOTICE BOARD
SLAM!
WHO SCHEDULED THAT?
AND WHY DO THEY HATE KENNY CHESNEY?
RIP! RIP! RIP!
"PICK OUT KESSLER PARTY DISGUISES."
CHECK!
"REPORT TO NEW ROOM IN ENTRY-LEVEL DORMS."
CHECK!
KLIK!

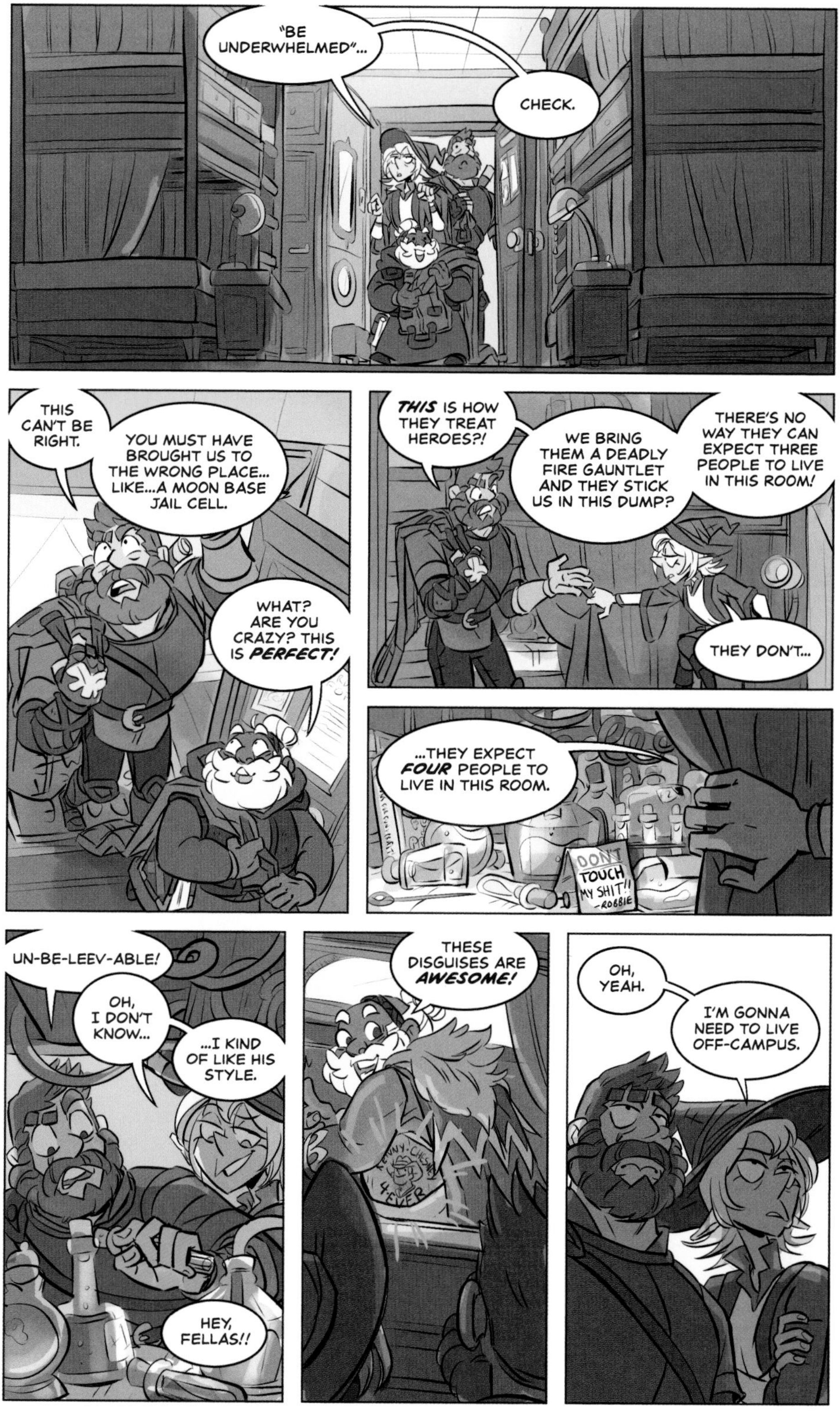
"BE UNDERWHELMED"...
CHECK.
THIS CAN'T BE RIGHT.
YOU MUST HAVE BROUGHT US TO THE WRONG PLACE... LIKE...A MOON BASE JAIL CELL.
WHAT? ARE YOU CRAZY? THIS IS PERFECT!
THIS IS HOW THEY TREAT HEROES?!
WE BRING THEM A DEADLY FIRE GAUNTLET AND THEY STICK US IN THIS DUMP?
THERE'S NO WAY THEY CAN EXPECT THREE PEOPLE TO LIVE IN THIS ROOM!
THEY DON'T...
...THEY EXPECT FOUR PEOPLE TO LIVE IN THIS ROOM.
DON'T TOUCH MY SHIT!! -ROBBIE
UN-BE-LEEV-ABLE!
OH, I DON'T KNOW...
...I KIND OF LIKE HIS STYLE.
HEY, FELLAS!!
THESE DISGUISES ARE AWESOME!
OH, YEAH.
I'M GONNA NEED TO LIVE OFF-CAMPUS.

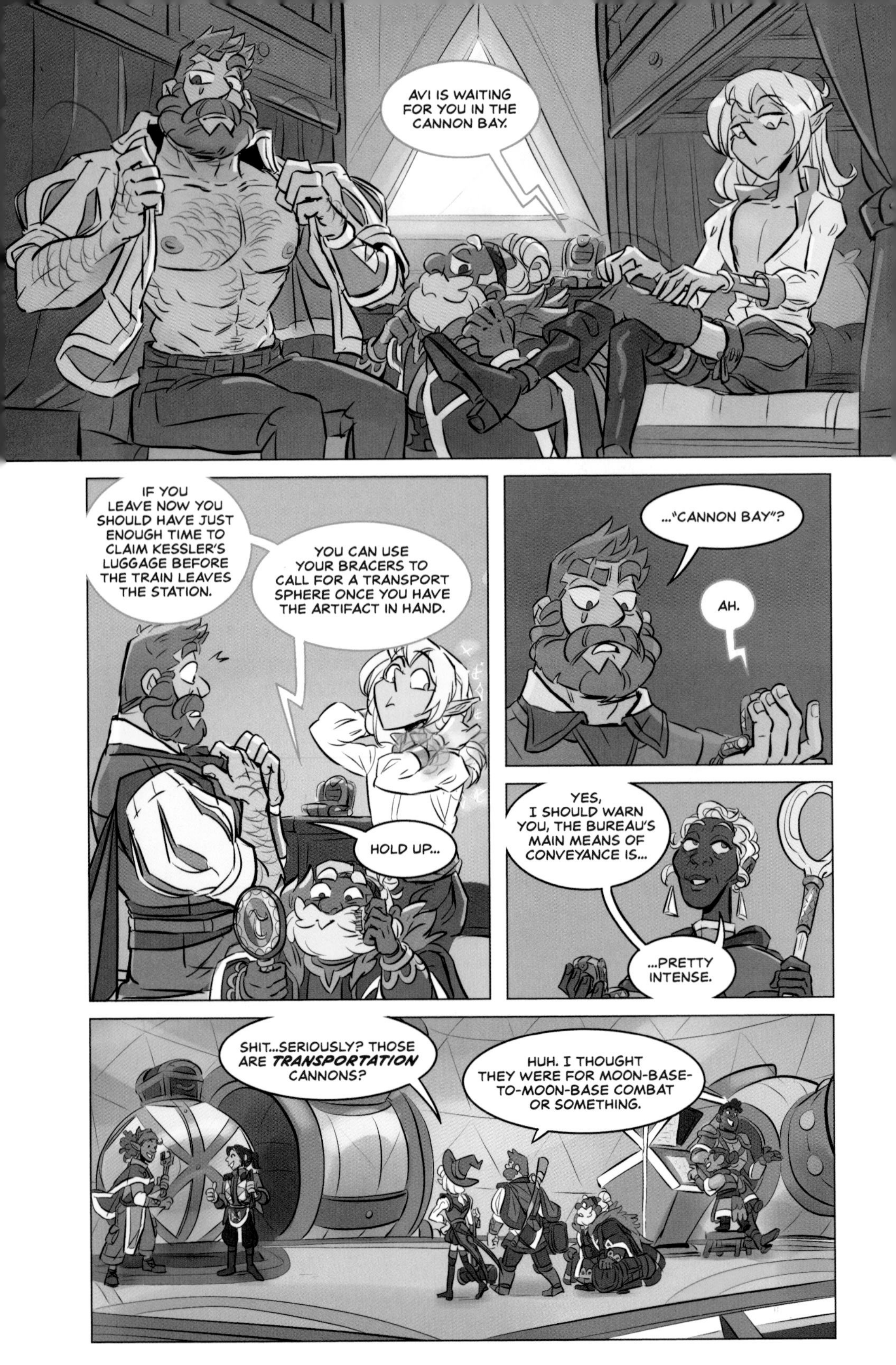
AVI IS WAITING FOR YOU IN THE CANNON BAY.
IF YOU LEAVE NOW YOU SHOULD HAVE JUST ENOUGH TIME TO CLAIM KESSLER'S LUGGAGE BEFORE THE TRAIN LEAVES THE STATION.
YOU CAN USE YOUR BRACERS TO CALL FOR A TRANSPORT SPHERE ONCE YOU HAVE THE ARTIFACT IN HAND.
HOLD UP...
..."CANNON BAY"?
AH.
YES, I SHOULD WARN YOU, THE BUREAU'S MAIN MEANS OF CONVEYANCE IS...
...PRETTY INTENSE.
SHIT...SERIOUSLY? THOSE ARE *TRANSPORTATION* CANNONS?
HUH. I THOUGHT THEY WERE FOR MOON-BASE-TO-MOON-BASE COMBAT OR SOMETHING.

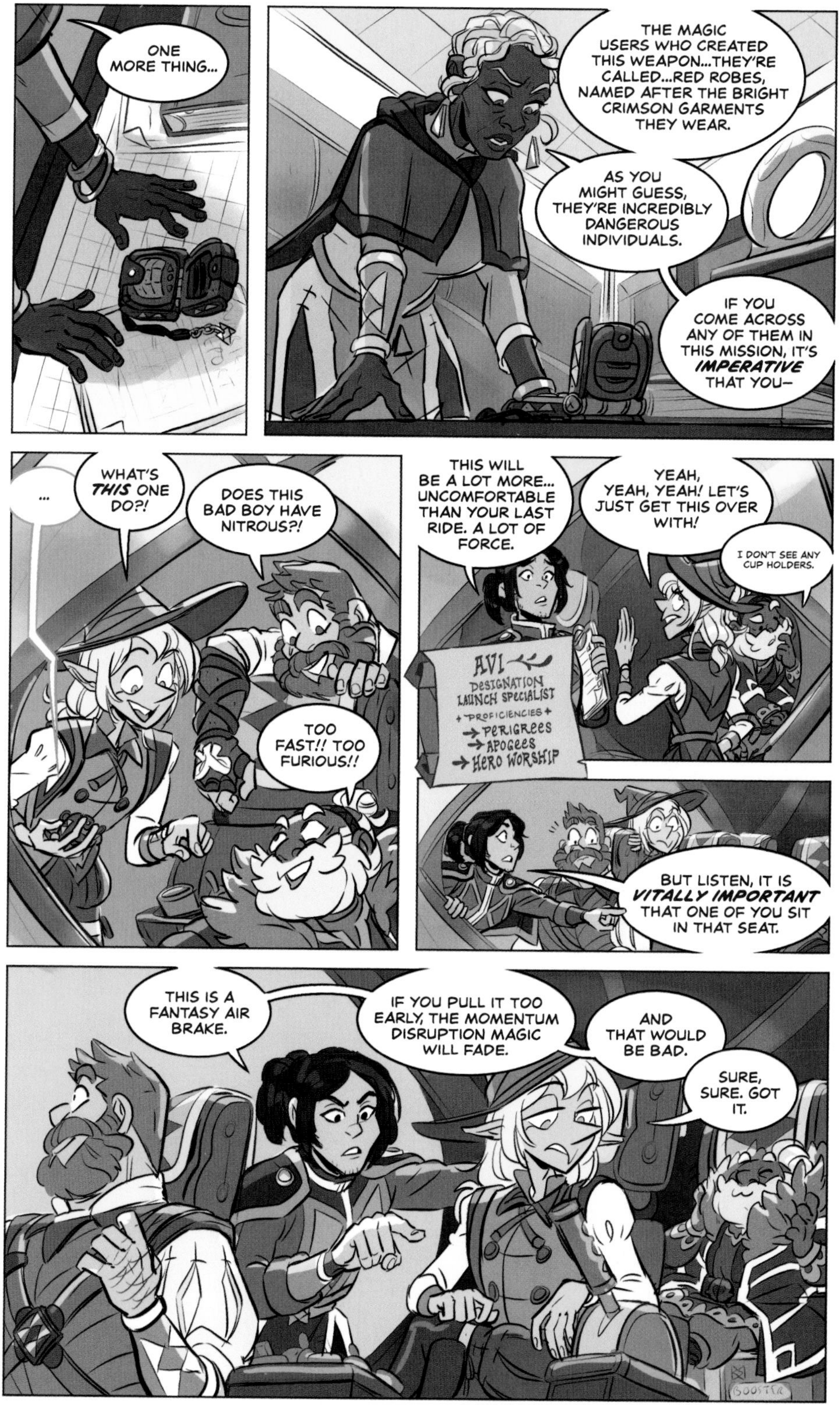
ONE MORE THING...
THE MAGIC USERS WHO CREATED THIS WEAPON...THEY'RE CALLED...RED ROBES, NAMED AFTER THE BRIGHT CRIMSON GARMENTS THEY WEAR.
AS YOU MIGHT GUESS, THEY'RE INCREDIBLY DANGEROUS INDIVIDUALS.
IF YOU COME ACROSS ANY OF THEM IN THIS MISSION, IT'S IMPERATIVE THAT YOU—
...
WHAT'S THIS ONE DO?!
DOES THIS BAD BOY HAVE NITROUS?!
TOO FAST!! TOO FURIOUS!!
THIS WILL BE A LOT MORE... UNCOMFORTABLE THAN YOUR LAST RIDE. A LOT OF FORCE.
YEAH, YEAH, YEAH! LET'S JUST GET THIS OVER WITH!
I DON'T SEE ANY CUP HOLDERS.
AVI
DESIGNATION LAUNCH SPECIALIST
PROFICIENCIES
PERIGREES
APOGEES
HERO WORSHIP
BUT LISTEN, IT IS VITALLY IMPORTANT THAT ONE OF YOU SIT IN THAT SEAT.
THIS IS A FANTASY AIR BRAKE.
IF YOU PULL IT TOO EARLY, THE MOMENTUM DISRUPTION MAGIC WILL FADE.
AND THAT WOULD BE BAD.
SURE, SURE. GOT IT.
BOOSTER

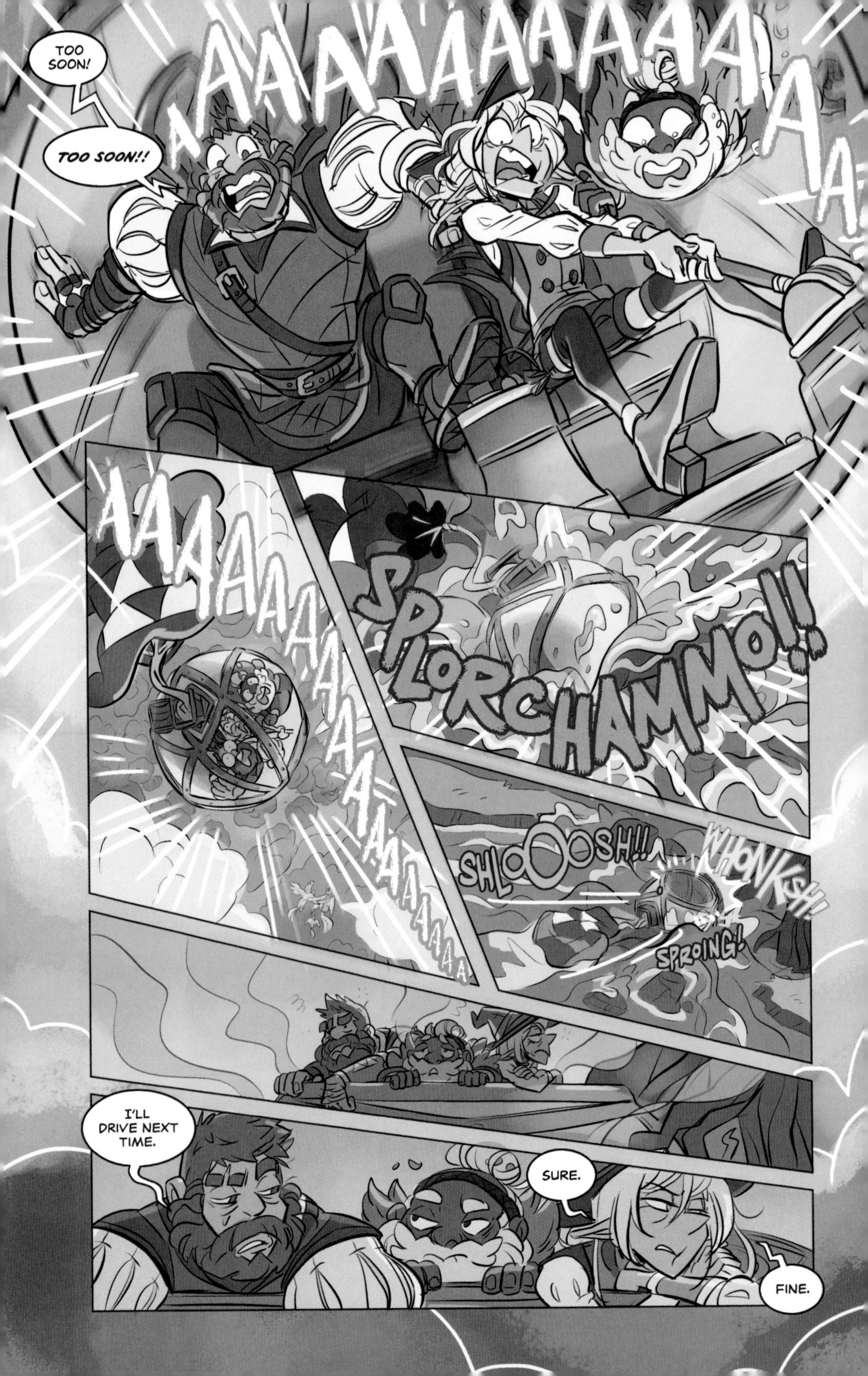
TOO SOON!
TOO SOON!!
AAAAAAAAAAAAA
AAAAAAAAAAAAAAAAAAAA
SPLORCHAMMO!!
SHLOOOOSH!!
WHONKSH!!
SPROING!
I'LL DRIVE NEXT TIME.
SURE.
FINE.

Chapter 2

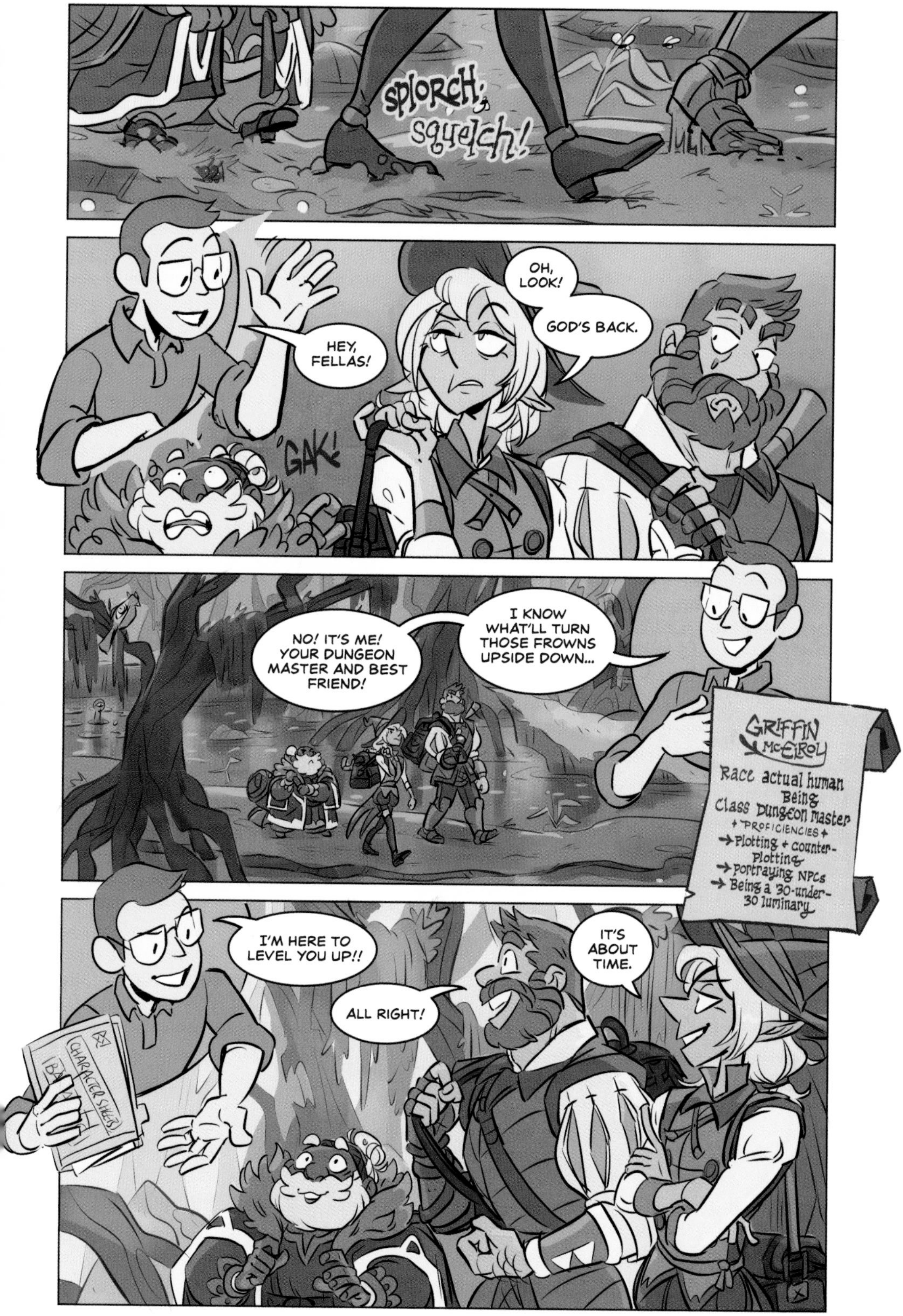
SPLORCH, squelch!
HEY, FELLAS!
OH, LOOK!
GOD'S BACK.
GAK!
NO! IT'S ME! YOUR DUNGEON MASTER AND BEST FRIEND!
I KNOW WHAT'LL TURN THOSE FROWNS UPSIDE DOWN...
GRIFFIN McELROY
Race actual human Being
Class Dungeon master
PROFICIENCIES
Plotting + counter-Plotting
Portraying NPCs
Being a 30-under-30 luminary
I'M HERE TO LEVEL YOU UP!!
IT'S ABOUT TIME.
ALL RIGHT!
CHARACTER SHEETS

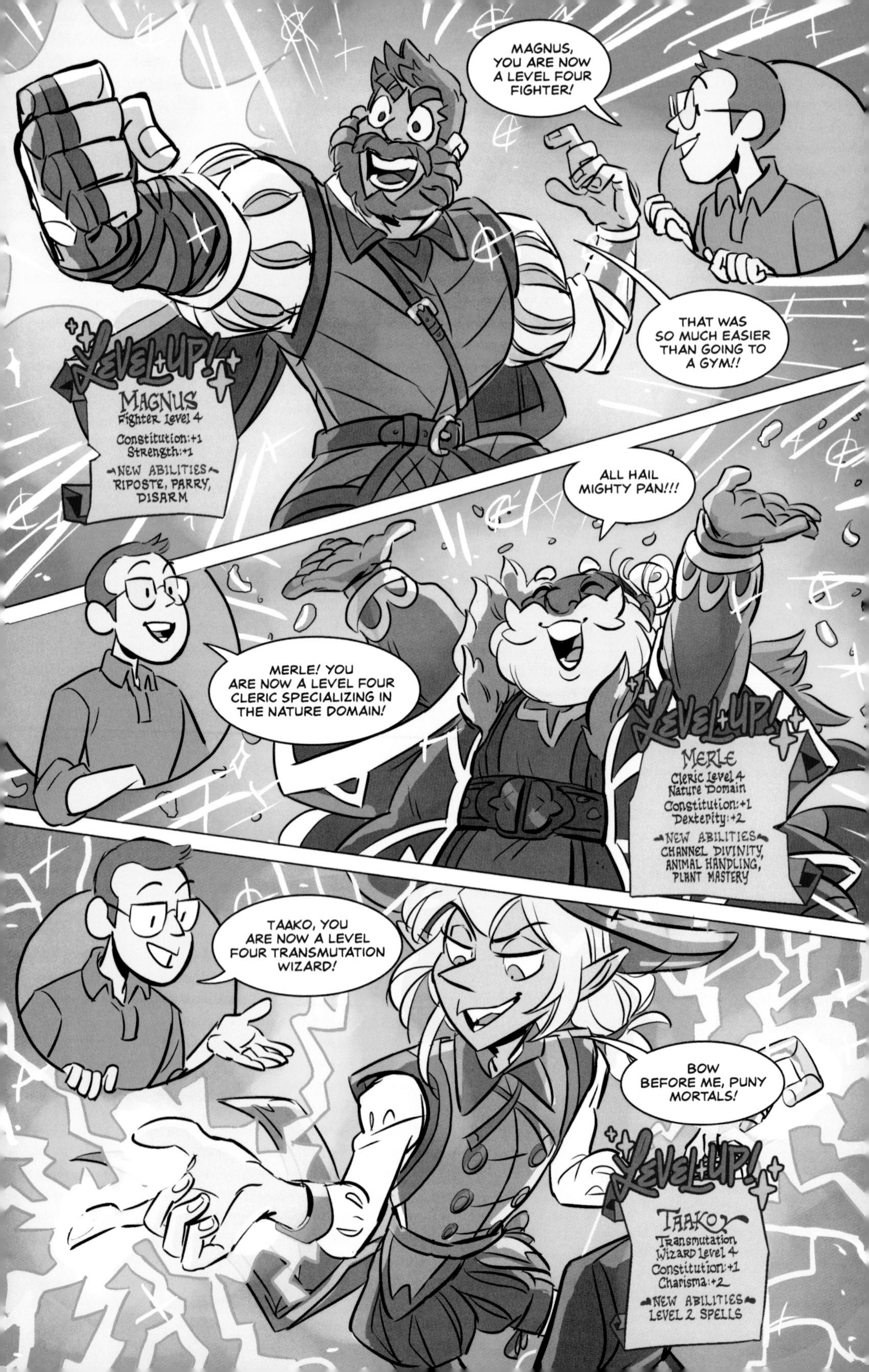
MAGNUS, YOU ARE NOW A LEVEL FOUR FIGHTER!
THAT WAS SO MUCH EASIER THAN GOING TO A GYM!!
LEVEL UP!
MAGNUS
Fighter Level 4
Constitution: +1
Strength: +1
NEW ABILITIES
RIPOSTE, PARRY, DISARM
ALL HAIL MIGHTY PAN!!!
MERLE! YOU ARE NOW A LEVEL FOUR CLERIC SPECIALIZING IN THE NATURE DOMAIN!
LEVEL UP!
MERLE
Cleric Level 4
Nature Domain
Constitution: +1
Dexterity: +2
NEW ABILITIES
CHANNEL DIVINITY, ANIMAL HANDLING, PLANT MASTERY
TAAKO, YOU ARE NOW A LEVEL FOUR TRANSMUTATION WIZARD!
BOW BEFORE ME, PUNY MORTALS!
LEVEL UP!
TAAKO
Transmutation Wizard Level 4
Constitution: +1
Charisma: +2
NEW ABILITIES
LEVEL 2 SPELLS

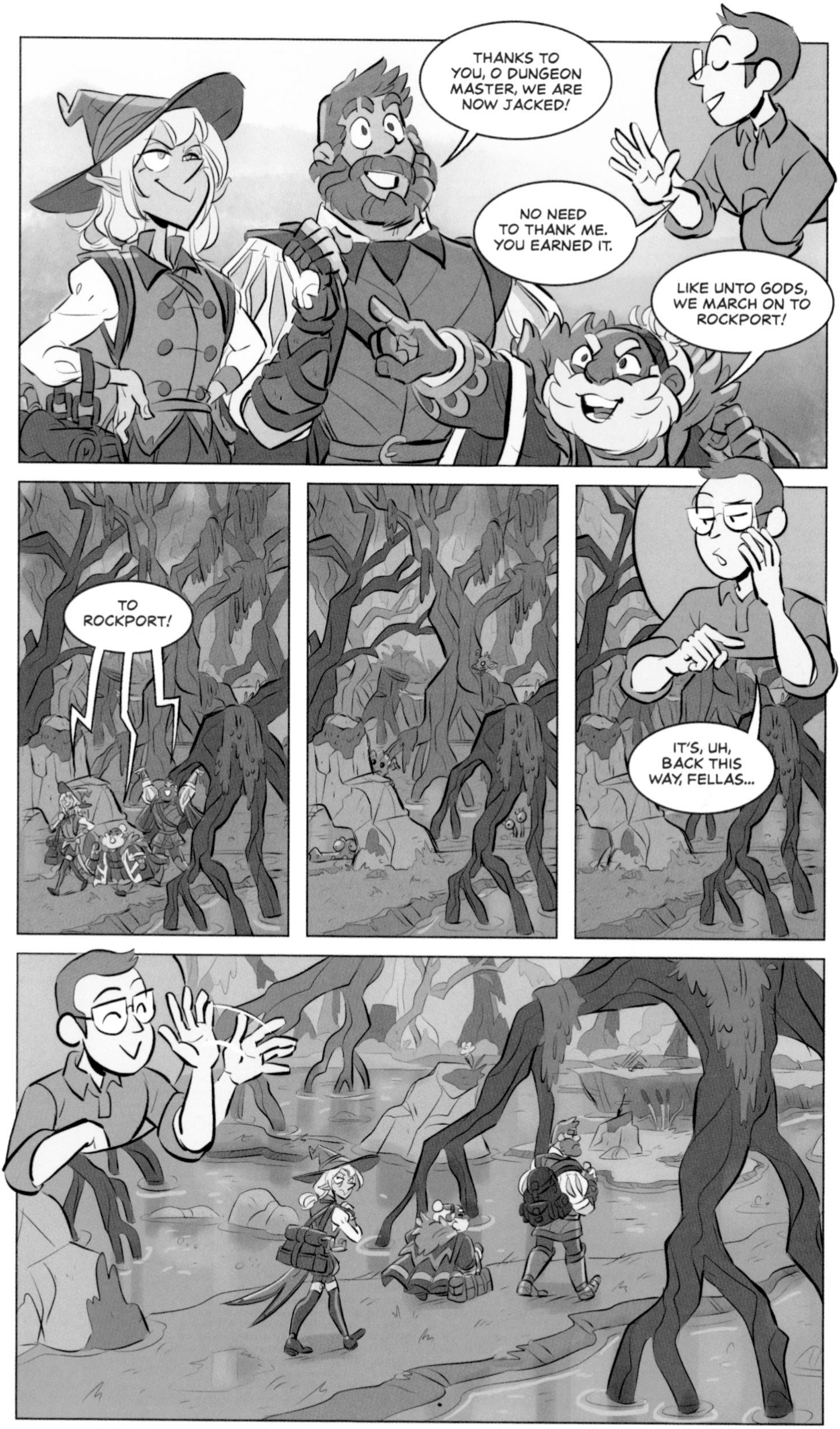
THANKS TO YOU, O DUNGEON MASTER, WE ARE NOW JACKED!
NO NEED TO THANK ME. YOU EARNED IT.
LIKE UNTO GODS, WE MARCH ON TO ROCKPORT!
TO ROCKPORT!
IT'S, UH, BACK THIS WAY, FELLAS...

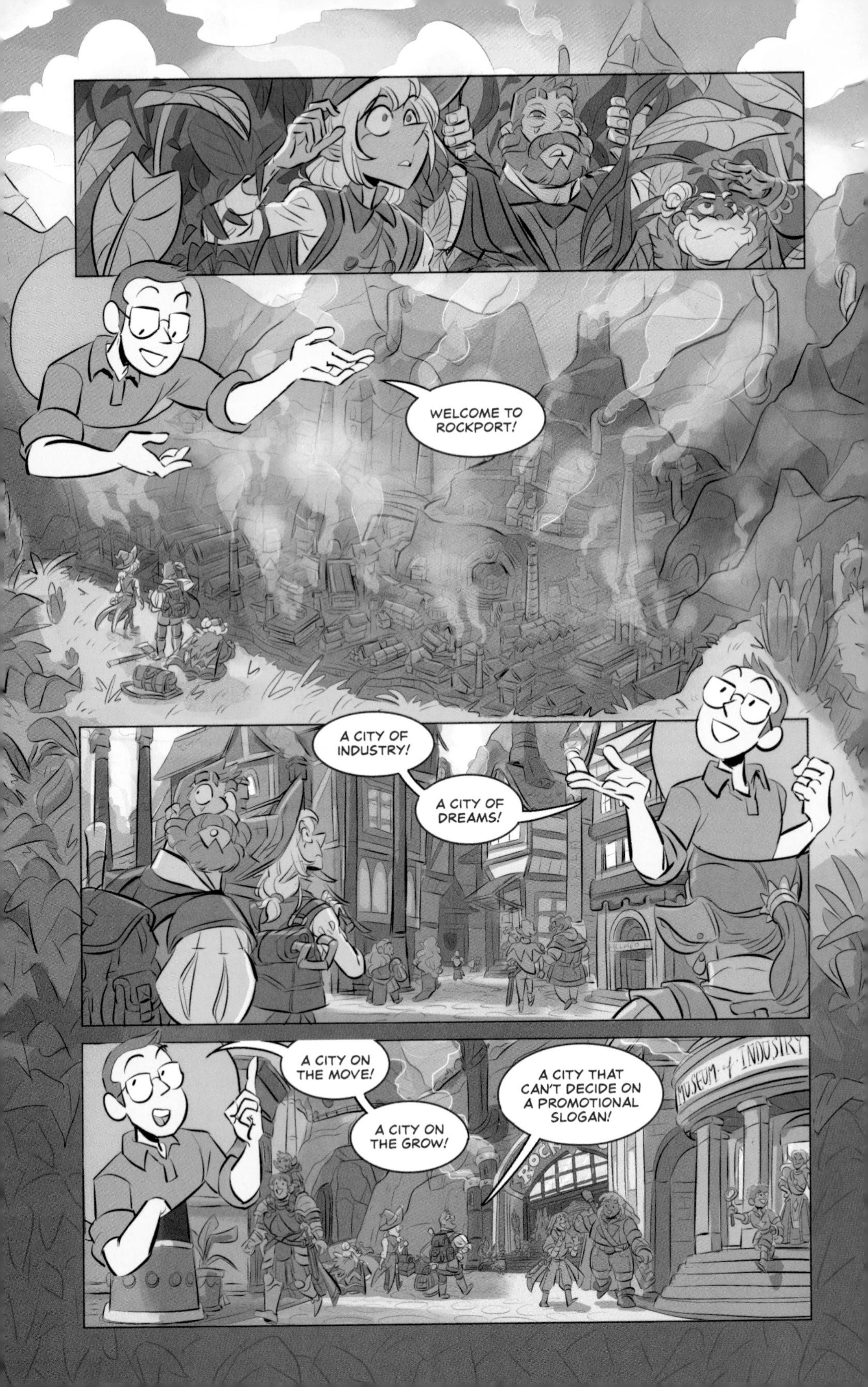
WELCOME TO ROCKPORT!
A CITY OF INDUSTRY!
A CITY OF DREAMS!
A CITY ON THE MOVE!
A CITY ON THE GROW!
A CITY THAT CAN'T DECIDE ON A PROMOTIONAL SLOGAN!
MUSEUM of INDUSTRY

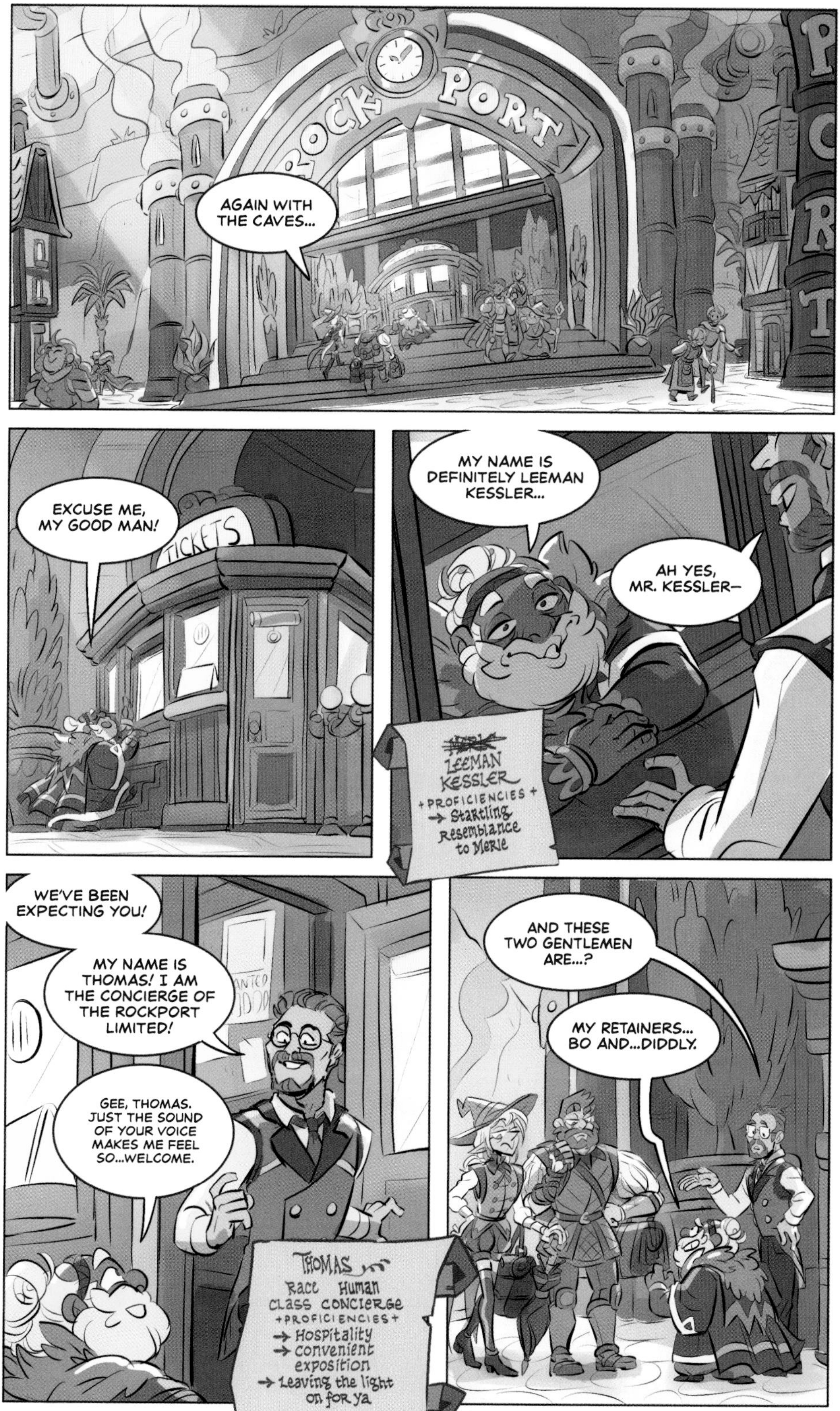
ROCK PORT
AGAIN WITH THE CAVES...
TICKETS
EXCUSE ME, MY GOOD MAN!
MY NAME IS DEFINITELY LEEMAN KESSLER...
AH YES, MR. KESSLER—
LEEMAN KESSLER
+PROFICIENCIES+
→ Startling Resemblance to Merle
WE'VE BEEN EXPECTING YOU!
MY NAME IS THOMAS! I AM THE CONCIERGE OF THE ROCKPORT LIMITED!
GEE, THOMAS. JUST THE SOUND OF YOUR VOICE MAKES ME FEEL SO...WELCOME.
THOMAS
Race Human
Class Concierge
+PROFICIENCIES+
→ Hospitality
→ convenient exposition
→ Leaving the light on for ya
AND THESE TWO GENTLEMEN ARE...?
MY RETAINERS... BO AND...DIDDLY.

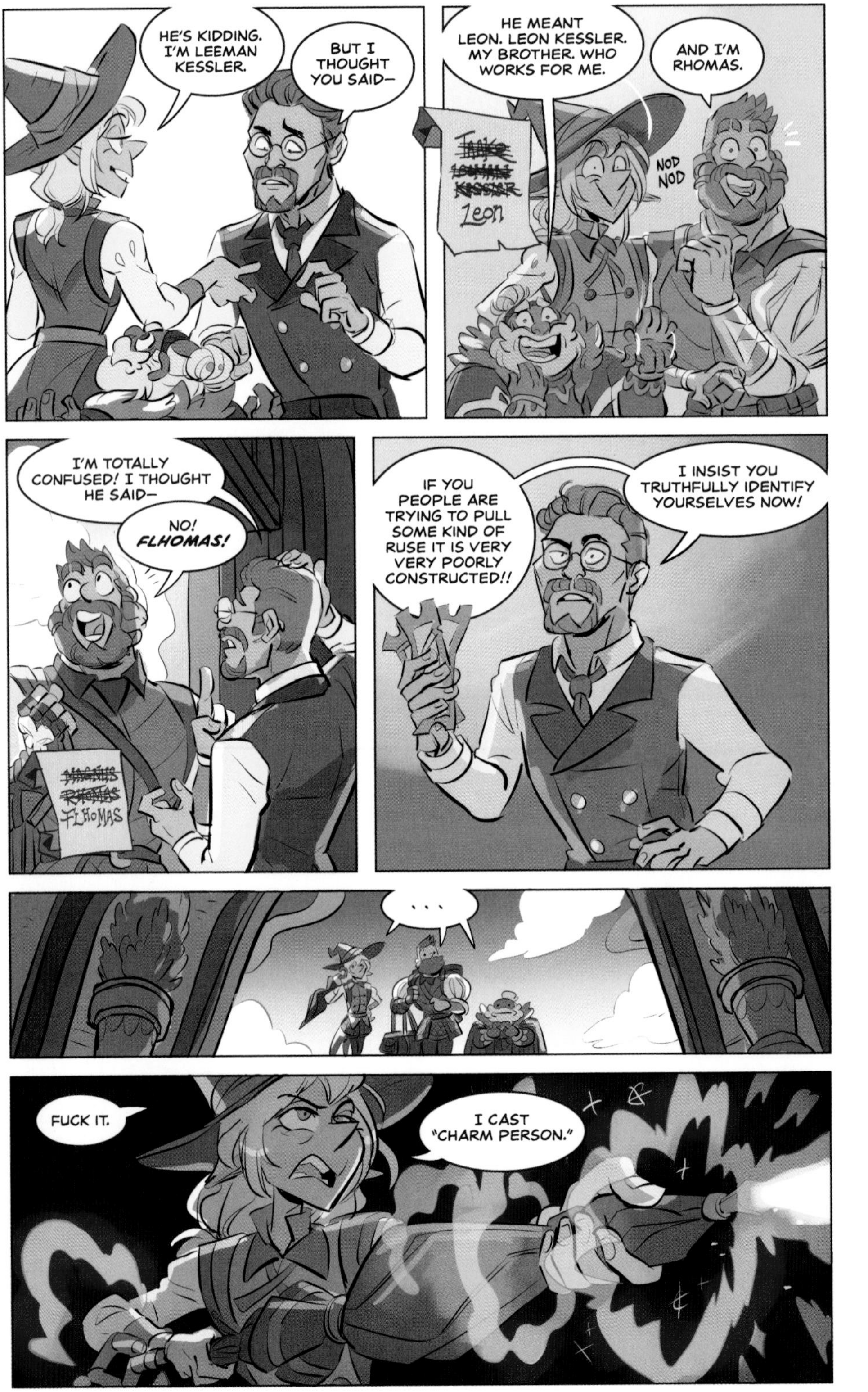
HE'S KIDDING. I'M LEEMAN KESSLER.
BUT I THOUGHT YOU SAID—
HE MEANT LEON. LEON KESSLER. MY BROTHER. WHO WORKS FOR ME.
AND I'M RHOMAS.
Leon
NOD NOD
I'M TOTALLY CONFUSED! I THOUGHT HE SAID—
NO! ***FLHOMAS!***
FLHOMAS
IF YOU PEOPLE ARE TRYING TO PULL SOME KIND OF RUSE IT IS VERY VERY POORLY CONSTRUCTED!!
I INSIST YOU TRUTHFULLY IDENTIFY YOURSELVES NOW!
. . .
FUCK IT.
I CAST "CHARM PERSON."

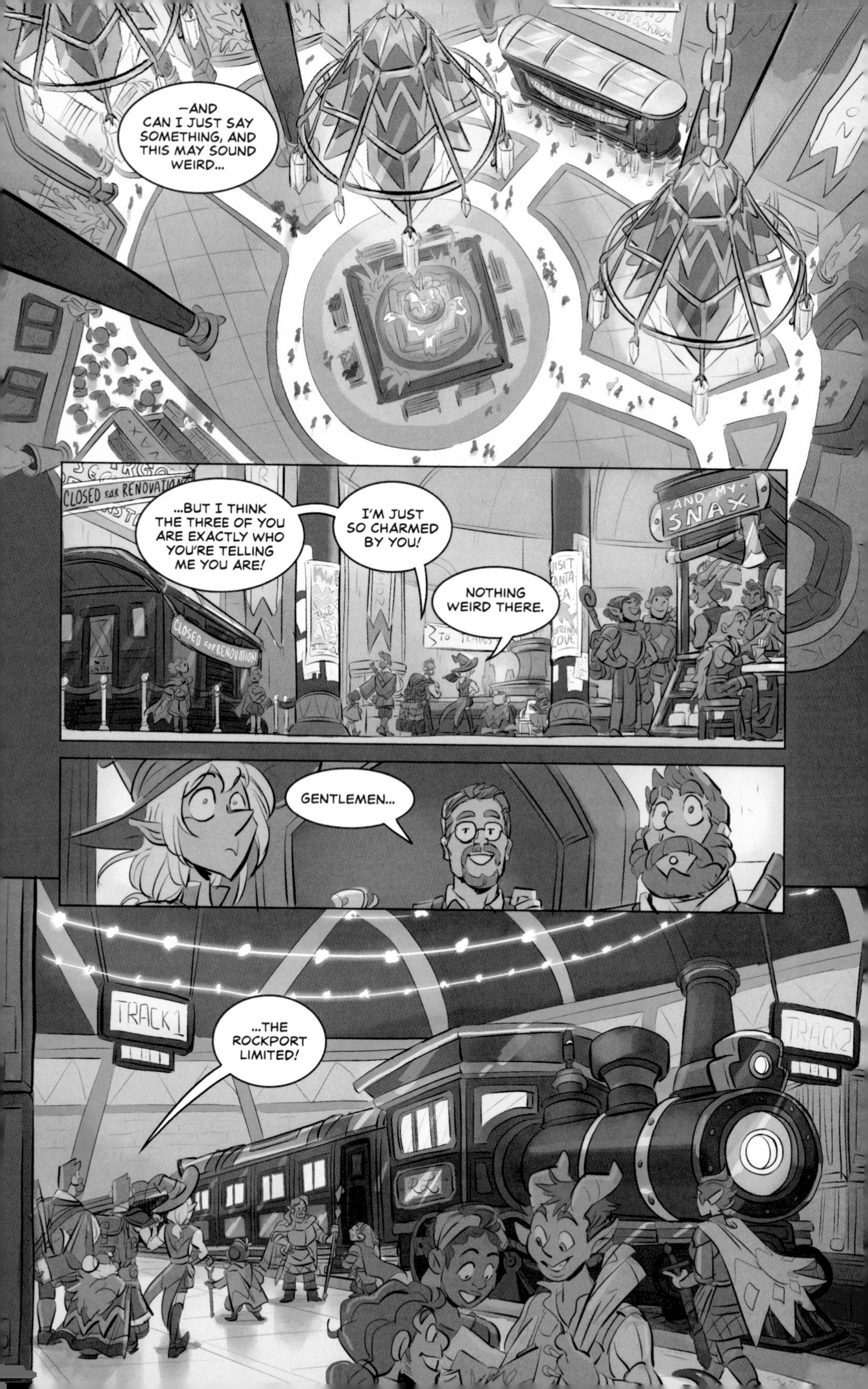
—AND CAN I JUST SAY SOMETHING, AND THIS MAY SOUND WEIRD...
CLOSED FOR RENOVATION
CLOSED FOR RENOVATION
...BUT I THINK THE THREE OF YOU ARE EXACTLY WHO YOU'RE TELLING ME YOU ARE!
I'M JUST SO CHARMED BY YOU!
AND MY SNAX
NOTHING WEIRD THERE.
CLOSED FOR RENOVATION
TO TRAINS
GENTLEMEN...
TRACK 1
...THE ROCKPORT LIMITED!
TRACK 2

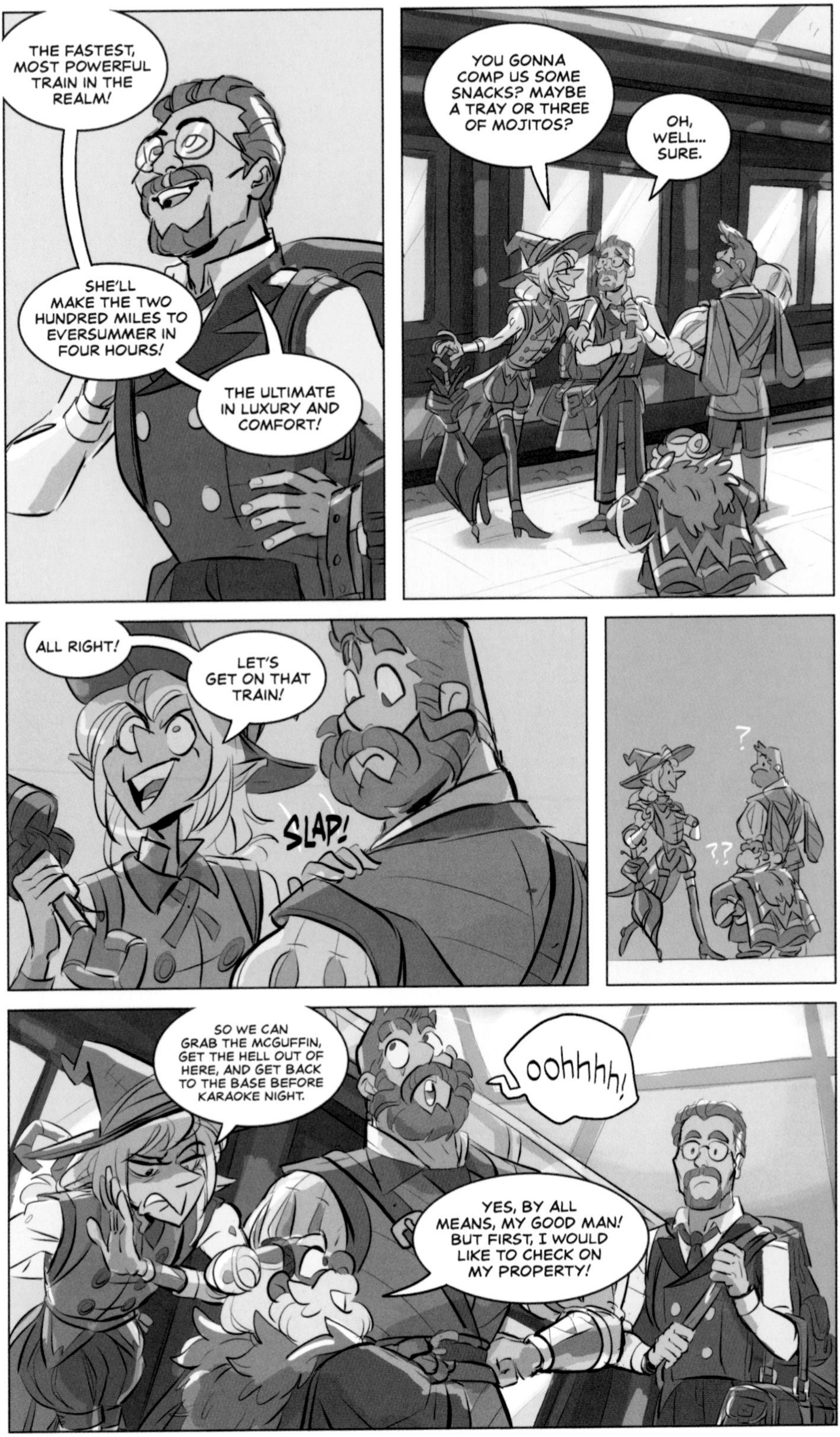
THE FASTEST, MOST POWERFUL TRAIN IN THE REALM!
SHE'LL MAKE THE TWO HUNDRED MILES TO EVERSUMMER IN FOUR HOURS!
THE ULTIMATE IN LUXURY AND COMFORT!
YOU GONNA COMP US SOME SNACKS? MAYBE A TRAY OR THREE OF MOJITOS?
OH, WELL... SURE.
ALL RIGHT!
LET'S GET ON THAT TRAIN!
SLAP!
?
??
SO WE CAN GRAB THE MCGUFFIN, GET THE HELL OUT OF HERE, AND GET BACK TO THE BASE BEFORE KARAOKE NIGHT.
oohhhh!
YES, BY ALL MEANS, MY GOOD MAN! BUT FIRST, I WOULD LIKE TO CHECK ON MY PROPERTY!

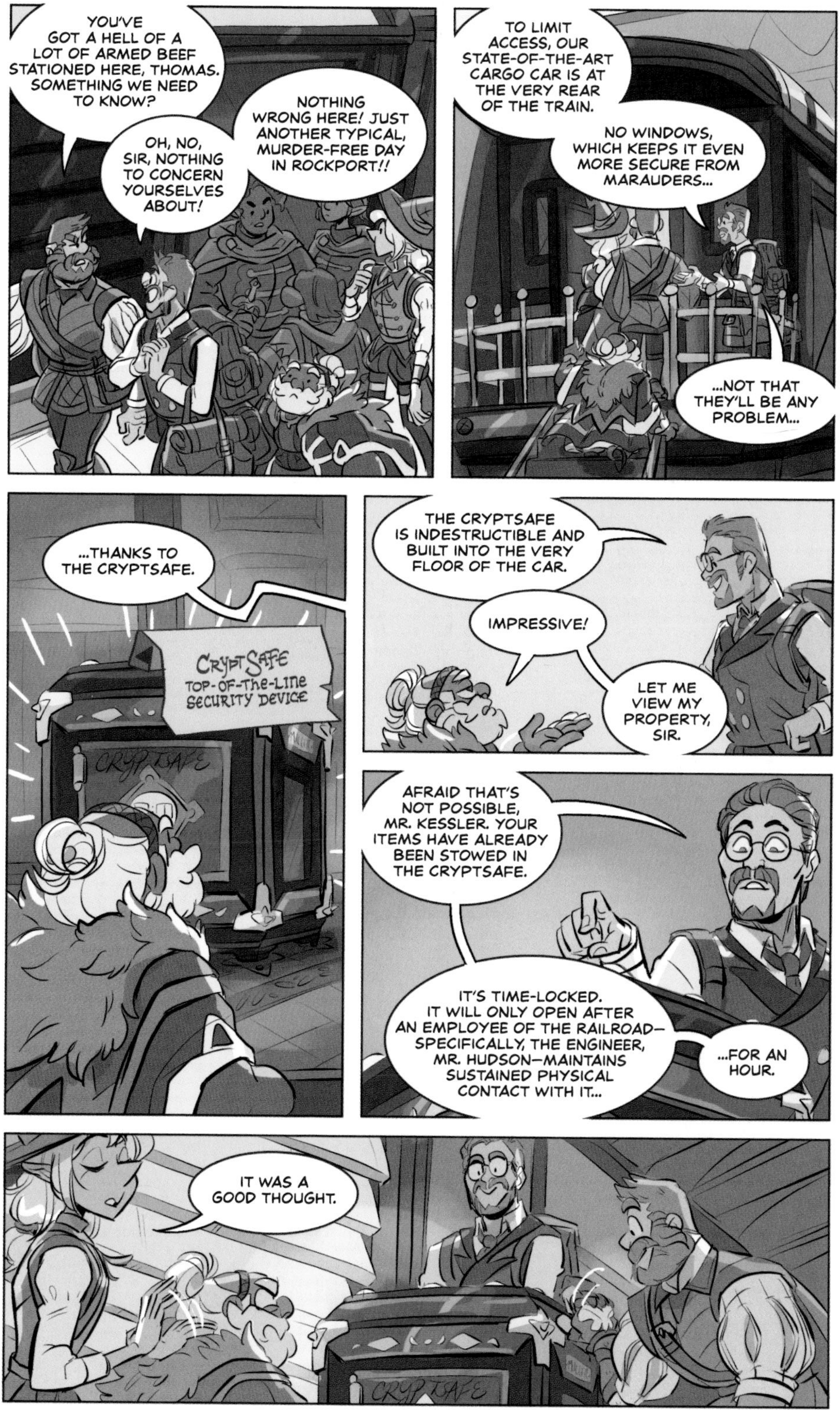
YOU'VE GOT A HELL OF A LOT OF ARMED BEEF STATIONED HERE, THOMAS. SOMETHING WE NEED TO KNOW?
OH, NO, SIR, NOTHING TO CONCERN YOURSELVES ABOUT!
NOTHING WRONG HERE! JUST ANOTHER TYPICAL, MURDER-FREE DAY IN ROCKPORT!!
TO LIMIT ACCESS, OUR STATE-OF-THE-ART CARGO CAR IS AT THE VERY REAR OF THE TRAIN.
NO WINDOWS, WHICH KEEPS IT EVEN MORE SECURE FROM MARAUDERS...
...NOT THAT THEY'LL BE ANY PROBLEM...
...THANKS TO THE CRYPTSAFE.
CRYPTSAFE
TOP-OF-THE-LINE SECURITY DEVICE
CRYPTSAFE
THE CRYPTSAFE IS INDESTRUCTIBLE AND BUILT INTO THE VERY FLOOR OF THE CAR.
IMPRESSIVE!
LET ME VIEW MY PROPERTY, SIR.
AFRAID THAT'S NOT POSSIBLE, MR. KESSLER. YOUR ITEMS HAVE ALREADY BEEN STOWED IN THE CRYPTSAFE.
IT'S TIME-LOCKED. IT WILL ONLY OPEN AFTER AN EMPLOYEE OF THE RAILROAD—SPECIFICALLY, THE ENGINEER, MR. HUDSON—MAINTAINS SUSTAINED PHYSICAL CONTACT WITH IT...
...FOR AN HOUR.
IT WAS A GOOD THOUGHT.
CRYPTSAFE

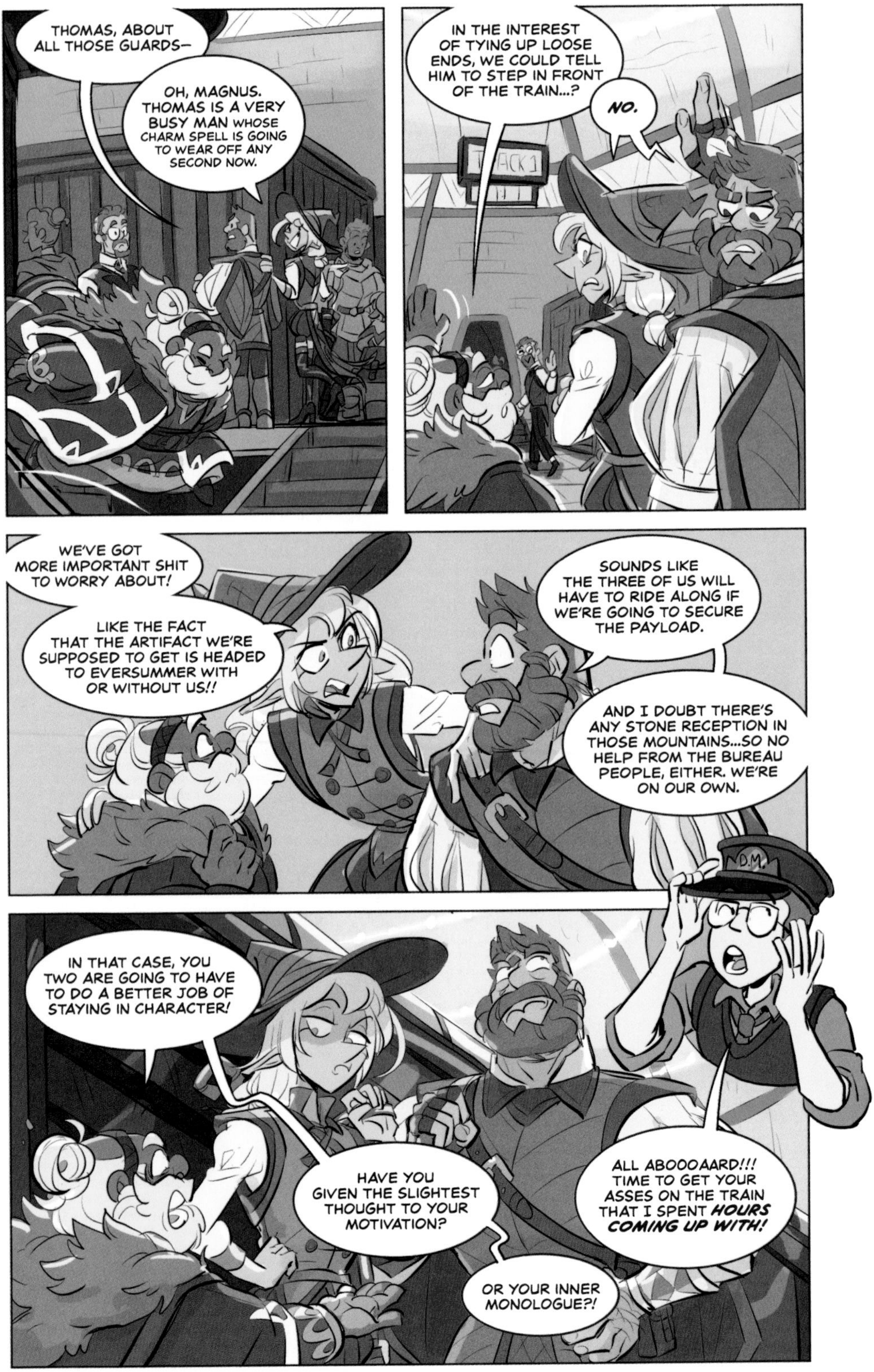
THOMAS, ABOUT ALL THOSE GUARDS—
OH, MAGNUS. THOMAS IS A VERY BUSY MAN WHOSE CHARM SPELL IS GOING TO WEAR OFF ANY SECOND NOW.
IN THE INTEREST OF TYING UP LOOSE ENDS, WE COULD TELL HIM TO STEP IN FRONT OF THE TRAIN...?
NO.
WE'VE GOT MORE IMPORTANT SHIT TO WORRY ABOUT!
LIKE THE FACT THAT THE ARTIFACT WE'RE SUPPOSED TO GET IS HEADED TO EVERSUMMER WITH OR WITHOUT US!!
SOUNDS LIKE THE THREE OF US WILL HAVE TO RIDE ALONG IF WE'RE GOING TO SECURE THE PAYLOAD.
AND I DOUBT THERE'S ANY STONE RECEPTION IN THOSE MOUNTAINS...SO NO HELP FROM THE BUREAU PEOPLE, EITHER. WE'RE ON OUR OWN.
D.M.
IN THAT CASE, YOU TWO ARE GOING TO HAVE TO DO A BETTER JOB OF STAYING IN CHARACTER!
HAVE YOU GIVEN THE SLIGHTEST THOUGHT TO YOUR MOTIVATION?
OR YOUR INNER MONOLOGUE?!
ALL ABOOOAARD!!! TIME TO GET YOUR ASSES ON THE TRAIN THAT I SPENT HOURS COMING UP WITH!

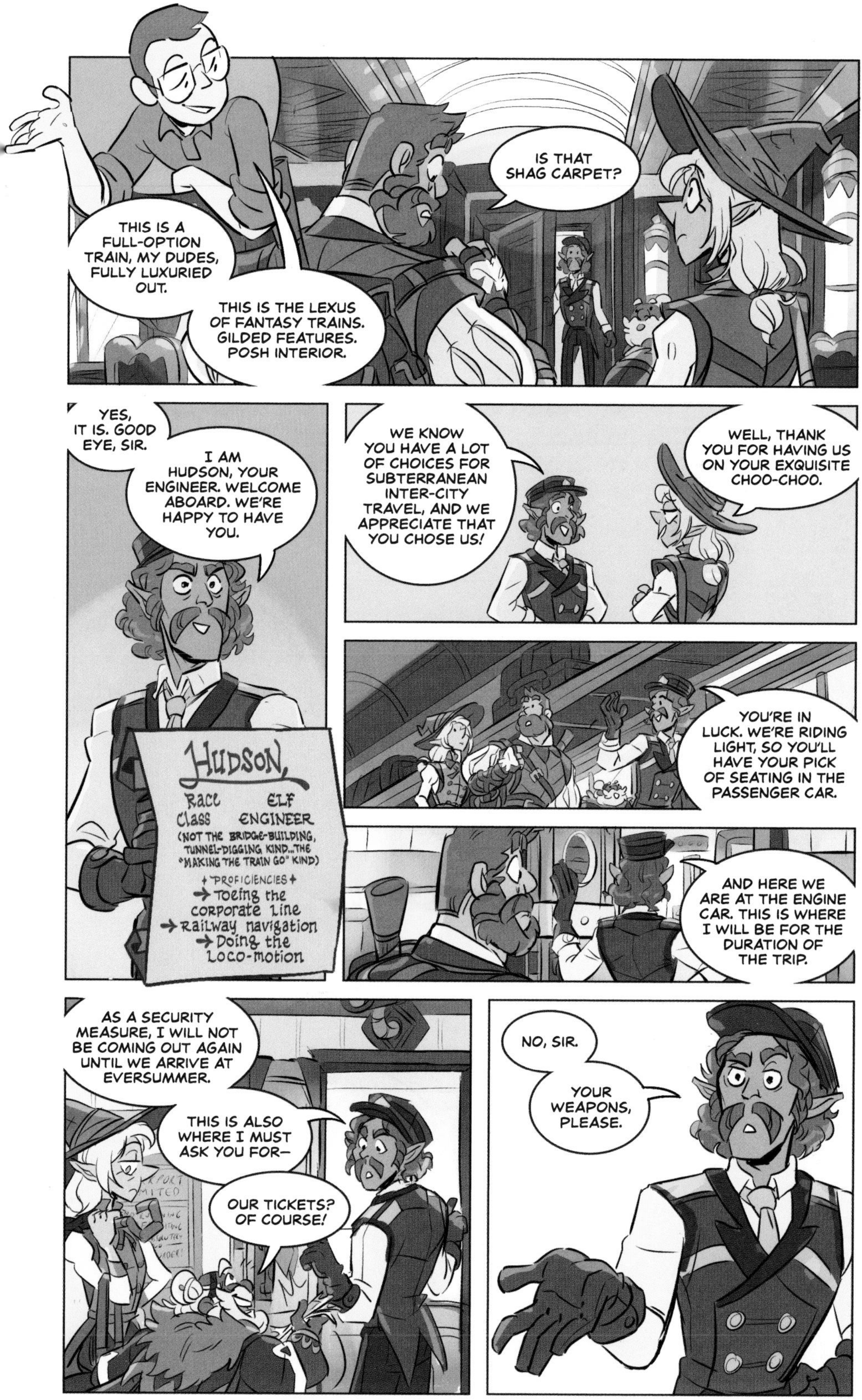
IS THAT SHAG CARPET?
THIS IS A FULL-OPTION TRAIN, MY DUDES, FULLY LUXURIED OUT.
THIS IS THE LEXUS OF FANTASY TRAINS. GILDED FEATURES. POSH INTERIOR.
YES, IT IS. GOOD EYE, SIR.
I AM HUDSON, YOUR ENGINEER. WELCOME ABOARD. WE'RE HAPPY TO HAVE YOU.
HUDSON,
Race ELF
Class ENGINEER
(NOT THE BRIDGE-BUILDING, TUNNEL-DIGGING KIND...THE "MAKING THE TRAIN GO" KIND)
PROFICIENCIES
→ Toeing the corporate Line
→ Railway navigation
→ Doing the Loco-motion
WE KNOW YOU HAVE A LOT OF CHOICES FOR SUBTERRANEAN INTER-CITY TRAVEL, AND WE APPRECIATE THAT YOU CHOSE US!
WELL, THANK YOU FOR HAVING US ON YOUR EXQUISITE CHOO-CHOO.
YOU'RE IN LUCK. WE'RE RIDING LIGHT, SO YOU'LL HAVE YOUR PICK OF SEATING IN THE PASSENGER CAR.
AND HERE WE ARE AT THE ENGINE CAR. THIS IS WHERE I WILL BE FOR THE DURATION OF THE TRIP.
AS A SECURITY MEASURE, I WILL NOT BE COMING OUT AGAIN UNTIL WE ARRIVE AT EVERSUMMER.
THIS IS ALSO WHERE I MUST ASK YOU FOR—
OUR TICKETS? OF COURSE!
NO, SIR.
YOUR WEAPONS, PLEASE.

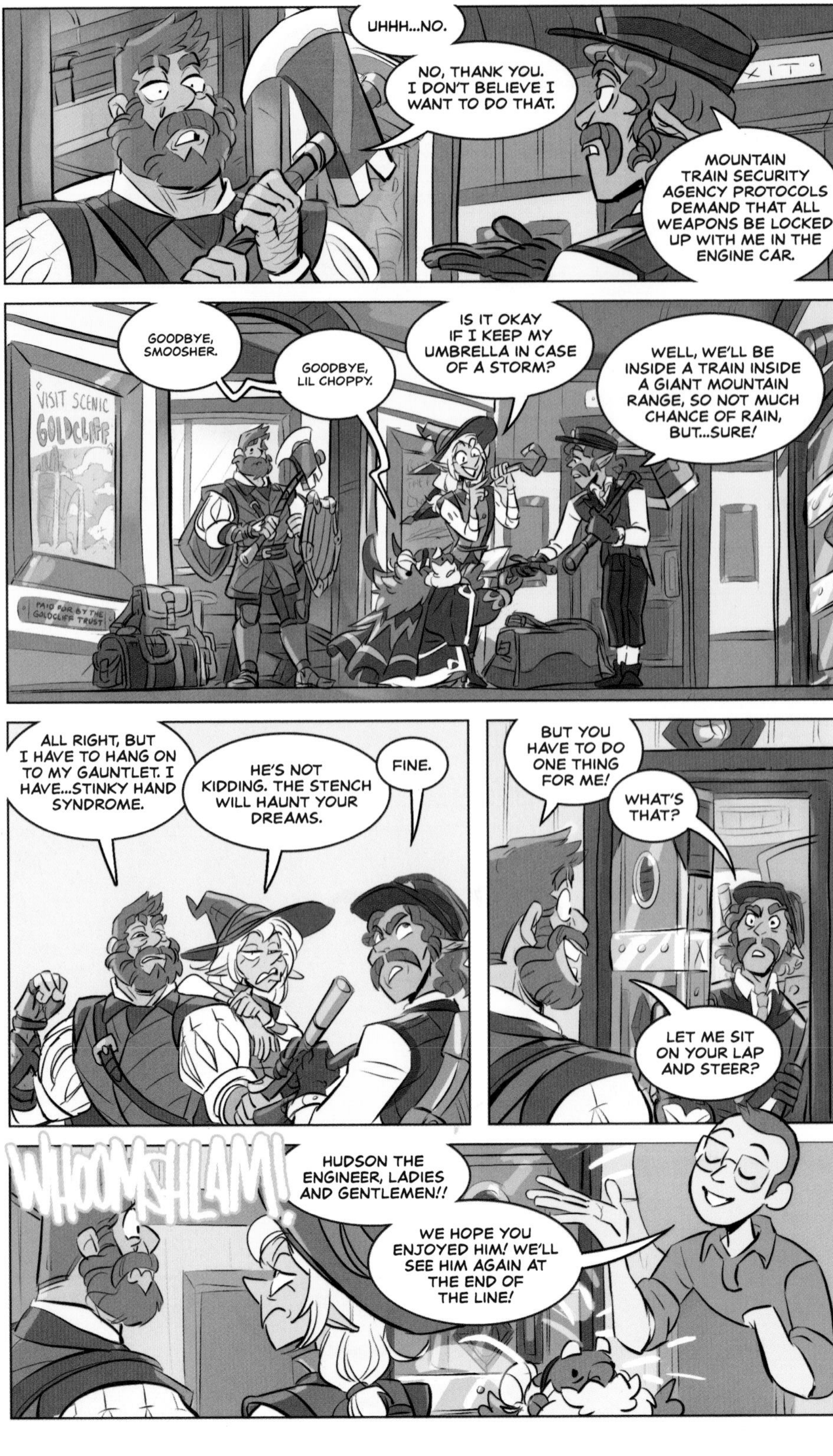
UHHH...NO.
NO, THANK YOU. I DON'T BELIEVE I WANT TO DO THAT.
MOUNTAIN TRAIN SECURITY AGENCY PROTOCOLS DEMAND THAT ALL WEAPONS BE LOCKED UP WITH ME IN THE ENGINE CAR.
VISIT SCENIC GOLDCLIFF
PAID FOR BY THE GOLDCLIFF TRUST
GOODBYE, SMOOSHER.
GOODBYE, LIL CHOPPY.
IS IT OKAY IF I KEEP MY UMBRELLA IN CASE OF A STORM?
WELL, WE'LL BE INSIDE A TRAIN INSIDE A GIANT MOUNTAIN RANGE, SO NOT MUCH CHANCE OF RAIN, BUT...SURE!
ALL RIGHT, BUT I HAVE TO HANG ON TO MY GAUNTLET. I HAVE...STINKY HAND SYNDROME.
HE'S NOT KIDDING. THE STENCH WILL HAUNT YOUR DREAMS.
FINE.
BUT YOU HAVE TO DO ONE THING FOR ME!
WHAT'S THAT?
LET ME SIT ON YOUR LAP AND STEER?
WHOOMSHLAM!
HUDSON THE ENGINEER, LADIES AND GENTLEMEN!!
WE HOPE YOU ENJOYED HIM! WE'LL SEE HIM AGAIN AT THE END OF THE LINE!

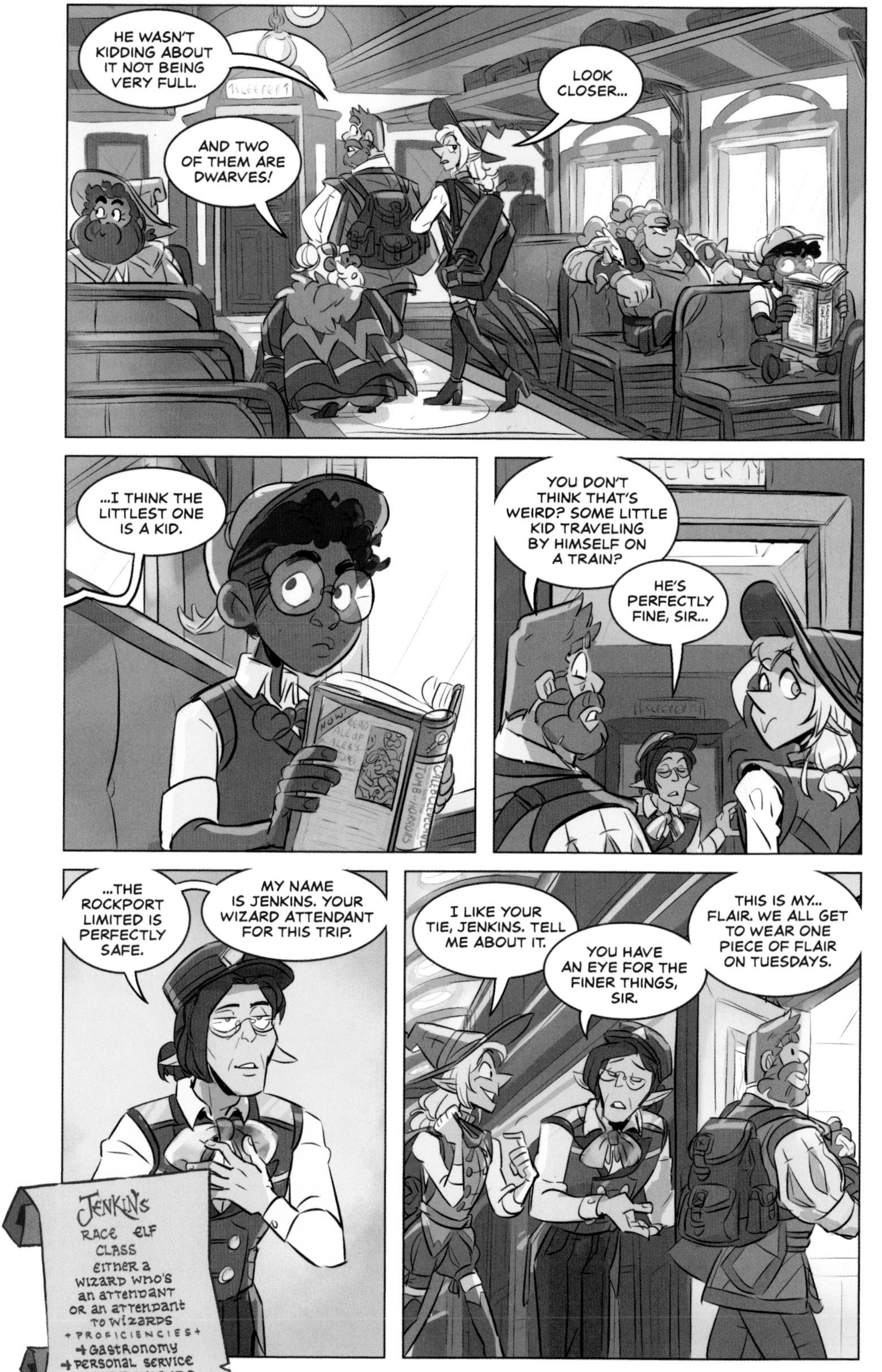
HE WASN'T KIDDING ABOUT IT NOT BEING VERY FULL.
AND TWO OF THEM ARE DWARVES!
LOOK CLOSER...
...I THINK THE LITTLEST ONE IS A KID.
YOU DON'T THINK THAT'S WEIRD? SOME LITTLE KID TRAVELING BY HIMSELF ON A TRAIN?
HE'S PERFECTLY FINE, SIR...
...THE ROCKPORT LIMITED IS PERFECTLY SAFE.
MY NAME IS JENKINS. YOUR WIZARD ATTENDANT FOR THIS TRIP.
JENKINS
RACE ELF
CLASS
Either a wizard who's an attendant or an attendant to wizards
PROFICIENCIES
Gastronomy
Personal service
HORTICULTURE
I LIKE YOUR TIE, JENKINS. TELL ME ABOUT IT.
YOU HAVE AN EYE FOR THE FINER THINGS, SIR.
THIS IS MY... FLAIR. WE ALL GET TO WEAR ONE PIECE OF FLAIR ON TUESDAYS.

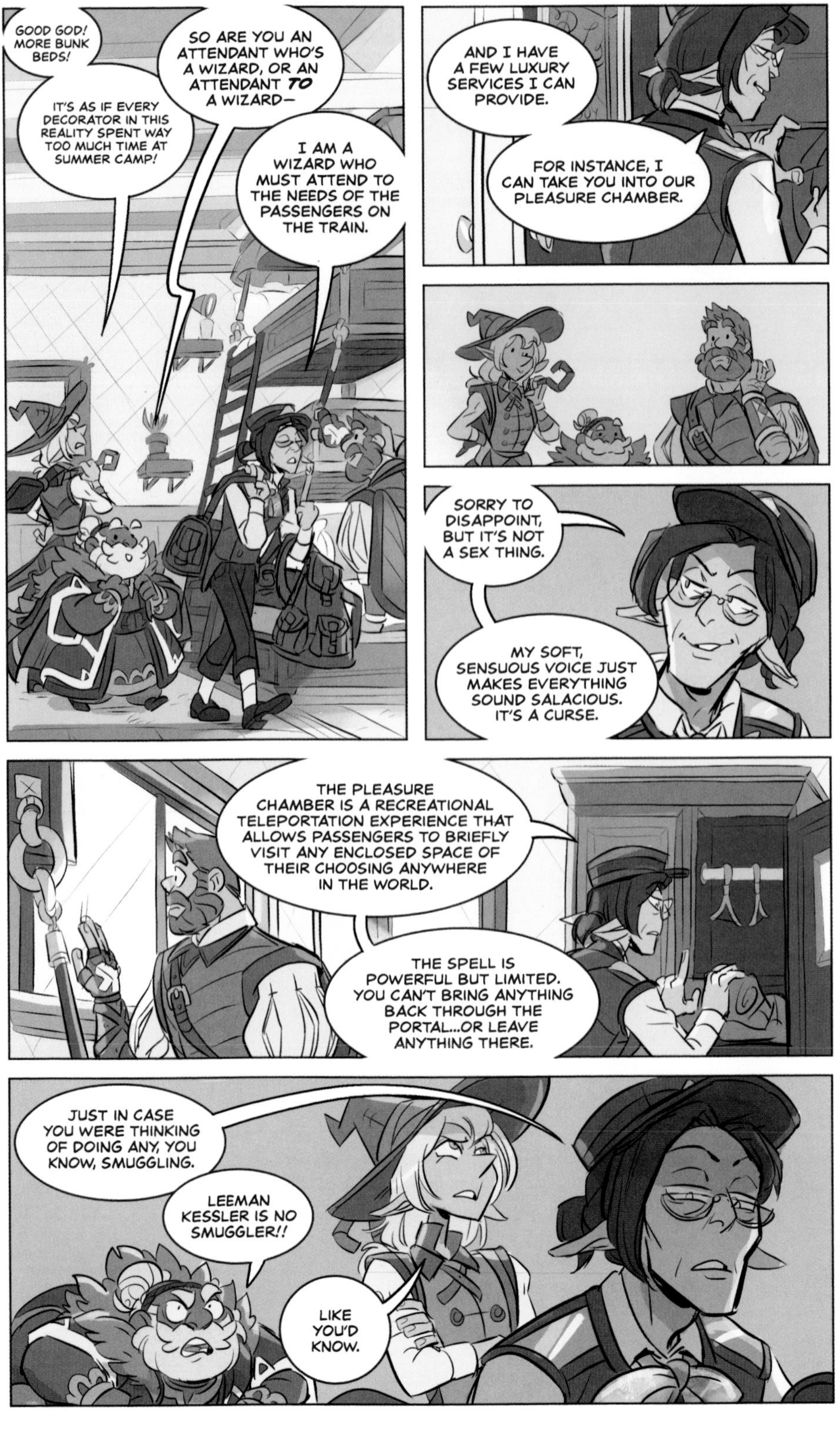
GOOD GOD! MORE BUNK BEDS!
IT'S AS IF EVERY DECORATOR IN THIS REALITY SPENT WAY TOO MUCH TIME AT SUMMER CAMP!
SO ARE YOU AN ATTENDANT WHO'S A WIZARD, OR AN ATTENDANT *TO* A WIZARD—
I AM A WIZARD WHO MUST ATTEND TO THE NEEDS OF THE PASSENGERS ON THE TRAIN.
AND I HAVE A FEW LUXURY SERVICES I CAN PROVIDE.
FOR INSTANCE, I CAN TAKE YOU INTO OUR PLEASURE CHAMBER.
SORRY TO DISAPPOINT, BUT IT'S NOT A SEX THING.
MY SOFT, SENSUOUS VOICE JUST MAKES EVERYTHING SOUND SALACIOUS. IT'S A CURSE.
THE PLEASURE CHAMBER IS A RECREATIONAL TELEPORTATION EXPERIENCE THAT ALLOWS PASSENGERS TO BRIEFLY VISIT ANY ENCLOSED SPACE OF THEIR CHOOSING ANYWHERE IN THE WORLD.
THE SPELL IS POWERFUL BUT LIMITED. YOU CAN'T BRING ANYTHING BACK THROUGH THE PORTAL...OR LEAVE ANYTHING THERE.
JUST IN CASE YOU WERE THINKING OF DOING ANY, YOU KNOW, SMUGGLING.
LEEMAN KESSLER IS NO SMUGGLER!!
LIKE YOU'D KNOW.

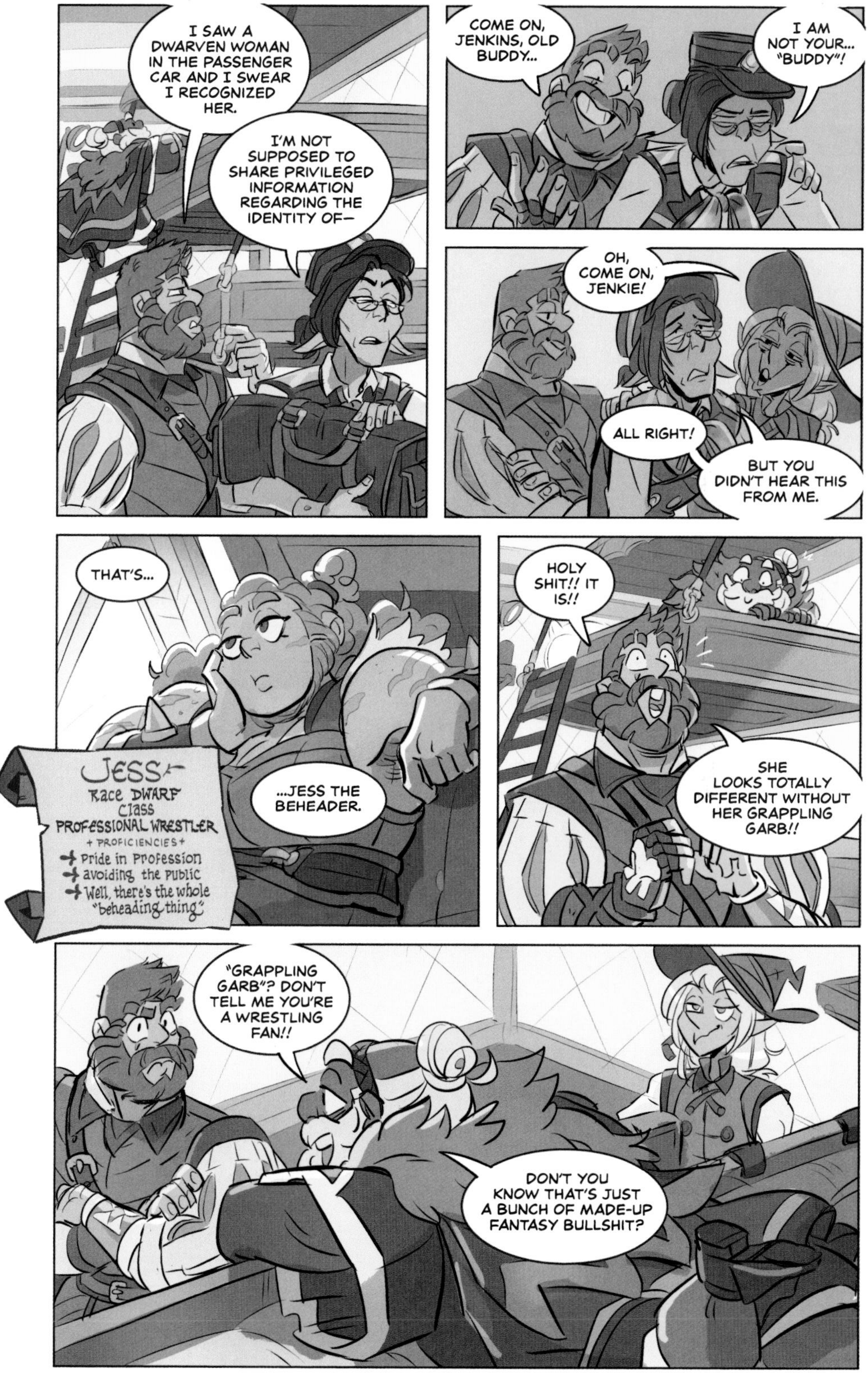

I SAW A DWARVEN WOMAN IN THE PASSENGER CAR AND I SWEAR I RECOGNIZED HER.
I'M NOT SUPPOSED TO SHARE PRIVILEGED INFORMATION REGARDING THE IDENTITY OF—
COME ON, JENKINS, OLD BUDDY...
I AM NOT YOUR... "BUDDY"!
OH, COME ON, JENKIE!
ALL RIGHT!
BUT YOU DIDN'T HEAR THIS FROM ME.
THAT'S...
...JESS THE BEHEADER.
JESS
Race DWARF
Class PROFESSIONAL WRESTLER
+ PROFICIENCIES +
Pride in Profession
avoiding the public
Well, there's the whole "beheading thing"
HOLY SHIT!! IT IS!!
SHE LOOKS TOTALLY DIFFERENT WITHOUT HER GRAPPLING GARB!!
"GRAPPLING GARB"? DON'T TELL ME YOU'RE A WRESTLING FAN!!
DON'T YOU KNOW THAT'S JUST A BUNCH OF MADE-UP FANTASY BULLSHIT?

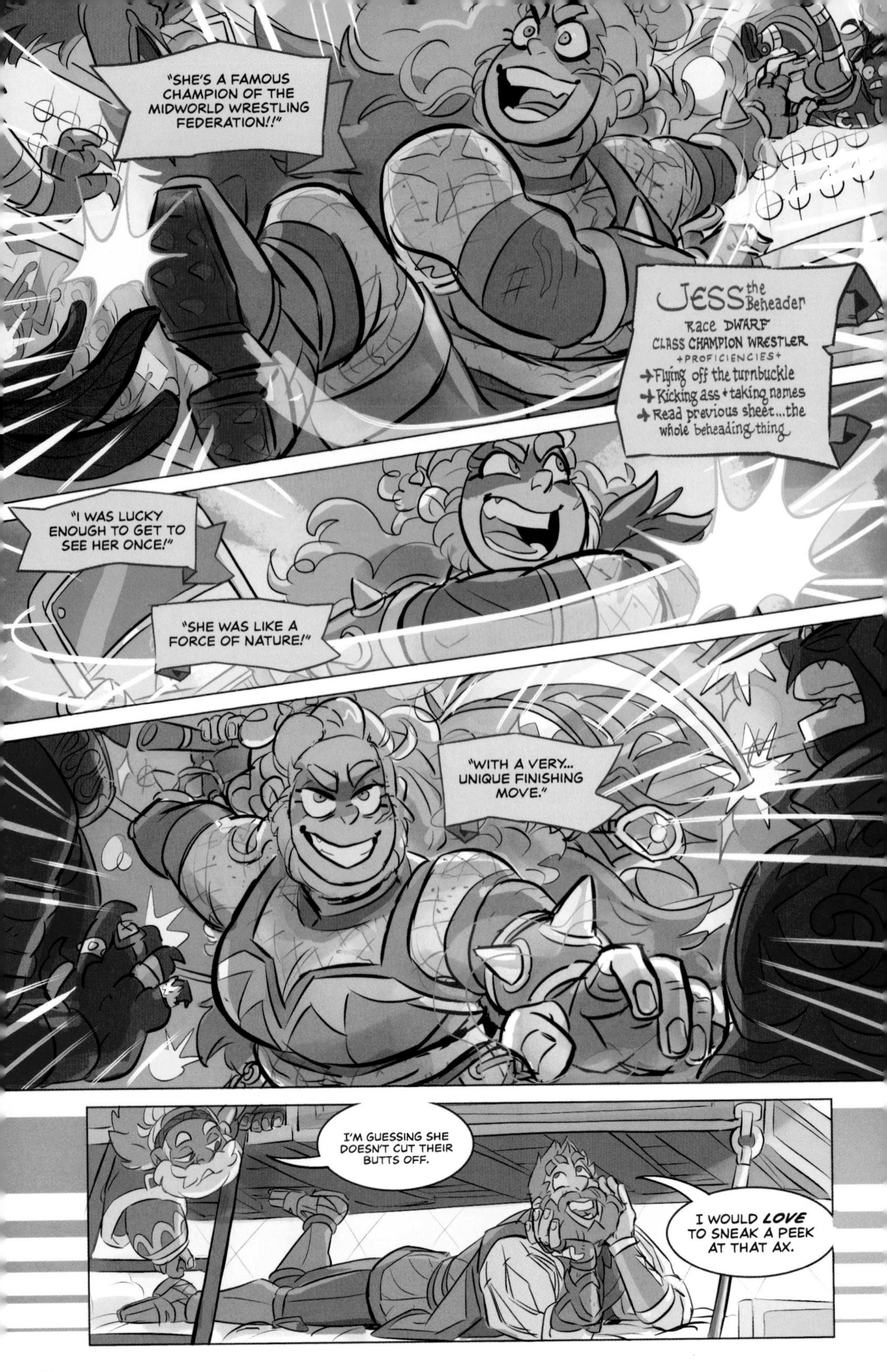
"SHE'S A FAMOUS CHAMPION OF THE MIDWORLD WRESTLING FEDERATION!!"
JESS the Beheader
RACE DWARF
CLASS CHAMPION WRESTLER
+PROFICIENCIES+
→Flying off the turnbuckle
→Kicking ass + taking names
→Read previous sheet...the whole beheading thing
"I WAS LUCKY ENOUGH TO GET TO SEE HER ONCE!"
"SHE WAS LIKE A FORCE OF NATURE!"
"WITH A VERY... UNIQUE FINISHING MOVE."
I'M GUESSING SHE DOESN'T CUT THEIR BUTTS OFF.
I WOULD ***LOVE*** TO SNEAK A PEEK AT THAT AX.

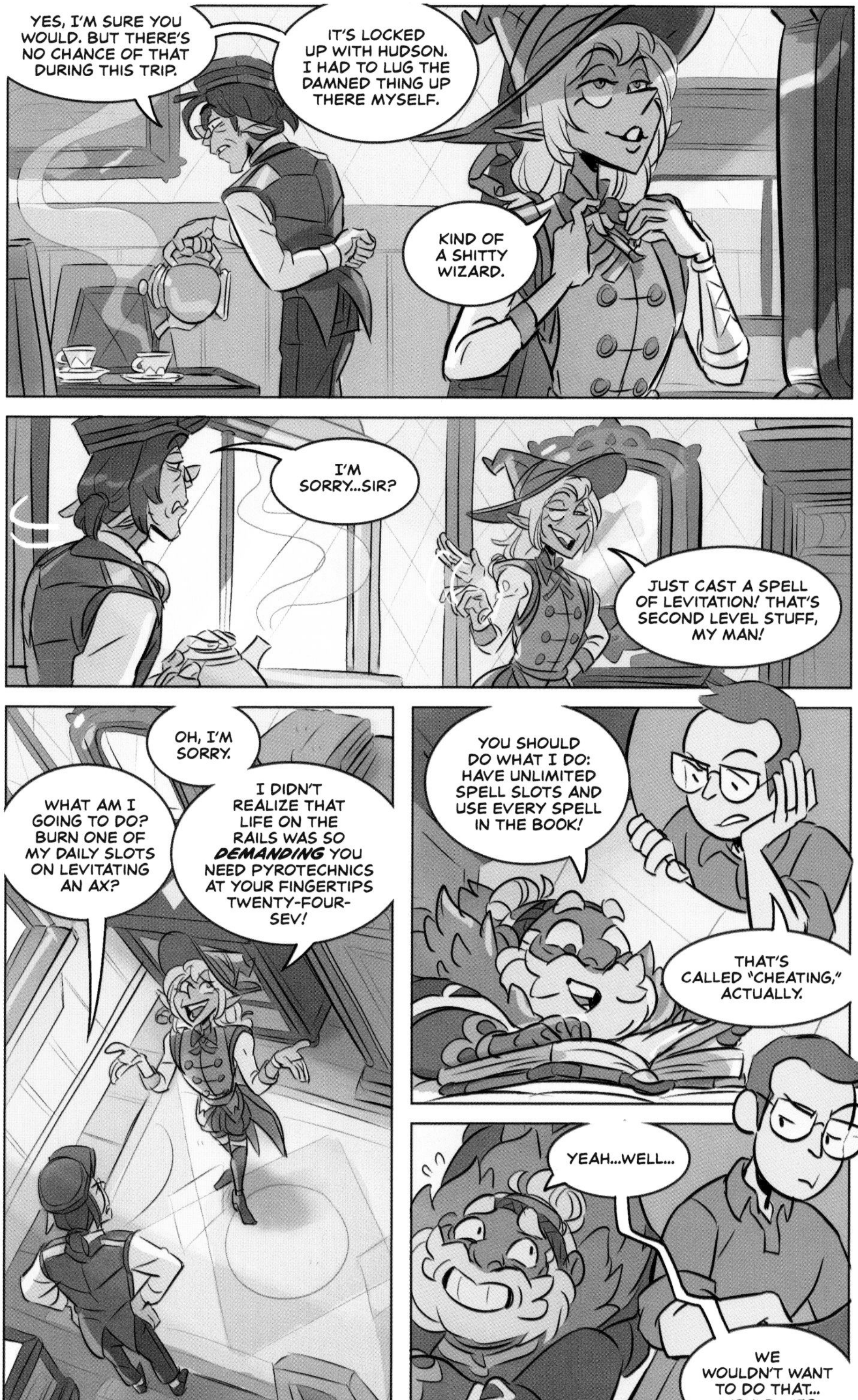
YES, I'M SURE YOU WOULD. BUT THERE'S NO CHANCE OF THAT DURING THIS TRIP.
IT'S LOCKED UP WITH HUDSON. I HAD TO LUG THE DAMNED THING UP THERE MYSELF.
KIND OF A SHITTY WIZARD.
I'M SORRY...SIR?
JUST CAST A SPELL OF LEVITATION! THAT'S SECOND LEVEL STUFF, MY MAN!
OH, I'M SORRY.
WHAT AM I GOING TO DO? BURN ONE OF MY DAILY SLOTS ON LEVITATING AN AX?
I DIDN'T REALIZE THAT LIFE ON THE RAILS WAS SO *DEMANDING* YOU NEED PYROTECHNICS AT YOUR FINGERTIPS TWENTY-FOUR-SEV!
YOU SHOULD DO WHAT I DO: HAVE UNLIMITED SPELL SLOTS AND USE EVERY SPELL IN THE BOOK!
THAT'S CALLED "CHEATING," ACTUALLY.
YEAH...WELL...
WE WOULDN'T WANT TO DO THAT... WOULD WE?

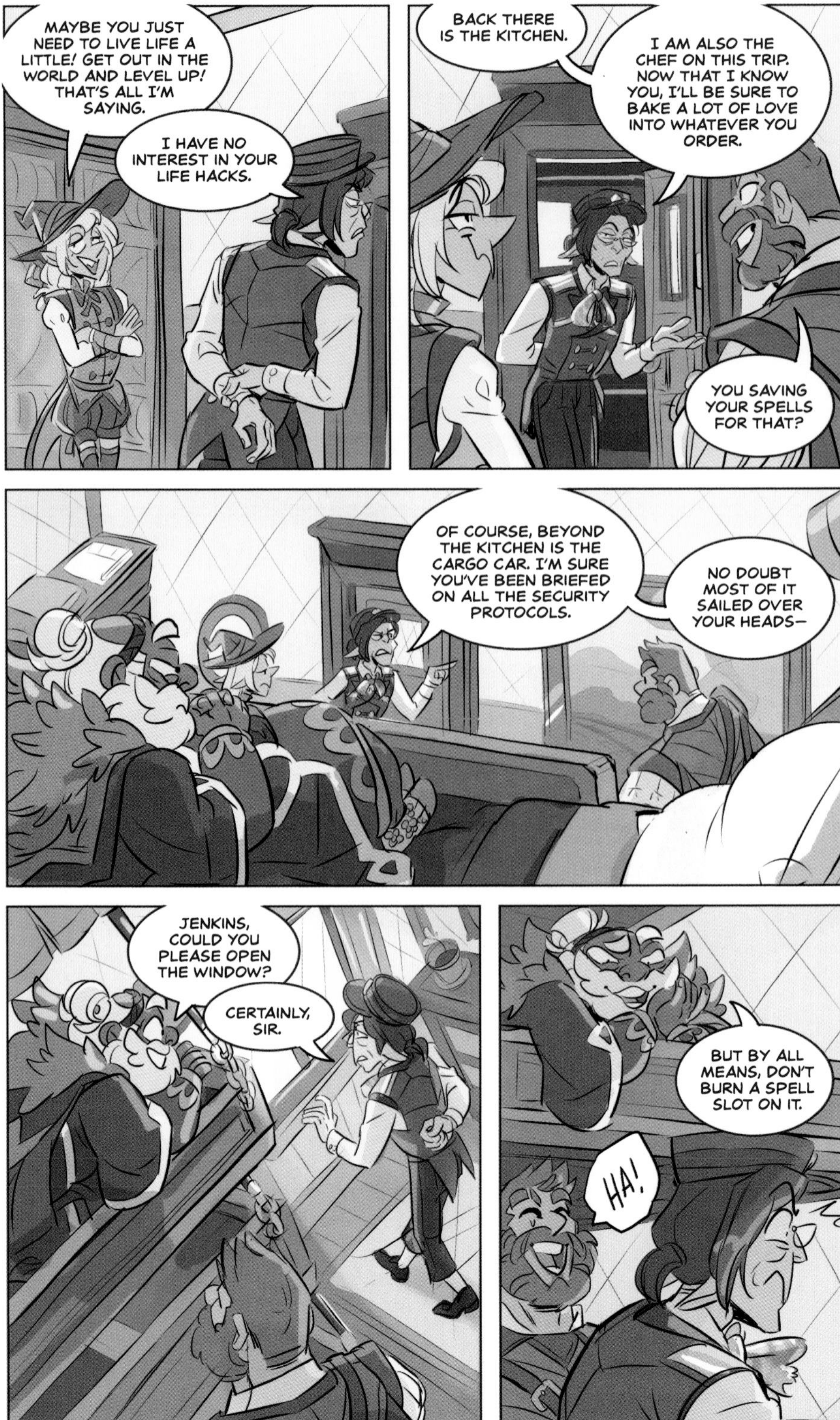
MAYBE YOU JUST NEED TO LIVE LIFE A LITTLE! GET OUT IN THE WORLD AND LEVEL UP! THAT'S ALL I'M SAYING.
I HAVE NO INTEREST IN YOUR LIFE HACKS.
BACK THERE IS THE KITCHEN.
I AM ALSO THE CHEF ON THIS TRIP. NOW THAT I KNOW YOU, I'LL BE SURE TO BAKE A LOT OF LOVE INTO WHATEVER YOU ORDER.
YOU SAVING YOUR SPELLS FOR THAT?
OF COURSE, BEYOND THE KITCHEN IS THE CARGO CAR. I'M SURE YOU'VE BEEN BRIEFED ON ALL THE SECURITY PROTOCOLS.
NO DOUBT MOST OF IT SAILED OVER YOUR HEADS—
JENKINS, COULD YOU PLEASE OPEN THE WINDOW?
CERTAINLY, SIR.
BUT BY ALL MEANS, DON'T BURN A SPELL SLOT ON IT.
HA!

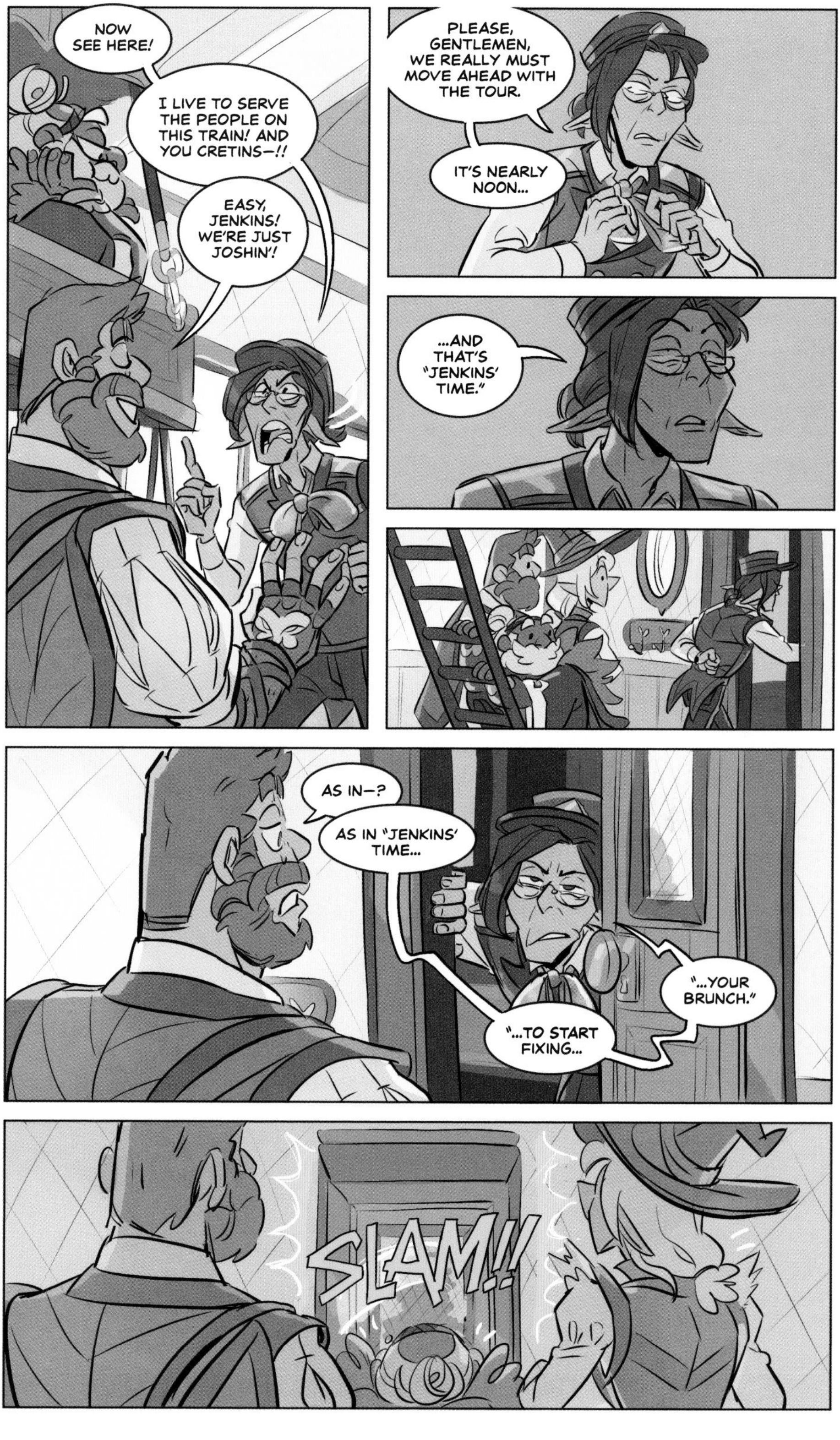
NOW SEE HERE!
I LIVE TO SERVE THE PEOPLE ON THIS TRAIN! AND YOU CRETINS—!!
EASY, JENKINS! WE'RE JUST JOSHIN'!
PLEASE, GENTLEMEN, WE REALLY MUST MOVE AHEAD WITH THE TOUR.
IT'S NEARLY NOON...
...AND THAT'S "JENKINS' TIME."
AS IN—?
AS IN "JENKINS' TIME...
"...TO START FIXING...
"...YOUR BRUNCH."
SLAM!!

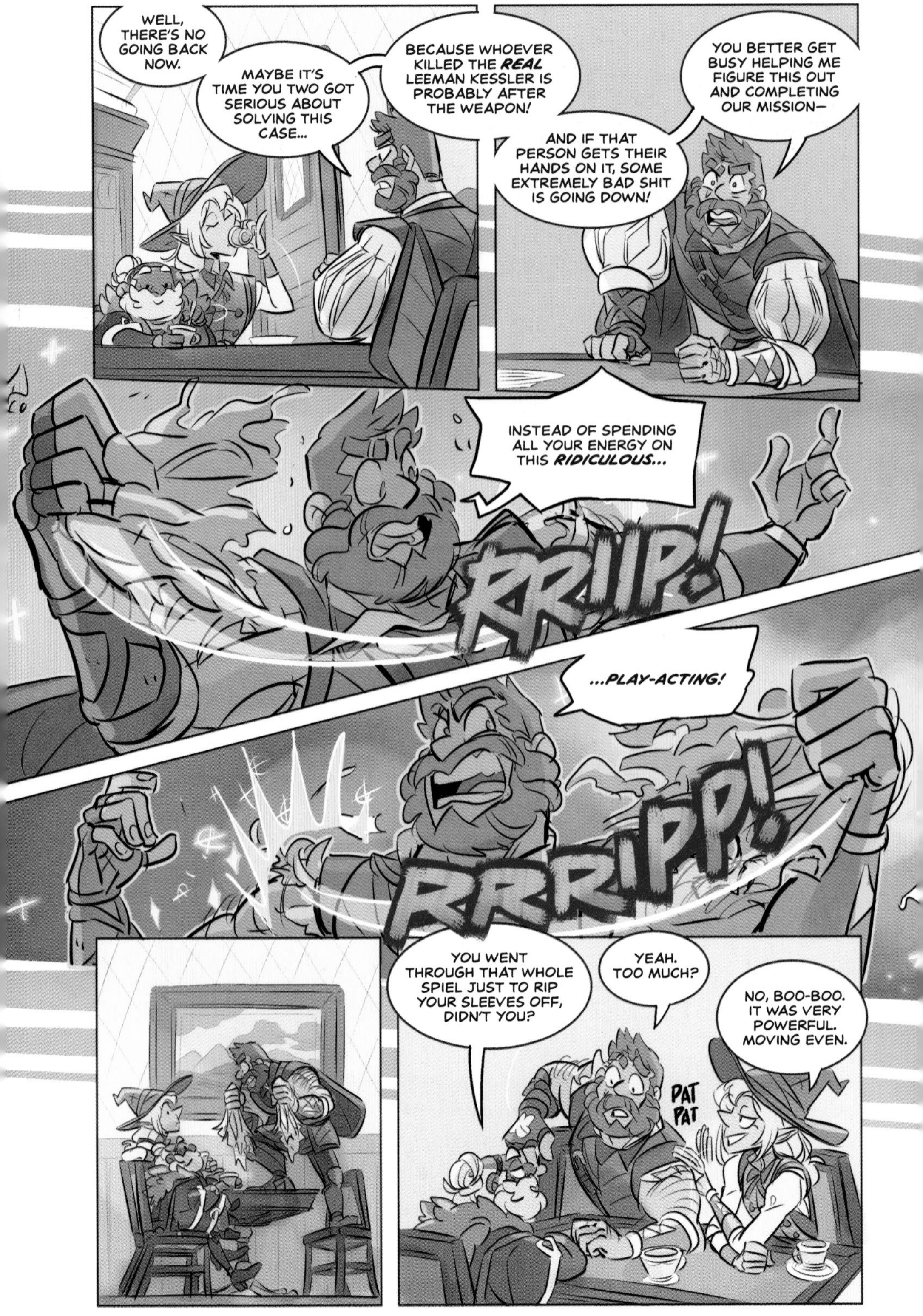

WELL, THERE'S NO GOING BACK NOW.
MAYBE IT'S TIME YOU TWO GOT SERIOUS ABOUT SOLVING THIS CASE...
BECAUSE WHOEVER KILLED THE REAL LEEMAN KESSLER IS PROBABLY AFTER THE WEAPON!
AND IF THAT PERSON GETS THEIR HANDS ON IT, SOME EXTREMELY BAD SHIT IS GOING DOWN!
YOU BETTER GET BUSY HELPING ME FIGURE THIS OUT AND COMPLETING OUR MISSION—
INSTEAD OF SPENDING ALL YOUR ENERGY ON THIS RIDICULOUS...
RRIIP!
...PLAY-ACTING!
RRRIPP!
YOU WENT THROUGH THAT WHOLE SPIEL JUST TO RIP YOUR SLEEVES OFF, DIDN'T YOU?
YEAH. TOO MUCH?
PAT PAT
NO, BOO-BOO. IT WAS VERY POWERFUL. MOVING EVEN.

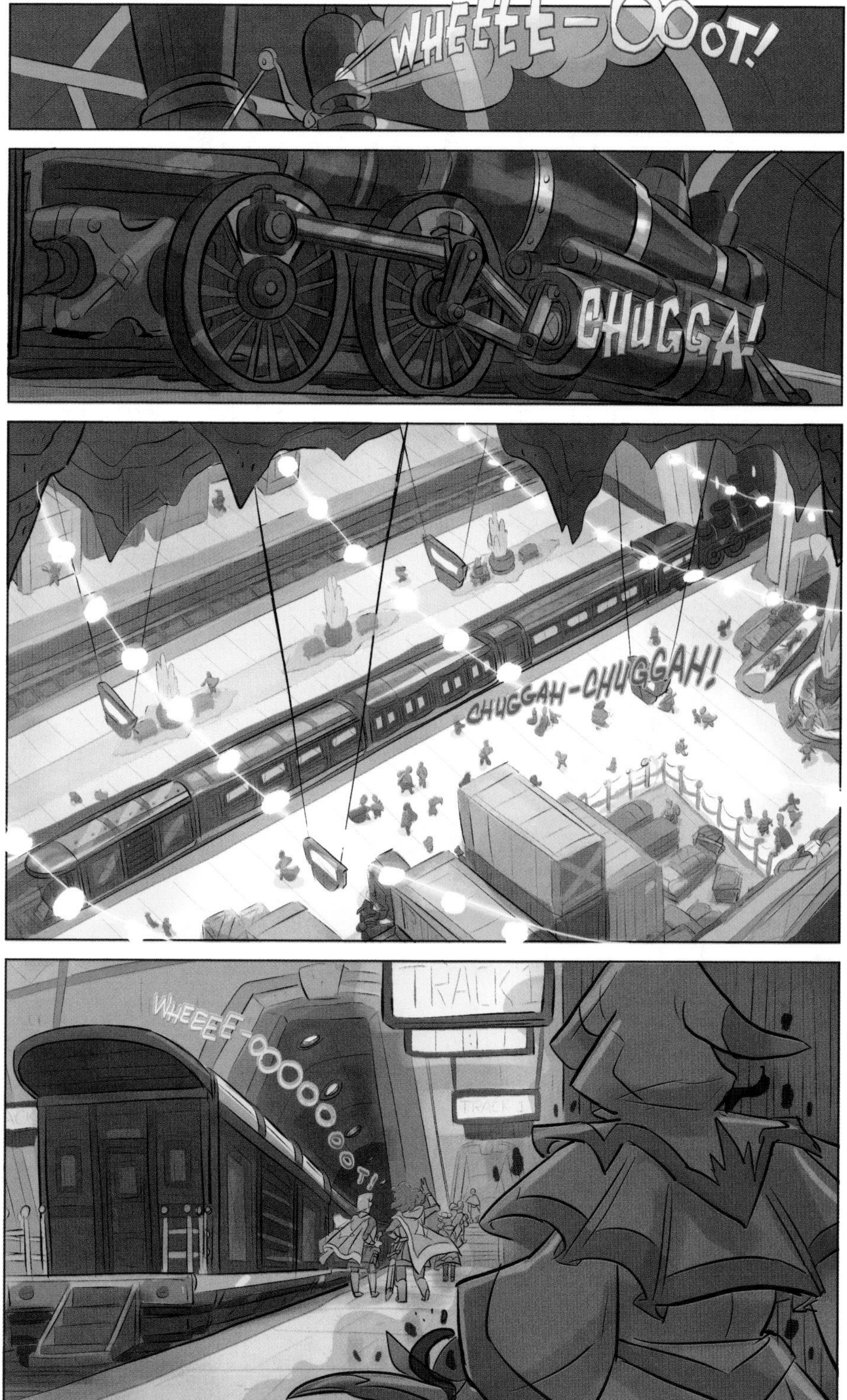
WHEEEE-OOOOT!
CHUGGA!
CHUGGAH-CHUGGAH!
TRACK 1
WHEEEE-OOOOOOOOT!

Chapter 3

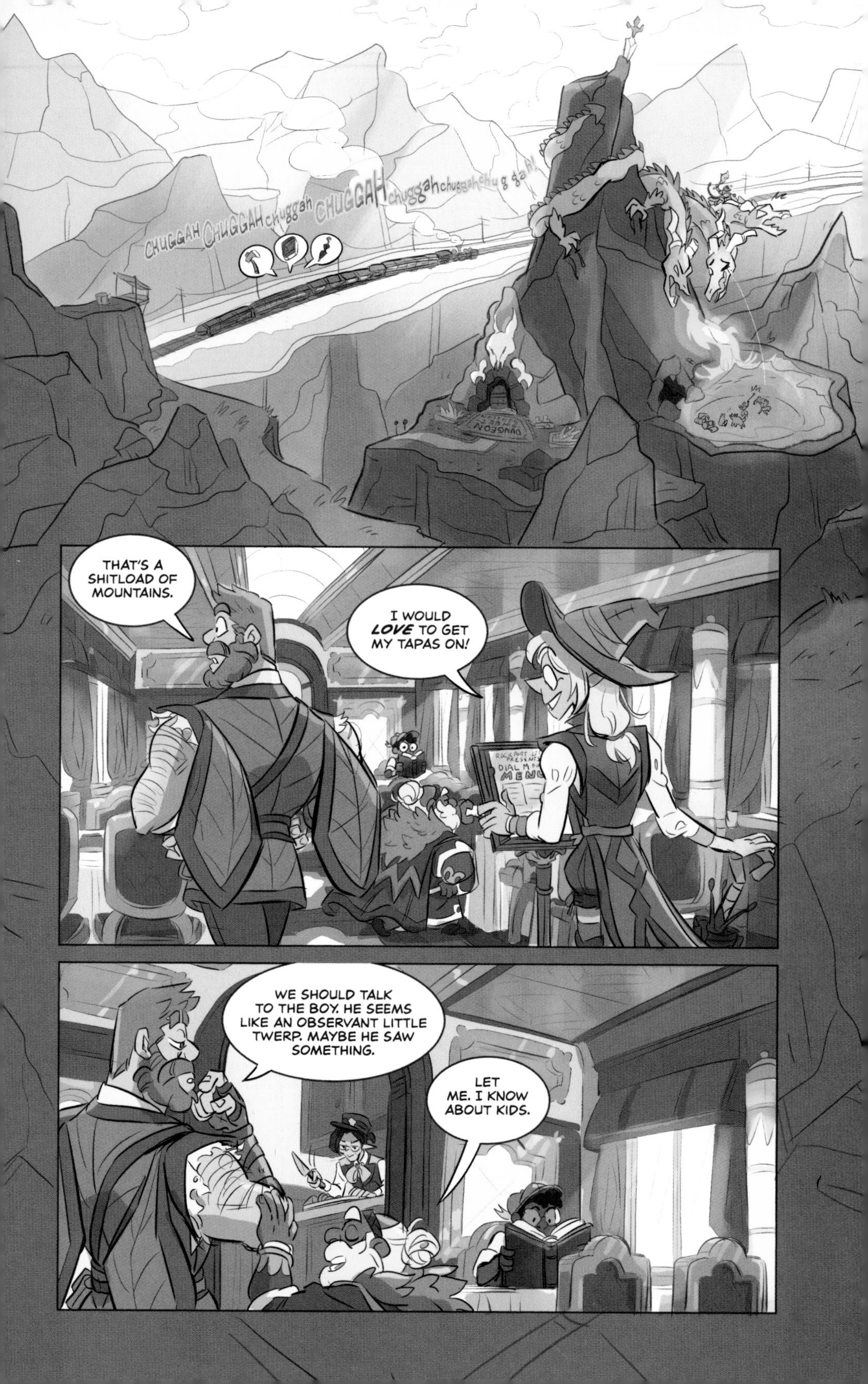
CHUGGAH CHUGGAH chuggah CHUGGAH chuggahchuggahchug g ah!
DUNGEON
THAT'S A SHITLOAD OF MOUNTAINS.
I WOULD LOVE TO GET MY TAPAS ON!
WE SHOULD TALK TO THE BOY. HE SEEMS LIKE AN OBSERVANT LITTLE TWERP. MAYBE HE SAW SOMETHING.
LET ME. I KNOW ABOUT KIDS.

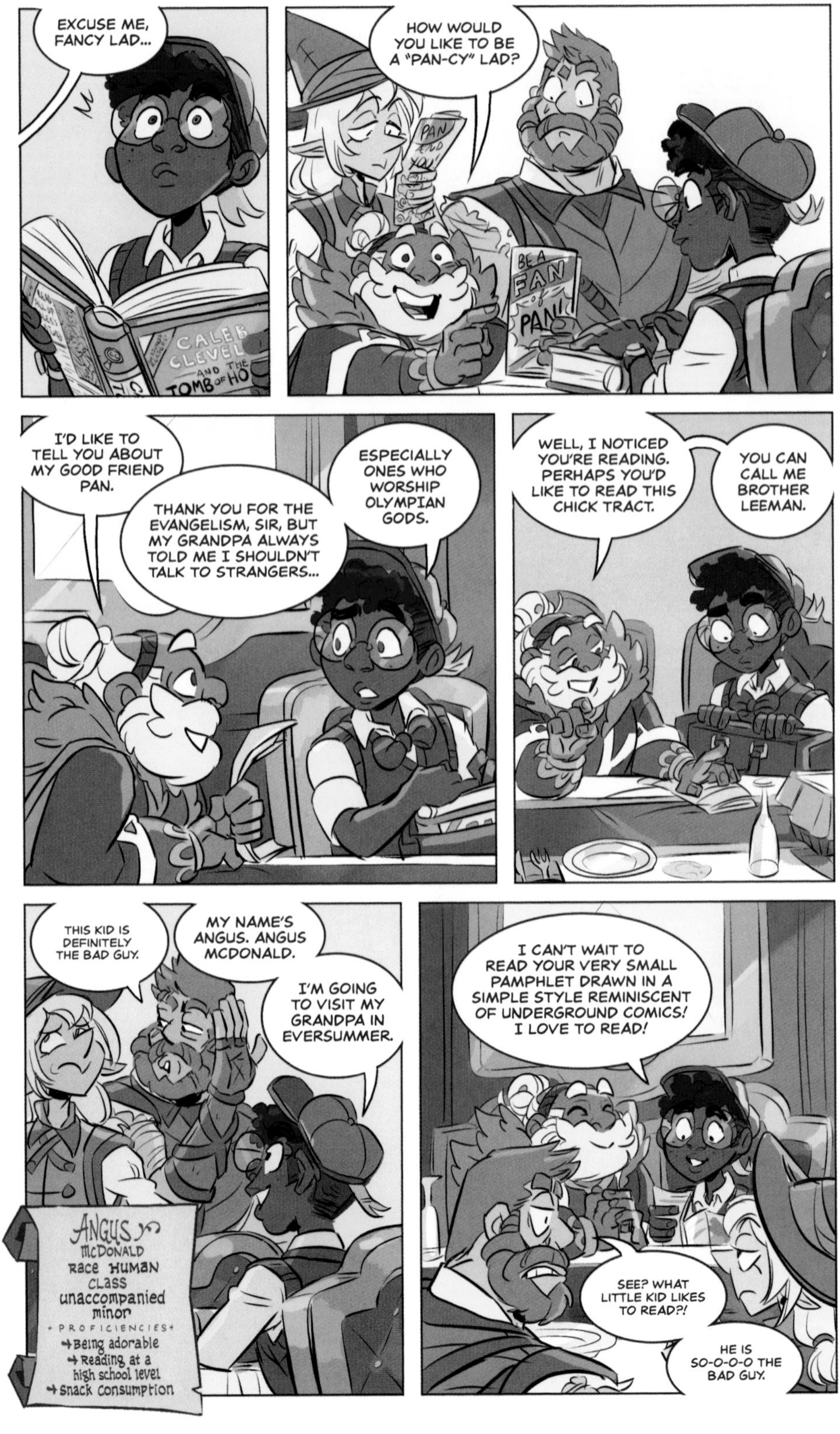
EXCUSE ME, FANCY LAD...
HOW WOULD YOU LIKE TO BE A "PAN-CY" LAD?
PAN AND YOU
BE A FAN of PAN!
I'D LIKE TO TELL YOU ABOUT MY GOOD FRIEND PAN.
THANK YOU FOR THE EVANGELISM, SIR, BUT MY GRANDPA ALWAYS TOLD ME I SHOULDN'T TALK TO STRANGERS...
ESPECIALLY ONES WHO WORSHIP OLYMPIAN GODS.
WELL, I NOTICED YOU'RE READING. PERHAPS YOU'D LIKE TO READ THIS CHICK TRACT.
YOU CAN CALL ME BROTHER LEEMAN.
THIS KID IS DEFINITELY THE BAD GUY.
MY NAME'S ANGUS. ANGUS MCDONALD.
I'M GOING TO VISIT MY GRANDPA IN EVERSUMMER.
ANGUS McDONALD
Race HUMAN
CLASS unaccompanied minor
PROFICIENCIES
Being adorable
Reading at a high school level
Snack consumption
I CAN'T WAIT TO READ YOUR VERY SMALL PAMPHLET DRAWN IN A SIMPLE STYLE REMINISCENT OF UNDERGROUND COMICS! I LOVE TO READ!
SEE? WHAT LITTLE KID LIKES TO READ?!
HE IS SO-O-O-O THE BAD GUY.

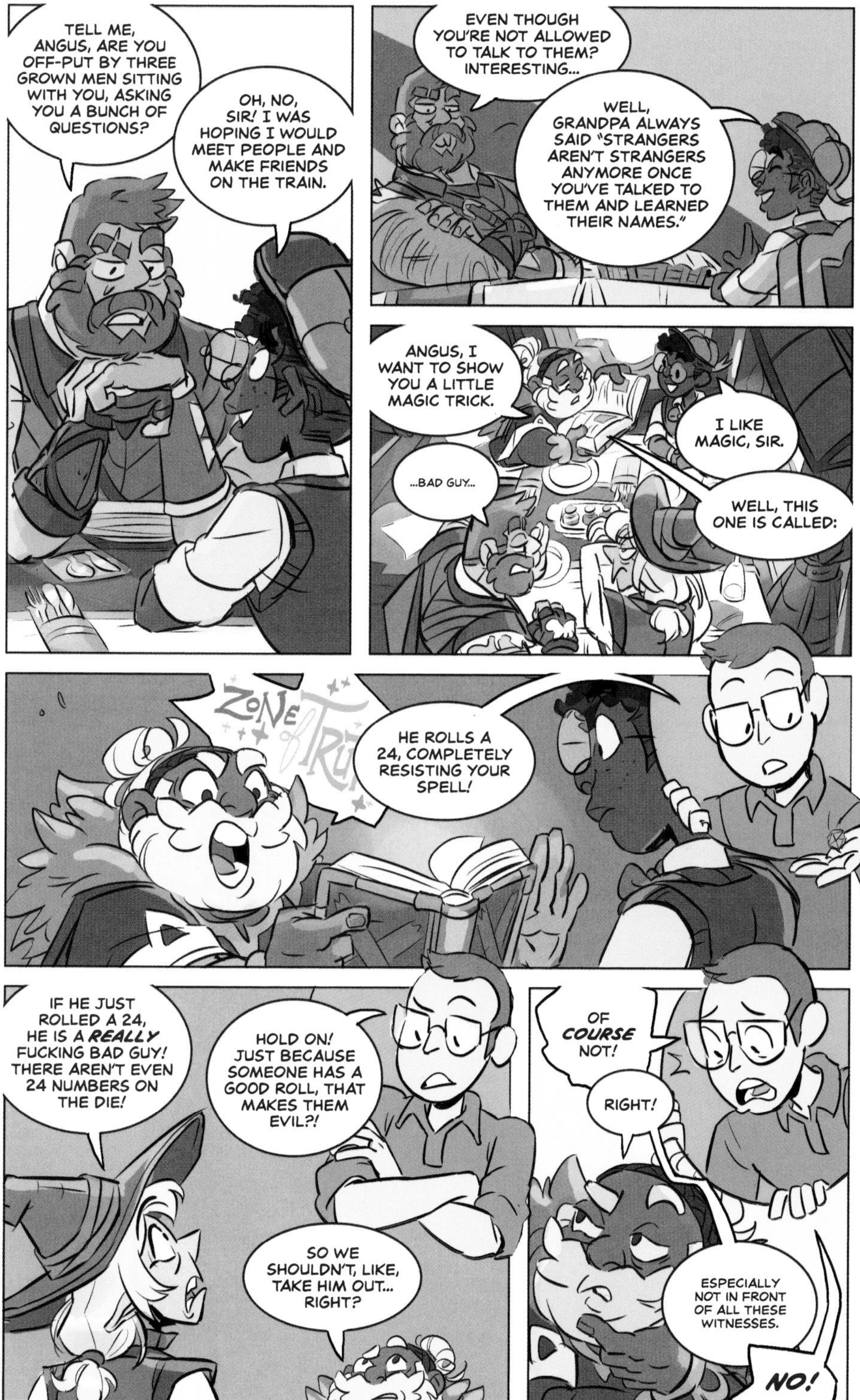
TELL ME, ANGUS, ARE YOU OFF-PUT BY THREE GROWN MEN SITTING WITH YOU, ASKING YOU A BUNCH OF QUESTIONS?
OH, NO, SIR! I WAS HOPING I WOULD MEET PEOPLE AND MAKE FRIENDS ON THE TRAIN.
EVEN THOUGH YOU'RE NOT ALLOWED TO TALK TO THEM? INTERESTING...
WELL, GRANDPA ALWAYS SAID "STRANGERS AREN'T STRANGERS ANYMORE ONCE YOU'VE TALKED TO THEM AND LEARNED THEIR NAMES."
ANGUS, I WANT TO SHOW YOU A LITTLE MAGIC TRICK.
I LIKE MAGIC, SIR.
...BAD GUY...
WELL, THIS ONE IS CALLED:
ZONE of TRU
HE ROLLS A 24, COMPLETELY RESISTING YOUR SPELL!
IF HE JUST ROLLED A 24, HE IS A REALLY FUCKING BAD GUY! THERE AREN'T EVEN 24 NUMBERS ON THE DIE!
HOLD ON! JUST BECAUSE SOMEONE HAS A GOOD ROLL, THAT MAKES THEM EVIL?!
SO WE SHOULDN'T, LIKE, TAKE HIM OUT... RIGHT?
OF COURSE NOT!
RIGHT!
ESPECIALLY NOT IN FRONT OF ALL THESE WITNESSES.
NO!

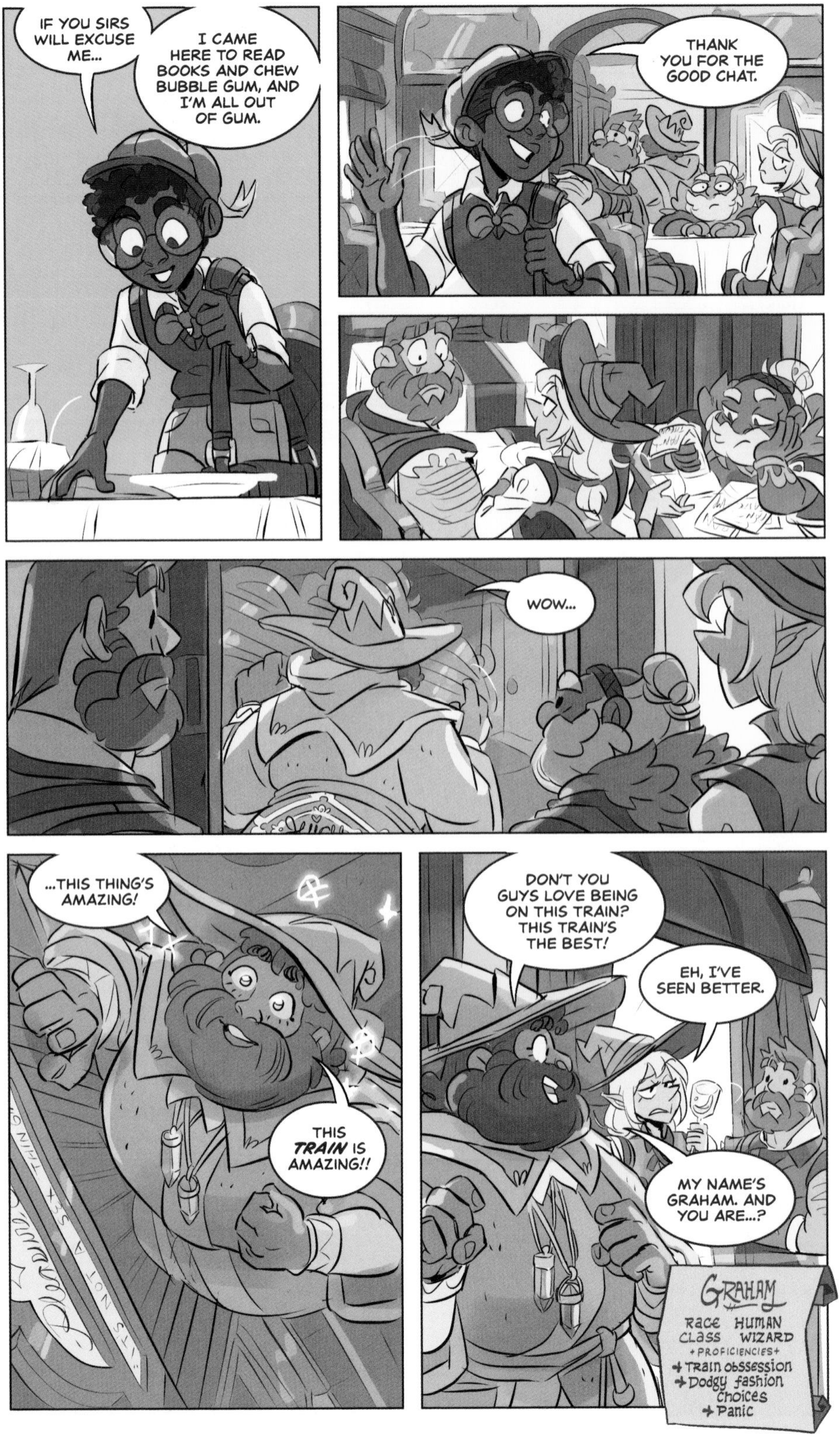
IF YOU SIRS WILL EXCUSE ME...
I CAME HERE TO READ BOOKS AND CHEW BUBBLE GUM, AND I'M ALL OUT OF GUM.
THANK YOU FOR THE GOOD CHAT.
WOW...
...THIS THING'S AMAZING!
THIS *TRAIN* IS AMAZING!!
DON'T YOU GUYS LOVE BEING ON THIS TRAIN? THIS TRAIN'S THE BEST!
EH, I'VE SEEN BETTER.
MY NAME'S GRAHAM. AND YOU ARE...?
GRAHAM
RACE HUMAN
CLASS WIZARD
+PROFICIENCIES+
+ Train obsession
+ Dodgy fashion choices
+ Panic

I'M LEEMAN KESSLER. AND THESE ARE MY ATTENDANTS: FLHOMAS—

—OF COURSE, DIDDLY. AND THIS IS—

DIDDLY.

JUSTIN!

~~VIRGIL~~ ~~RACHEL~~ ~~FLHOMAS~~ DIDDLY

~~FLAKE~~ ~~LEEMAN KESSLER~~ ~~JUST~~ I QUIT!! —PERSON WRITING THESE CHARACTER SHEETS!!

I CAN'T HELP BUT NOTICE YOUR GARB. YOUR HAT AND ALL.

ARE YOU PERCHANCE A WIZARD, TOO?

YEAH. NO DOUBT YOU RECOGNIZE ME.

I'M ACTUALLY TAAKO. YOU KNOW, FROM TV.

YES IT IS, MY DUDE.

HOLY SHIT! IT IS YOU!

WHEN I TRAVEL I USE MY REAL NAME...JUSTIN KESSLER.

YOUR SHOW IS LIKE, MY SECOND FAVORITE THING IN THE WORLD.

IT'S ALWAYS GOOD TO MEET A FAN—

WAIT! *SECOND?!* WHAT'S *FIRST?*

TRAINS!

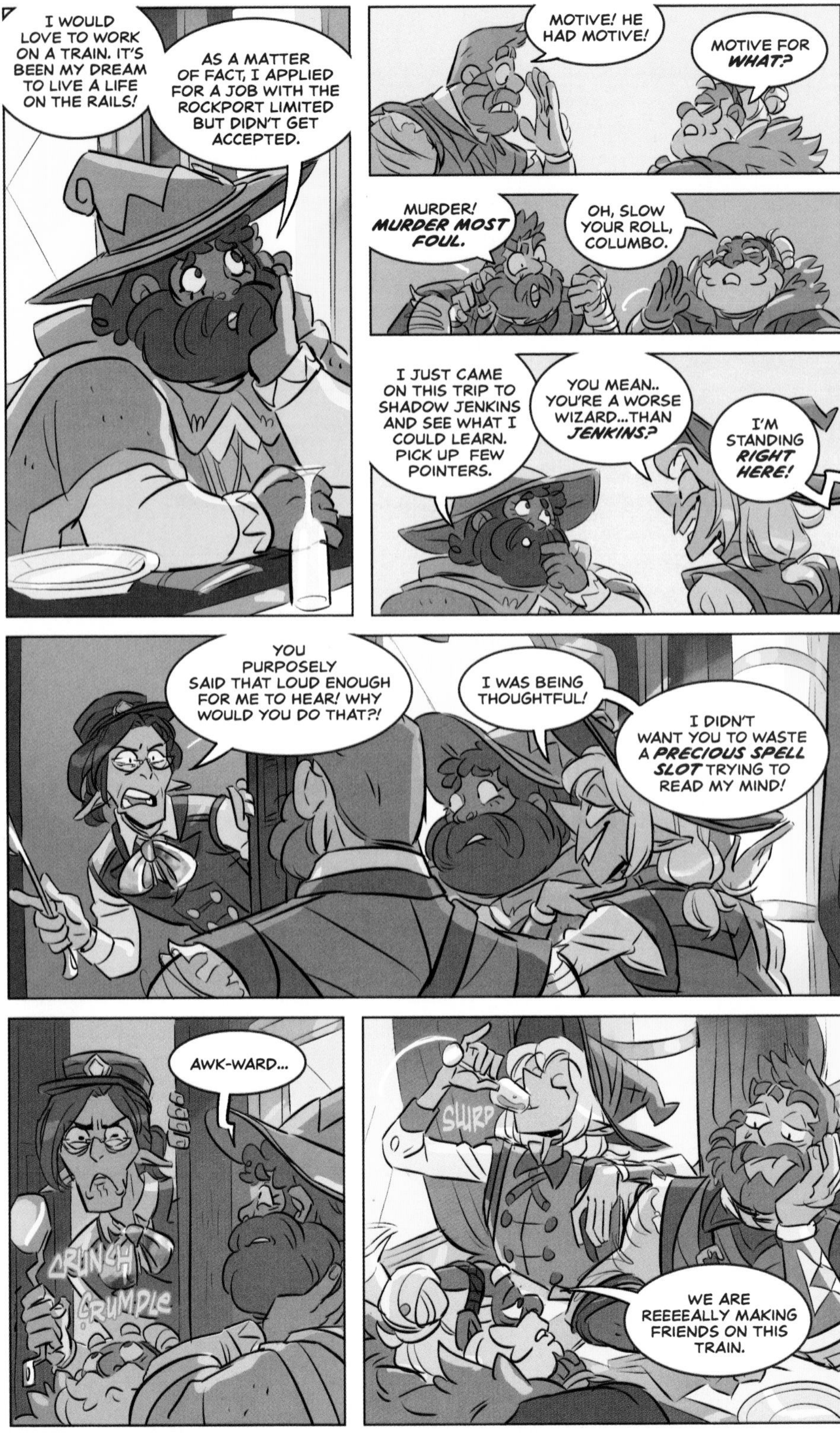
I WOULD LOVE TO WORK ON A TRAIN. IT'S BEEN MY DREAM TO LIVE A LIFE ON THE RAILS!
AS A MATTER OF FACT, I APPLIED FOR A JOB WITH THE ROCKPORT LIMITED BUT DIDN'T GET ACCEPTED.
MOTIVE! HE HAD MOTIVE!
MOTIVE FOR WHAT?
MURDER! MURDER MOST FOUL.
OH, SLOW YOUR ROLL, COLUMBO.
I JUST CAME ON THIS TRIP TO SHADOW JENKINS AND SEE WHAT I COULD LEARN. PICK UP FEW POINTERS.
YOU MEAN.. YOU'RE A WORSE WIZARD...THAN JENKINS?
I'M STANDING RIGHT HERE!
YOU PURPOSELY SAID THAT LOUD ENOUGH FOR ME TO HEAR! WHY WOULD YOU DO THAT?!
I WAS BEING THOUGHTFUL!
I DIDN'T WANT YOU TO WASTE A PRECIOUS SPELL SLOT TRYING TO READ MY MIND!
AWK-WARD...
CRUNCH
CRUMPLE
SLURP
WE ARE REEEEALLY MAKING FRIENDS ON THIS TRAIN.

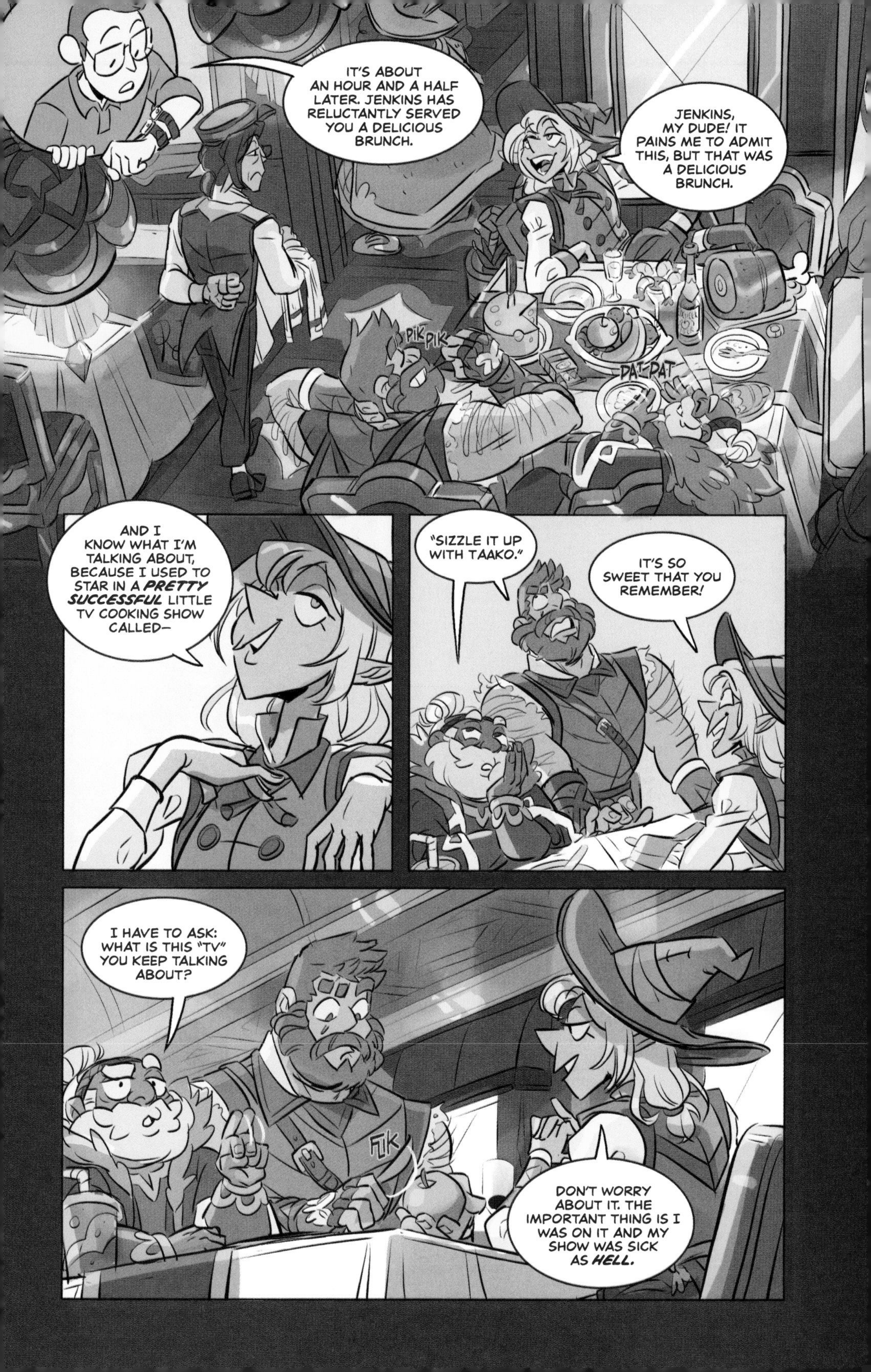
IT'S ABOUT AN HOUR AND A HALF LATER. JENKINS HAS RELUCTANTLY SERVED YOU A DELICIOUS BRUNCH.
JENKINS, MY DUDE! IT PAINS ME TO ADMIT THIS, BUT THAT WAS A DELICIOUS BRUNCH.
PIK PIK
DAT DAT
AND I KNOW WHAT I'M TALKING ABOUT, BECAUSE I USED TO STAR IN A PRETTY SUCCESSFUL LITTLE TV COOKING SHOW CALLED—
"SIZZLE IT UP WITH TAAKO."
IT'S SO SWEET THAT YOU REMEMBER!
I HAVE TO ASK: WHAT IS THIS "TV" YOU KEEP TALKING ABOUT?
DON'T WORRY ABOUT IT. THE IMPORTANT THING IS I WAS ON IT AND MY SHOW WAS SICK AS HELL.

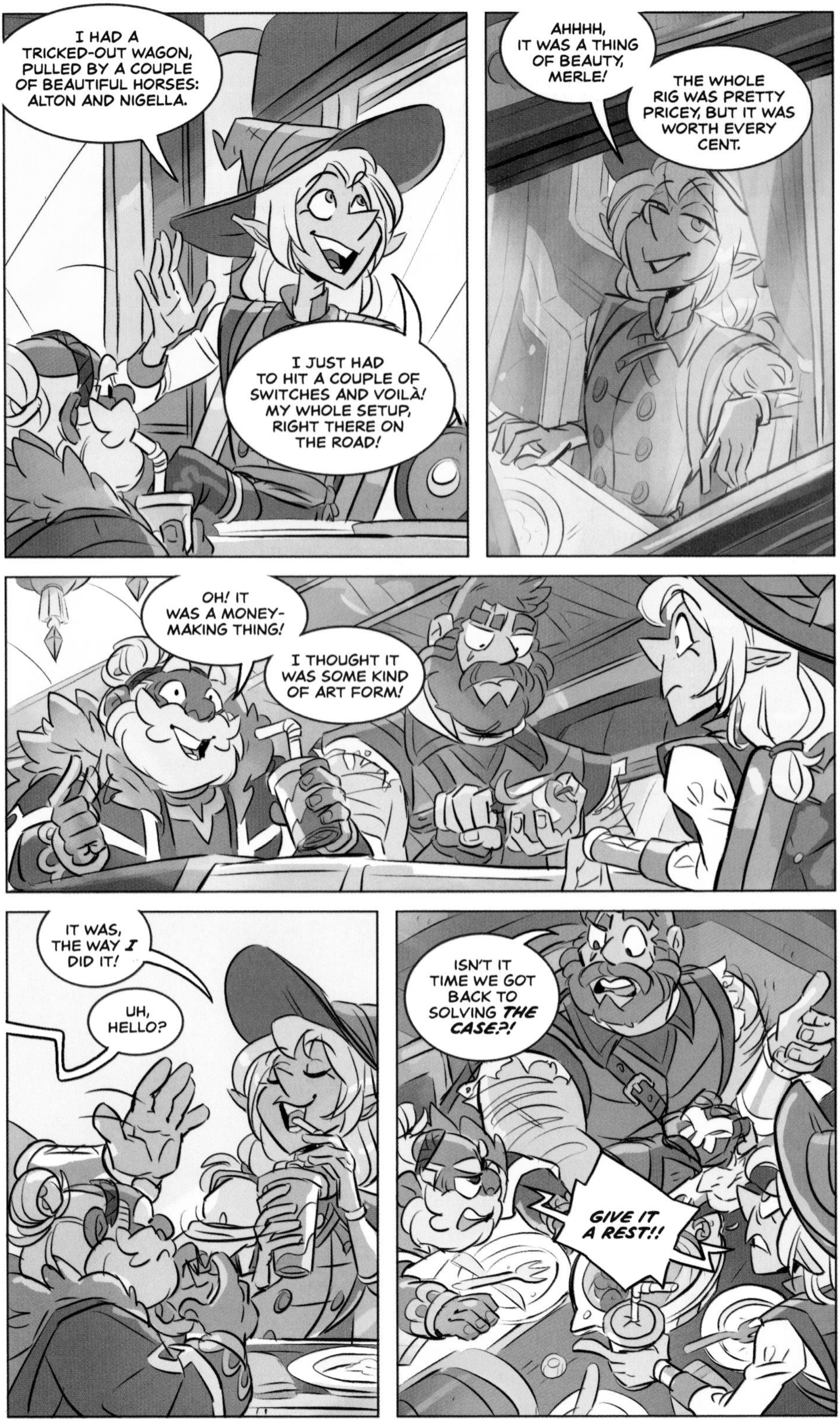
I HAD A TRICKED-OUT WAGON, PULLED BY A COUPLE OF BEAUTIFUL HORSES: ALTON AND NIGELLA.
I JUST HAD TO HIT A COUPLE OF SWITCHES AND VOILÀ! MY WHOLE SETUP, RIGHT THERE ON THE ROAD!
AHHHH, IT WAS A THING OF BEAUTY, MERLE!
THE WHOLE RIG WAS PRETTY PRICEY, BUT IT WAS WORTH EVERY CENT.
OH! IT WAS A MONEY-MAKING THING!
I THOUGHT IT WAS SOME KIND OF ART FORM!
IT WAS, THE WAY I DID IT!
UH, HELLO?
ISN'T IT TIME WE GOT BACK TO SOLVING THE CASE?!
GIVE IT A REST!!

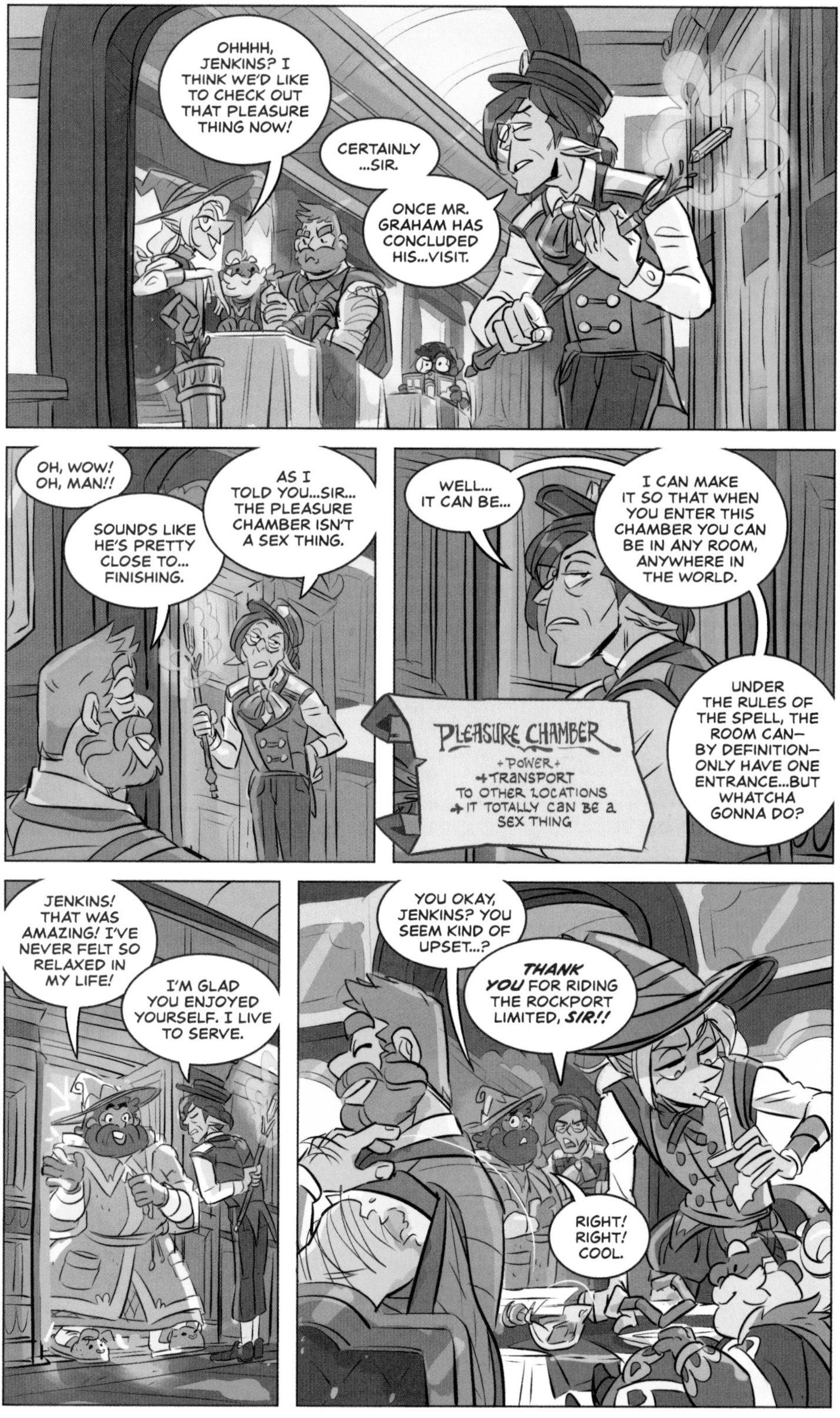

OHHHH, JENKINS? I THINK WE'D LIKE TO CHECK OUT THAT PLEASURE THING NOW!
CERTAINLY ...SIR.
ONCE MR. GRAHAM HAS CONCLUDED HIS...VISIT.
OH, WOW! OH, MAN!!
SOUNDS LIKE HE'S PRETTY CLOSE TO... FINISHING.
AS I TOLD YOU...SIR... THE PLEASURE CHAMBER ISN'T A SEX THING.
WELL... IT CAN BE...
I CAN MAKE IT SO THAT WHEN YOU ENTER THIS CHAMBER YOU CAN BE IN ANY ROOM, ANYWHERE IN THE WORLD.
PLEASURE CHAMBER
+POWER+
+TRANSPORT TO OTHER LOCATIONS
+IT TOTALLY CAN BE A SEX THING
UNDER THE RULES OF THE SPELL, THE ROOM CAN— BY DEFINITION— ONLY HAVE ONE ENTRANCE...BUT WHATCHA GONNA DO?
JENKINS! THAT WAS AMAZING! I'VE NEVER FELT SO RELAXED IN MY LIFE!
I'M GLAD YOU ENJOYED YOURSELF. I LIVE TO SERVE.
YOU OKAY, JENKINS? YOU SEEM KIND OF UPSET...?
THANK YOU FOR RIDING THE ROCKPORT LIMITED, SIR!!
RIGHT! RIGHT! COOL.

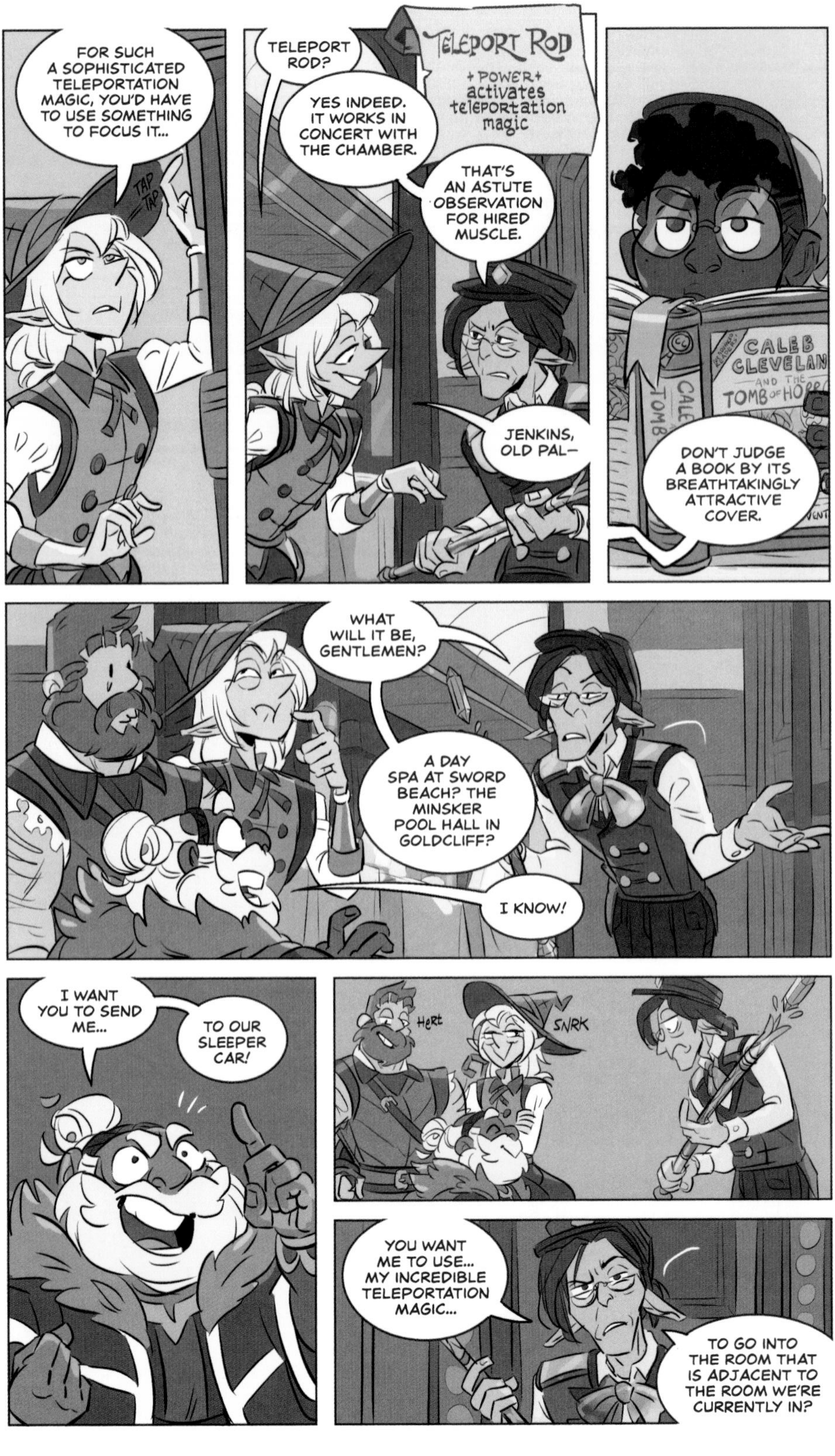
FOR SUCH A SOPHISTICATED TELEPORTATION MAGIC, YOU'D HAVE TO USE SOMETHING TO FOCUS IT...
TAP TAP
TELEPORT ROD?
TELEPORT ROD
+POWER+ activates teleportation magic
YES INDEED. IT WORKS IN CONCERT WITH THE CHAMBER.
THAT'S AN ASTUTE OBSERVATION FOR HIRED MUSCLE.
JENKINS, OLD PAL—
CALEB CLEVELAN AND THE TOMB OF HORR
DON'T JUDGE A BOOK BY ITS BREATHTAKINGLY ATTRACTIVE COVER.
WHAT WILL IT BE, GENTLEMEN?
A DAY SPA AT SWORD BEACH? THE MINSKER POOL HALL IN GOLDCLIFF?
I KNOW!
I WANT YOU TO SEND ME...
TO OUR SLEEPER CAR!
HeRt
SNRK
YOU WANT ME TO USE... MY INCREDIBLE TELEPORTATION MAGIC...
TO GO INTO THE ROOM THAT IS ADJACENT TO THE ROOM WE'RE CURRENTLY IN?

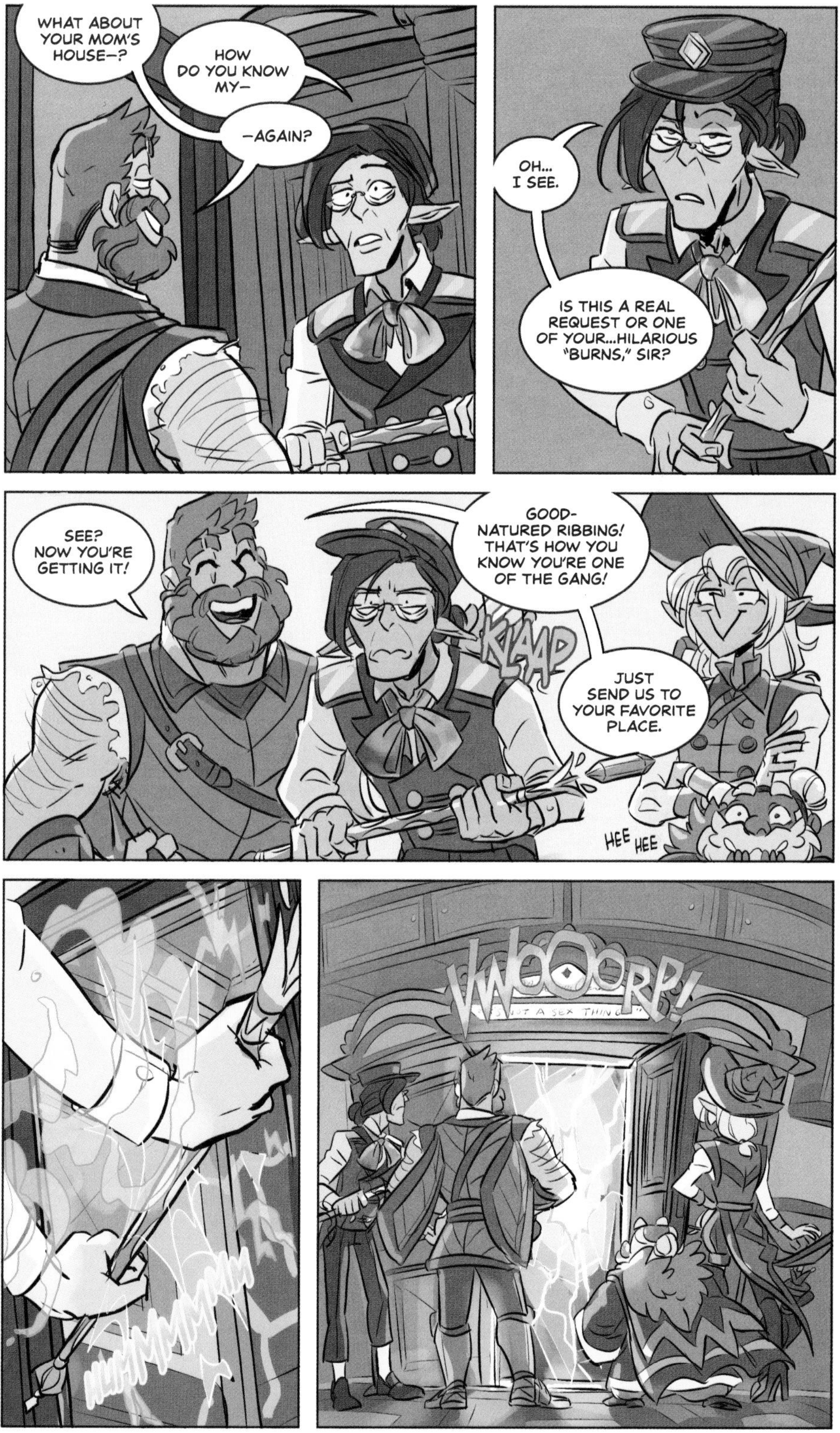

WHAT ABOUT YOUR MOM'S HOUSE—?
HOW DO YOU KNOW MY—
—AGAIN?
OH... I SEE.
IS THIS A REAL REQUEST OR ONE OF YOUR...HILARIOUS "BURNS," SIR?
SEE? NOW YOU'RE GETTING IT!
GOOD-NATURED RIBBING! THAT'S HOW YOU KNOW YOU'RE ONE OF THE GANG!
KLAAP
JUST SEND US TO YOUR FAVORITE PLACE.
HEE HEE
HMMMMMMM
VWOOORP!

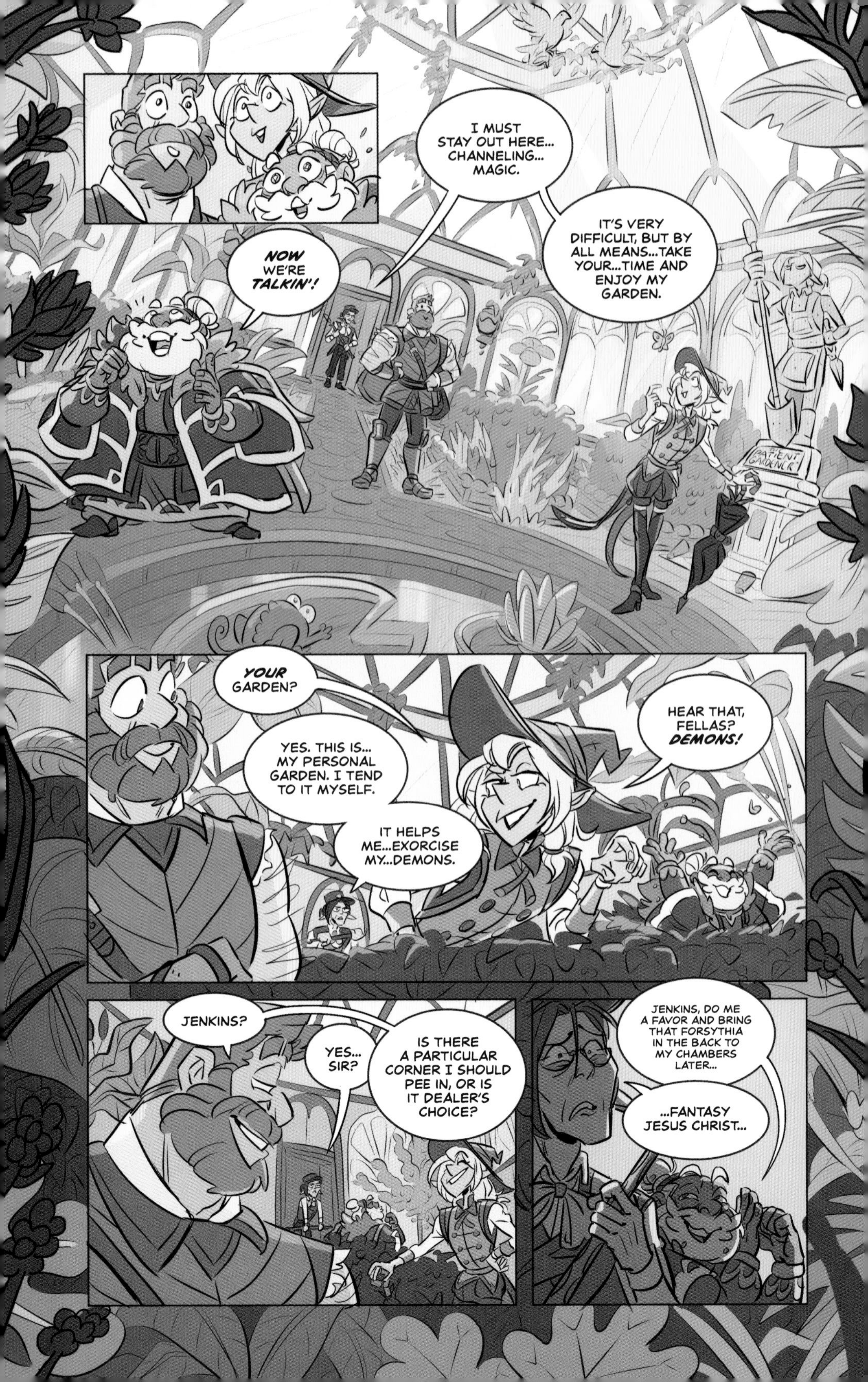

I MUST STAY OUT HERE... CHANNELING... MAGIC.
IT'S VERY DIFFICULT, BUT BY ALL MEANS...TAKE YOUR...TIME AND ENJOY MY GARDEN.
NOW WE'RE TALKIN'!
PATIENT GARDENER
YOUR GARDEN?
YES. THIS IS... MY PERSONAL GARDEN. I TEND TO IT MYSELF.
IT HELPS ME...EXORCISE MY...DEMONS.
HEAR THAT, FELLAS? DEMONS!
JENKINS?
YES... SIR?
IS THERE A PARTICULAR CORNER I SHOULD PEE IN, OR IS IT DEALER'S CHOICE?
JENKINS, DO ME A FAVOR AND BRING THAT FORSYTHIA IN THE BACK TO MY CHAMBERS LATER...
...FANTASY JESUS CHRIST...

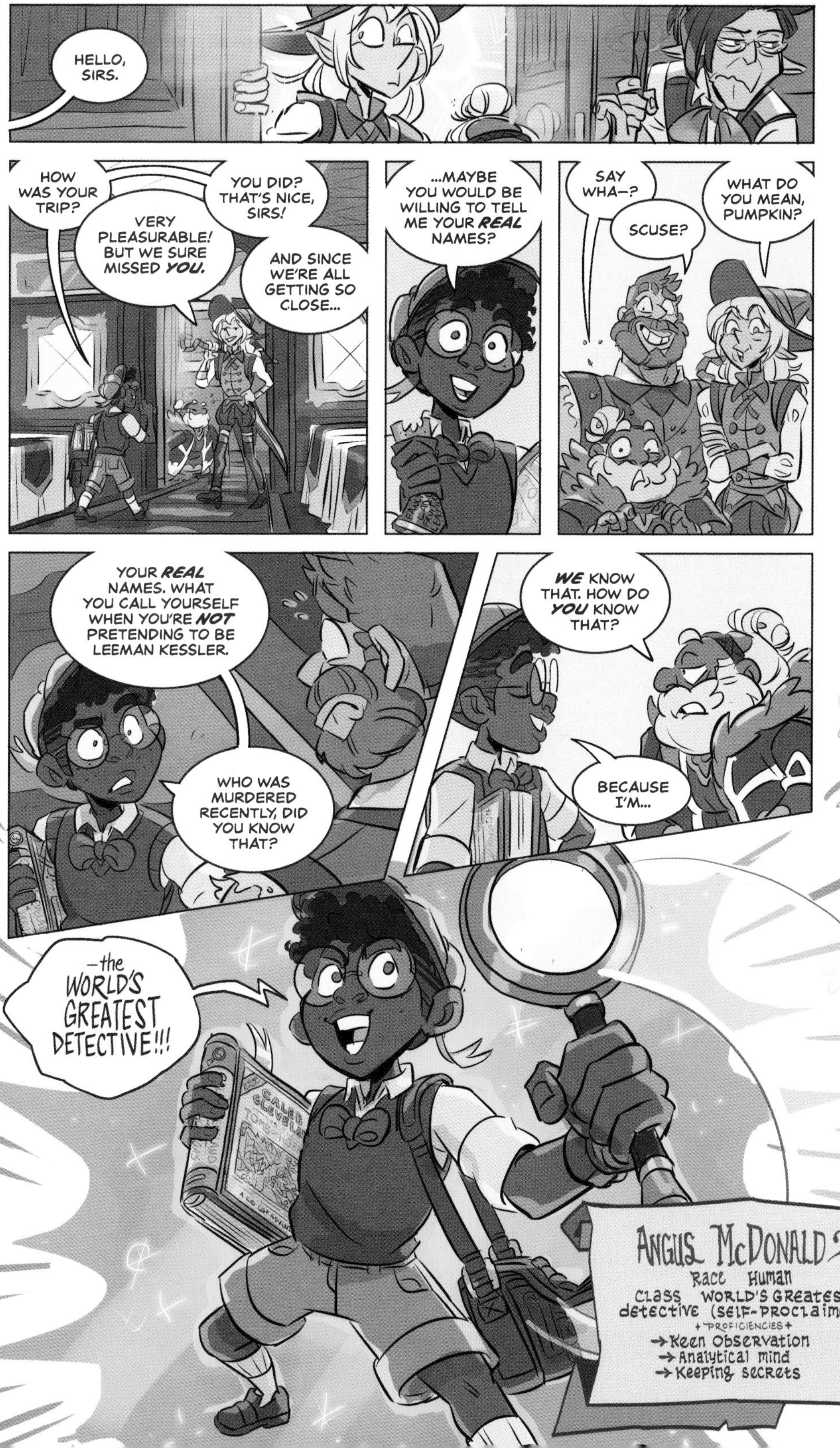
HELLO, SIRS.
HOW WAS YOUR TRIP?
VERY PLEASURABLE! BUT WE SURE MISSED YOU.
YOU DID? THAT'S NICE, SIRS!
AND SINCE WE'RE ALL GETTING SO CLOSE...
...MAYBE YOU WOULD BE WILLING TO TELL ME YOUR REAL NAMES?
SAY WHA—?
SCUSE?
WHAT DO YOU MEAN, PUMPKIN?
YOUR REAL NAMES. WHAT YOU CALL YOURSELF WHEN YOU'RE NOT PRETENDING TO BE LEEMAN KESSLER.
WHO WAS MURDERED RECENTLY, DID YOU KNOW THAT?
WE KNOW THAT. HOW DO YOU KNOW THAT?
BECAUSE I'M...
—the WORLD'S GREATEST DETECTIVE!!!
ANGUS McDONALD
Race Human
Class World's Greatest detective (self-proclaimed)
+ PROFICIENCIES +
→Keen Observation
→Analytical mind
→Keeping secrets

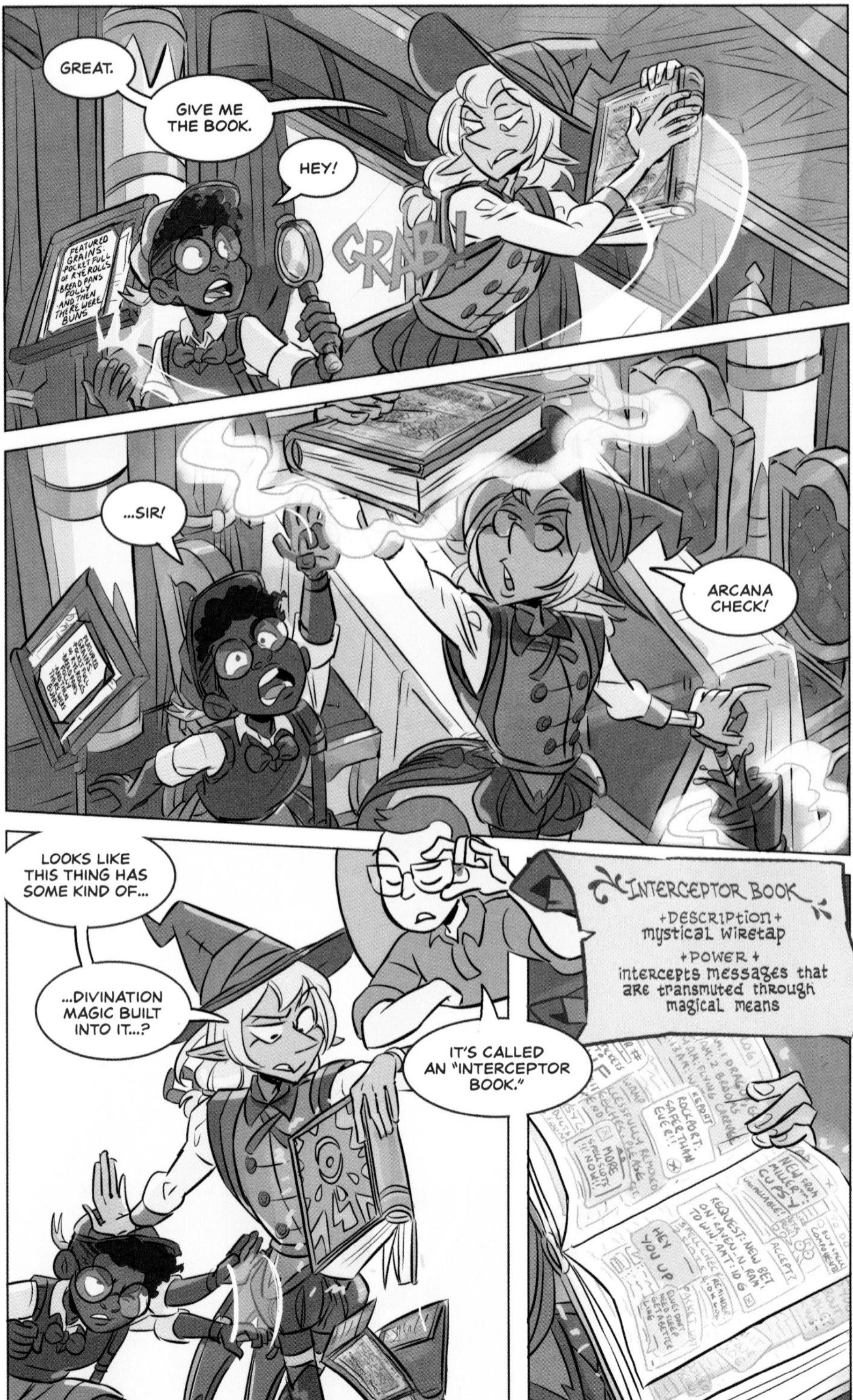
GREAT.
GIVE ME THE BOOK.
HEY!
FEATURED GRAINS: POCKETFUL OF RYE ROLLS - BREAD PANS FOLLY - AND THEN THERE WERE BUNS
GRAB!
...SIR!
ARCANA CHECK!
LOOKS LIKE THIS THING HAS SOME KIND OF...
...DIVINATION MAGIC BUILT INTO IT...?
IT'S CALLED AN "INTERCEPTOR BOOK."
INTERCEPTOR BOOK
+DESCRIPTION+
mystical wiretap
+POWER+
intercepts messages that are transmuted through magical means

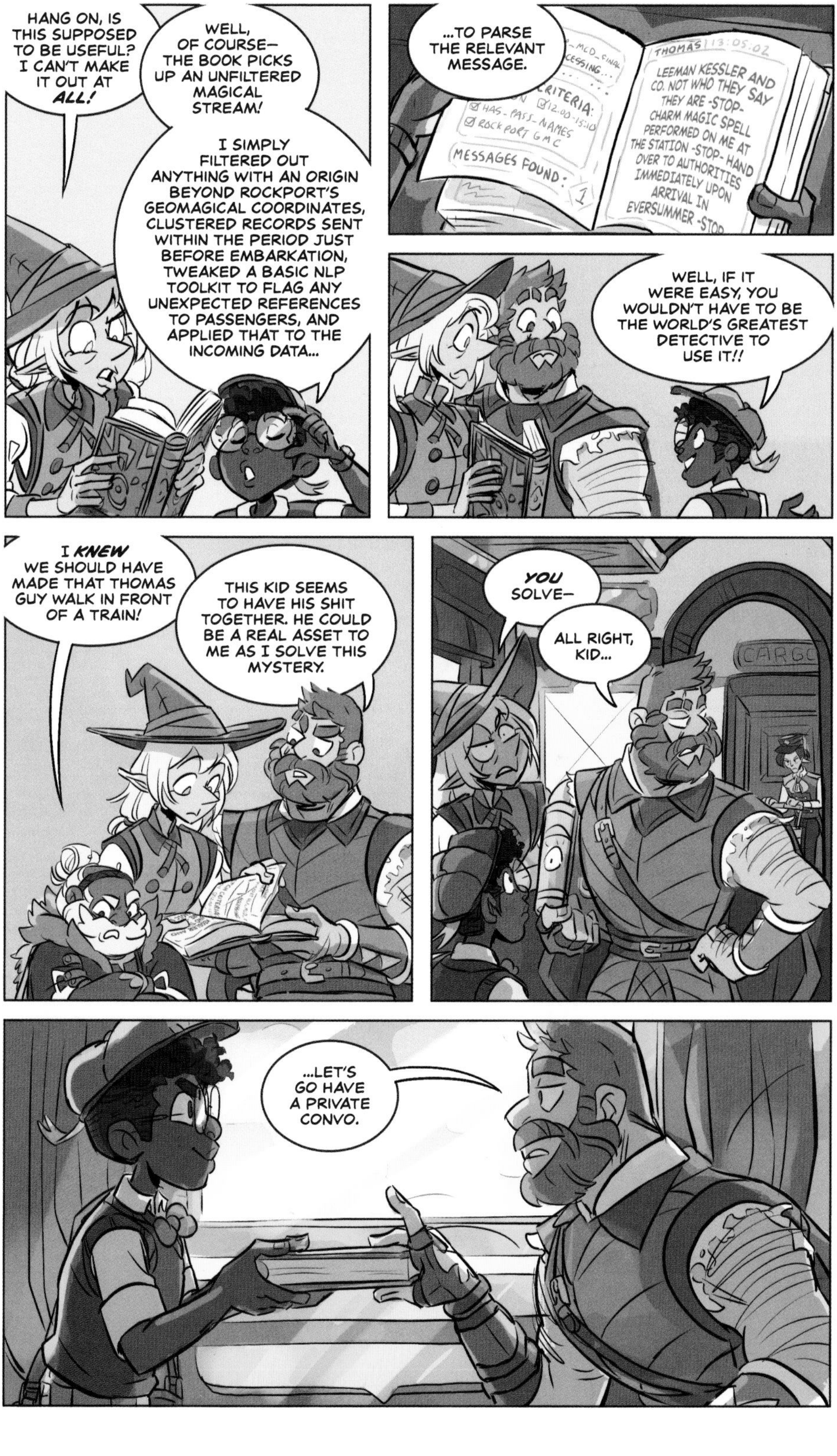
HANG ON, IS THIS SUPPOSED TO BE USEFUL? I CAN'T MAKE IT OUT AT ALL!
WELL, OF COURSE— THE BOOK PICKS UP AN UNFILTERED MAGICAL STREAM!
I SIMPLY FILTERED OUT ANYTHING WITH AN ORIGIN BEYOND ROCKPORT'S GEOMAGICAL COORDINATES, CLUSTERED RECORDS SENT WITHIN THE PERIOD JUST BEFORE EMBARKATION, TWEAKED A BASIC NLP TOOLKIT TO FLAG ANY UNEXPECTED REFERENCES TO PASSENGERS, AND APPLIED THAT TO THE INCOMING DATA...
...TO PARSE THE RELEVANT MESSAGE.
CRITERIA:
HAS-PASS-NAMES
12:00-15:10
ROCKPORT GMC
MESSAGES FOUND: 1
THOMAS 13:05:02
LEEMAN KESSLER AND CO. NOT WHO THEY SAY THEY ARE -STOP- CHARM MAGIC SPELL PERFORMED ON ME AT THE STATION -STOP- HAND OVER TO AUTHORITIES IMMEDIATELY UPON ARRIVAL IN EVERSUMMER -STOP
WELL, IF IT WERE EASY, YOU WOULDN'T HAVE TO BE THE WORLD'S GREATEST DETECTIVE TO USE IT!!
I KNEW WE SHOULD HAVE MADE THAT THOMAS GUY WALK IN FRONT OF A TRAIN!
THIS KID SEEMS TO HAVE HIS SHIT TOGETHER. HE COULD BE A REAL ASSET TO ME AS I SOLVE THIS MYSTERY.
YOU SOLVE—
ALL RIGHT, KID...
CARGO
...LET'S GO HAVE A PRIVATE CONVO.

Chapter 4

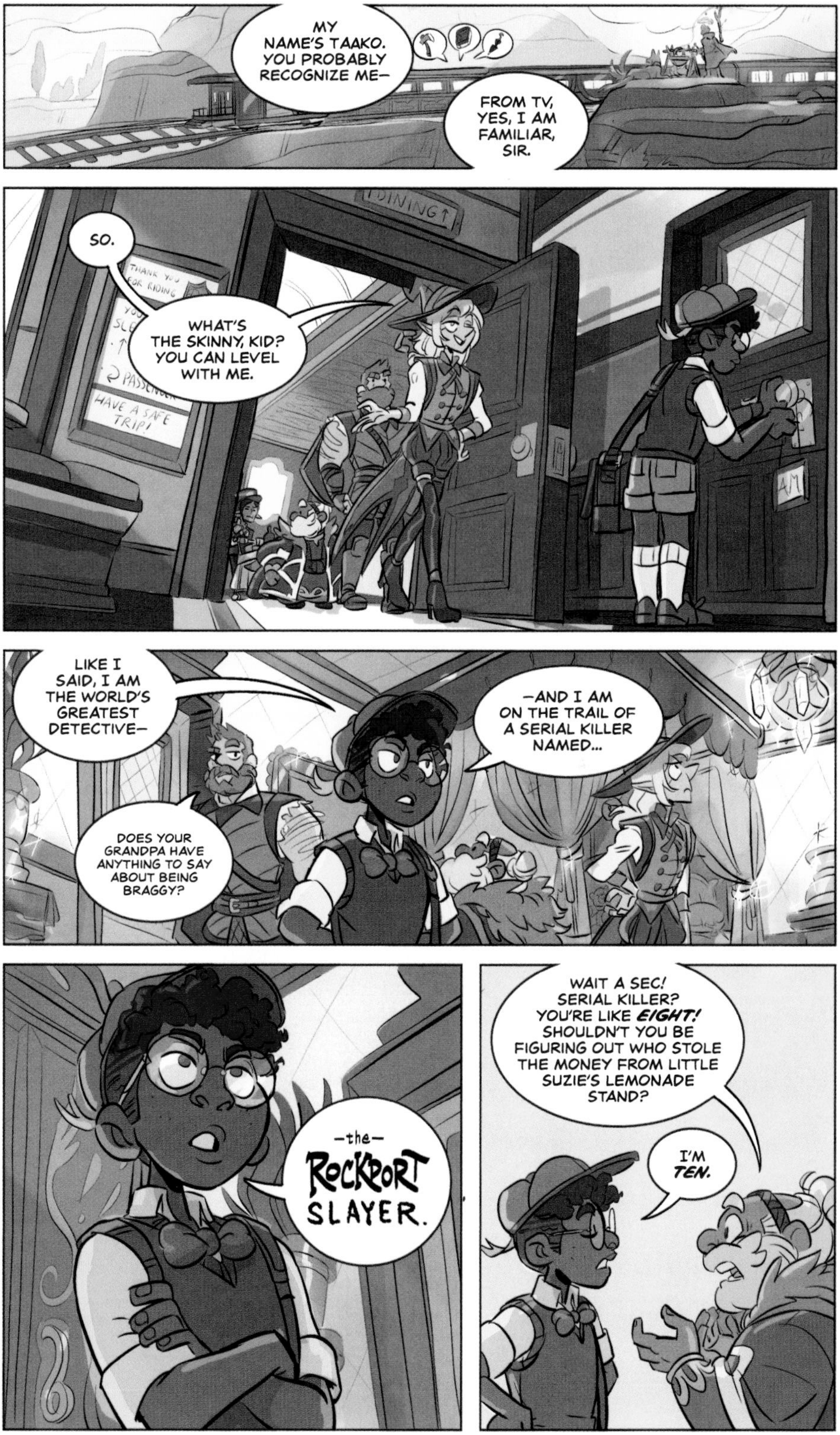
MY NAME'S TAAKO. YOU PROBABLY RECOGNIZE ME—
FROM TV, YES, I AM FAMILIAR, SIR.
DINING
SO.
THANK YOU FOR RIDING
HAVE A SAFE TRIP!
WHAT'S THE SKINNY, KID? YOU CAN LEVEL WITH ME.
AM
LIKE I SAID, I AM THE WORLD'S GREATEST DETECTIVE—
—AND I AM ON THE TRAIL OF A SERIAL KILLER NAMED...
DOES YOUR GRANDPA HAVE ANYTHING TO SAY ABOUT BEING BRAGGY?
—the— ROCKPORT SLAYER.
WAIT A SEC! SERIAL KILLER? YOU'RE LIKE *EIGHT!* SHOULDN'T YOU BE FIGURING OUT WHO STOLE THE MONEY FROM LITTLE SUZIE'S LEMONADE STAND?
I'M *TEN.*

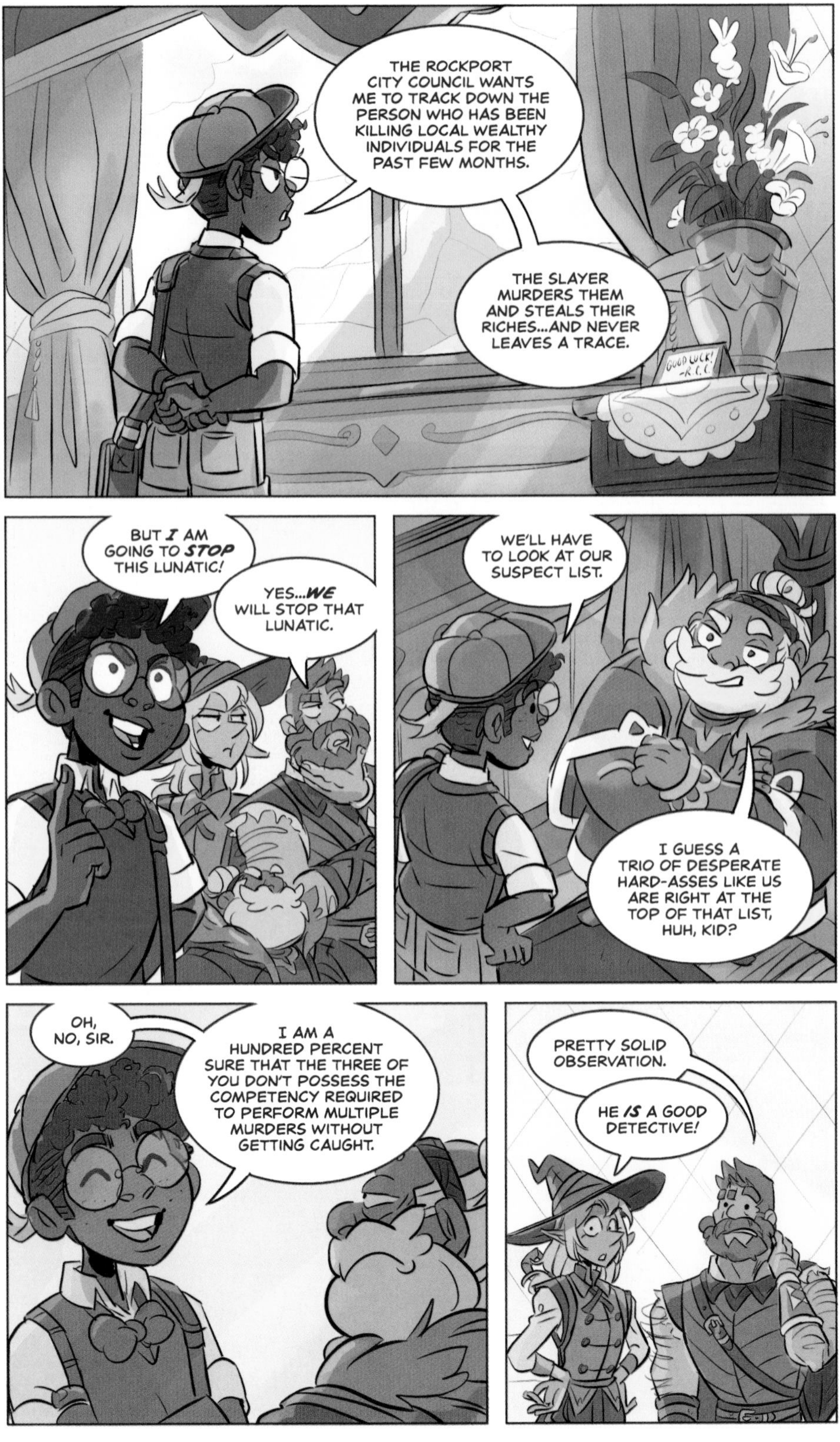
THE ROCKPORT CITY COUNCIL WANTS ME TO TRACK DOWN THE PERSON WHO HAS BEEN KILLING LOCAL WEALTHY INDIVIDUALS FOR THE PAST FEW MONTHS.
THE SLAYER MURDERS THEM AND STEALS THEIR RICHES...AND NEVER LEAVES A TRACE.
GOOD LUCK! -R.C.C.
BUT *I* AM GOING TO ***STOP*** THIS LUNATIC!
YES...***WE*** WILL STOP THAT LUNATIC.
WE'LL HAVE TO LOOK AT OUR SUSPECT LIST.
I GUESS A TRIO OF DESPERATE HARD-ASSES LIKE US ARE RIGHT AT THE TOP OF THAT LIST, HUH, KID?
OH, NO, SIR.
I AM A HUNDRED PERCENT SURE THAT THE THREE OF YOU DON'T POSSESS THE COMPETENCY REQUIRED TO PERFORM MULTIPLE MURDERS WITHOUT GETTING CAUGHT.
PRETTY SOLID OBSERVATION.
HE *IS* A GOOD DETECTIVE!

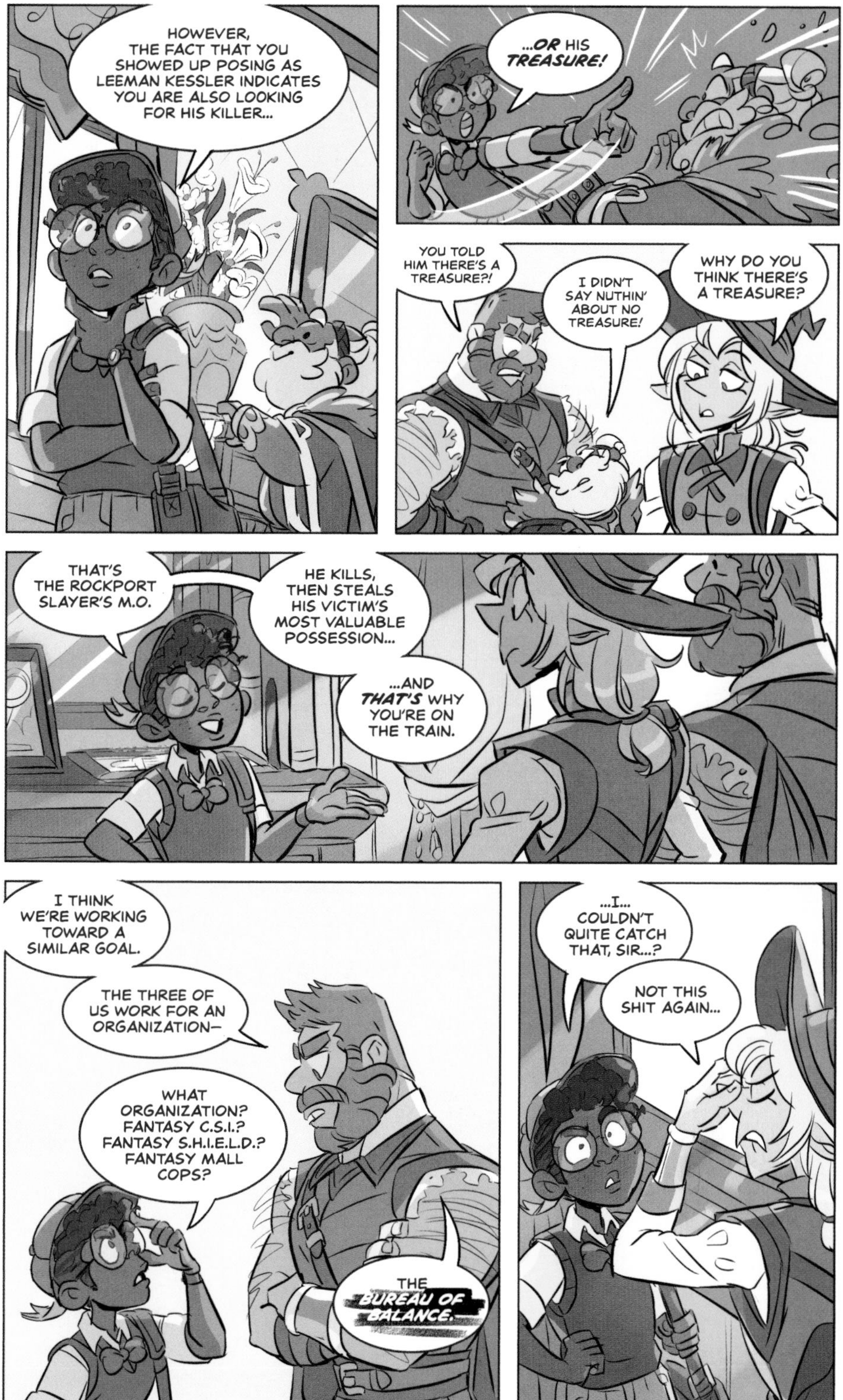
HOWEVER, THE FACT THAT YOU SHOWED UP POSING AS LEEMAN KESSLER INDICATES YOU ARE ALSO LOOKING FOR HIS KILLER...
...OR HIS TREASURE!
YOU TOLD HIM THERE'S A TREASURE?!
I DIDN'T SAY NUTHIN' ABOUT NO TREASURE!
WHY DO YOU THINK THERE'S A TREASURE?
THAT'S THE ROCKPORT SLAYER'S M.O.
HE KILLS, THEN STEALS HIS VICTIM'S MOST VALUABLE POSSESSION...
...AND THAT'S WHY YOU'RE ON THE TRAIN.
I THINK WE'RE WORKING TOWARD A SIMILAR GOAL.
THE THREE OF US WORK FOR AN ORGANIZATION—
WHAT ORGANIZATION? FANTASY C.S.I.? FANTASY S.H.I.E.L.D.? FANTASY MALL COPS?
THE BUREAU OF BALANCE.
...I... COULDN'T QUITE CATCH THAT, SIR...?
NOT THIS SHIT AGAIN...

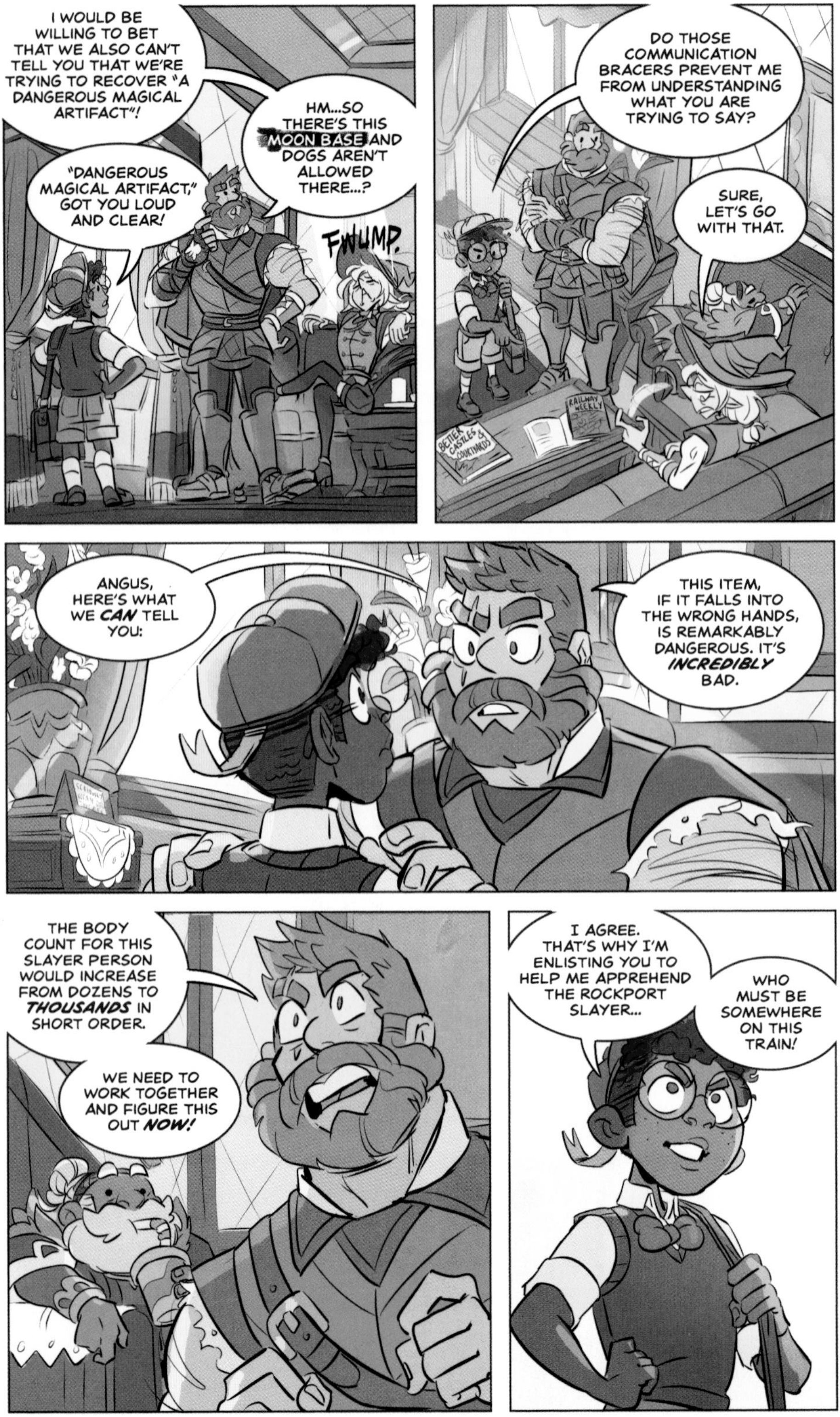

I WOULD BE WILLING TO BET THAT WE ALSO CAN'T TELL YOU THAT WE'RE TRYING TO RECOVER "A DANGEROUS MAGICAL ARTIFACT"!
HM...SO THERE'S THIS MOON BASE AND DOGS AREN'T ALLOWED THERE...?
"DANGEROUS MAGICAL ARTIFACT," GOT YOU LOUD AND CLEAR!
FWUMP.
DO THOSE COMMUNICATION BRACERS PREVENT ME FROM UNDERSTANDING WHAT YOU ARE TRYING TO SAY?
SURE, LET'S GO WITH THAT.
BETTER CASTLES & COURTYARDS
RAILWAY WEEKLY
ANGUS, HERE'S WHAT WE *CAN* TELL YOU:
THIS ITEM, IF IT FALLS INTO THE WRONG HANDS, IS REMARKABLY DANGEROUS. IT'S *INCREDIBLY* BAD.
THE BODY COUNT FOR THIS SLAYER PERSON WOULD INCREASE FROM DOZENS TO *THOUSANDS* IN SHORT ORDER.
WE NEED TO WORK TOGETHER AND FIGURE THIS OUT *NOW!*
I AGREE. THAT'S WHY I'M ENLISTING YOU TO HELP ME APPREHEND THE ROCKPORT SLAYER...
WHO MUST BE SOMEWHERE ON THIS TRAIN!

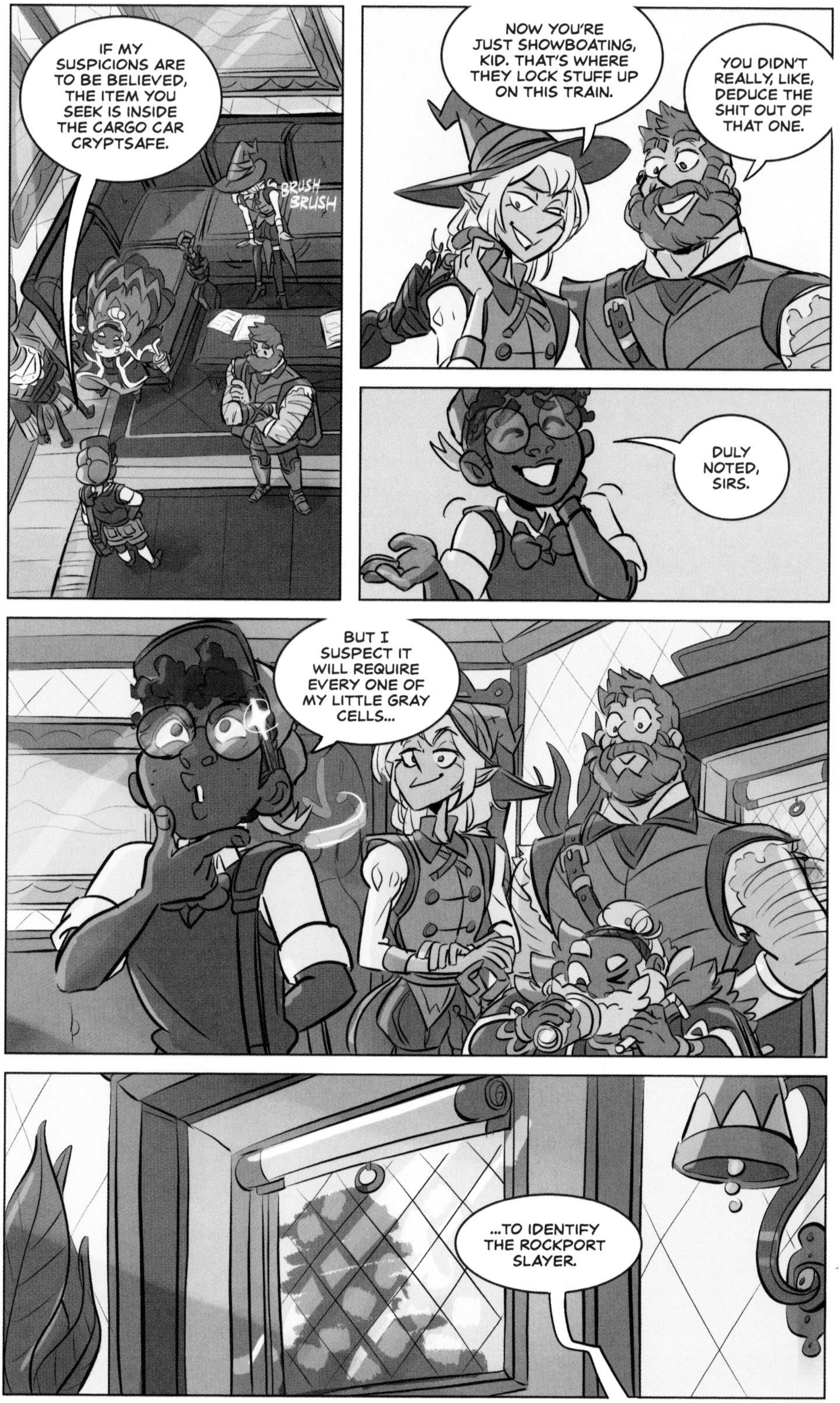
IF MY SUSPICIONS ARE TO BE BELIEVED, THE ITEM YOU SEEK IS INSIDE THE CARGO CAR CRYPTSAFE.
BRUSH BRUSH
NOW YOU'RE JUST SHOWBOATING, KID. THAT'S WHERE THEY LOCK STUFF UP ON THIS TRAIN.
YOU DIDN'T REALLY, LIKE, DEDUCE THE SHIT OUT OF THAT ONE.
DULY NOTED, SIRS.
BUT I SUSPECT IT WILL REQUIRE EVERY ONE OF MY LITTLE GRAY CELLS...
...TO IDENTIFY THE ROCKPORT SLAYER.

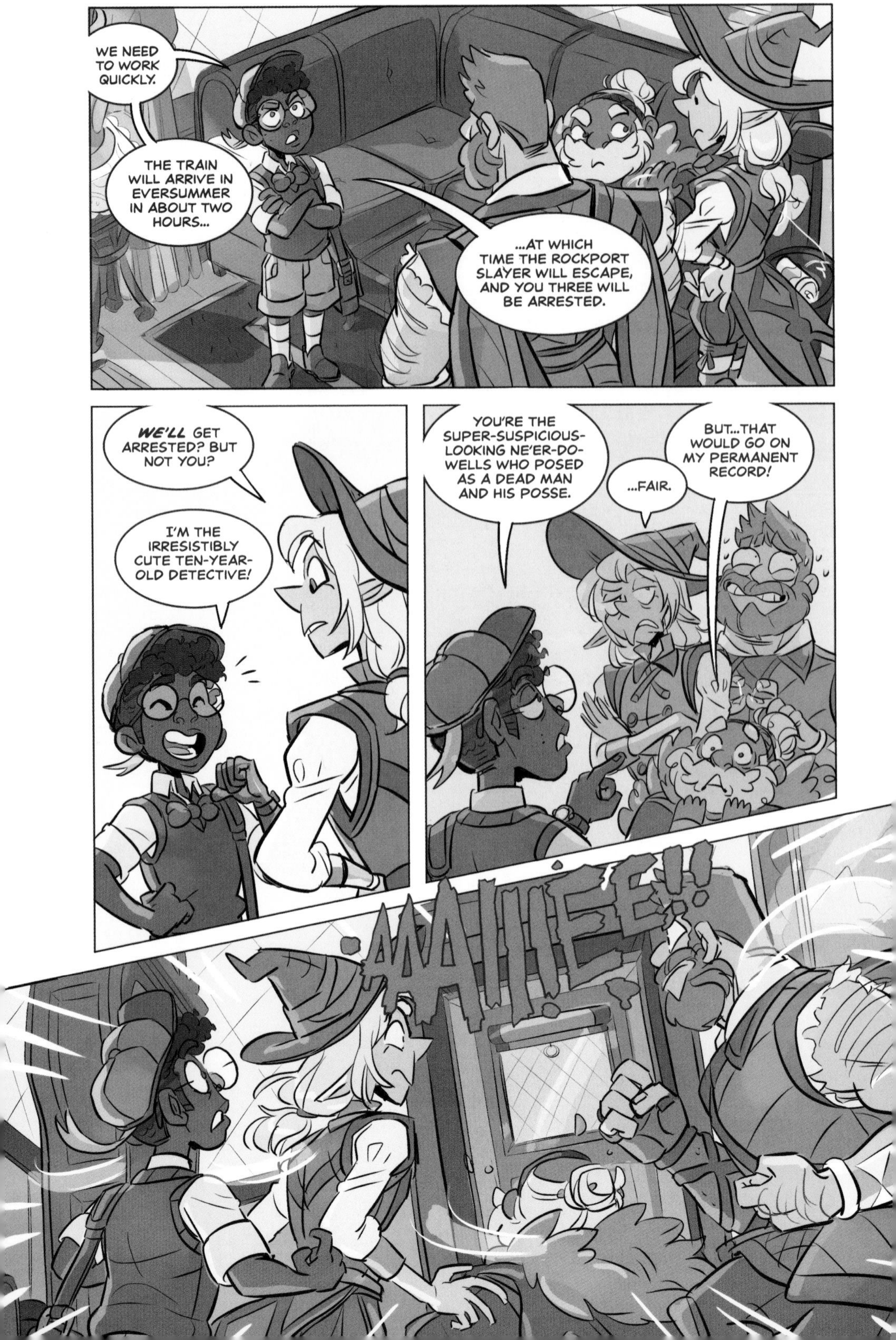
WE NEED TO WORK QUICKLY.
THE TRAIN WILL ARRIVE IN EVERSUMMER IN ABOUT TWO HOURS...
...AT WHICH TIME THE ROCKPORT SLAYER WILL ESCAPE, AND YOU THREE WILL BE ARRESTED.
WE'LL GET ARRESTED? BUT NOT YOU?
I'M THE IRRESISTIBLY CUTE TEN-YEAR-OLD DETECTIVE!
YOU'RE THE SUPER-SUSPICIOUS-LOOKING NE'ER-DO-WELLS WHO POSED AS A DEAD MAN AND HIS POSSE.
...FAIR.
BUT...THAT WOULD GO ON MY PERMANENT RECORD!
AAAIIIEEE!!

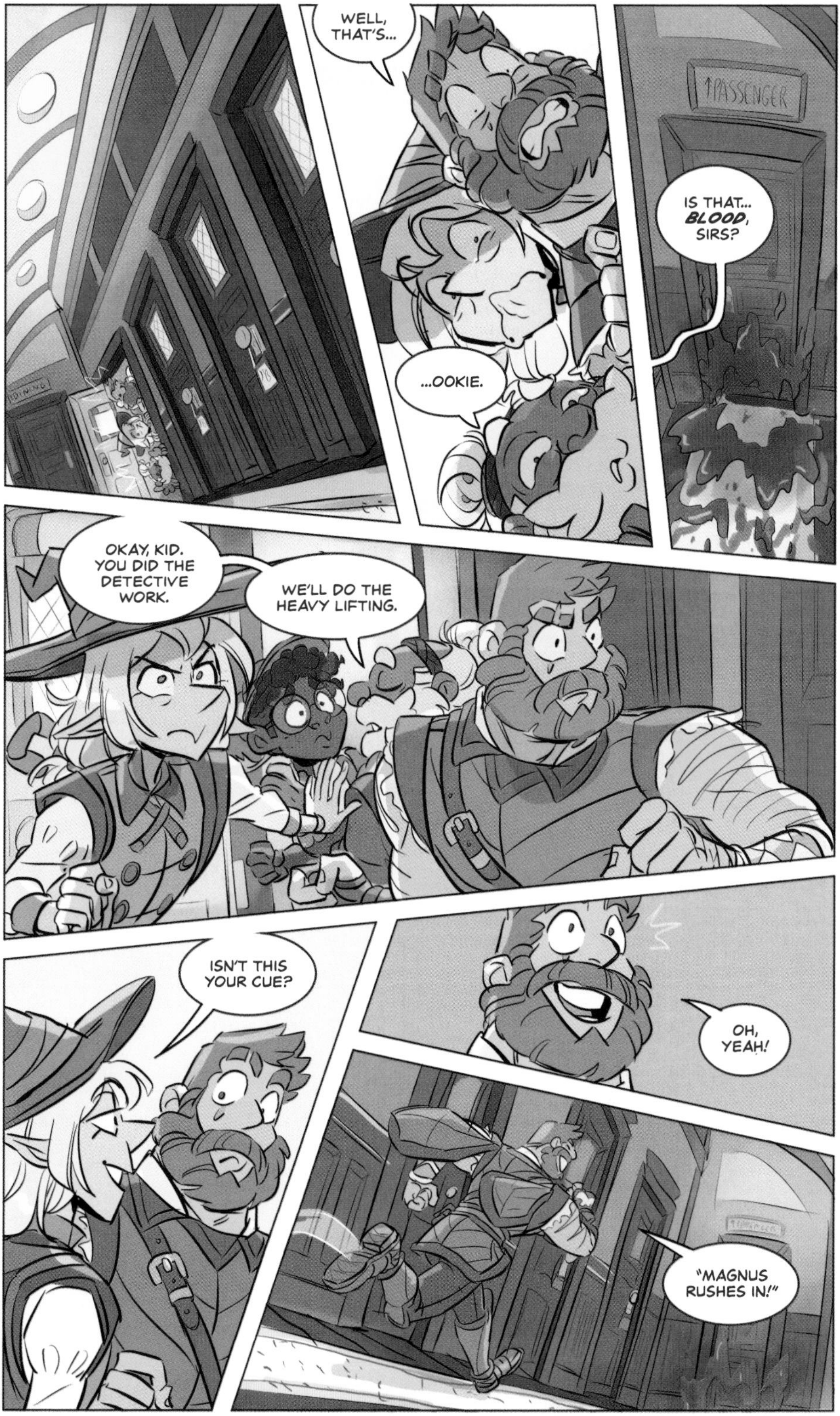
DINING
PASSENGER
WELL, THAT'S...
...OOKIE.
IS THAT... *BLOOD*, SIRS?
OKAY, KID. YOU DID THE DETECTIVE WORK.
WE'LL DO THE HEAVY LIFTING.
ISN'T THIS YOUR CUE?
OH, YEAH!
"MAGNUS RUSHES IN!"

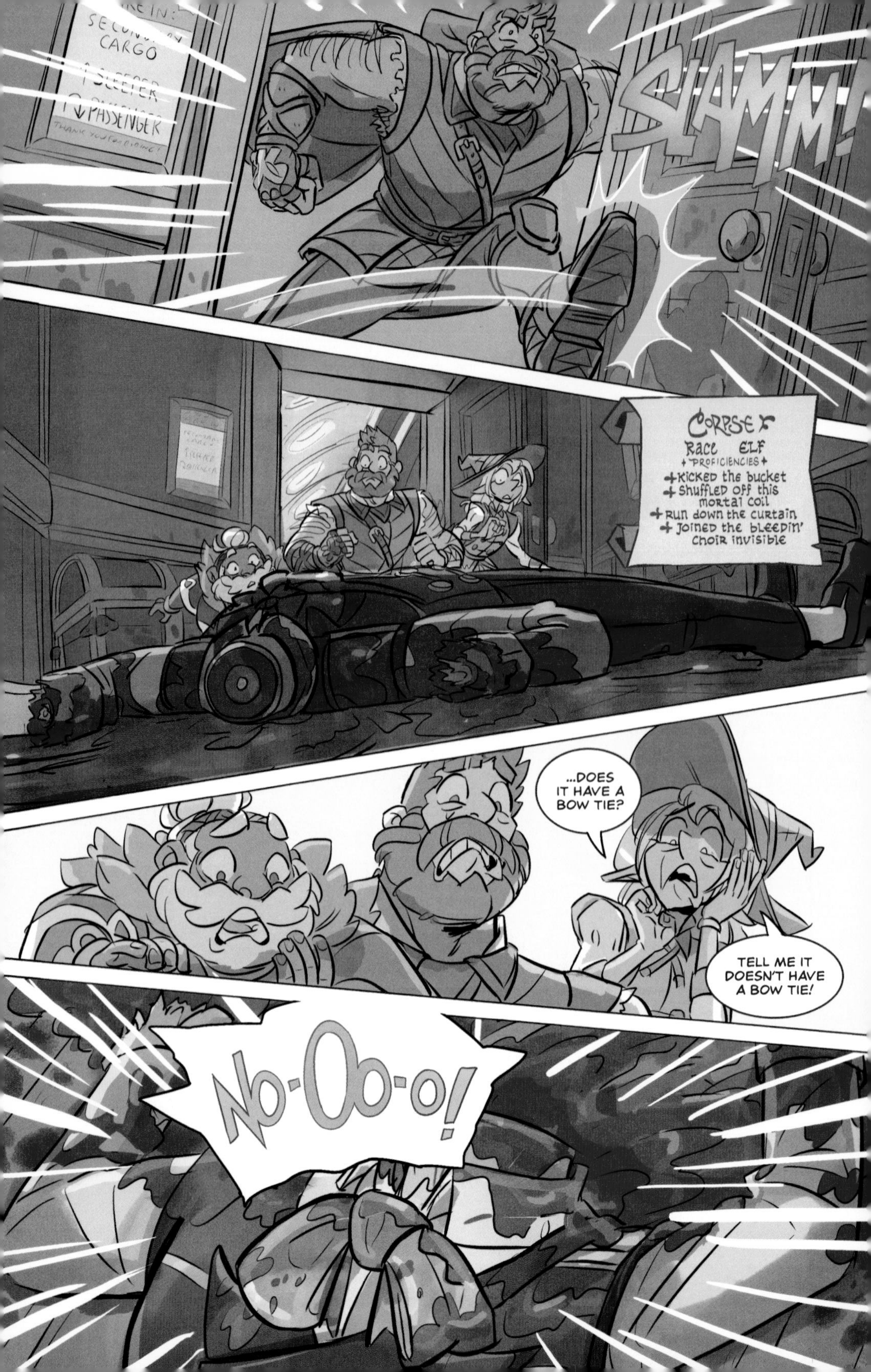
CARGO
SLEEPER
PASSENGER
SLAMM!
CORPSE
RACE ELF
PROFICIENCIES
KICKED THE BUCKET
SHUFFLED OFF THIS MORTAL COIL
RUN DOWN THE CURTAIN
JOINED THE BLEEDIN' CHOIR INVISIBLE
...DOES IT HAVE A BOW TIE?
TELL ME IT DOESN'T HAVE A BOW TIE!
NO-OO-O!

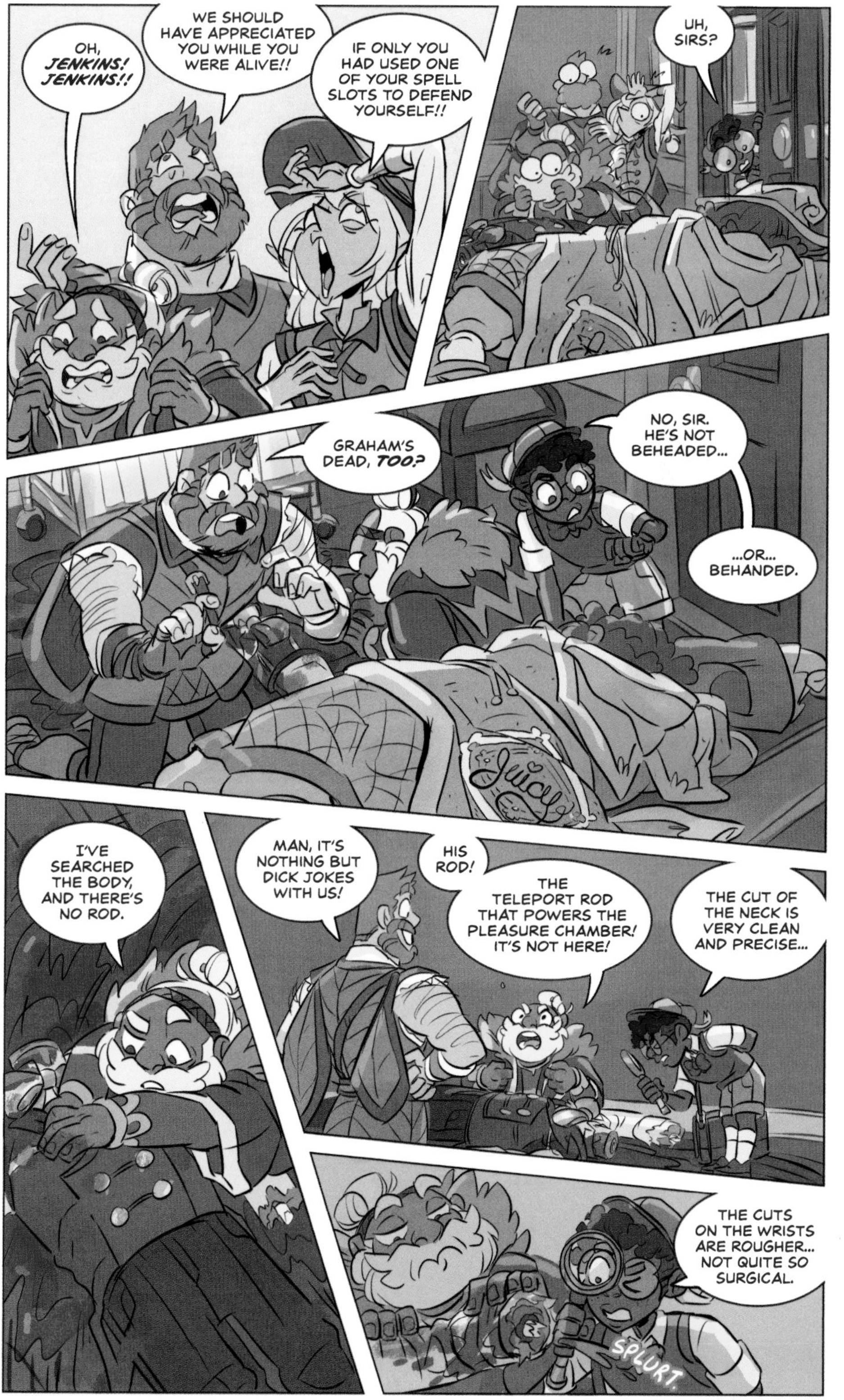
OH, JENKINS! JENKINS!!
WE SHOULD HAVE APPRECIATED YOU WHILE YOU WERE ALIVE!!
IF ONLY YOU HAD USED ONE OF YOUR SPELL SLOTS TO DEFEND YOURSELF!!
UH, SIRS?
GRAHAM'S DEAD, TOO?
NO, SIR. HE'S NOT BEHEADED...
...OR... BEHANDED.
JUICY
I'VE SEARCHED THE BODY, AND THERE'S NO ROD.
MAN, IT'S NOTHING BUT DICK JOKES WITH US!
HIS ROD!
THE TELEPORT ROD THAT POWERS THE PLEASURE CHAMBER! IT'S NOT HERE!
THE CUT OF THE NECK IS VERY CLEAN AND PRECISE...
THE CUTS ON THE WRISTS ARE ROUGHER... NOT QUITE SO SURGICAL.
SPLURT.

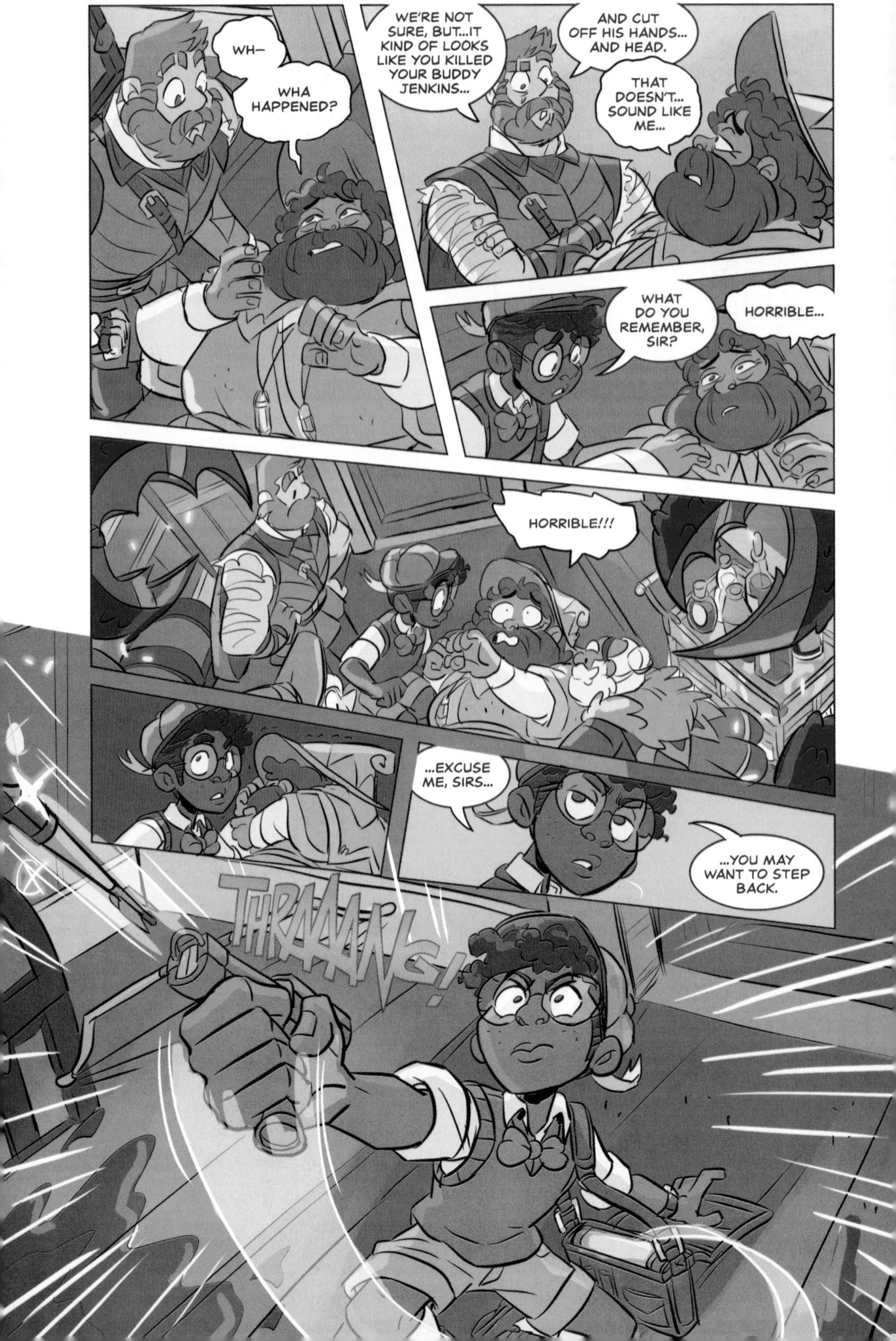
WH—
WHA HAPPENED?
WE'RE NOT SURE, BUT...IT KIND OF LOOKS LIKE YOU KILLED YOUR BUDDY JENKINS...
AND CUT OFF HIS HANDS... AND HEAD.
THAT DOESN'T... SOUND LIKE ME...
WHAT DO YOU REMEMBER, SIR?
HORRIBLE...
HORRIBLE!!!
...EXCUSE ME, SIRS...
...YOU MAY WANT TO STEP BACK.
THRAAAANG!

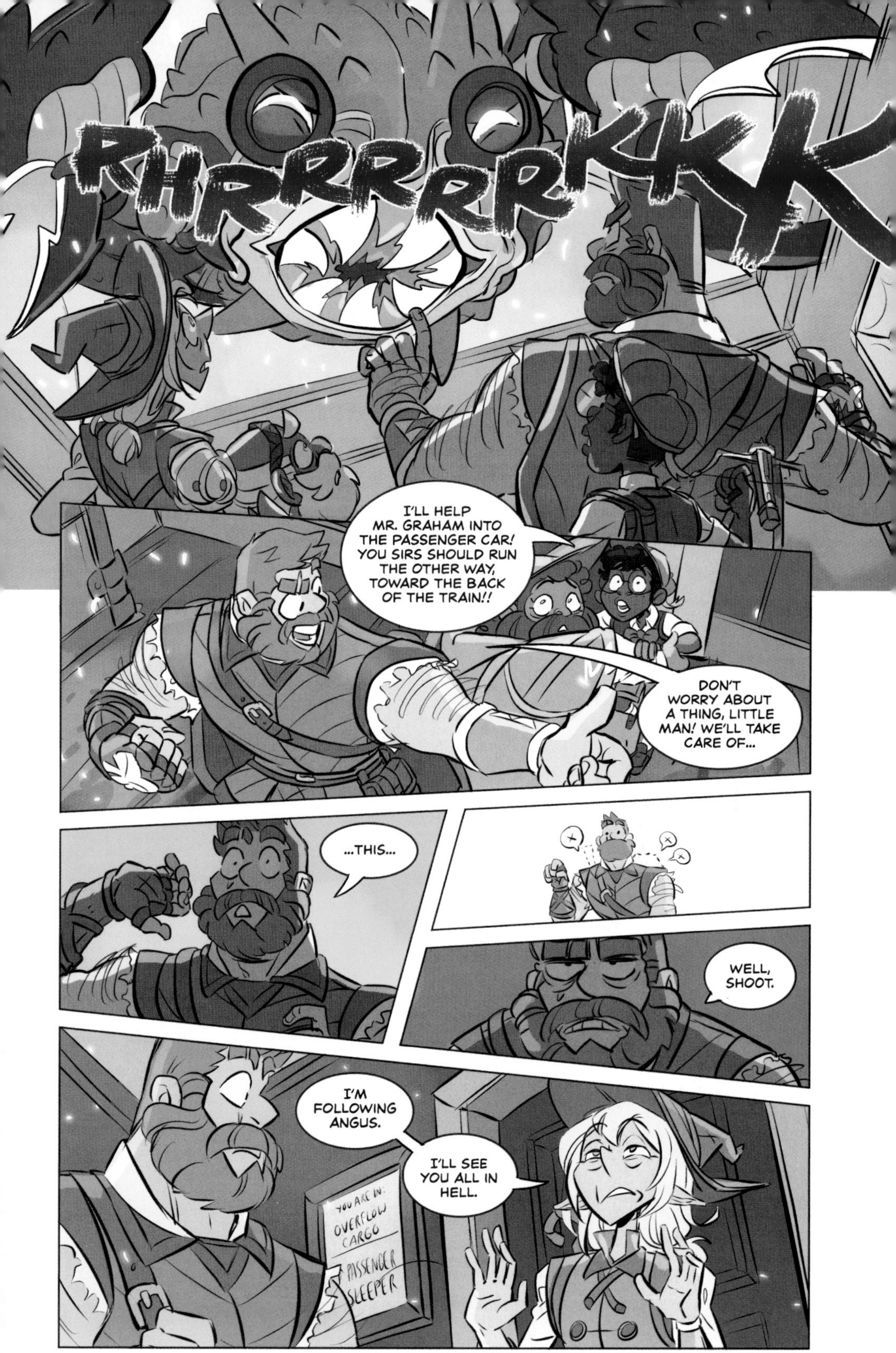
PHRRRRRKKKK
I'LL HELP MR. GRAHAM INTO THE PASSENGER CAR! YOU SIRS SHOULD RUN THE OTHER WAY, TOWARD THE BACK OF THE TRAIN!!
DON'T WORRY ABOUT A THING, LITTLE MAN! WE'LL TAKE CARE OF...
...THIS...
WELL, SHOOT.
I'M FOLLOWING ANGUS.
I'LL SEE YOU ALL IN HELL.
YOU ARE IN: OVERFLOW CARGO
PASSENGER SLEEPER

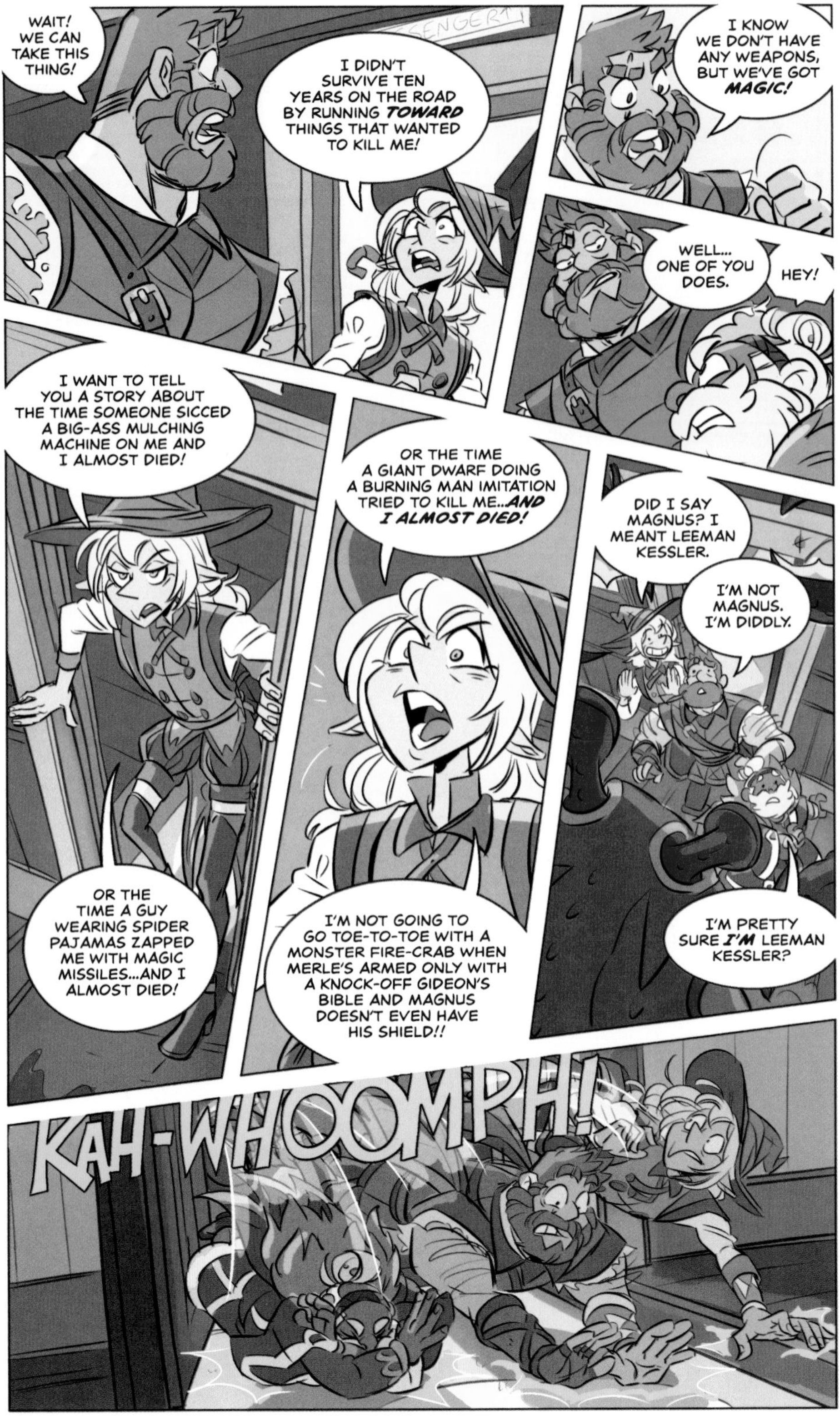
WAIT! WE CAN TAKE THIS THING!
I DIDN'T SURVIVE TEN YEARS ON THE ROAD BY RUNNING **TOWARD** THINGS THAT WANTED TO KILL ME!
I KNOW WE DON'T HAVE ANY WEAPONS, BUT WE'VE GOT **MAGIC!**
WELL... ONE OF YOU DOES.
HEY!
I WANT TO TELL YOU A STORY ABOUT THE TIME SOMEONE SICCED A BIG-ASS MULCHING MACHINE ON ME AND I ALMOST DIED!
OR THE TIME A GIANT DWARF DOING A BURNING MAN IMITATION TRIED TO KILL ME...**AND I ALMOST DIED!**
DID I SAY MAGNUS? I MEANT LEEMAN KESSLER.
I'M NOT MAGNUS. I'M DIDDLY.
OR THE TIME A GUY WEARING SPIDER PAJAMAS ZAPPED ME WITH MAGIC MISSILES...AND I ALMOST DIED!
I'M NOT GOING TO GO TOE-TO-TOE WITH A MONSTER FIRE-CRAB WHEN MERLE'S ARMED ONLY WITH A KNOCK-OFF GIDEON'S BIBLE AND MAGNUS DOESN'T EVEN HAVE HIS SHIELD!!
I'M PRETTY SURE **I'M** LEEMAN KESSLER?
KAH-WHOOMPH!

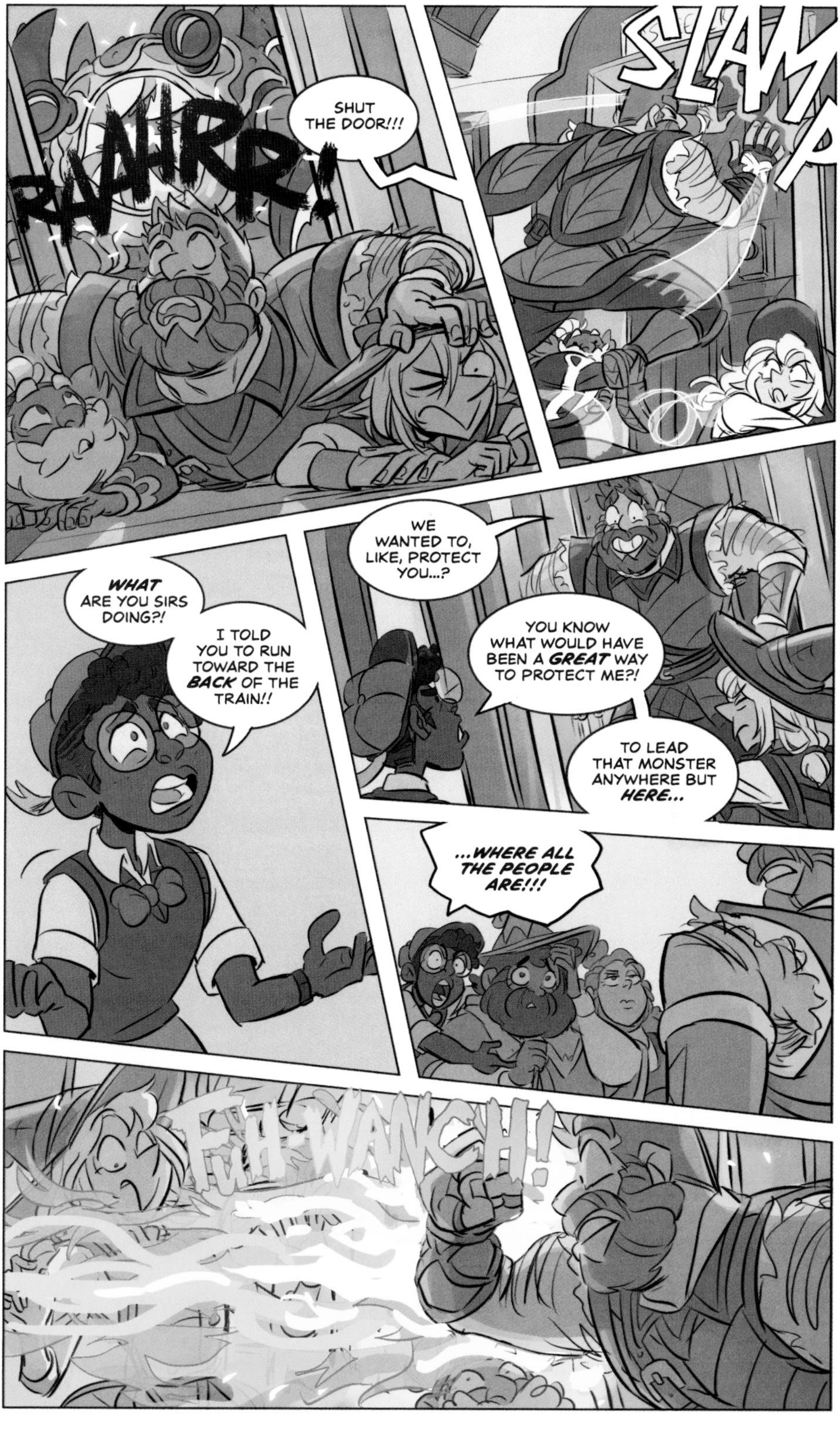
RAAHRR!
SHUT THE DOOR!!!
SLAM!
WHAT ARE YOU SIRS DOING?!
I TOLD YOU TO RUN TOWARD THE BACK OF THE TRAIN!!
WE WANTED TO, LIKE, PROTECT YOU...?
YOU KNOW WHAT WOULD HAVE BEEN A GREAT WAY TO PROTECT ME?!
TO LEAD THAT MONSTER ANYWHERE BUT HERE...
...WHERE ALL THE PEOPLE ARE!!!
FUH-WANCH!

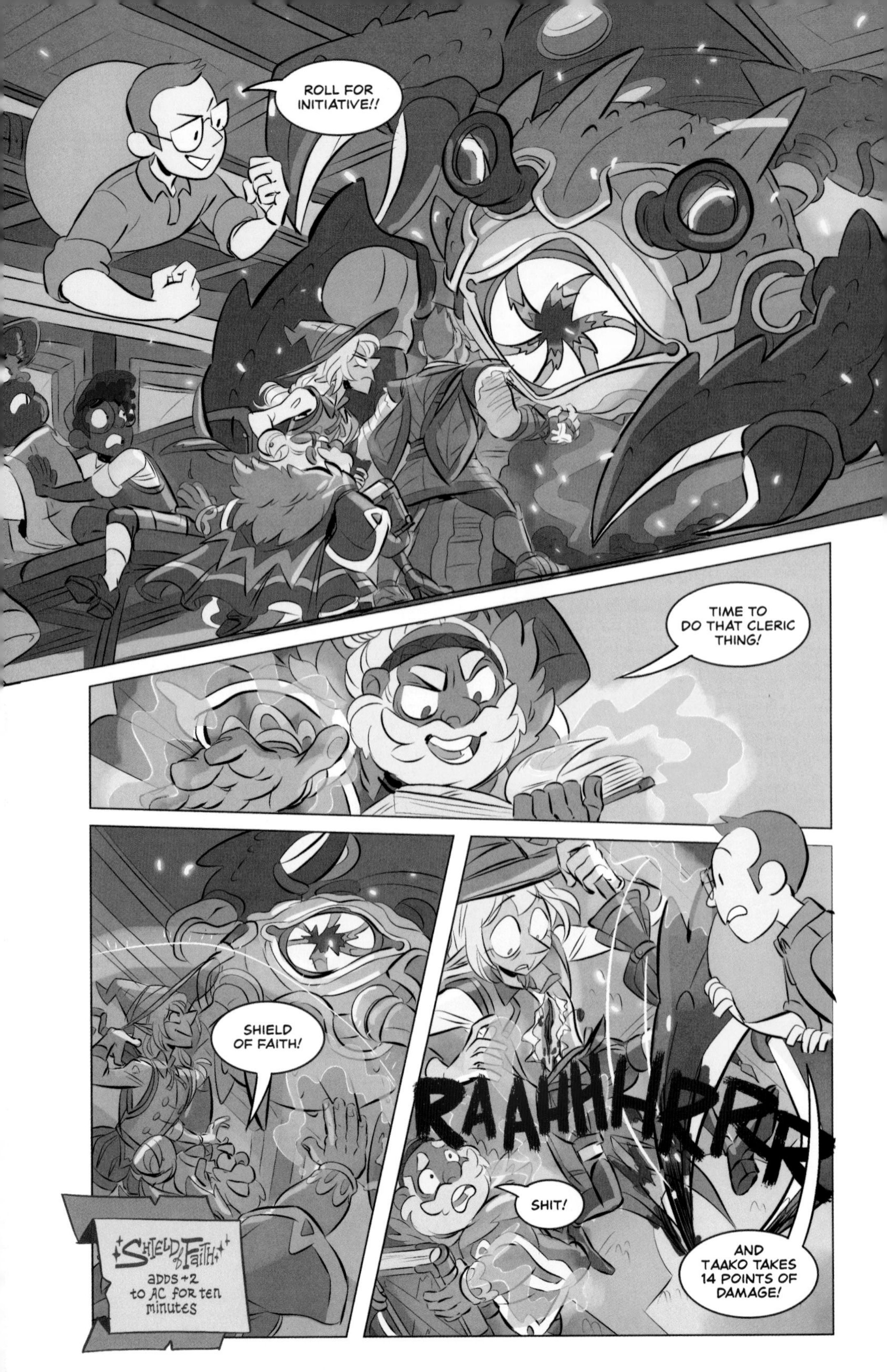
ROLL FOR INITIATIVE!!
TIME TO DO THAT CLERIC THING!
SHIELD OF FAITH!
SHIELD OF FAITH
ADDS +2 TO AC FOR TEN MINUTES
RAAHHHRRR
SHIT!
AND TAAKO TAKES 14 POINTS OF DAMAGE!

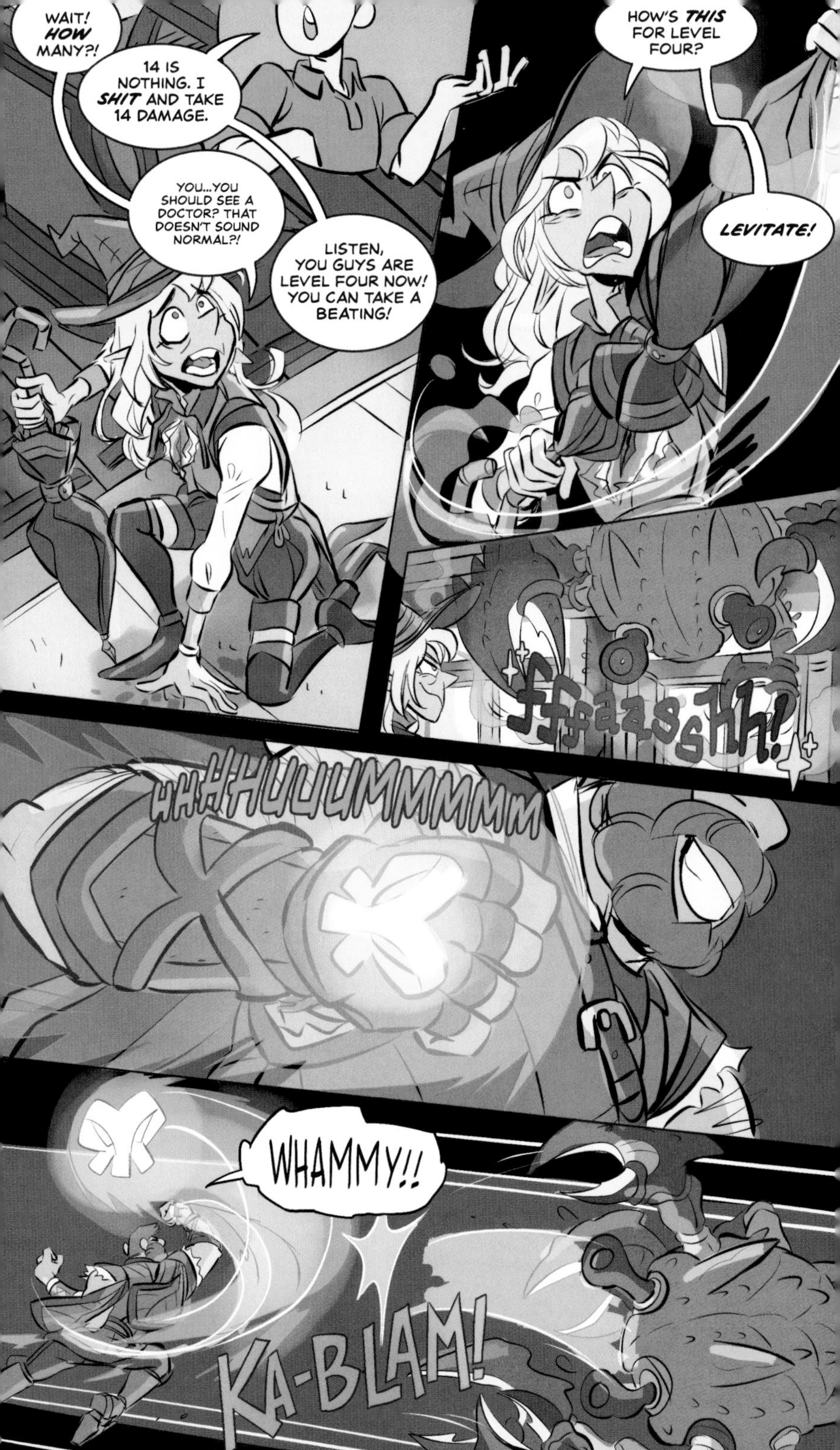

WAIT! HOW MANY?!
14 IS NOTHING. I SHIT AND TAKE 14 DAMAGE.
YOU...YOU SHOULD SEE A DOCTOR? THAT DOESN'T SOUND NORMAL?!
LISTEN, YOU GUYS ARE LEVEL FOUR NOW! YOU CAN TAKE A BEATING!
HOW'S THIS FOR LEVEL FOUR?
LEVITATE!
fffaaasshh!
HHHHUUUUMMMMMM
WHAMMY!!
KA-BLAM!

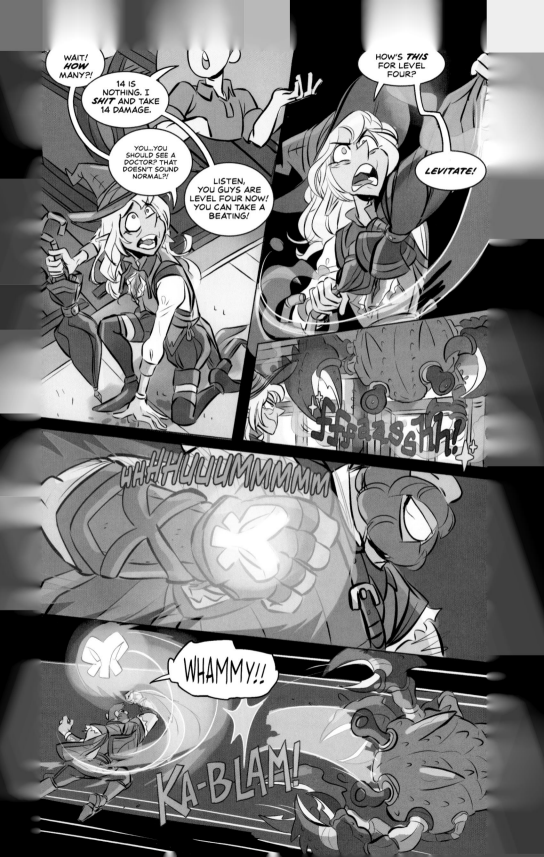

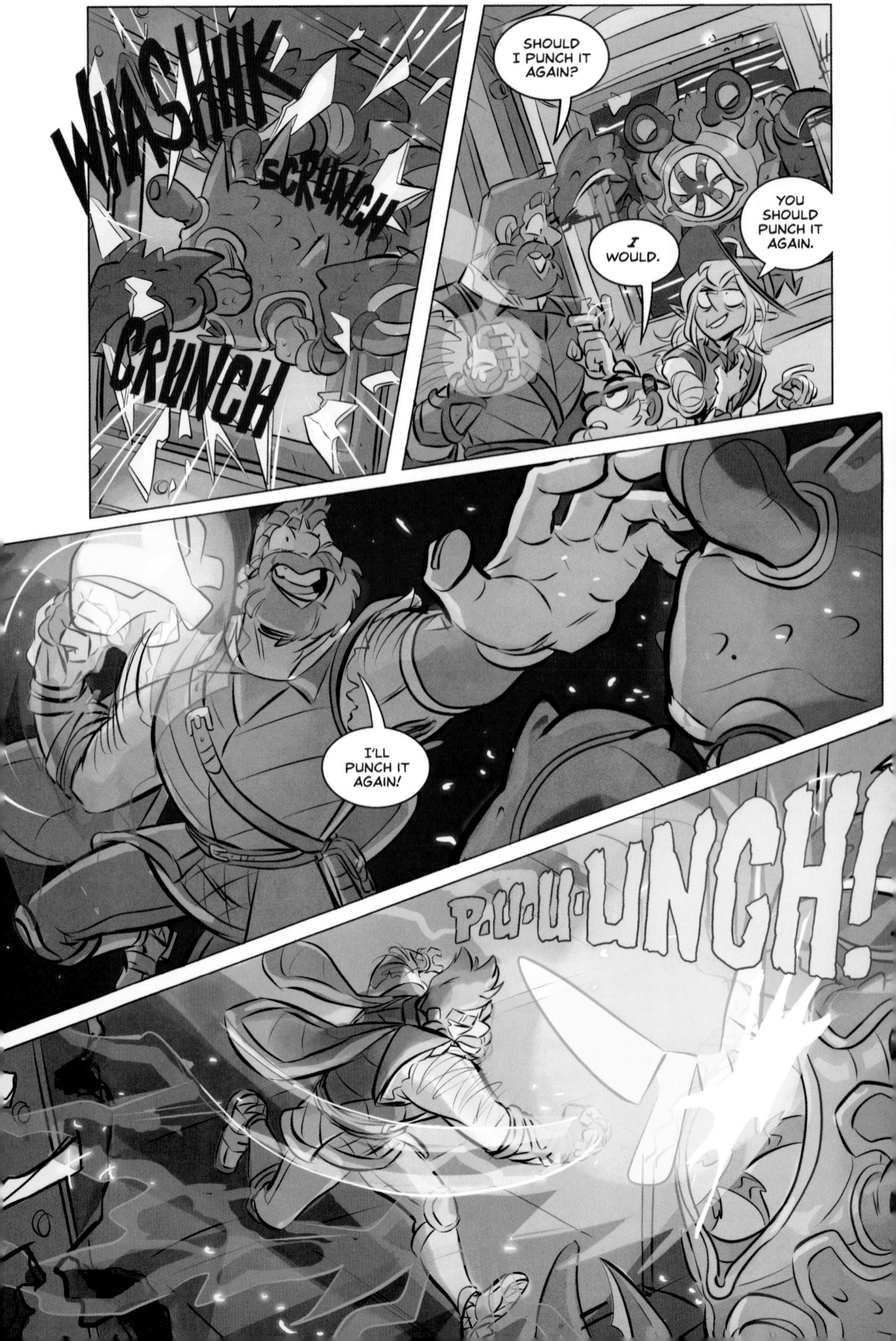
WHASHHK
SCRUNCH
CRUNCH
SHOULD I PUNCH IT AGAIN?
YOU SHOULD PUNCH IT AGAIN.
I WOULD.
I'LL PUNCH IT AGAIN!
P-U-U-UNCH!

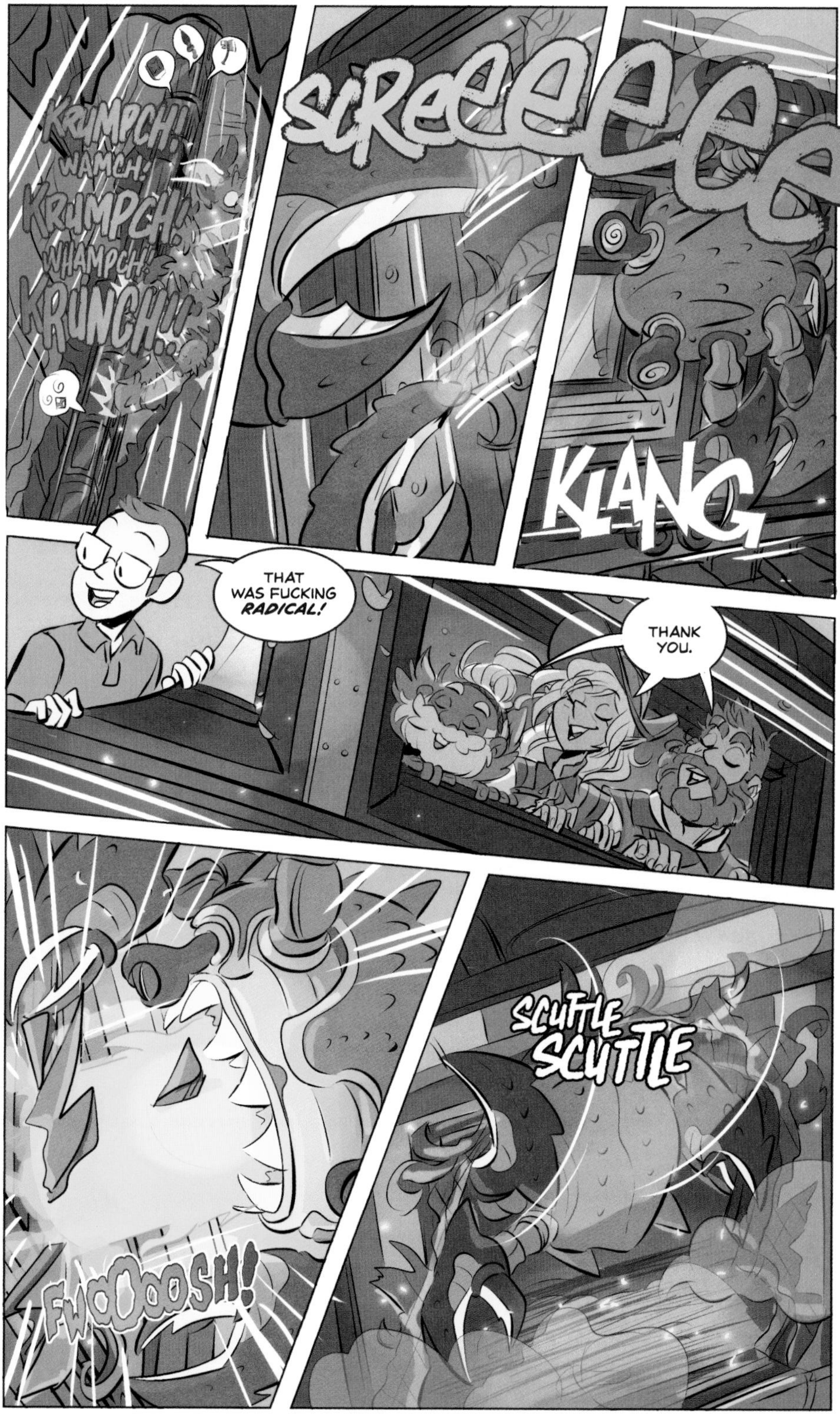
KRUMPCH!
WAMCH!
KRUMPCH!
WHAMPCH!
KRUNCH!!
SCREEEEEE
KLANG
THAT WAS FUCKING RADICAL!
THANK YOU.
FWOOOOSH!
SCUTTLE SCUTTLE

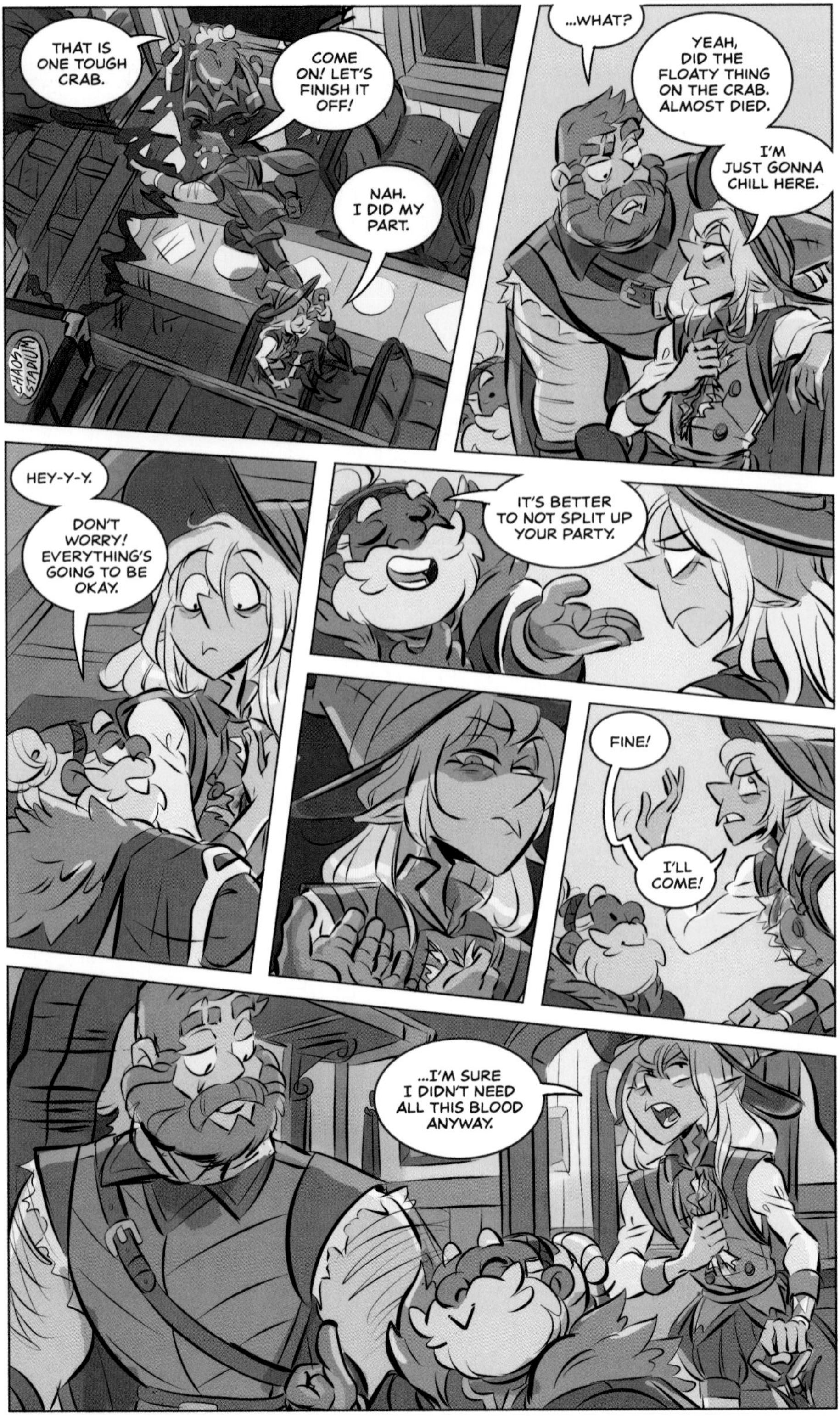

THAT IS ONE TOUGH CRAB.
COME ON! LET'S FINISH IT OFF!
NAH. I DID MY PART.
CHAOS STADIUM
...WHAT?
YEAH, DID THE FLOATY THING ON THE CRAB. ALMOST DIED.
I'M JUST GONNA CHILL HERE.
HEY-Y-Y.
DON'T WORRY! EVERYTHING'S GOING TO BE OKAY.
IT'S BETTER TO NOT SPLIT UP YOUR PARTY.
FINE!
I'LL COME!
...I'M SURE I DIDN'T NEED ALL THIS BLOOD ANYWAY.

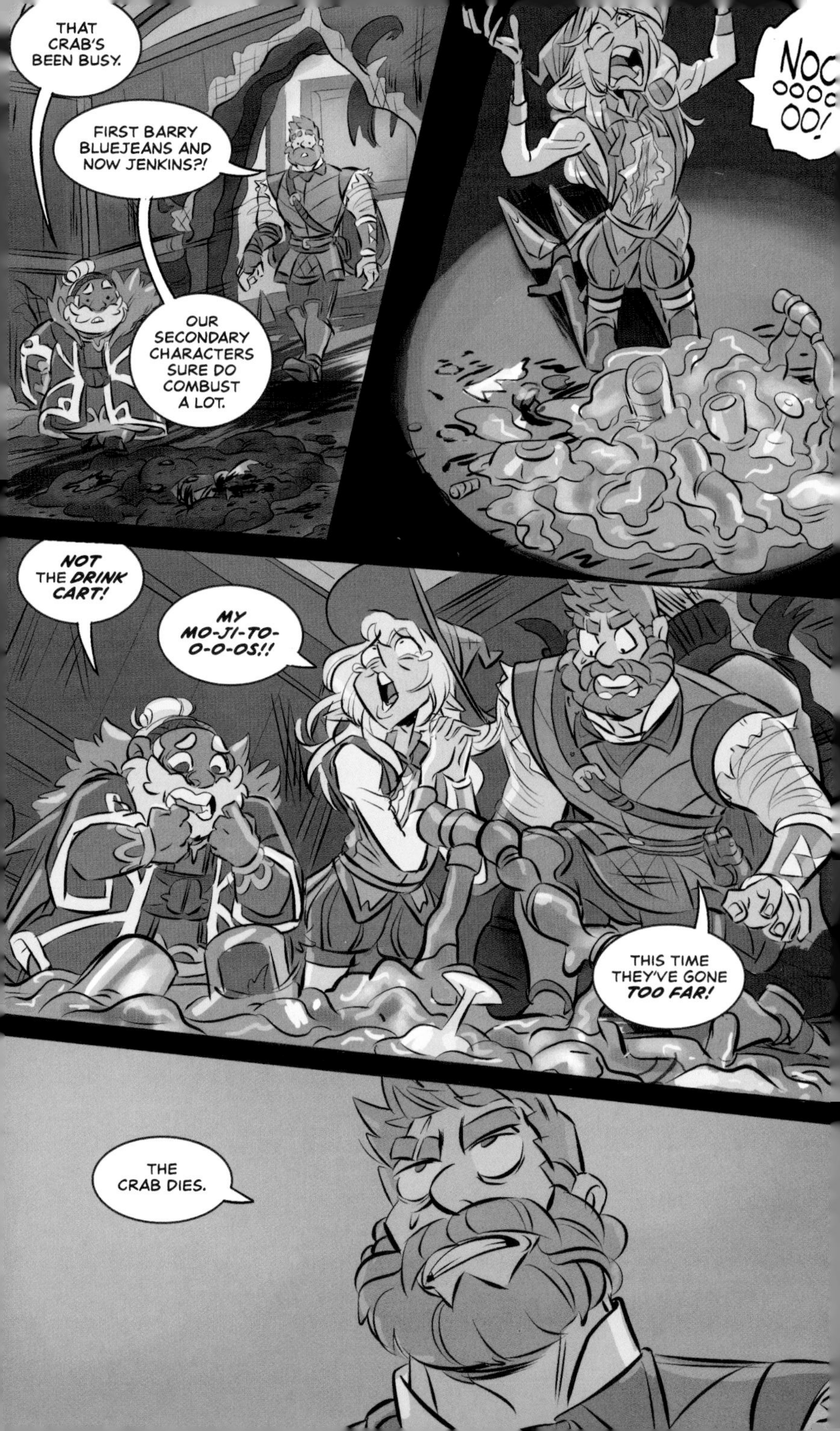
THAT CRAB'S BEEN BUSY.
FIRST BARRY BLUEJEANS AND NOW JENKINS?!
OUR SECONDARY CHARACTERS SURE DO COMBUST A LOT.
NOOOOOOOOO!
NOT THE DRINK CART!
MY MO-JI-TO-O-O-OS!!
THIS TIME THEY'VE GONE TOO FAR!
THE CRAB DIES.

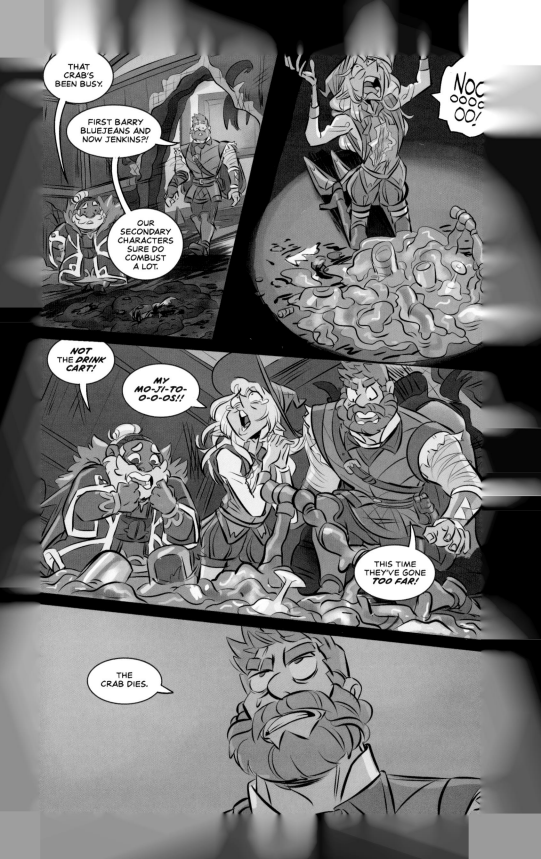

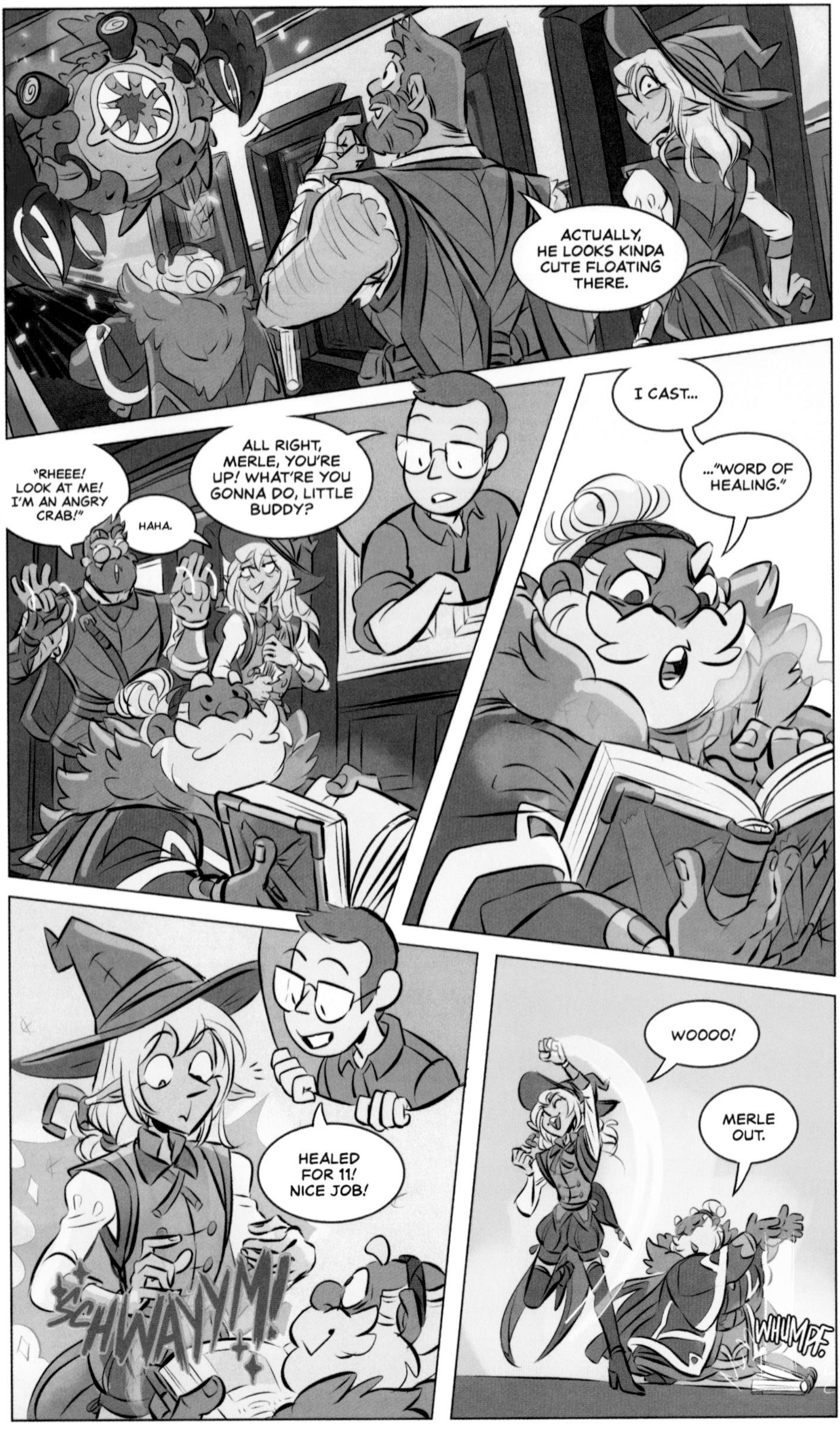
ACTUALLY, HE LOOKS KINDA CUTE FLOATING THERE.
"RHEEE! LOOK AT ME! I'M AN ANGRY CRAB!"
HAHA.
ALL RIGHT, MERLE, YOU'RE UP! WHAT'RE YOU GONNA DO, LITTLE BUDDY?
I CAST...
..."WORD OF HEALING."
HEALED FOR 11! NICE JOB!
SCHWAYYM!
WOOOO!
MERLE OUT.
WHUMPF.

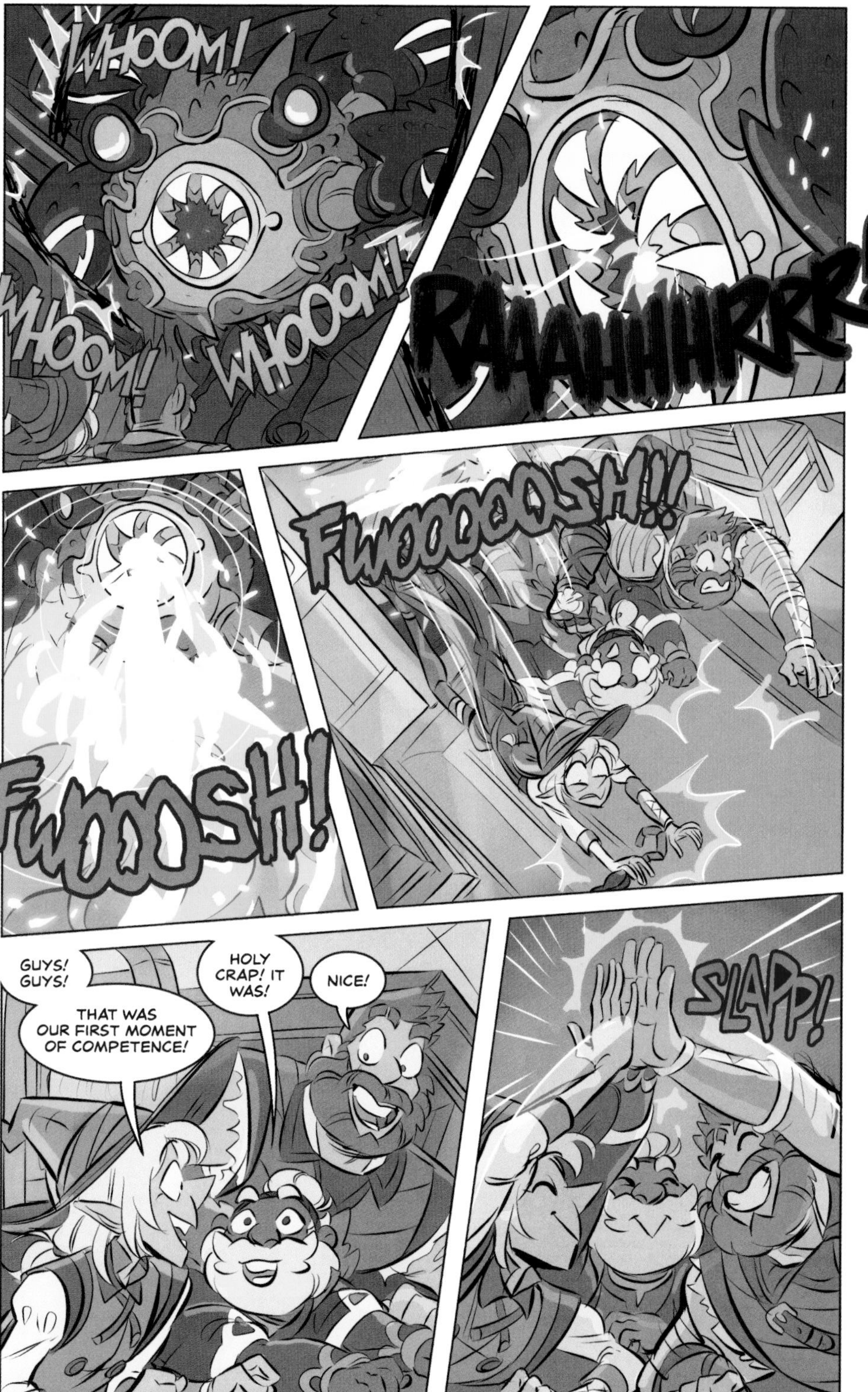
WHOOM!
WHOOM!
WHOOOM!
RAAAHHHHRRR!
FWOOOSH!
FWOOOOOOSH!!
GUYS! GUYS!
THAT WAS OUR FIRST MOMENT OF COMPETENCE!
HOLY CRAP! IT WAS!
NICE!
SLAPP!

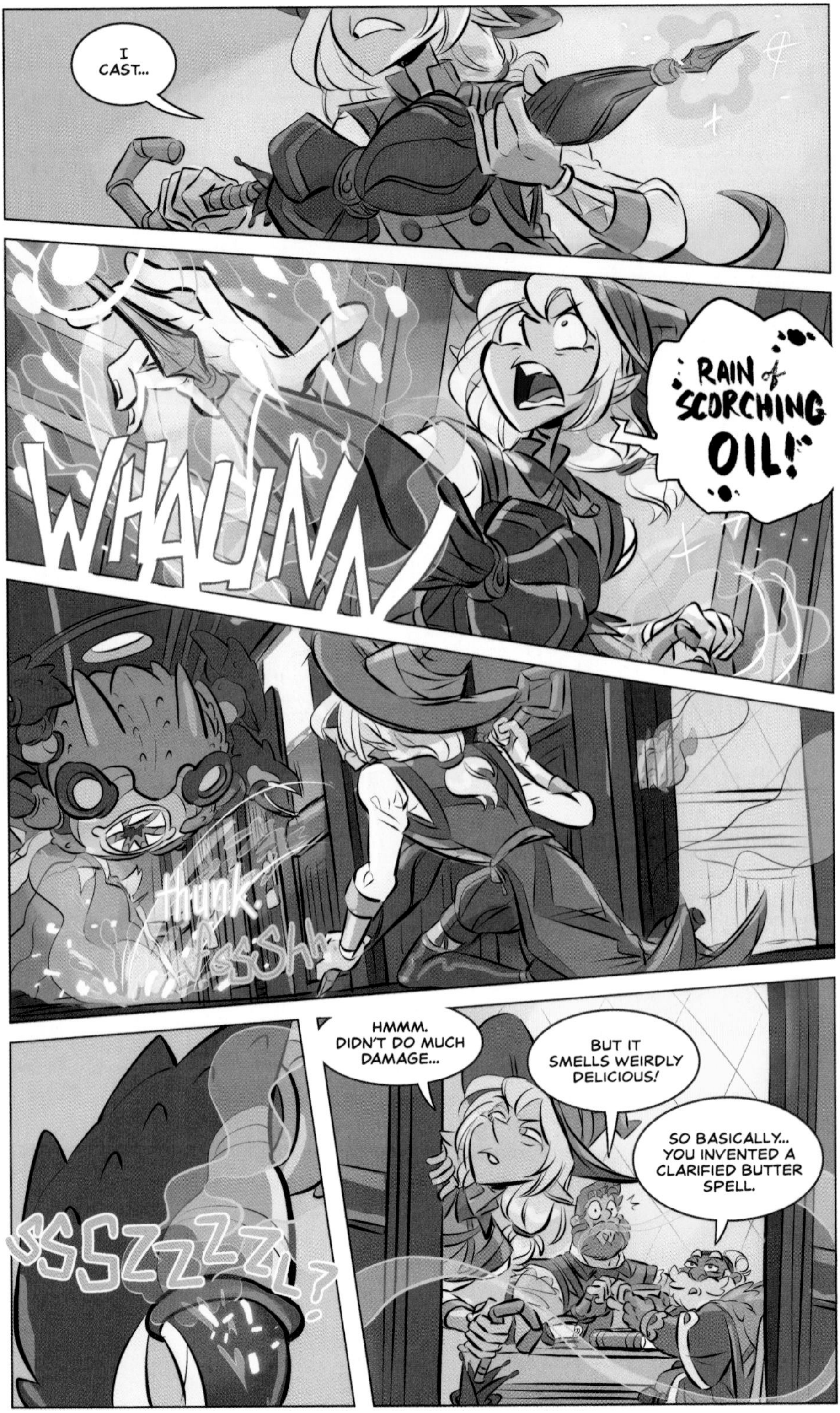
I CAST...
RAIN of SCORCHING OIL!
WHAUMM
thunk.
fssShh
HMMM. DIDN'T DO MUCH DAMAGE...
BUT IT SMELLS WEIRDLY DELICIOUS!
SO BASICALLY... YOU INVENTED A CLARIFIED BUTTER SPELL.
SSSZZZZL?

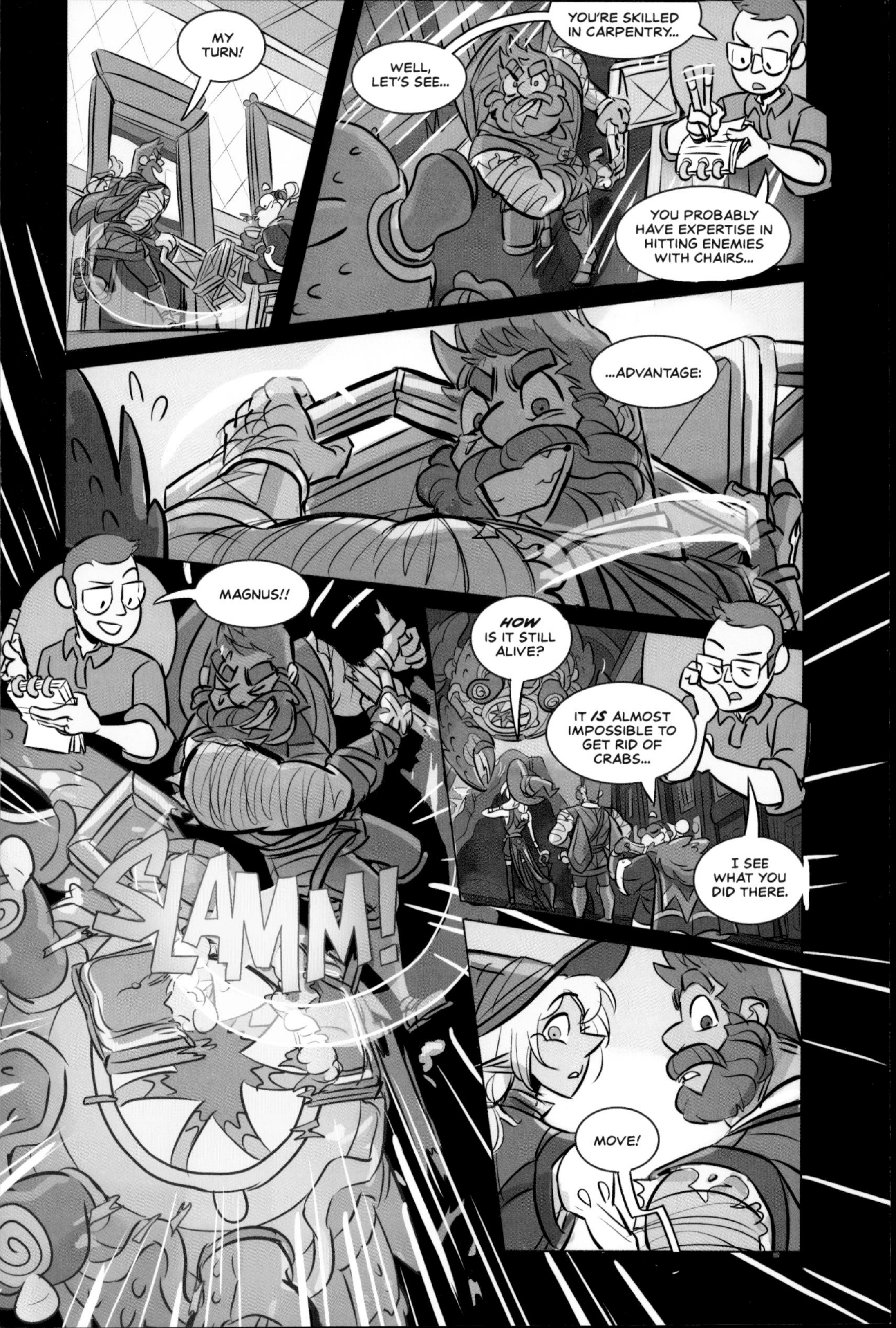
MY TURN!
YOU'RE SKILLED IN CARPENTRY...
WELL, LET'S SEE...
YOU PROBABLY HAVE EXPERTISE IN HITTING ENEMIES WITH CHAIRS...
...ADVANTAGE:
MAGNUS!!
SLAMM!
HOW IS IT STILL ALIVE?
IT IS ALMOST IMPOSSIBLE TO GET RID OF CRABS...
I SEE WHAT YOU DID THERE.
MOVE!

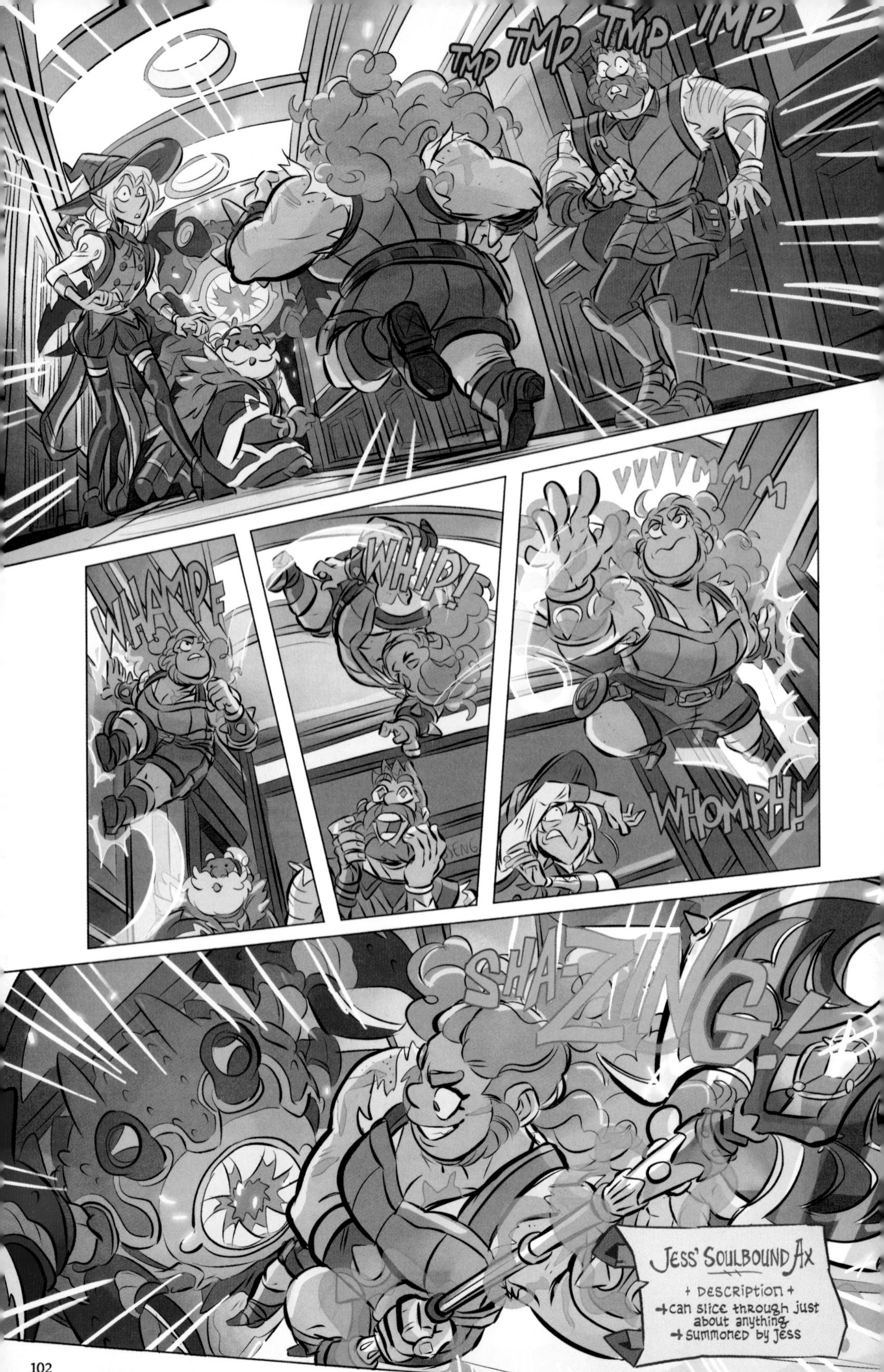
TMP TMP TMP TMP
VVVVVMMMM
WHAMP!
WHIP!
WHOMPH!
SHA-ZING!
Jess' Soulbound Ax
+ Description +
→ can slice through just about anything
→ summoned by Jess

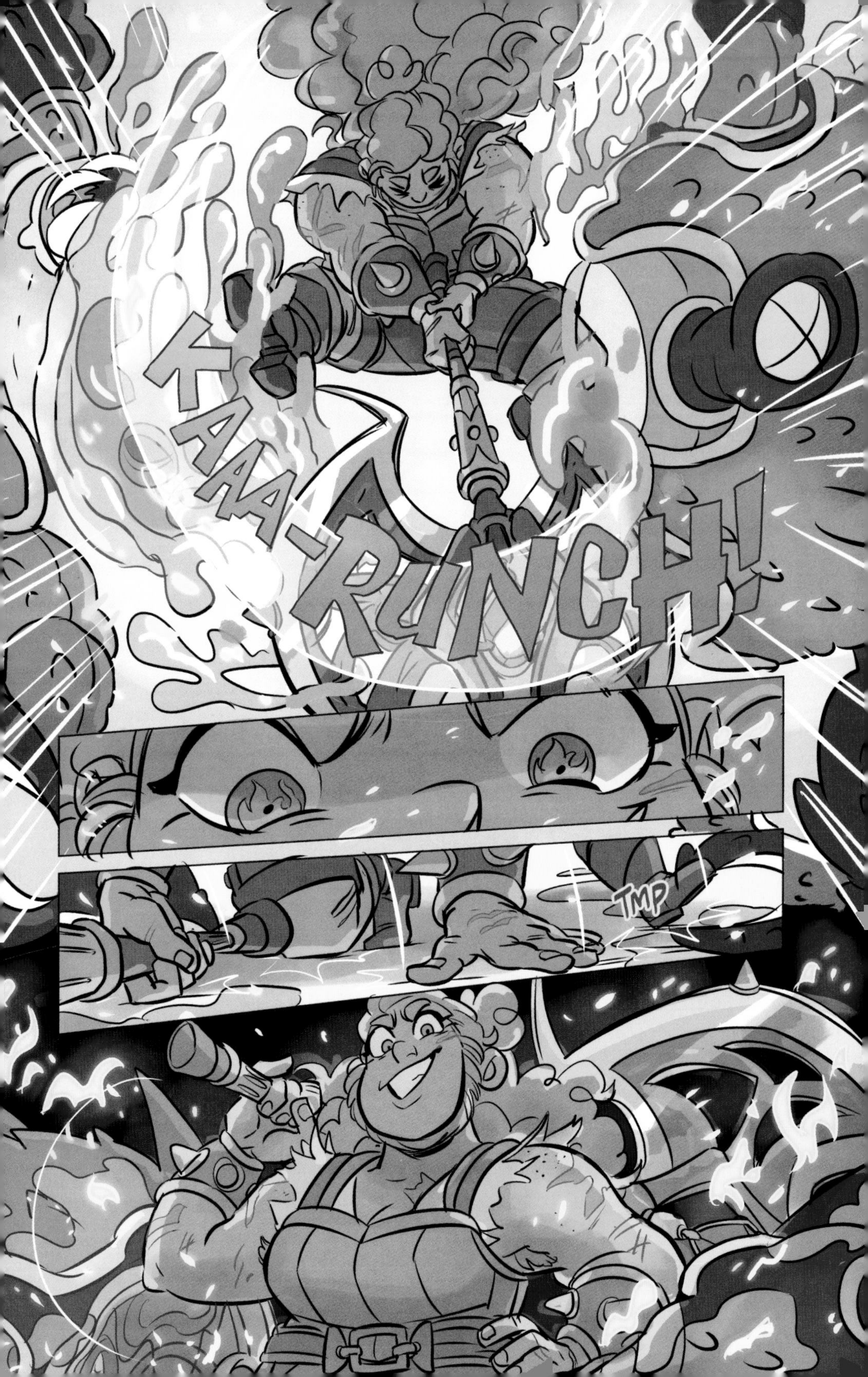
KAAA-RUNCH!
TMP

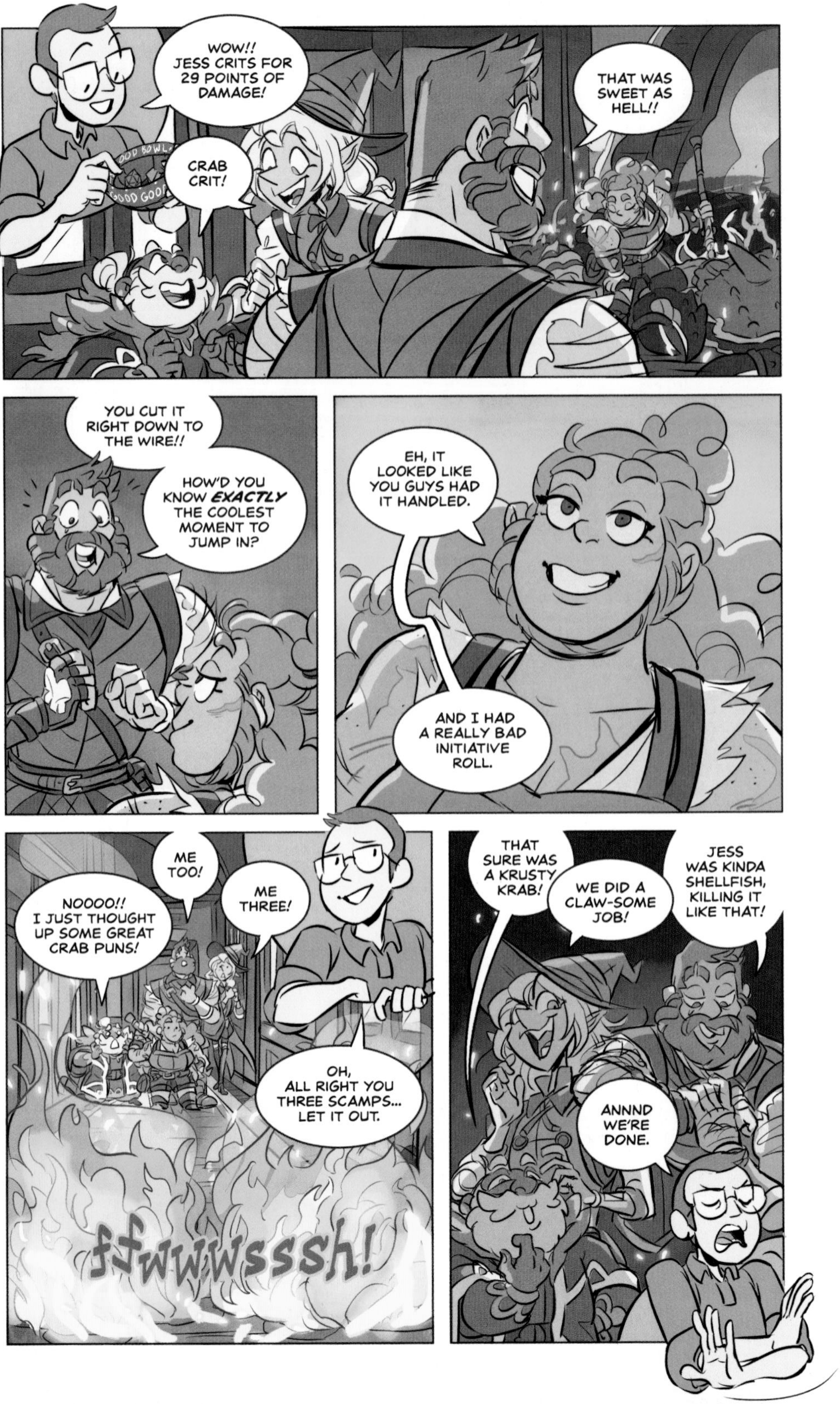
WOW!!
JESS CRITS FOR 29 POINTS OF DAMAGE!
GOOD BOWL
GOOD GOOD
CRAB CRIT!
THAT WAS SWEET AS HELL!!
YOU CUT IT RIGHT DOWN TO THE WIRE!!
HOW'D YOU KNOW *EXACTLY* THE COOLEST MOMENT TO JUMP IN?
EH, IT LOOKED LIKE YOU GUYS HAD IT HANDLED.
AND I HAD A REALLY BAD INITIATIVE ROLL.
NOOOO!! I JUST THOUGHT UP SOME GREAT CRAB PUNS!
ME TOO!
ME THREE!
OH, ALL RIGHT YOU THREE SCAMPS... LET IT OUT.
ffwwwsssh!
THAT SURE WAS A KRUSTY KRAB!
WE DID A CLAW-SOME JOB!
JESS WAS KINDA SHELLFISH, KILLING IT LIKE THAT!
ANNND WE'RE DONE.

Chapter 5

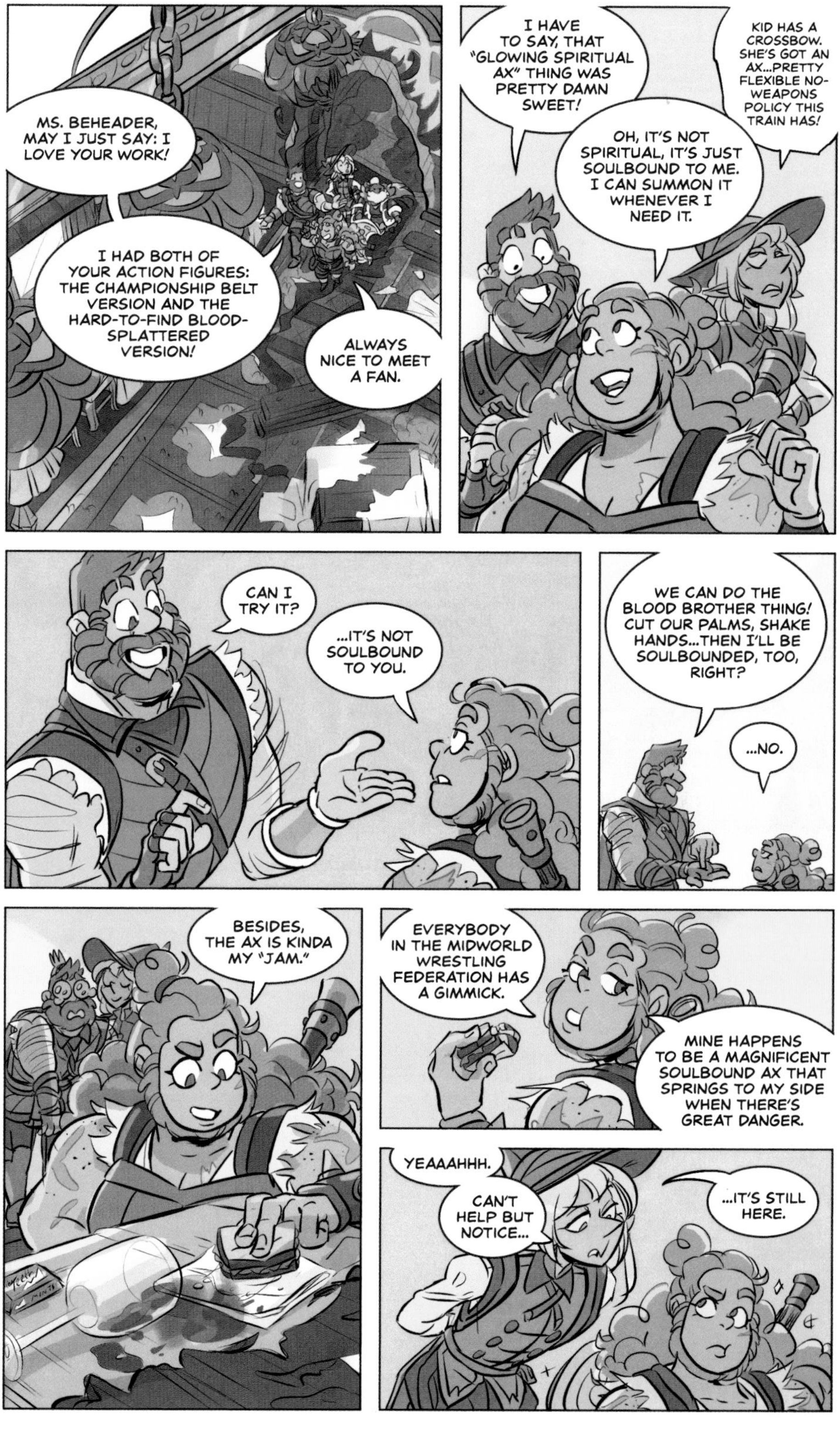
MS. BEHEADER, MAY I JUST SAY: I LOVE YOUR WORK!
I HAD BOTH OF YOUR ACTION FIGURES: THE CHAMPIONSHIP BELT VERSION AND THE HARD-TO-FIND BLOOD-SPLATTERED VERSION!
ALWAYS NICE TO MEET A FAN.
I HAVE TO SAY, THAT "GLOWING SPIRITUAL AX" THING WAS PRETTY DAMN SWEET!
OH, IT'S NOT SPIRITUAL, IT'S JUST SOULBOUND TO ME. I CAN SUMMON IT WHENEVER I NEED IT.
KID HAS A CROSSBOW. SHE'S GOT AN AX...PRETTY FLEXIBLE NO-WEAPONS POLICY THIS TRAIN HAS!
CAN I TRY IT?
...IT'S NOT SOULBOUND TO YOU.
WE CAN DO THE BLOOD BROTHER THING! CUT OUR PALMS, SHAKE HANDS...THEN I'LL BE SOULBOUNDED, TOO, RIGHT?
...NO.
BESIDES, THE AX IS KINDA MY "JAM."
EVERYBODY IN THE MIDWORLD WRESTLING FEDERATION HAS A GIMMICK.
MINE HAPPENS TO BE A MAGNIFICENT SOULBOUND AX THAT SPRINGS TO MY SIDE WHEN THERE'S GREAT DANGER.
YEAAAHHH.
CAN'T HELP BUT NOTICE...
...IT'S STILL HERE.

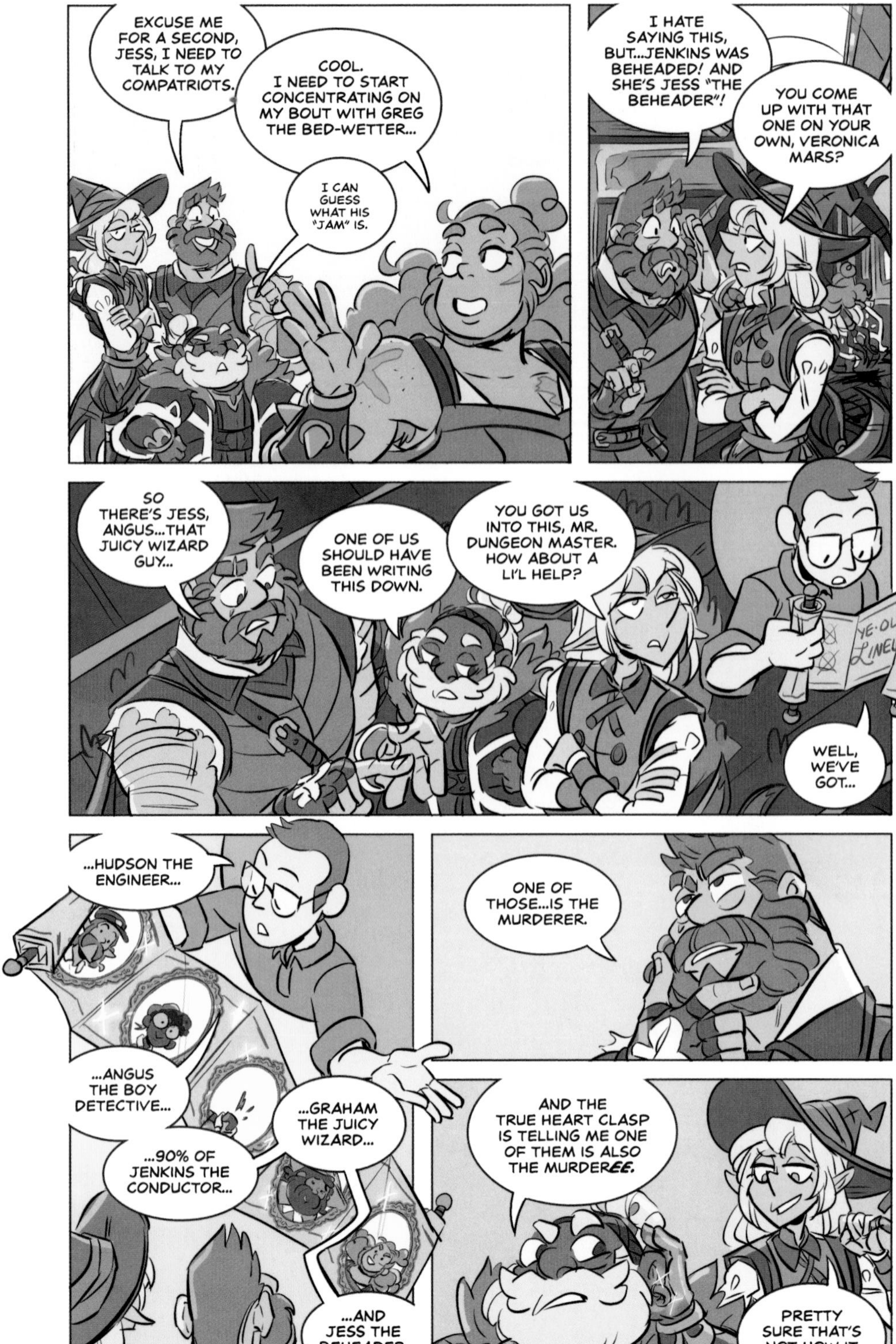
EXCUSE ME FOR A SECOND, JESS, I NEED TO TALK TO MY COMPATRIOTS.
COOL. I NEED TO START CONCENTRATING ON MY BOUT WITH GREG THE BED-WETTER...
I CAN GUESS WHAT HIS "JAM" IS.
I HATE SAYING THIS, BUT...JENKINS WAS BEHEADED! AND SHE'S JESS "THE BEHEADER"!
YOU COME UP WITH THAT ONE ON YOUR OWN, VERONICA MARS?
SO THERE'S JESS, ANGUS...THAT JUICY WIZARD GUY...
ONE OF US SHOULD HAVE BEEN WRITING THIS DOWN.
YOU GOT US INTO THIS, MR. DUNGEON MASTER. HOW ABOUT A LI'L HELP?
WELL, WE'VE GOT...
...HUDSON THE ENGINEER...
ONE OF THOSE...IS THE MURDERER.
...ANGUS THE BOY DETECTIVE...
...90% OF JENKINS THE CONDUCTOR...
...GRAHAM THE JUICY WIZARD...
...AND JESS THE BEHEADER.
AND THE TRUE HEART CLASP IS TELLING ME ONE OF THEM IS ALSO THE MURDER*EE.*
PRETTY SURE THAT'S NOT HOW IT WORKS.

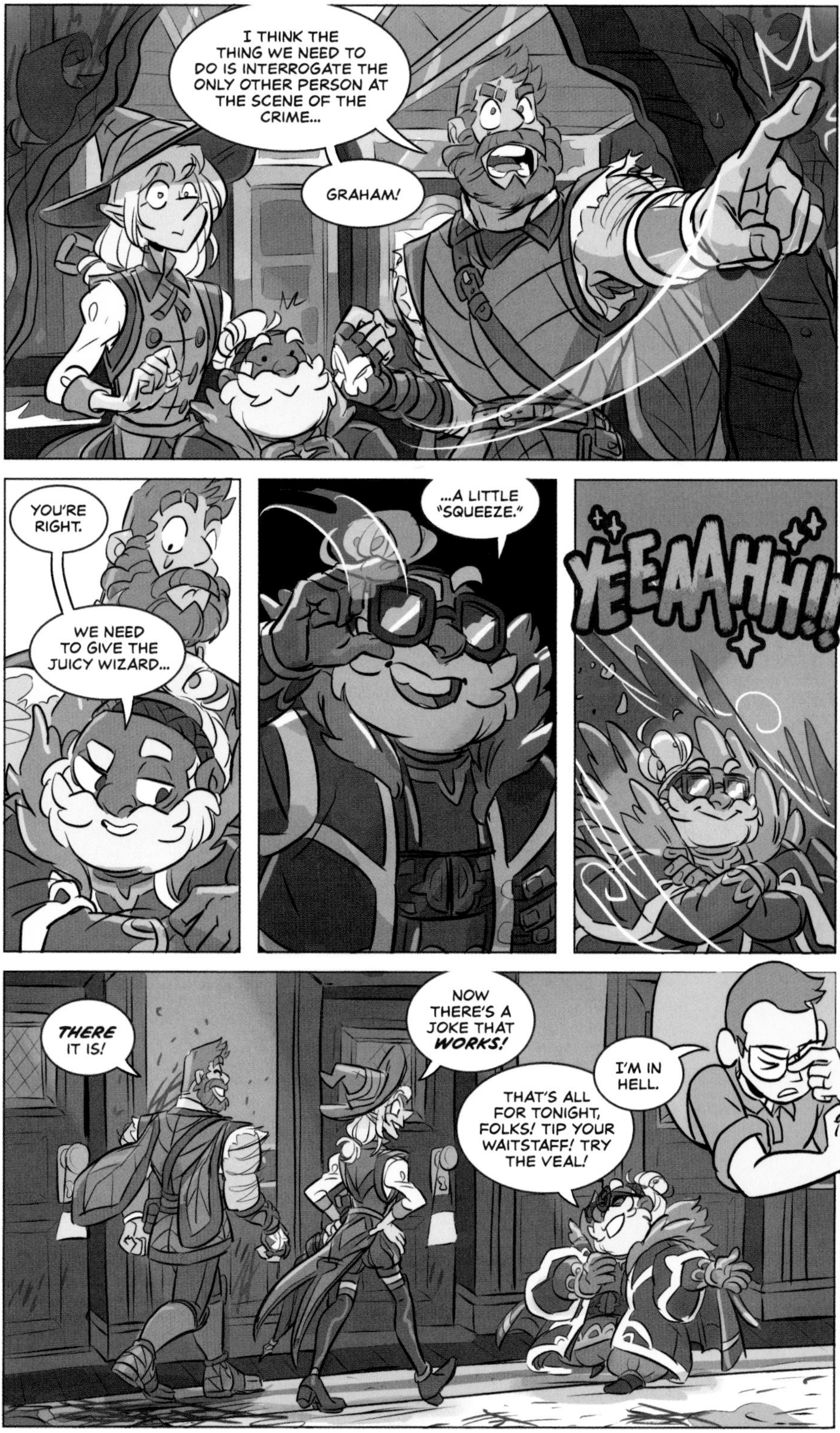
I THINK THE THING WE NEED TO DO IS INTERROGATE THE ONLY OTHER PERSON AT THE SCENE OF THE CRIME...
GRAHAM!
YOU'RE RIGHT.
WE NEED TO GIVE THE JUICY WIZARD...
...A LITTLE "SQUEEZE."
YEEAAHH!!
THERE IT IS!
NOW THERE'S A JOKE THAT WORKS!
I'M IN HELL.
THAT'S ALL FOR TONIGHT, FOLKS! TIP YOUR WAITSTAFF! TRY THE VEAL!

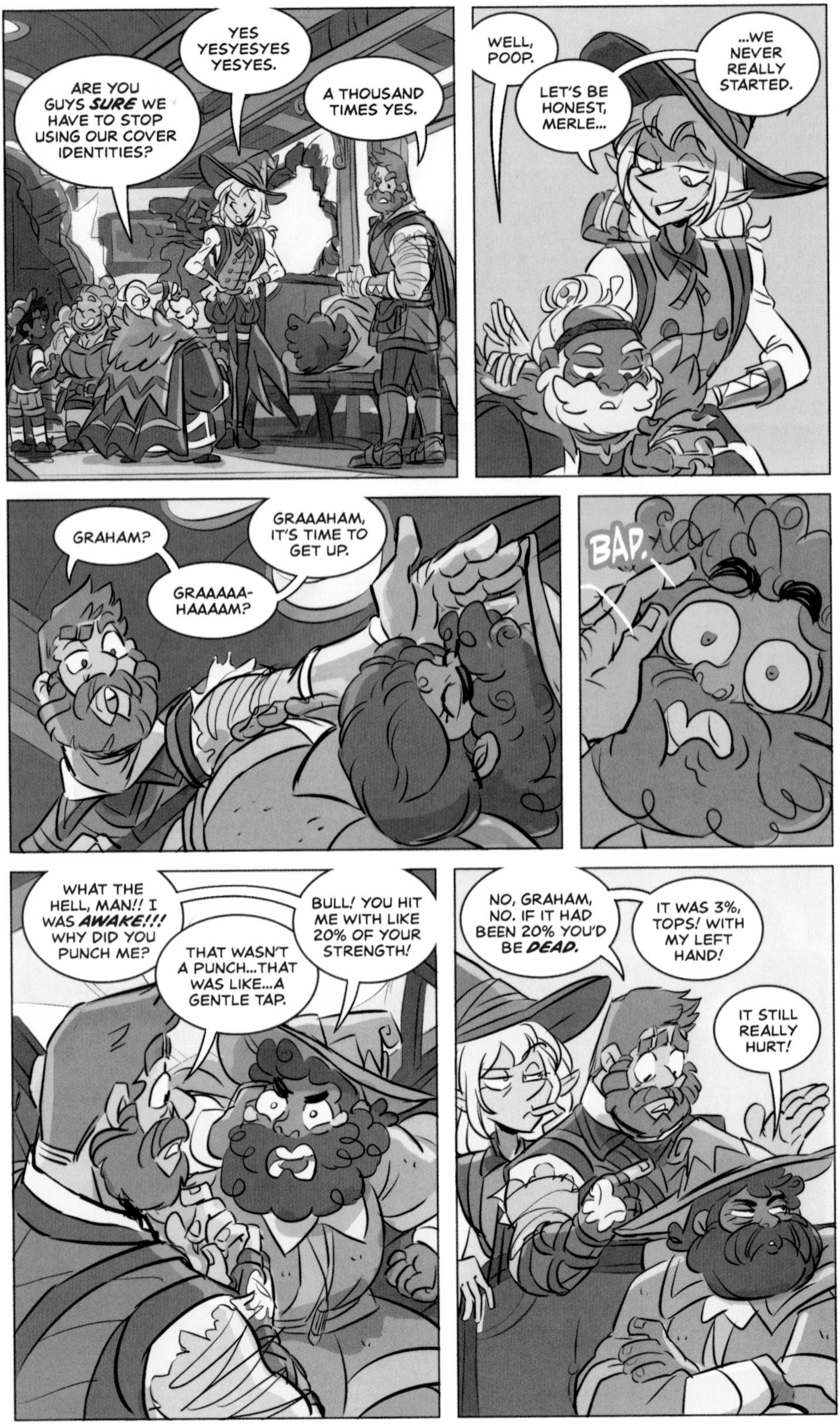
ARE YOU GUYS SURE WE HAVE TO STOP USING OUR COVER IDENTITIES?
YES YESYESYES YESYES.
A THOUSAND TIMES YES.
WELL, POOP.
LET'S BE HONEST, MERLE...
...WE NEVER REALLY STARTED.
GRAHAM?
GRAAAAA-HAAAAM?
GRAAAHAM, IT'S TIME TO GET UP.
BAP.
WHAT THE HELL, MAN!! I WAS AWAKE!!! WHY DID YOU PUNCH ME?
THAT WASN'T A PUNCH...THAT WAS LIKE...A GENTLE TAP.
BULL! YOU HIT ME WITH LIKE 20% OF YOUR STRENGTH!
NO, GRAHAM, NO. IF IT HAD BEEN 20% YOU'D BE DEAD.
IT WAS 3%, TOPS! WITH MY LEFT HAND!
IT STILL REALLY HURT!

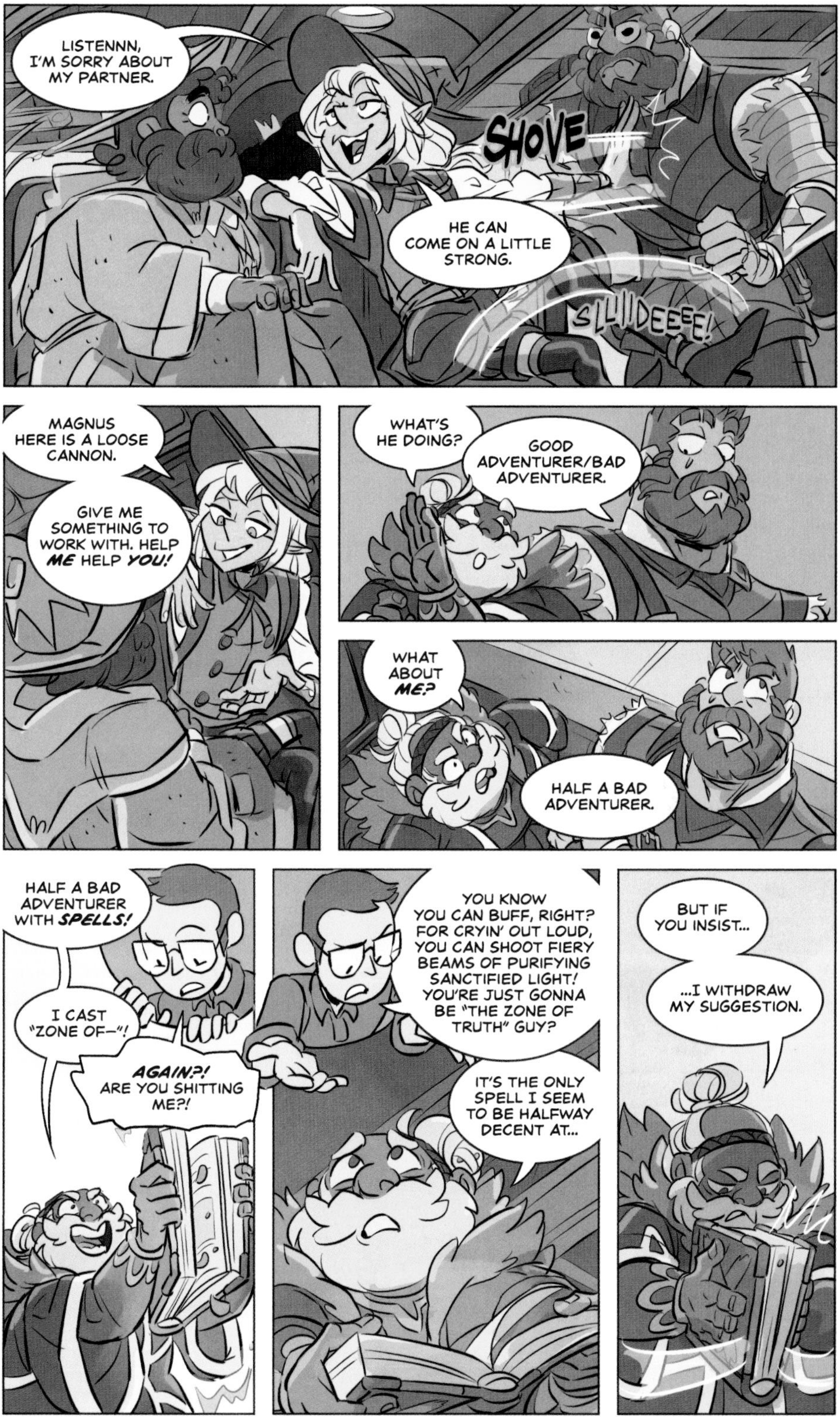
LISTENNN, I'M SORRY ABOUT MY PARTNER.
SHOVE
HE CAN COME ON A LITTLE STRONG.
SLIIIDEEEE!
MAGNUS HERE IS A LOOSE CANNON.
GIVE ME SOMETHING TO WORK WITH. HELP **ME** HELP **YOU!**
WHAT'S HE DOING?
GOOD ADVENTURER/BAD ADVENTURER.
WHAT ABOUT **ME?**
HALF A BAD ADVENTURER.
HALF A BAD ADVENTURER WITH **SPELLS!**
I CAST "ZONE OF–"!
AGAIN?! ARE YOU SHITTING ME?!
YOU KNOW YOU CAN BUFF, RIGHT? FOR CRYIN' OUT LOUD, YOU CAN SHOOT FIERY BEAMS OF PURIFYING SANCTIFIED LIGHT! YOU'RE JUST GONNA BE "THE ZONE OF TRUTH" GUY?
IT'S THE ONLY SPELL I SEEM TO BE HALFWAY DECENT AT...
BUT IF YOU INSIST...
...I WITHDRAW MY SUGGESTION.

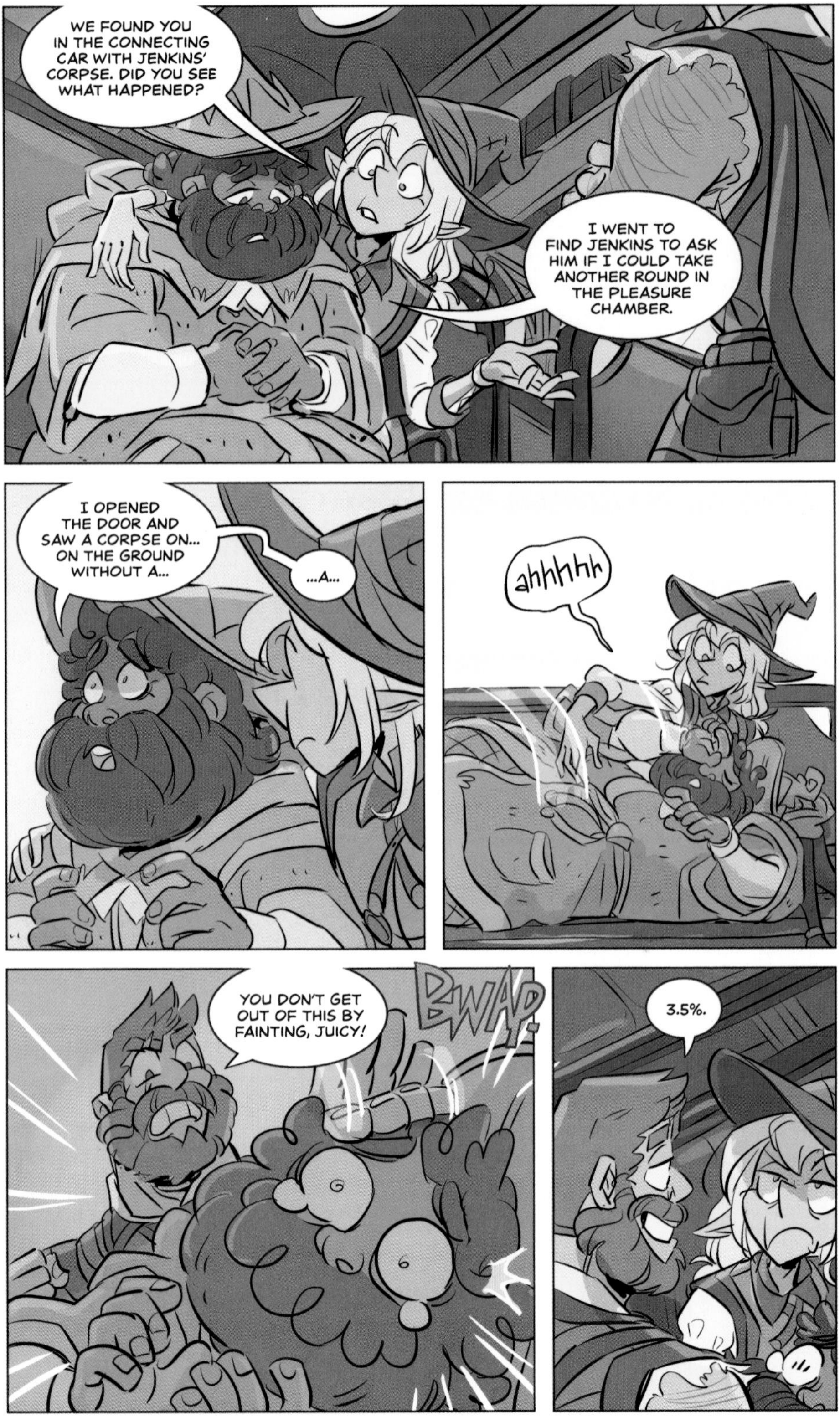
WE FOUND YOU IN THE CONNECTING CAR WITH JENKINS' CORPSE. DID YOU SEE WHAT HAPPENED?
I WENT TO FIND JENKINS TO ASK HIM IF I COULD TAKE ANOTHER ROUND IN THE PLEASURE CHAMBER.
I OPENED THE DOOR AND SAW A CORPSE ON... ON THE GROUND WITHOUT A...
...A...
ahhhhh
YOU DON'T GET OUT OF THIS BY FAINTING, JUICY!
BWAP
3.5%.

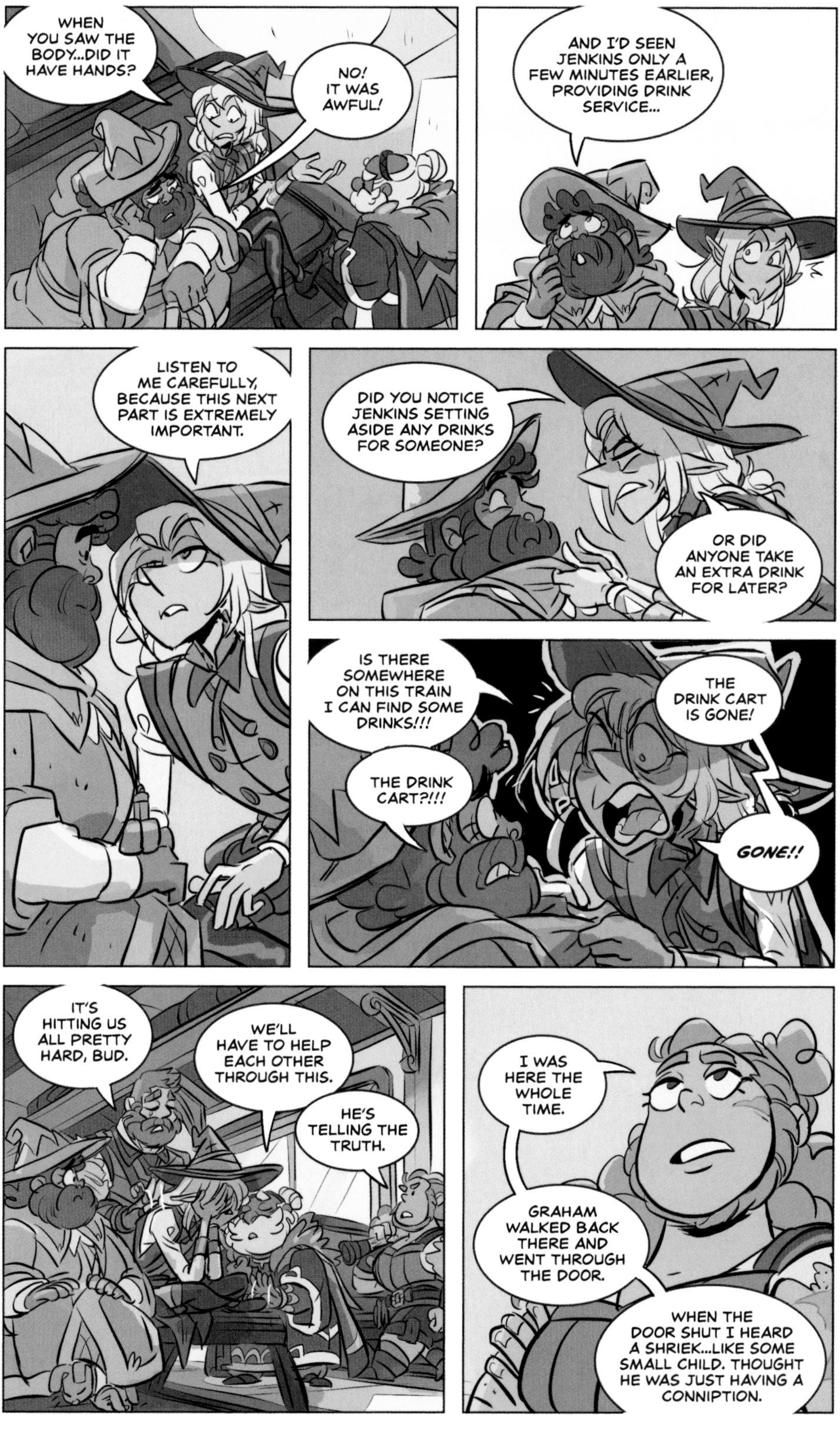
WHEN YOU SAW THE BODY...DID IT HAVE HANDS?
NO! IT WAS AWFUL!
AND I'D SEEN JENKINS ONLY A FEW MINUTES EARLIER, PROVIDING DRINK SERVICE...
LISTEN TO ME CAREFULLY, BECAUSE THIS NEXT PART IS EXTREMELY IMPORTANT.
DID YOU NOTICE JENKINS SETTING ASIDE ANY DRINKS FOR SOMEONE?
OR DID ANYONE TAKE AN EXTRA DRINK FOR LATER?
IS THERE SOMEWHERE ON THIS TRAIN I CAN FIND SOME DRINKS!!!
THE DRINK CART IS GONE!
THE DRINK CART?!!!
GONE!!
IT'S HITTING US ALL PRETTY HARD, BUD.
WE'LL HAVE TO HELP EACH OTHER THROUGH THIS.
HE'S TELLING THE TRUTH.
I WAS HERE THE WHOLE TIME.
GRAHAM WALKED BACK THERE AND WENT THROUGH THE DOOR.
WHEN THE DOOR SHUT I HEARD A SHRIEK...LIKE SOME SMALL CHILD. THOUGHT HE WAS JUST HAVING A CONNIPTION.

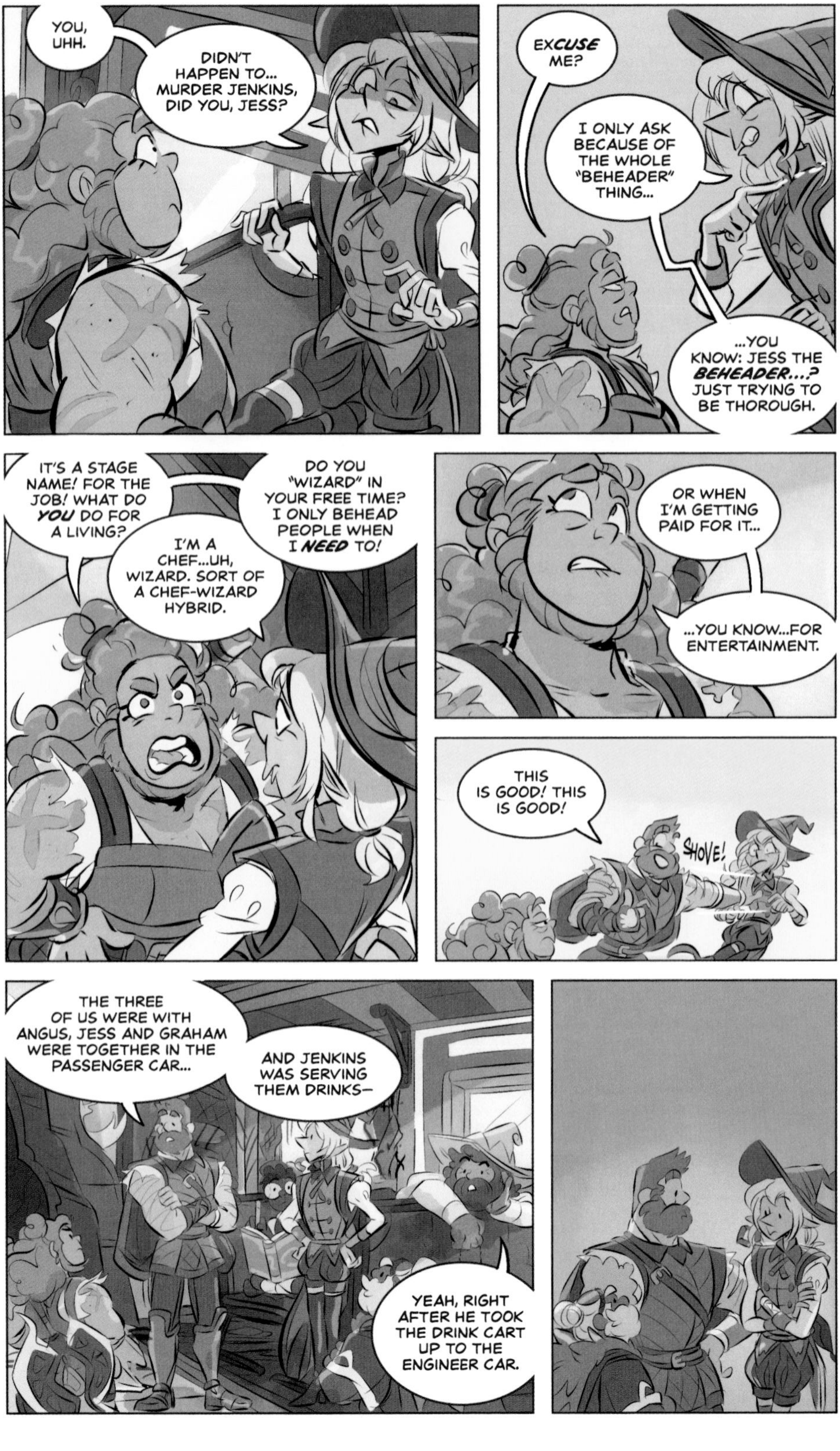
YOU, UHH.
DIDN'T HAPPEN TO... MURDER JENKINS, DID YOU, JESS?
EX*CUSE* ME?
I ONLY ASK BECAUSE OF THE WHOLE "BEHEADER" THING...
...YOU KNOW: JESS THE ***BEHEADER...?*** JUST TRYING TO BE THOROUGH.
IT'S A STAGE NAME! FOR THE JOB! WHAT DO ***YOU*** DO FOR A LIVING?
I'M A CHEF...UH, WIZARD. SORT OF A CHEF-WIZARD HYBRID.
DO YOU "WIZARD" IN YOUR FREE TIME? I ONLY BEHEAD PEOPLE WHEN I ***NEED*** TO!
OR WHEN I'M GETTING PAID FOR IT...
...YOU KNOW...FOR ENTERTAINMENT.
THIS IS GOOD! THIS IS GOOD!
SHOVE!
THE THREE OF US WERE WITH ANGUS, JESS AND GRAHAM WERE TOGETHER IN THE PASSENGER CAR...
AND JENKINS WAS SERVING THEM DRINKS—
YEAH, RIGHT AFTER HE TOOK THE DRINK CART UP TO THE ENGINEER CAR.

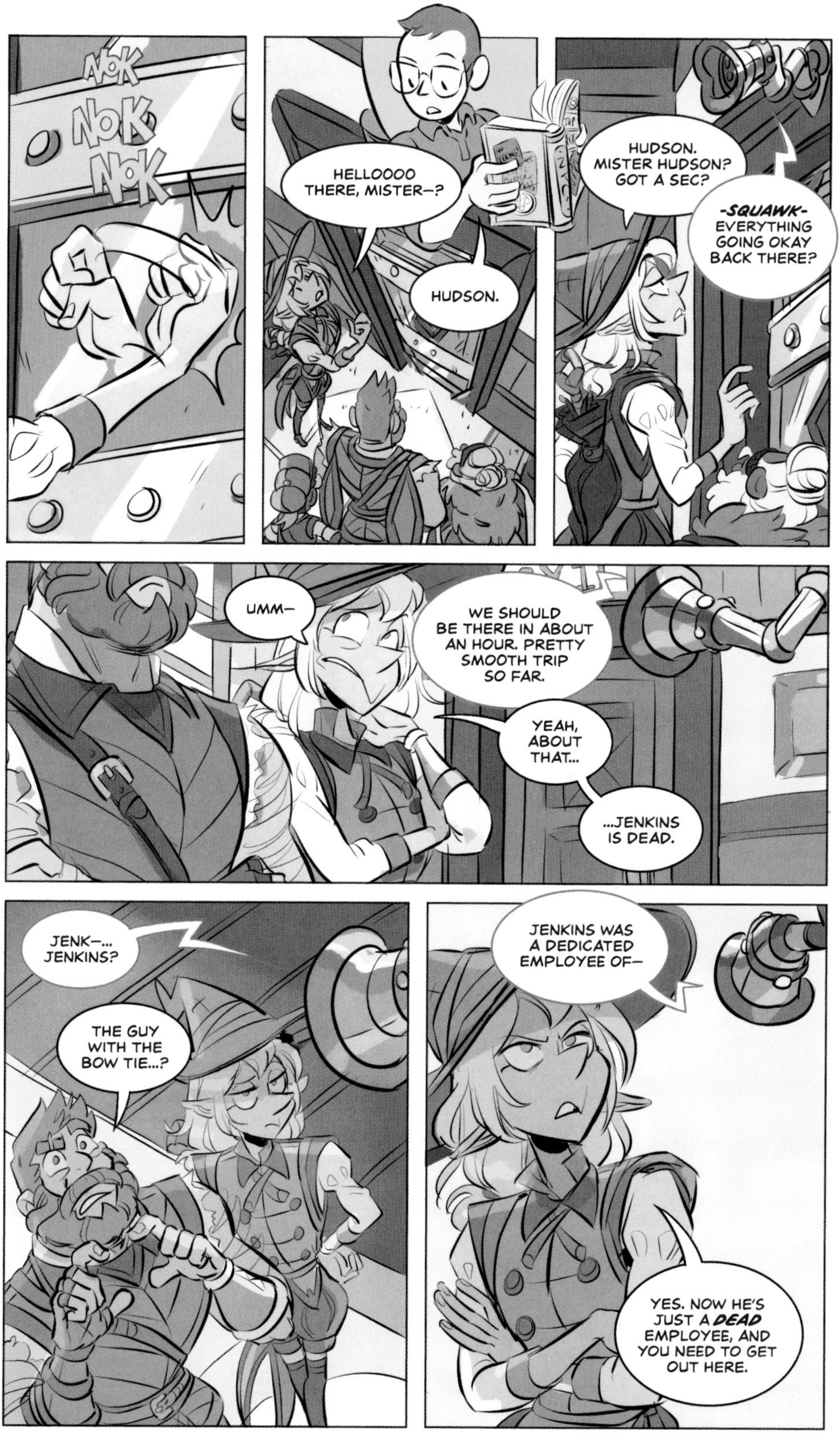
NOK
NOK NOK
HELLOOOO THERE, MISTER—?
HUDSON.
HUDSON. MISTER HUDSON? GOT A SEC?
-SQUAWK- EVERYTHING GOING OKAY BACK THERE?
UMM—
WE SHOULD BE THERE IN ABOUT AN HOUR. PRETTY SMOOTH TRIP SO FAR.
YEAH, ABOUT THAT...
...JENKINS IS DEAD.
JENK—... JENKINS?
THE GUY WITH THE BOW TIE...?
JENKINS WAS A DEDICATED EMPLOYEE OF—
YES. NOW HE'S JUST A DEAD EMPLOYEE, AND YOU NEED TO GET OUT HERE.

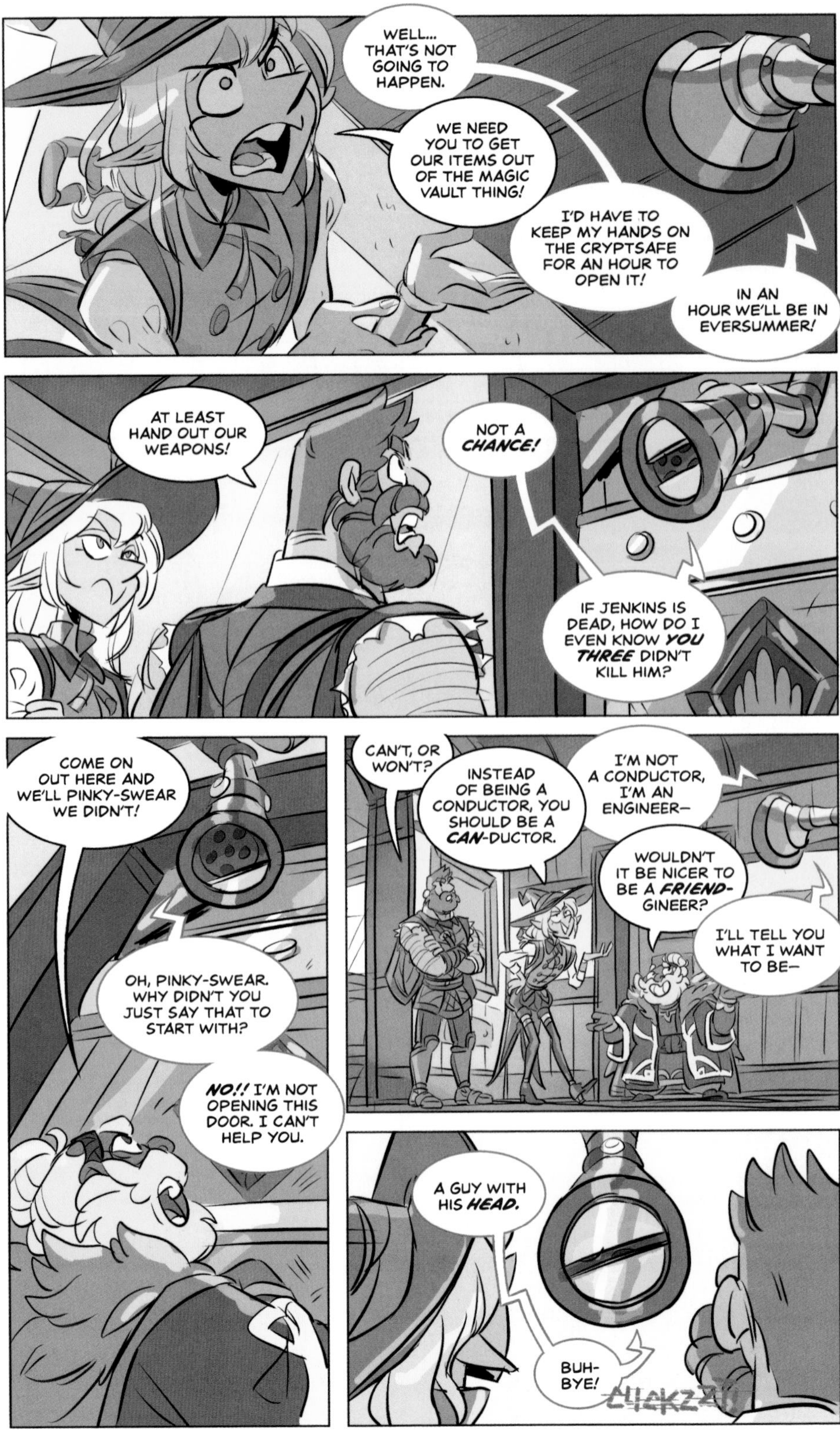
WELL... THAT'S NOT GOING TO HAPPEN.
WE NEED YOU TO GET OUR ITEMS OUT OF THE MAGIC VAULT THING!
I'D HAVE TO KEEP MY HANDS ON THE CRYPTSAFE FOR AN HOUR TO OPEN IT!
IN AN HOUR WE'LL BE IN EVERSUMMER!
AT LEAST HAND OUT OUR WEAPONS!
NOT A CHANCE!
IF JENKINS IS DEAD, HOW DO I EVEN KNOW YOU THREE DIDN'T KILL HIM?
COME ON OUT HERE AND WE'LL PINKY-SWEAR WE DIDN'T!
OH, PINKY-SWEAR. WHY DIDN'T YOU JUST SAY THAT TO START WITH?
NO!! I'M NOT OPENING THIS DOOR. I CAN'T HELP YOU.
CAN'T, OR WON'T?
INSTEAD OF BEING A CONDUCTOR, YOU SHOULD BE A CAN-DUCTOR.
I'M NOT A CONDUCTOR, I'M AN ENGINEER—
WOULDN'T IT BE NICER TO BE A FRIEND-GINEER?
I'LL TELL YOU WHAT I WANT TO BE—
A GUY WITH HIS HEAD.
BUH-BYE!
CLLAKZZH

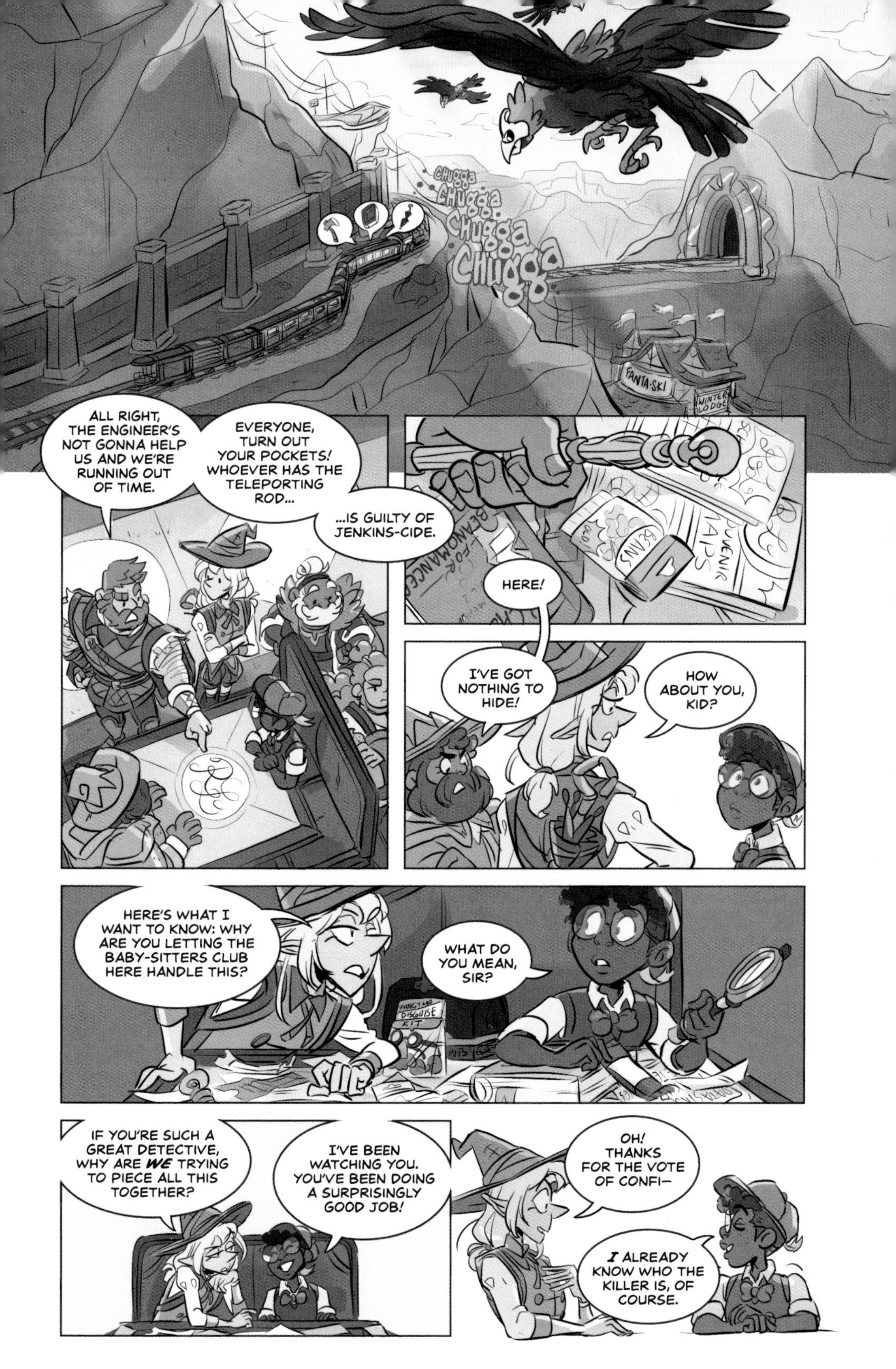

Chugga Chugga Chugga Chugga
FANTA·SKI
WINTER LODGE
ALL RIGHT, THE ENGINEER'S NOT GONNA HELP US AND WE'RE RUNNING OUT OF TIME.
EVERYONE, TURN OUT YOUR POCKETS! WHOEVER HAS THE TELEPORTING ROD...
...IS GUILTY OF JENKINS-CIDE.
HERE!
I'VE GOT NOTHING TO HIDE!
HOW ABOUT YOU, KID?
HERE'S WHAT I WANT TO KNOW: WHY ARE YOU LETTING THE BABY-SITTERS CLUB HERE HANDLE THIS?
WHAT DO YOU MEAN, SIR?
FANCY LAD DISGUISE KIT
IF YOU'RE SUCH A GREAT DETECTIVE, WHY ARE ***WE*** TRYING TO PIECE ALL THIS TOGETHER?
I'VE BEEN WATCHING YOU. YOU'VE BEEN DOING A SURPRISINGLY GOOD JOB!
OH! THANKS FOR THE VOTE OF CONFI—
I ALREADY KNOW WHO THE KILLER IS, OF COURSE.

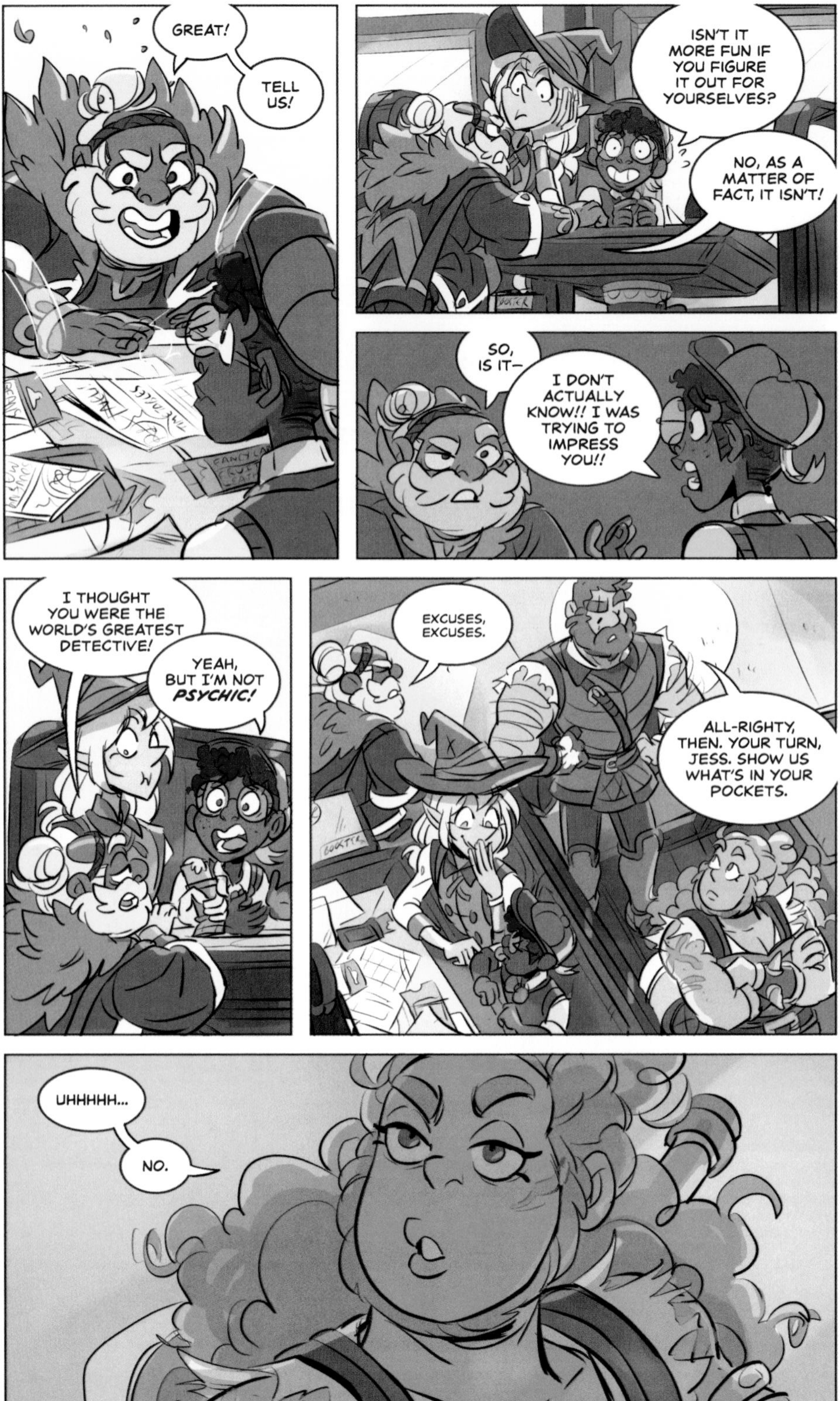
GREAT!
TELL US!
ISN'T IT MORE FUN IF YOU FIGURE IT OUT FOR YOURSELVES?
NO, AS A MATTER OF FACT, IT ISN'T!
SO, IS IT—
I DON'T ACTUALLY KNOW!! I WAS TRYING TO IMPRESS YOU!!
I THOUGHT YOU WERE THE WORLD'S GREATEST DETECTIVE!
YEAH, BUT I'M NOT **PSYCHIC!**
EXCUSES, EXCUSES.
ALL-RIGHTY, THEN. YOUR TURN, JESS. SHOW US WHAT'S IN YOUR POCKETS.
UHHHHH...
NO.

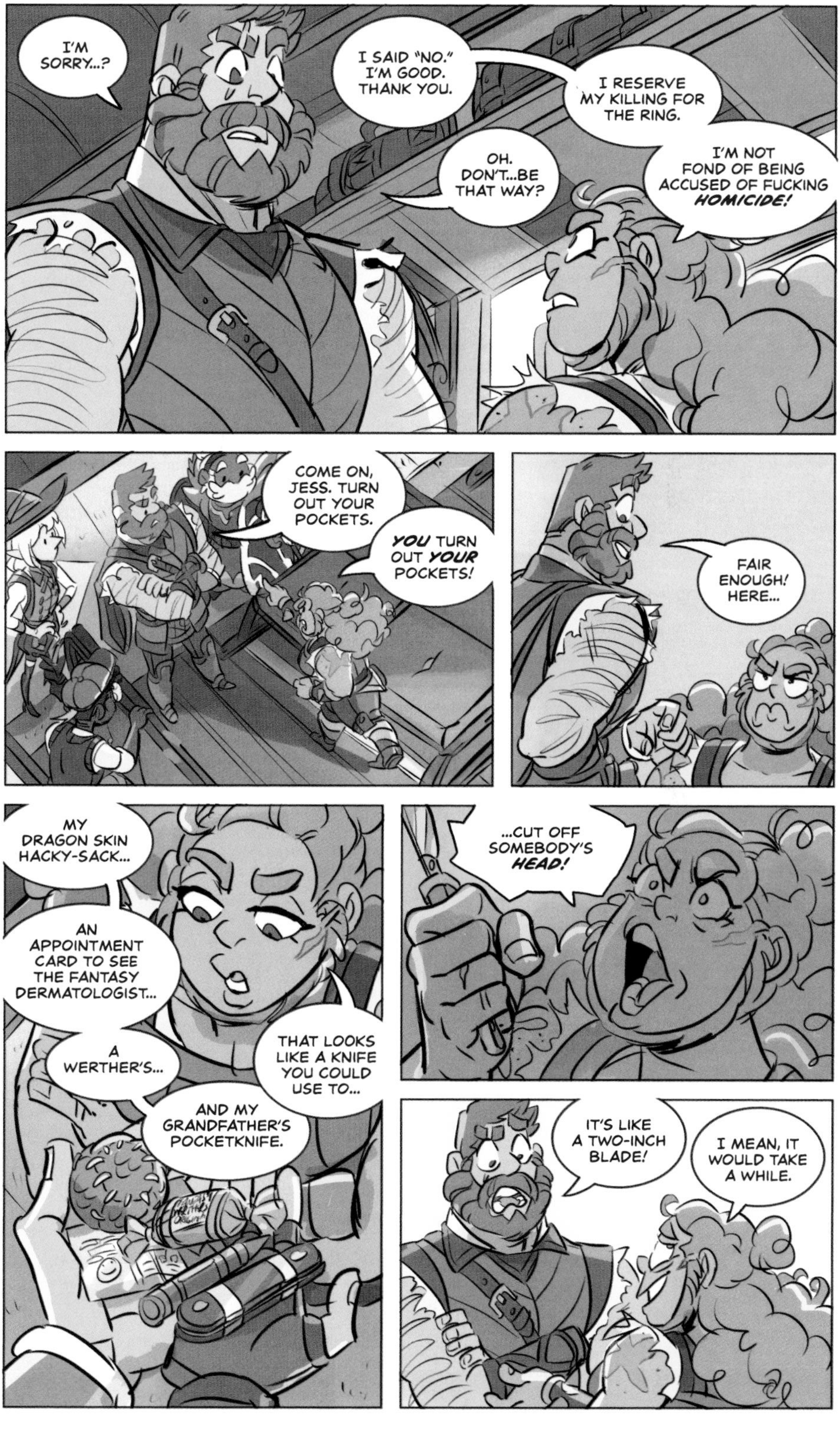
I'M SORRY...?
I SAID "NO." I'M GOOD. THANK YOU.
I RESERVE MY KILLING FOR THE RING.
OH. DON'T...BE THAT WAY?
I'M NOT FOND OF BEING ACCUSED OF FUCKING *HOMICIDE!*
COME ON, JESS. TURN OUT YOUR POCKETS.
YOU TURN OUT *YOUR* POCKETS!
FAIR ENOUGH! HERE...
MY DRAGON SKIN HACKY-SACK...
AN APPOINTMENT CARD TO SEE THE FANTASY DERMATOLOGIST...
A WERTHER'S...
AND MY GRANDFATHER'S POCKETKNIFE.
THAT LOOKS LIKE A KNIFE YOU COULD USE TO...
...CUT OFF SOMEBODY'S *HEAD!*
IT'S LIKE A TWO-INCH BLADE!
I MEAN, IT WOULD TAKE A WHILE.

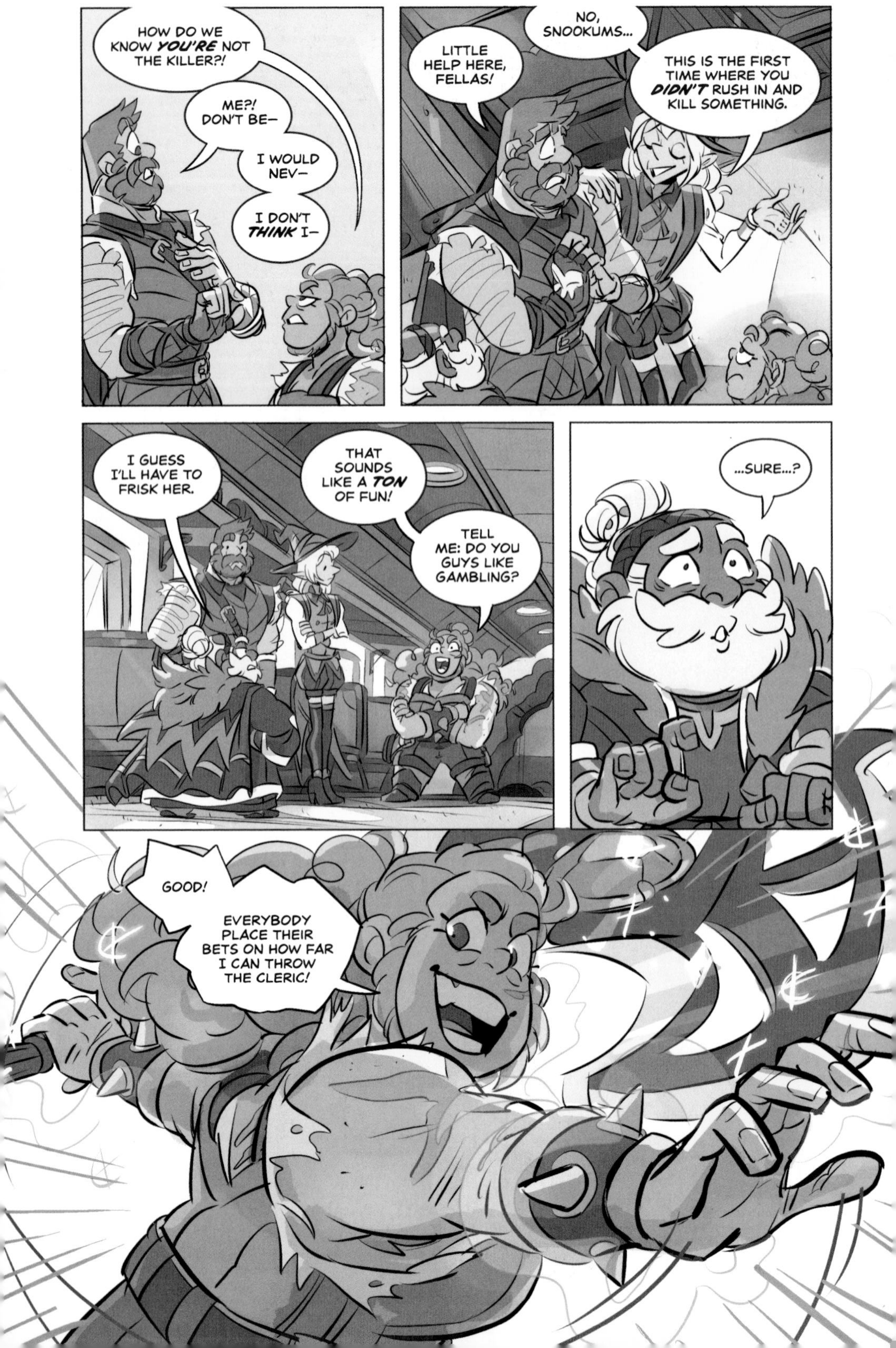
HOW DO WE KNOW *YOU'RE* NOT THE KILLER?!
ME?! DON'T BE—
I WOULD NEV—
I DON'T *THINK* I—
LITTLE HELP HERE, FELLAS!
NO, SNOOKUMS...
THIS IS THE FIRST TIME WHERE YOU *DIDN'T* RUSH IN AND KILL SOMETHING.
I GUESS I'LL HAVE TO FRISK HER.
THAT SOUNDS LIKE A *TON* OF FUN!
TELL ME: DO YOU GUYS LIKE GAMBLING?
...SURE...?
GOOD!
EVERYBODY PLACE THEIR BETS ON HOW FAR I CAN THROW THE CLERIC!

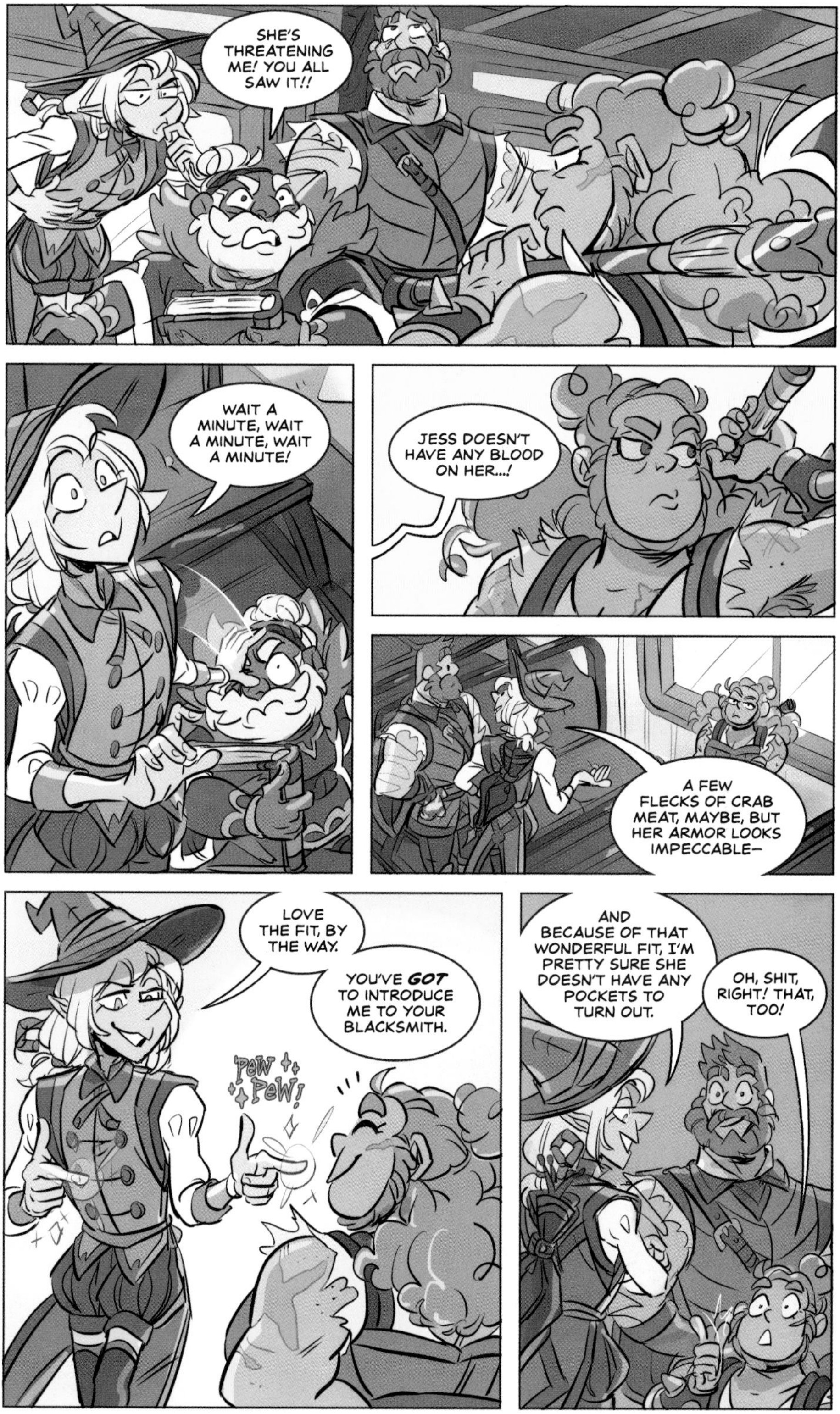
SHE'S THREATENING ME! YOU ALL SAW IT!!
WAIT A MINUTE, WAIT A MINUTE, WAIT A MINUTE!
JESS DOESN'T HAVE ANY BLOOD ON HER...!
A FEW FLECKS OF CRAB MEAT, MAYBE, BUT HER ARMOR LOOKS IMPECCABLE–
LOVE THE FIT, BY THE WAY.
YOU'VE GOT TO INTRODUCE ME TO YOUR BLACKSMITH.
PEW PEW!
AND BECAUSE OF THAT WONDERFUL FIT, I'M PRETTY SURE SHE DOESN'T HAVE ANY POCKETS TO TURN OUT.
OH, SHIT, RIGHT! THAT, TOO!

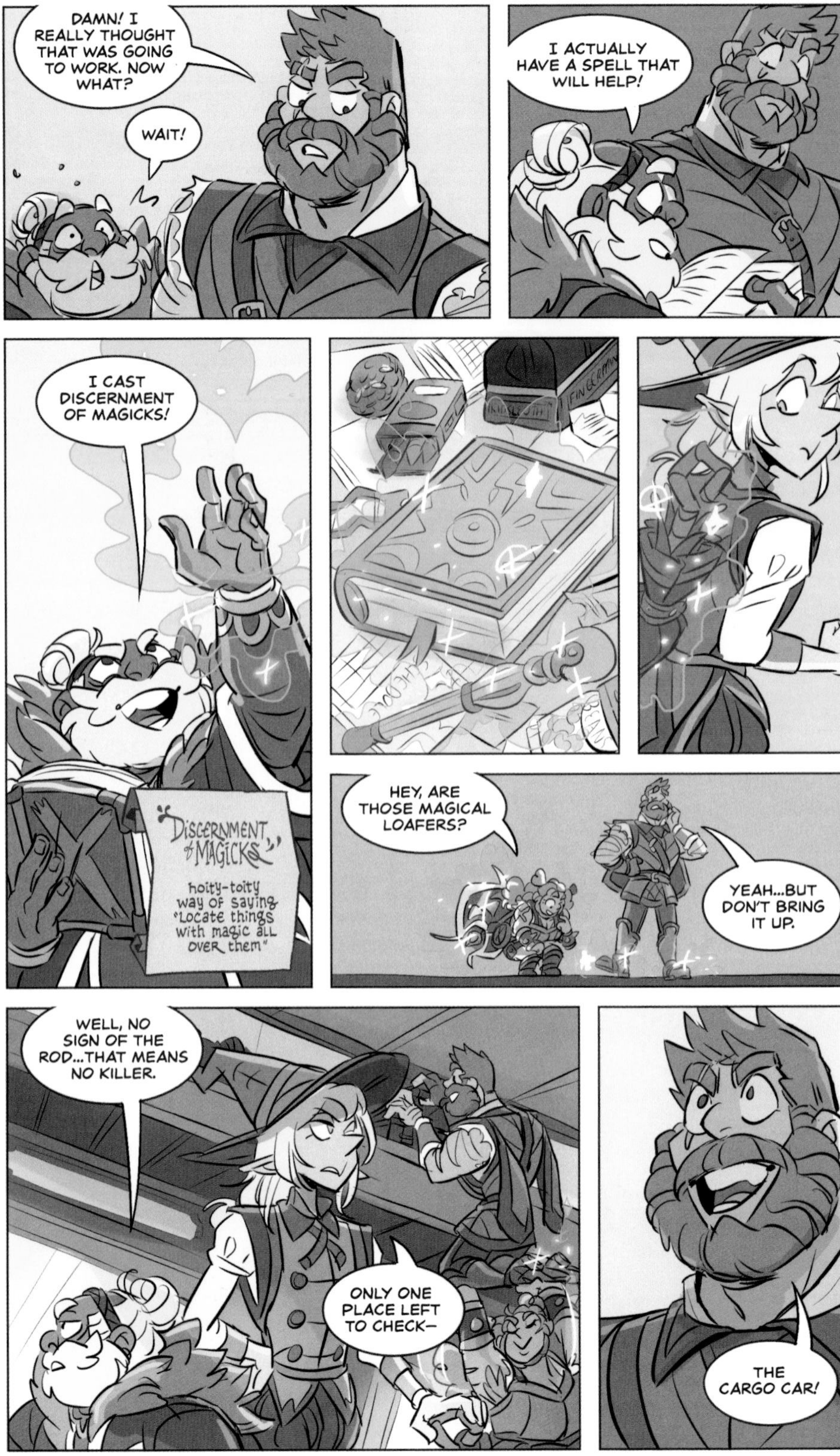
DAMN! I REALLY THOUGHT THAT WAS GOING TO WORK. NOW WHAT?
WAIT!
I ACTUALLY HAVE A SPELL THAT WILL HELP!
I CAST DISCERNMENT OF MAGICKS!
DISCERNMENT of MAGICKS
hoity-toity way of saying "Locate things with magic all over them"
HEY, ARE THOSE MAGICAL LOAFERS?
YEAH...BUT DON'T BRING IT UP.
WELL, NO SIGN OF THE ROD...THAT MEANS NO KILLER.
ONLY ONE PLACE LEFT TO CHECK—
THE CARGO CAR!

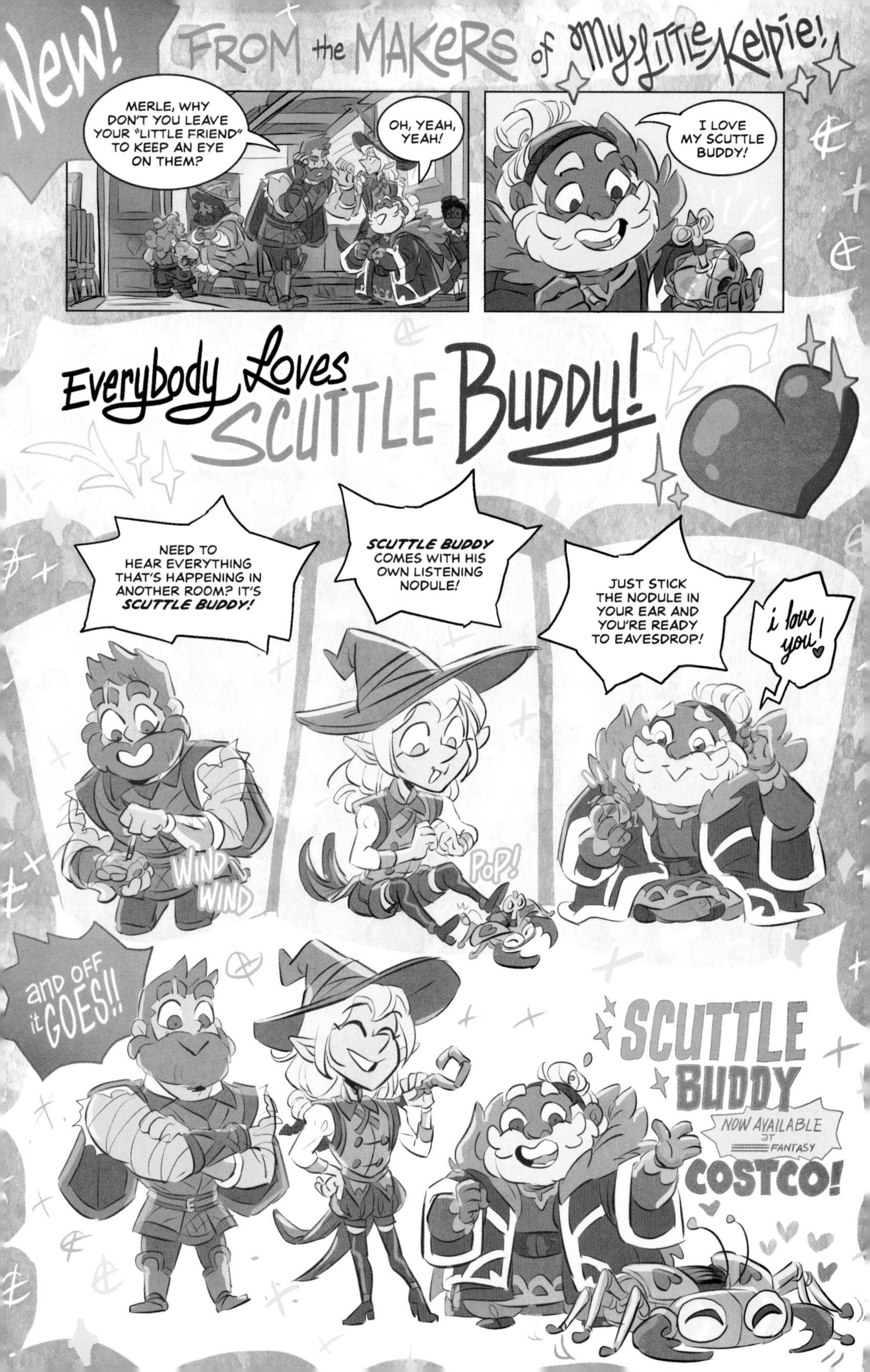
New!
FROM the MAKERS of My Little Kelpie!
MERLE, WHY DON'T YOU LEAVE YOUR "LITTLE FRIEND" TO KEEP AN EYE ON THEM?
OH, YEAH, YEAH!
I LOVE MY SCUTTLE BUDDY!
Everybody Loves SCUTTLE BUDDY!
NEED TO HEAR EVERYTHING THAT'S HAPPENING IN ANOTHER ROOM? IT'S SCUTTLE BUDDY!
WIND WIND
SCUTTLE BUDDY COMES WITH HIS OWN LISTENING NODULE!
POP!
JUST STICK THE NODULE IN YOUR EAR AND YOU'RE READY TO EAVESDROP!
i love you!
and off it GOES!!
SCUTTLE BUDDY
NOW AVAILABLE AT FANTASY
COSTCO!

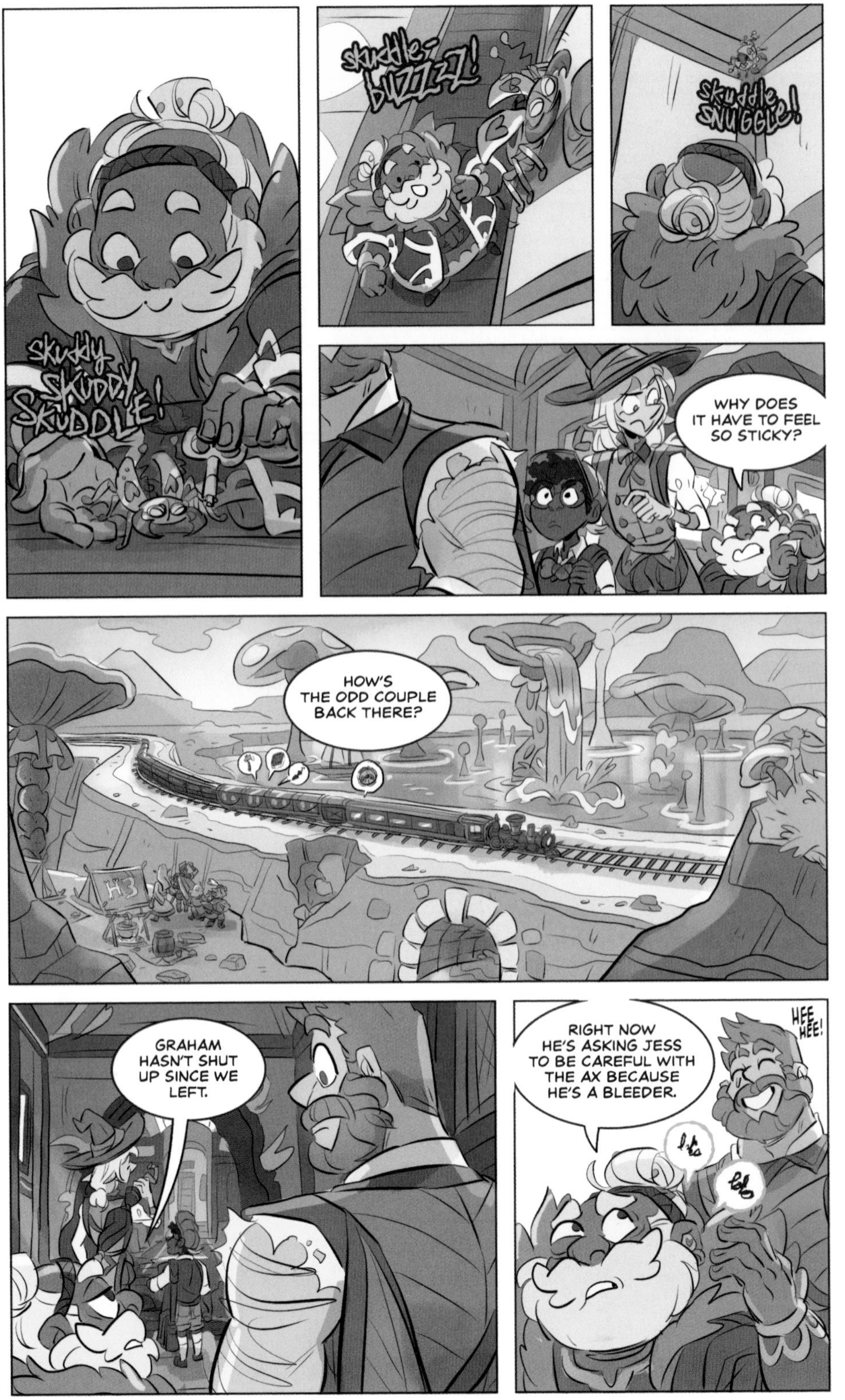
skuddly SKUDDY SKUDDLE!
skuddle-BUZZZZ!
skuddle SNUGGLE!
WHY DOES IT HAVE TO FEEL SO STICKY?
HOW'S THE ODD COUPLE BACK THERE?
H3
GRAHAM HASN'T SHUT UP SINCE WE LEFT.
RIGHT NOW HE'S ASKING JESS TO BE CAREFUL WITH THE AX BECAUSE HE'S A BLEEDER.
HEE HEE!

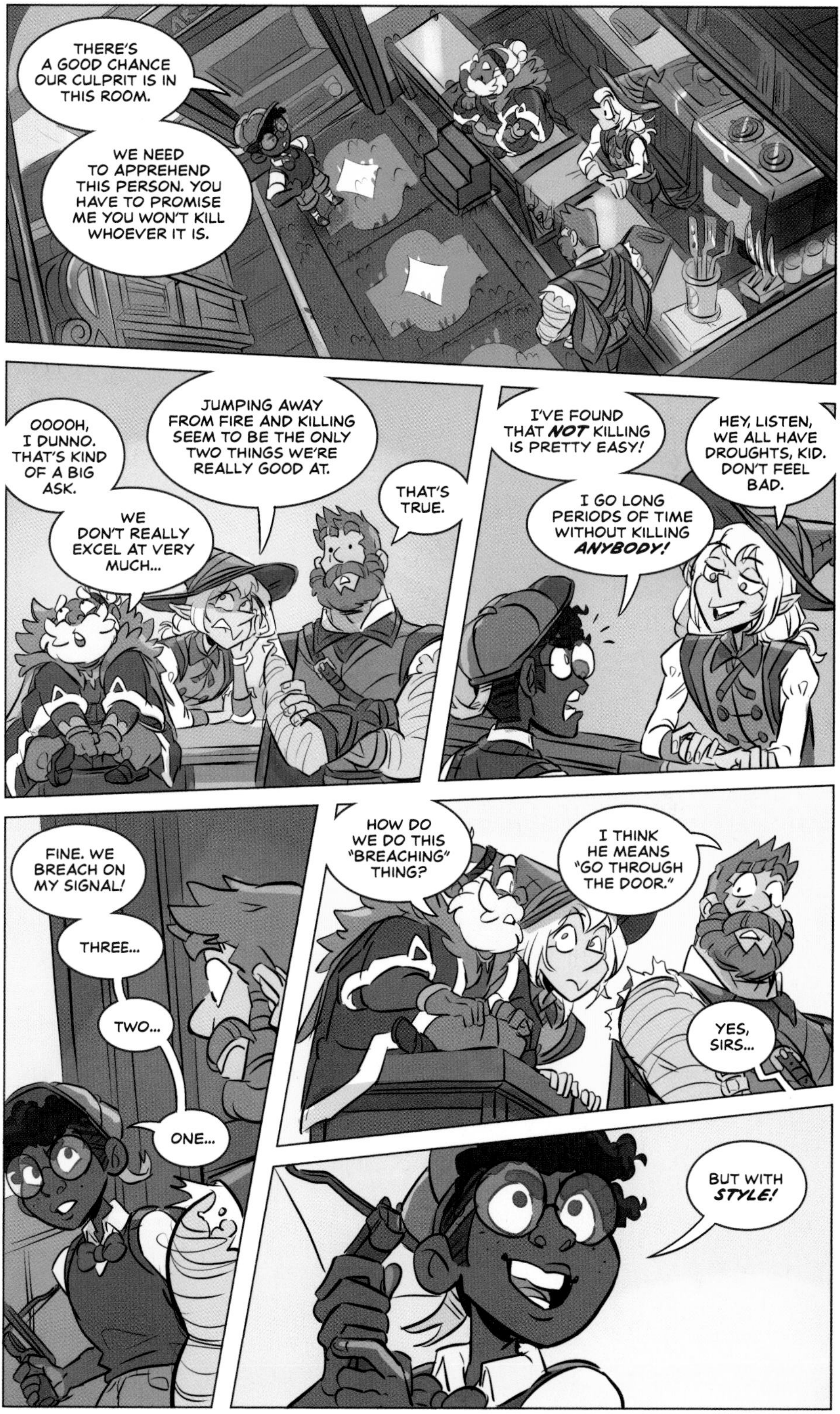
THERE'S A GOOD CHANCE OUR CULPRIT IS IN THIS ROOM.
WE NEED TO APPREHEND THIS PERSON. YOU HAVE TO PROMISE ME YOU WON'T KILL WHOEVER IT IS.
OOOOH, I DUNNO. THAT'S KIND OF A BIG ASK.
JUMPING AWAY FROM FIRE AND KILLING SEEM TO BE THE ONLY TWO THINGS WE'RE REALLY GOOD AT.
WE DON'T REALLY EXCEL AT VERY MUCH...
THAT'S TRUE.
I'VE FOUND THAT ***NOT*** KILLING IS PRETTY EASY!
HEY, LISTEN, WE ALL HAVE DROUGHTS, KID. DON'T FEEL BAD.
I GO LONG PERIODS OF TIME WITHOUT KILLING ***ANYBODY!***
FINE. WE BREACH ON MY SIGNAL!
THREE...
TWO...
ONE...
HOW DO WE DO THIS "BREACHING" THING?
I THINK HE MEANS "GO THROUGH THE DOOR."
YES, SIRS...
BUT WITH ***STYLE!***

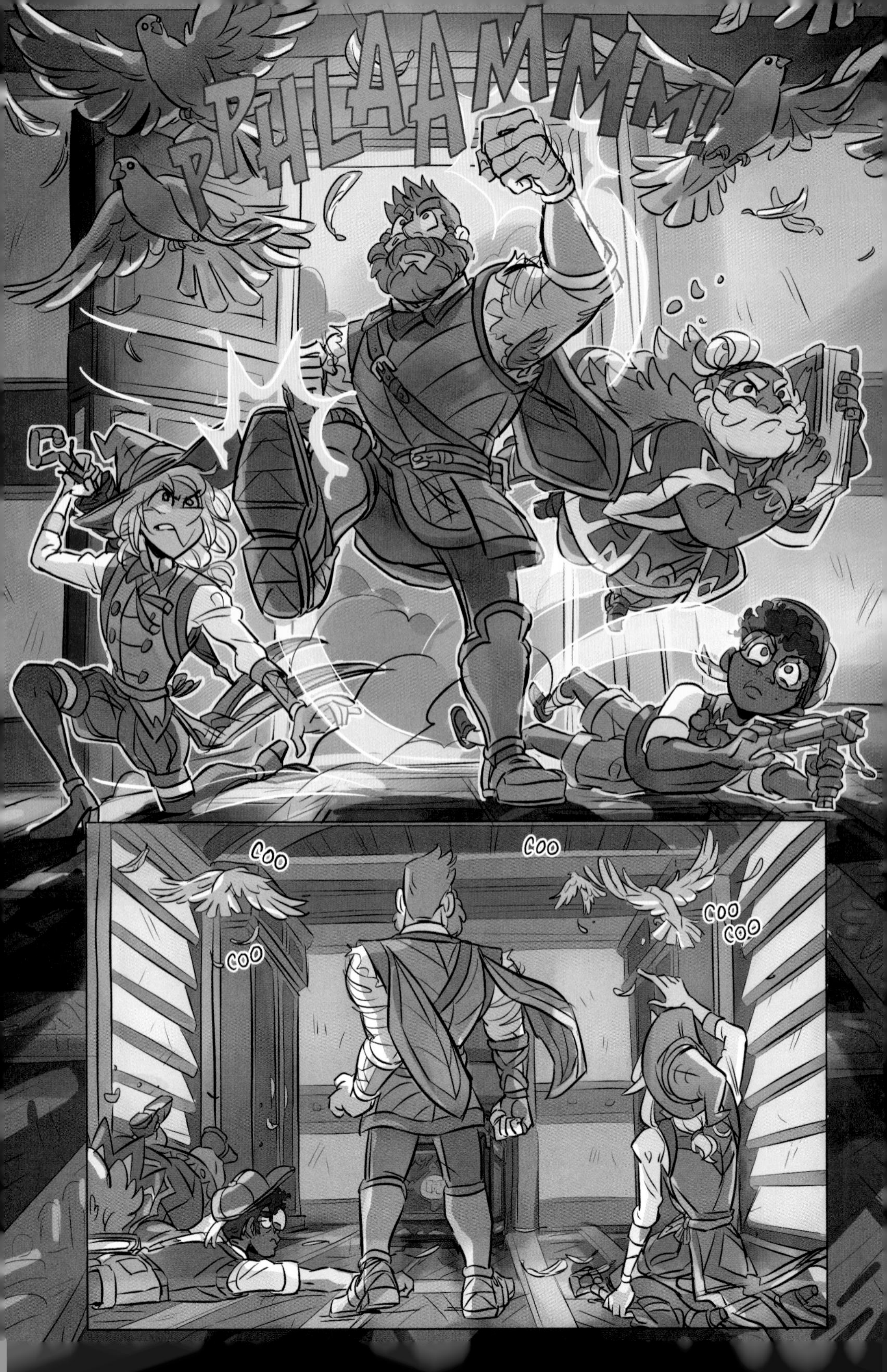
PHLAAMMM!!
COO
COO
COO
COO
COO

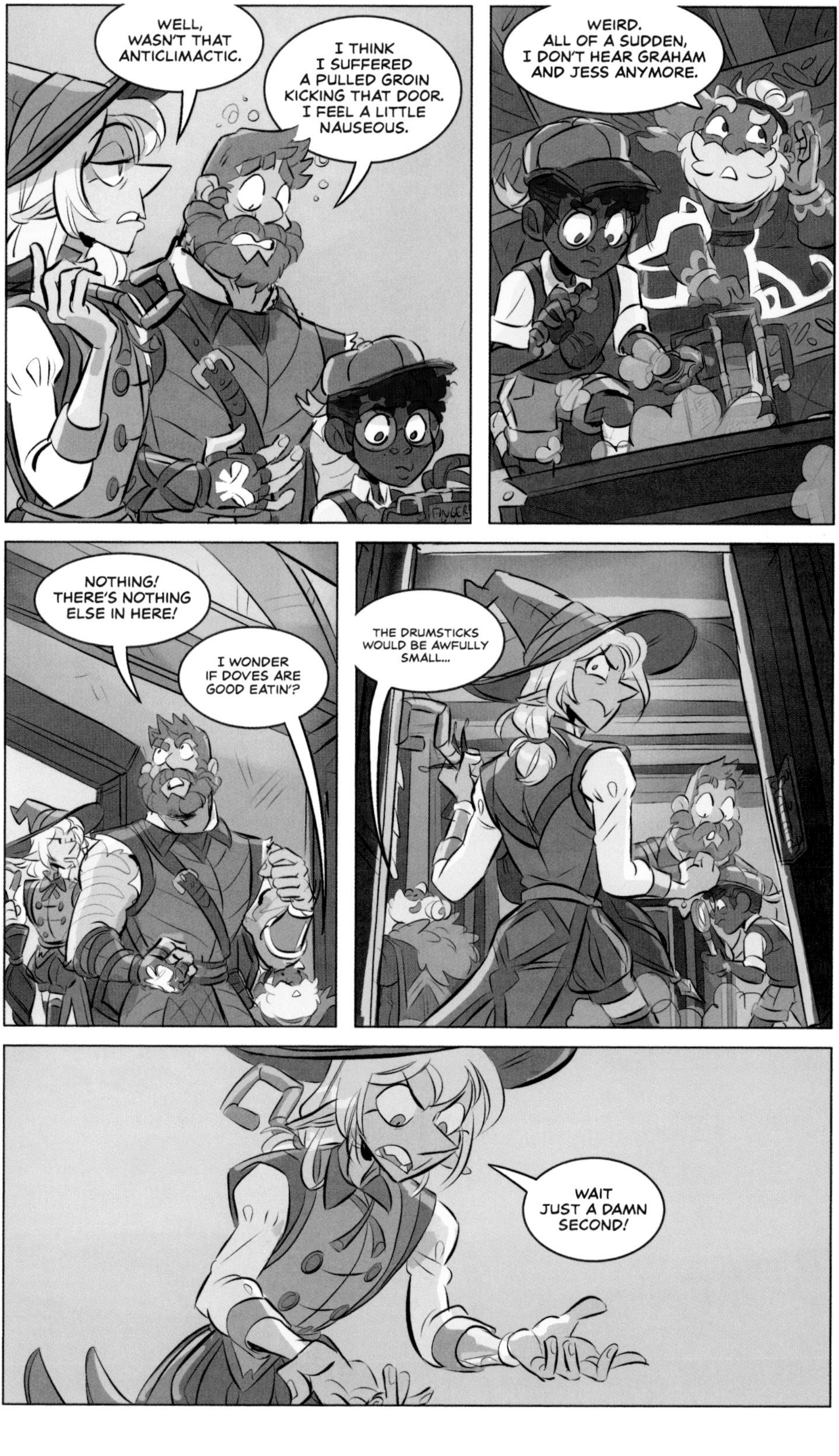
WELL, WASN'T THAT ANTICLIMACTIC.
I THINK I SUFFERED A PULLED GROIN KICKING THAT DOOR. I FEEL A LITTLE NAUSEOUS.
WEIRD. ALL OF A SUDDEN, I DON'T HEAR GRAHAM AND JESS ANYMORE.
NOTHING! THERE'S NOTHING ELSE IN HERE!
I WONDER IF DOVES ARE GOOD EATIN'?
THE DRUMSTICKS WOULD BE AWFULLY SMALL...
WAIT JUST A DAMN SECOND!

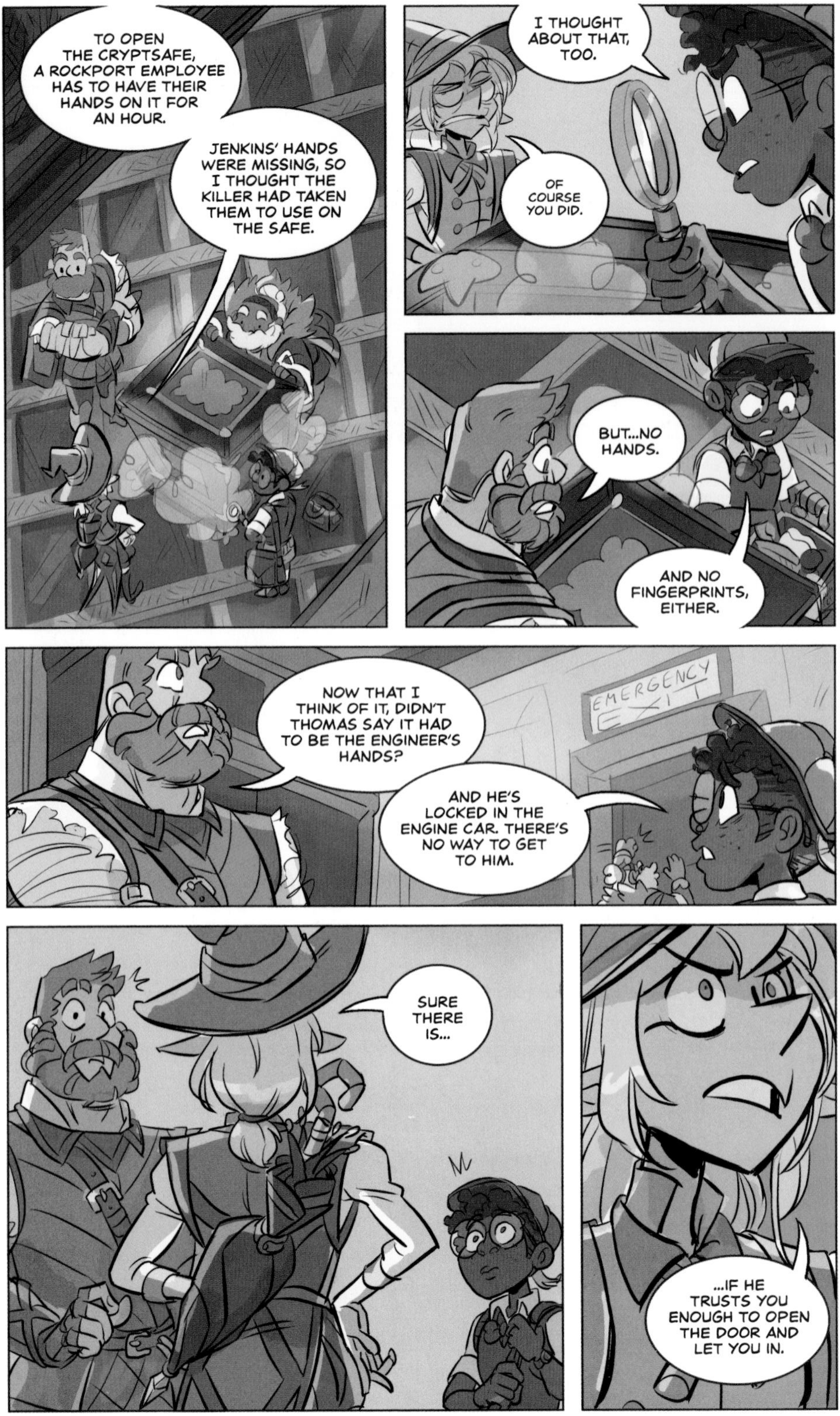
TO OPEN THE CRYPTSAFE, A ROCKPORT EMPLOYEE HAS TO HAVE THEIR HANDS ON IT FOR AN HOUR.
JENKINS' HANDS WERE MISSING, SO I THOUGHT THE KILLER HAD TAKEN THEM TO USE ON THE SAFE.
I THOUGHT ABOUT THAT, TOO.
OF COURSE YOU DID.
BUT...NO HANDS.
AND NO FINGERPRINTS, EITHER.
NOW THAT I THINK OF IT, DIDN'T THOMAS SAY IT HAD TO BE THE ENGINEER'S HANDS?
EMERGENCY EXIT
AND HE'S LOCKED IN THE ENGINE CAR. THERE'S NO WAY TO GET TO HIM.
SURE THERE IS...
...IF HE TRUSTS YOU ENOUGH TO OPEN THE DOOR AND LET YOU IN.

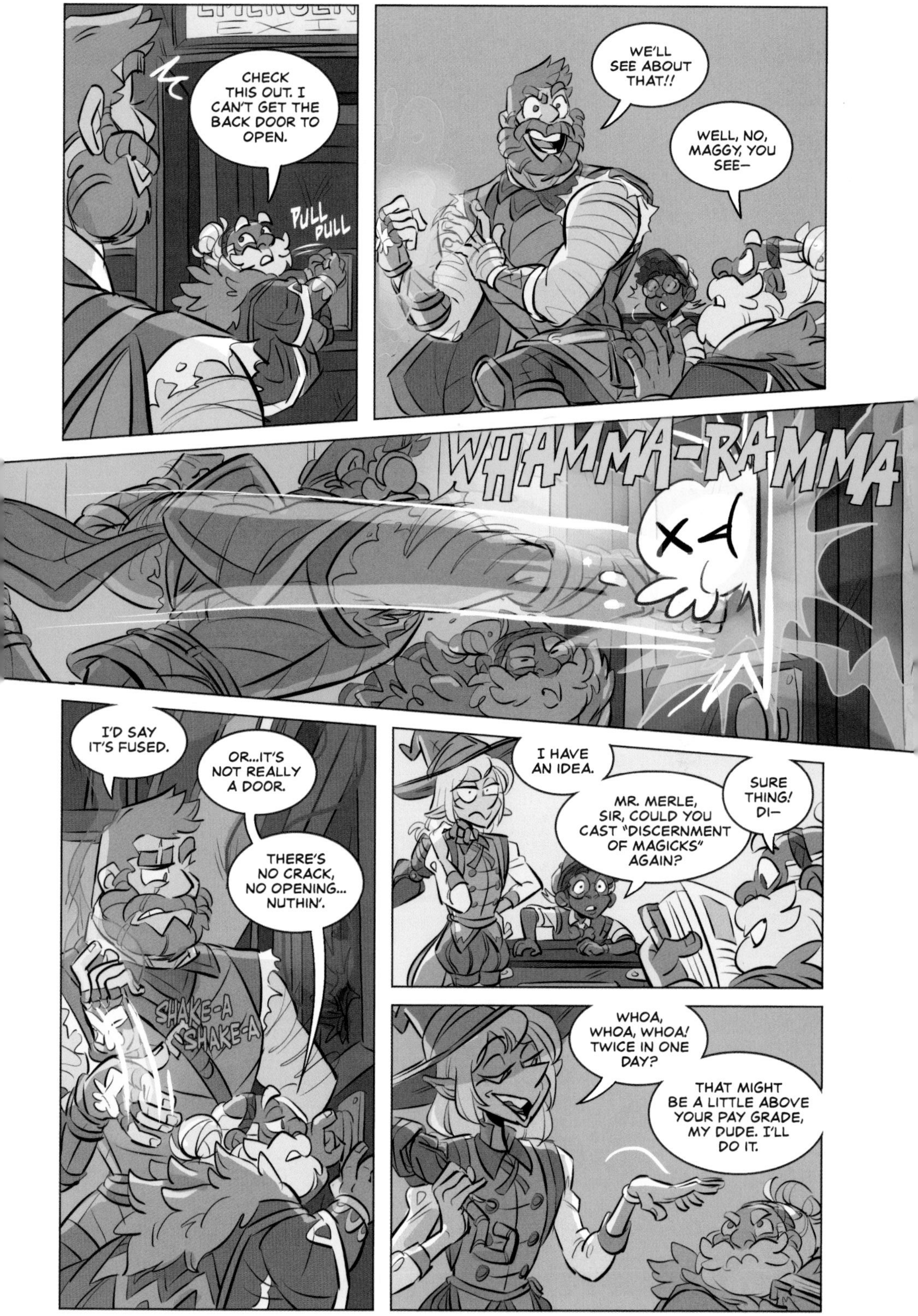
CHECK THIS OUT. I CAN'T GET THE BACK DOOR TO OPEN.
PULL PULL
WE'LL SEE ABOUT THAT!!
WELL, NO, MAGGY, YOU SEE–
WHAMMA-RAMMA
I'D SAY IT'S FUSED.
OR...IT'S NOT REALLY A DOOR.
THERE'S NO CRACK, NO OPENING... NUTHIN'.
SHAKE-A SHAKE-A
I HAVE AN IDEA.
MR. MERLE, SIR, COULD YOU CAST "DISCERNMENT OF MAGICKS" AGAIN?
SURE THING! DI–
WHOA, WHOA, WHOA! TWICE IN ONE DAY?
THAT MIGHT BE A LITTLE ABOVE YOUR PAY GRADE, MY DUDE. I'LL DO IT.

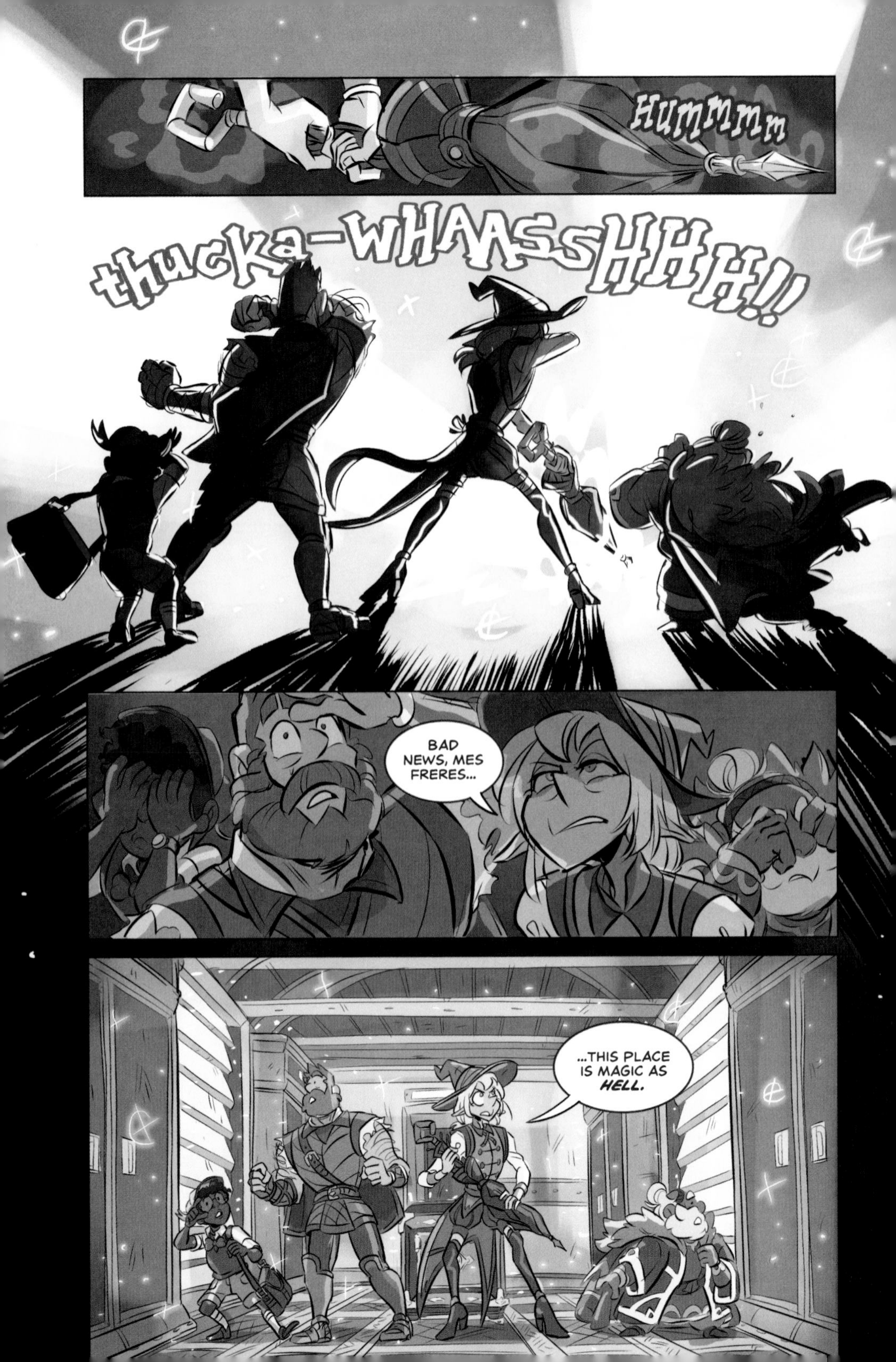

HUMMMM
thucka-WHAASSHHHH!!
BAD NEWS, MES FRERES...
...THIS PLACE IS MAGIC AS HELL.

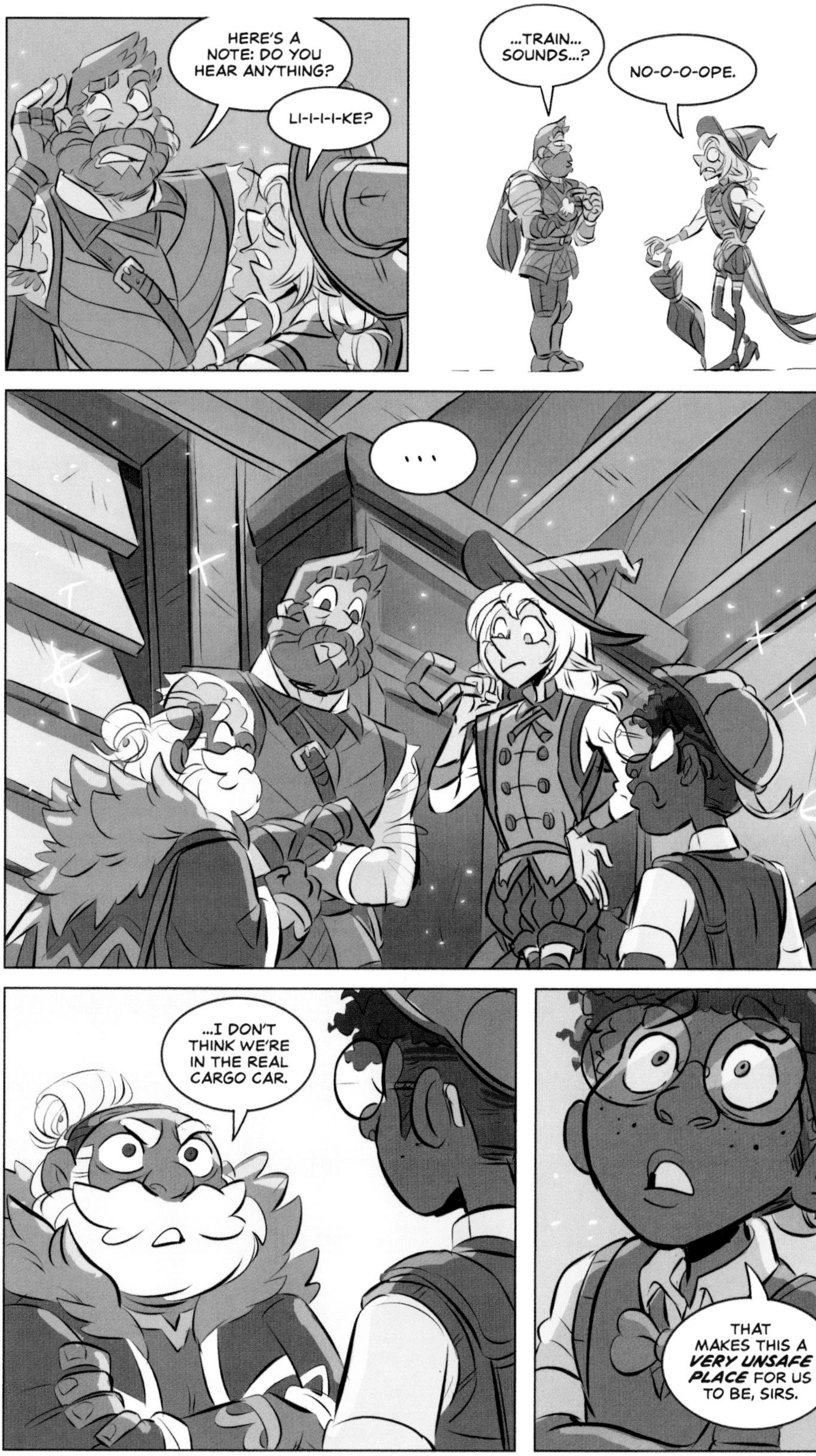
HERE'S A NOTE: DO YOU HEAR ANYTHING?
LI-I-I-I-KE?
...TRAIN... SOUNDS...?
NO-O-O-OPE.
...
...I DON'T THINK WE'RE IN THE REAL CARGO CAR.
THAT MAKES THIS A ***VERY UNSAFE PLACE*** FOR US TO BE, SIRS.

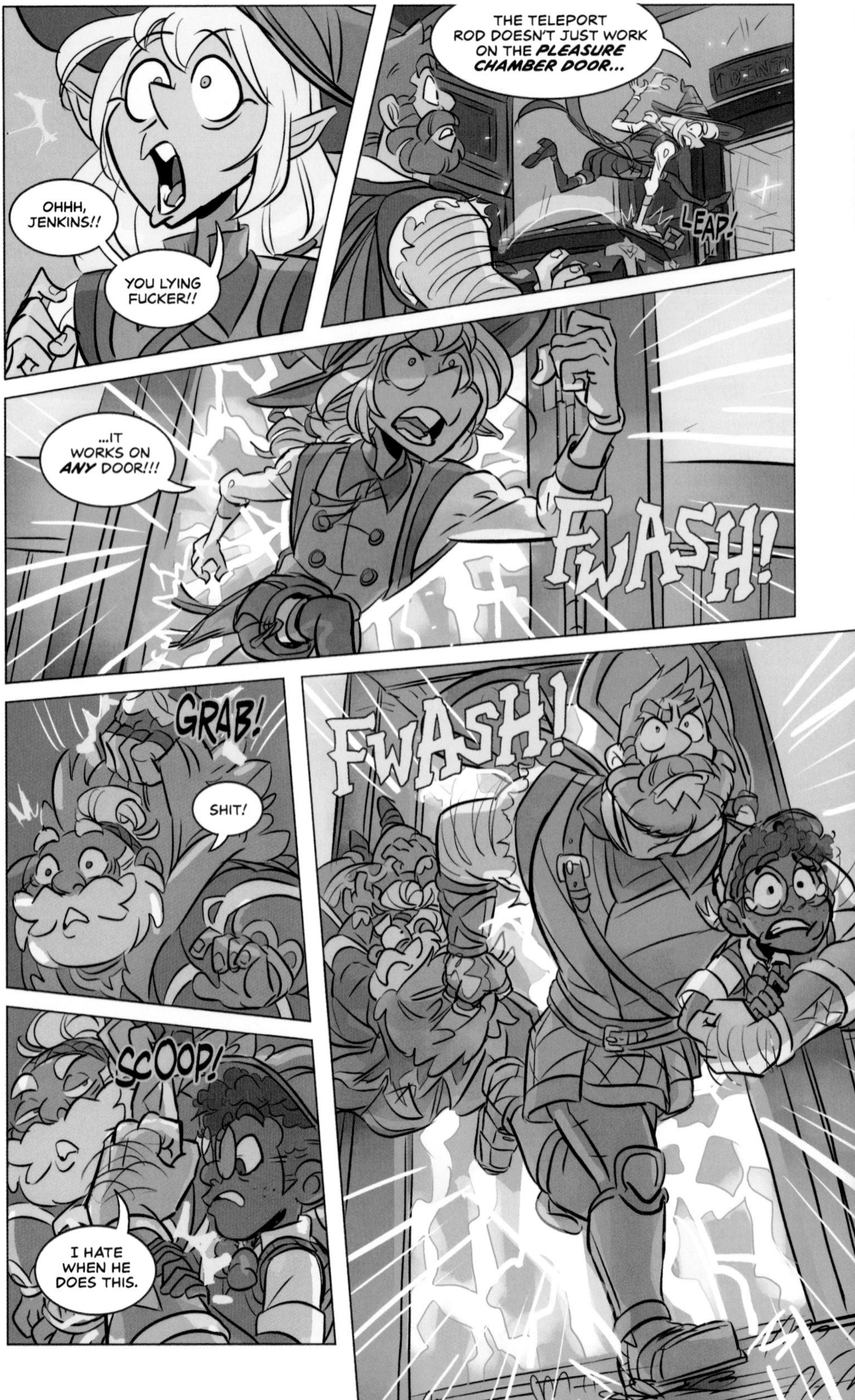
OHHH, JENKINS!!
YOU LYING FUCKER!!
THE TELEPORT ROD DOESN'T JUST WORK ON THE *PLEASURE CHAMBER DOOR*...
LEAP!
...IT WORKS ON *ANY* DOOR!!!
FWASH!
GRAB!
SHIT!
FWASH!
SCOOP!
I HATE WHEN HE DOES THIS.

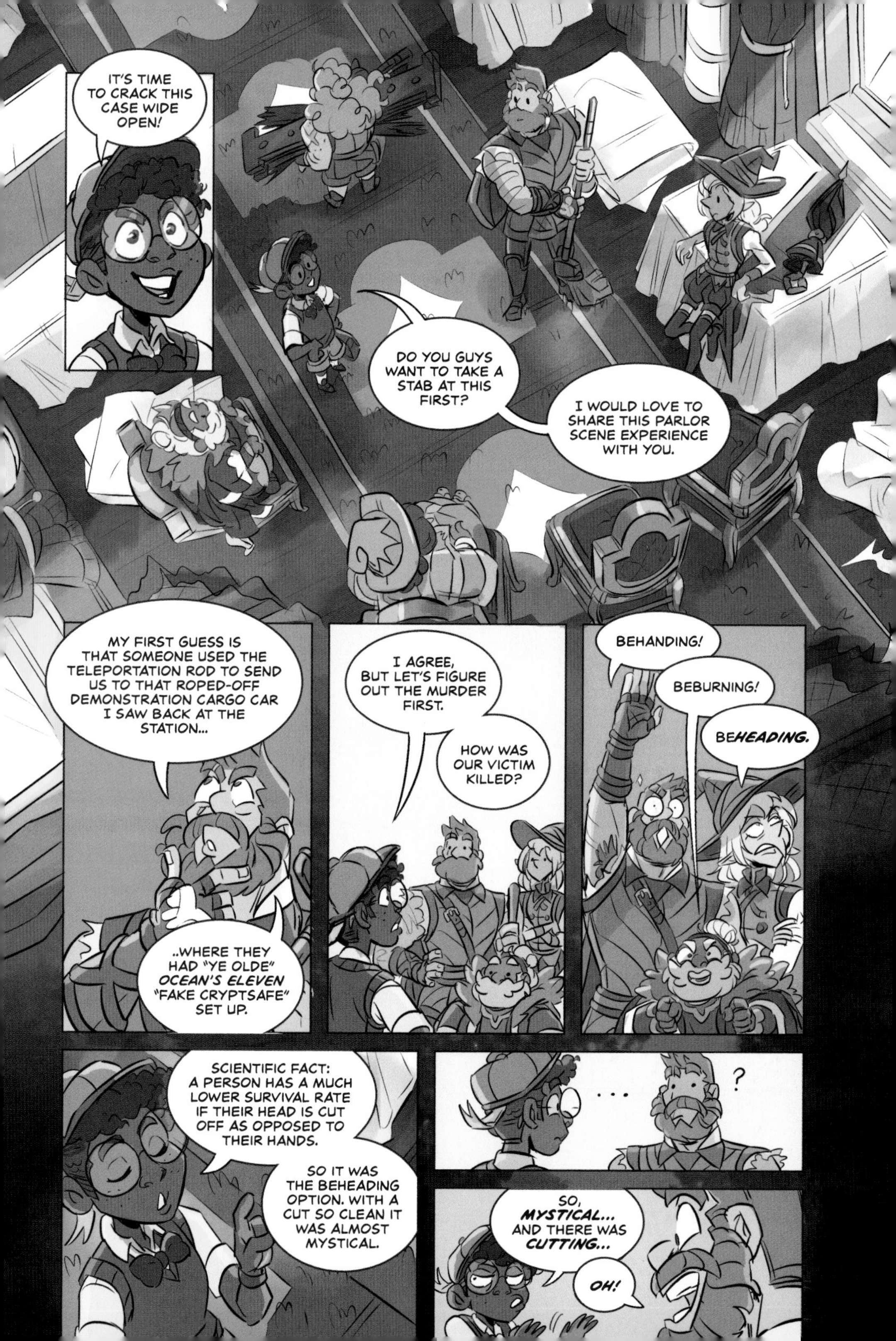
IT'S TIME TO CRACK THIS CASE WIDE OPEN!
DO YOU GUYS WANT TO TAKE A STAB AT THIS FIRST?
I WOULD LOVE TO SHARE THIS PARLOR SCENE EXPERIENCE WITH YOU.
MY FIRST GUESS IS THAT SOMEONE USED THE TELEPORTATION ROD TO SEND US TO THAT ROPED-OFF DEMONSTRATION CARGO CAR I SAW BACK AT THE STATION...
..WHERE THEY HAD "YE OLDE" *OCEAN'S ELEVEN* "FAKE CRYPTSAFE" SET UP.
I AGREE, BUT LET'S FIGURE OUT THE MURDER FIRST.
HOW WAS OUR VICTIM KILLED?
BEHANDING!
BEBURNING!
BE***HEADING.***
SCIENTIFIC FACT: A PERSON HAS A MUCH LOWER SURVIVAL RATE IF THEIR HEAD IS CUT OFF AS OPPOSED TO THEIR HANDS.
SO IT WAS THE BEHEADING OPTION. WITH A CUT SO CLEAN IT WAS ALMOST MYSTICAL.
. . .
?
SO, ***MYSTICAL...*** AND THERE WAS ***CUTTING...***
OH!

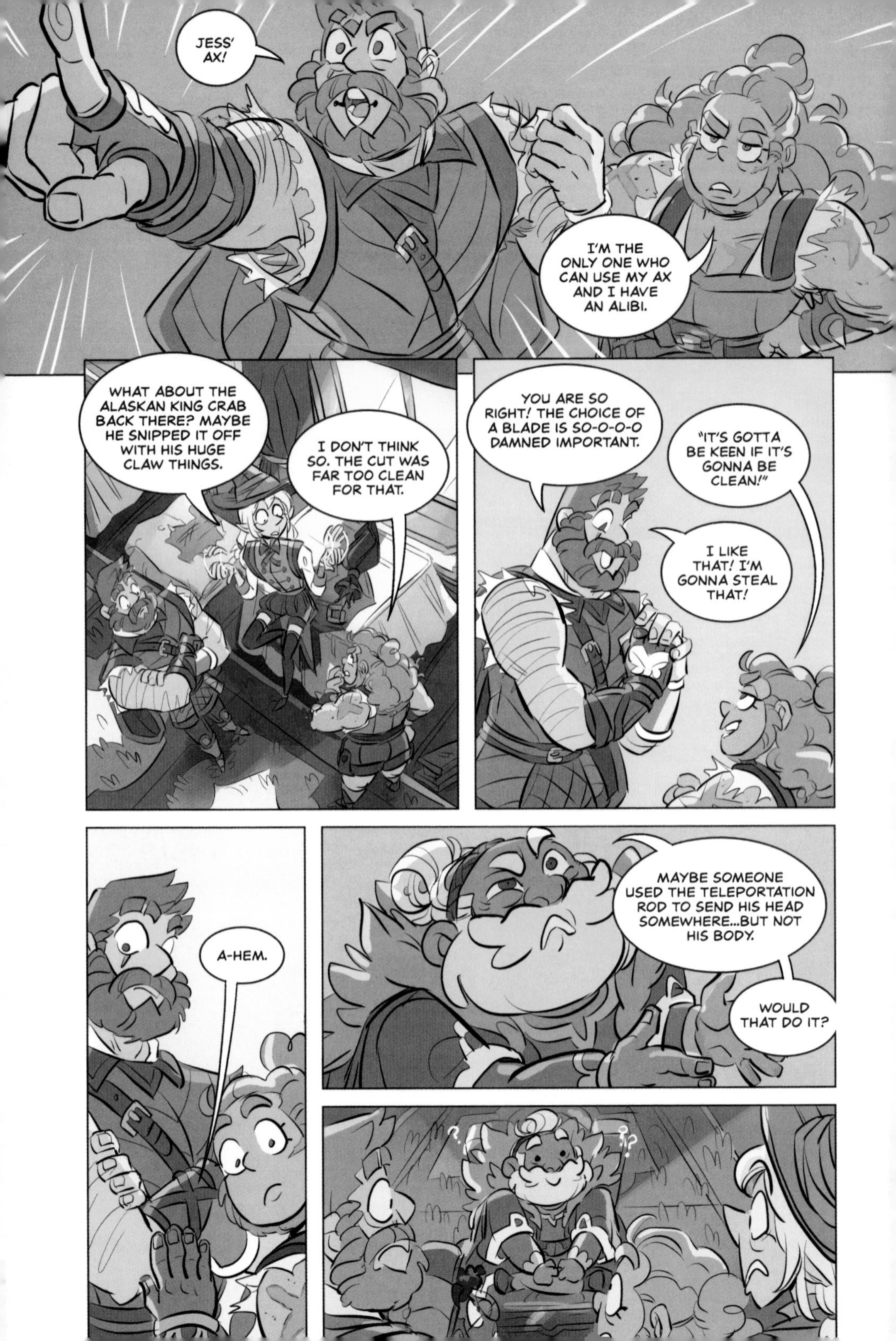
JESS' AX!
I'M THE ONLY ONE WHO CAN USE MY AX AND I HAVE AN ALIBI.
WHAT ABOUT THE ALASKAN KING CRAB BACK THERE? MAYBE HE SNIPPED IT OFF WITH HIS HUGE CLAW THINGS.
I DON'T THINK SO. THE CUT WAS FAR TOO CLEAN FOR THAT.
YOU ARE SO RIGHT! THE CHOICE OF A BLADE IS SO-O-O-O DAMNED IMPORTANT.
"IT'S GOTTA BE KEEN IF IT'S GONNA BE CLEAN!"
I LIKE THAT! I'M GONNA STEAL THAT!
A-HEM.
MAYBE SOMEONE USED THE TELEPORTATION ROD TO SEND HIS HEAD SOMEWHERE...BUT NOT HIS BODY.
WOULD THAT DO IT?

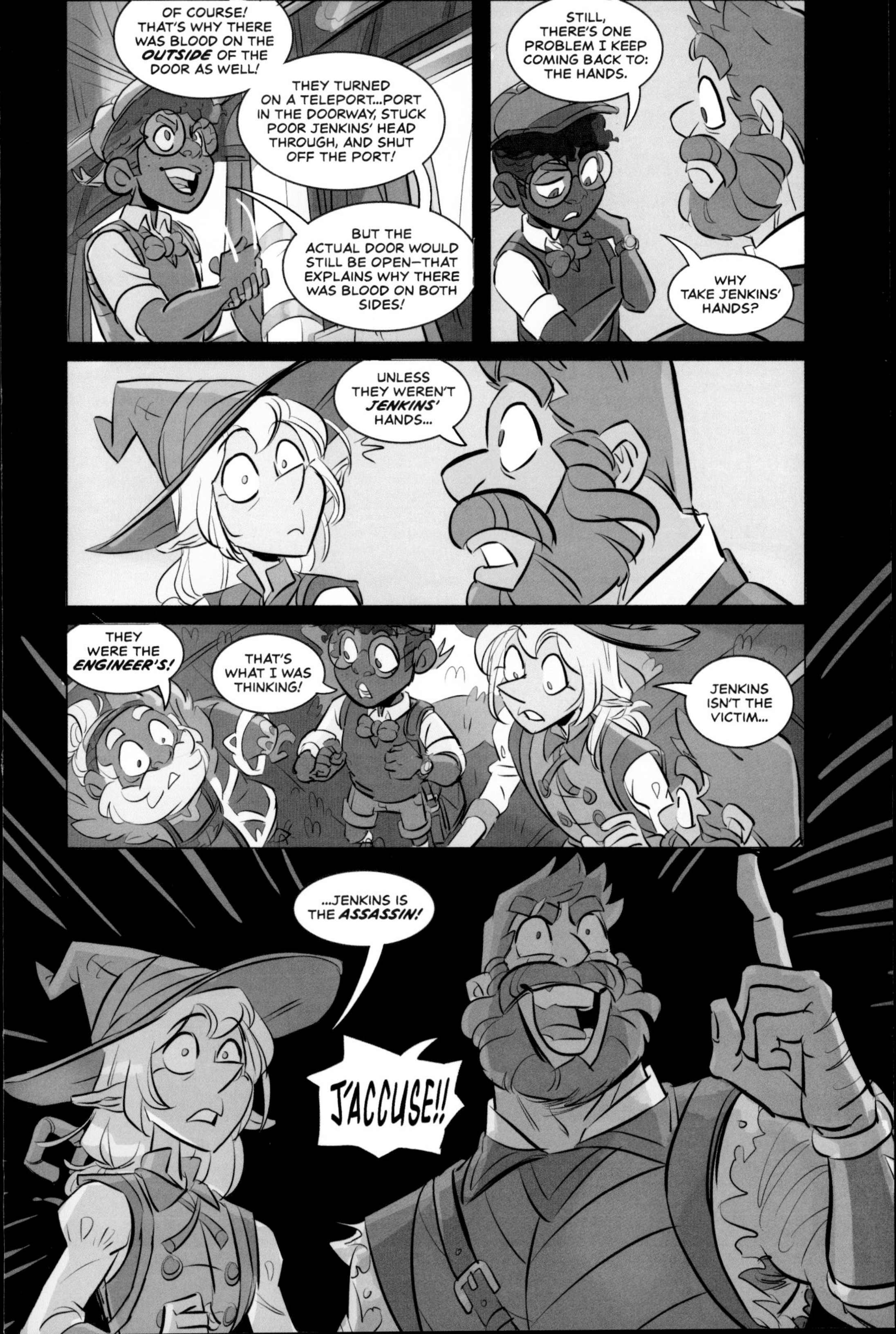
OF COURSE! THAT'S WHY THERE WAS BLOOD ON THE OUTSIDE OF THE DOOR AS WELL!
THEY TURNED ON A TELEPORT...PORT IN THE DOORWAY, STUCK POOR JENKINS' HEAD THROUGH, AND SHUT OFF THE PORT!
BUT THE ACTUAL DOOR WOULD STILL BE OPEN—THAT EXPLAINS WHY THERE WAS BLOOD ON BOTH SIDES!
STILL, THERE'S ONE PROBLEM I KEEP COMING BACK TO: THE HANDS.
WHY TAKE JENKINS' HANDS?
UNLESS THEY WEREN'T JENKINS' HANDS...
THEY WERE THE ENGINEER'S!
THAT'S WHAT I WAS THINKING!
JENKINS ISN'T THE VICTIM...
...JENKINS IS THE ASSASSIN!
J'ACCUSE!!

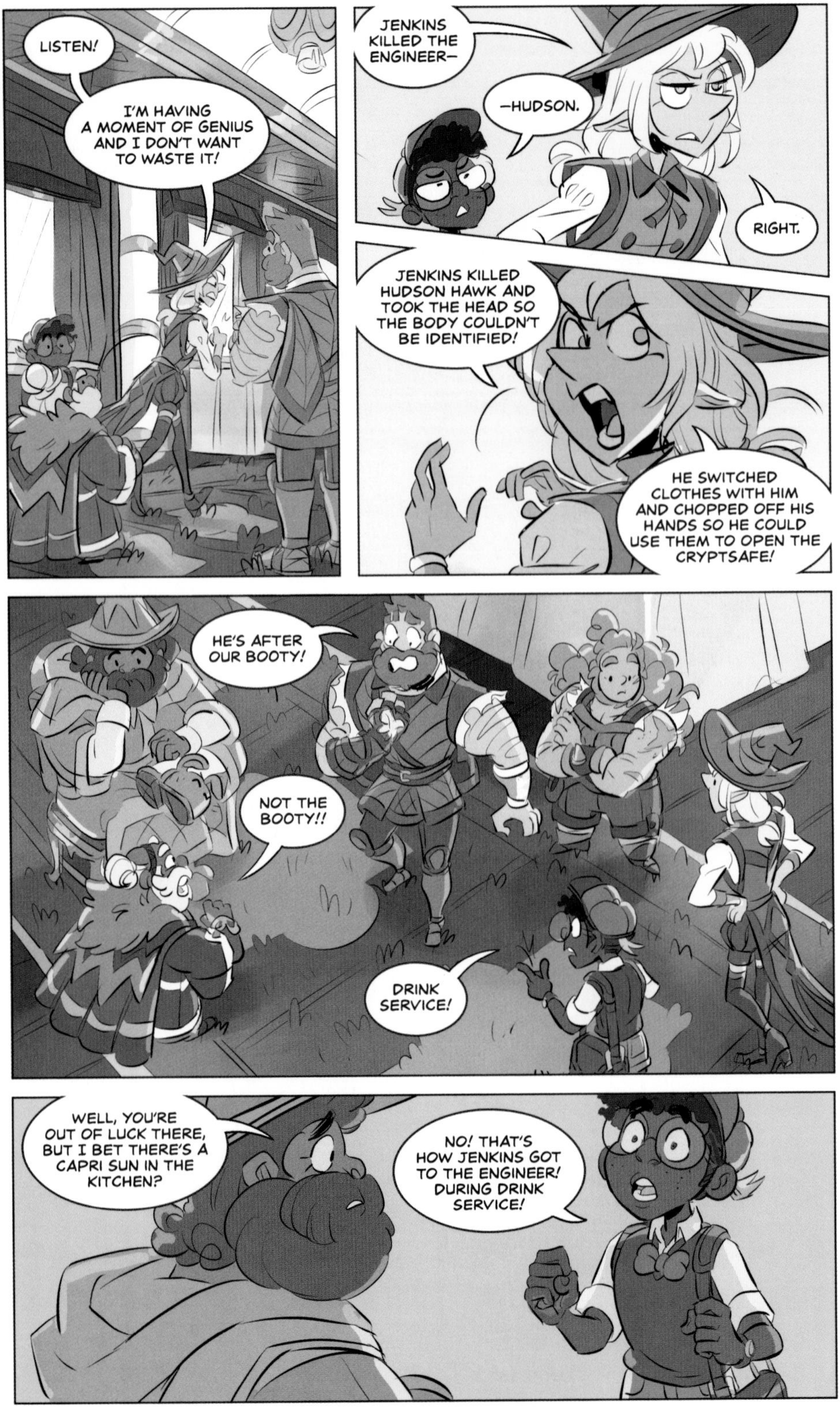
LISTEN!
I'M HAVING A MOMENT OF GENIUS AND I DON'T WANT TO WASTE IT!
JENKINS KILLED THE ENGINEER—
—HUDSON.
RIGHT.
JENKINS KILLED HUDSON HAWK AND TOOK THE HEAD SO THE BODY COULDN'T BE IDENTIFIED!
HE SWITCHED CLOTHES WITH HIM AND CHOPPED OFF HIS HANDS SO HE COULD USE THEM TO OPEN THE CRYPTSAFE!
HE'S AFTER OUR BOOTY!
NOT THE BOOTY!!
DRINK SERVICE!
WELL, YOU'RE OUT OF LUCK THERE, BUT I BET THERE'S A CAPRI SUN IN THE KITCHEN?
NO! THAT'S HOW JENKINS GOT TO THE ENGINEER! DURING DRINK SERVICE!

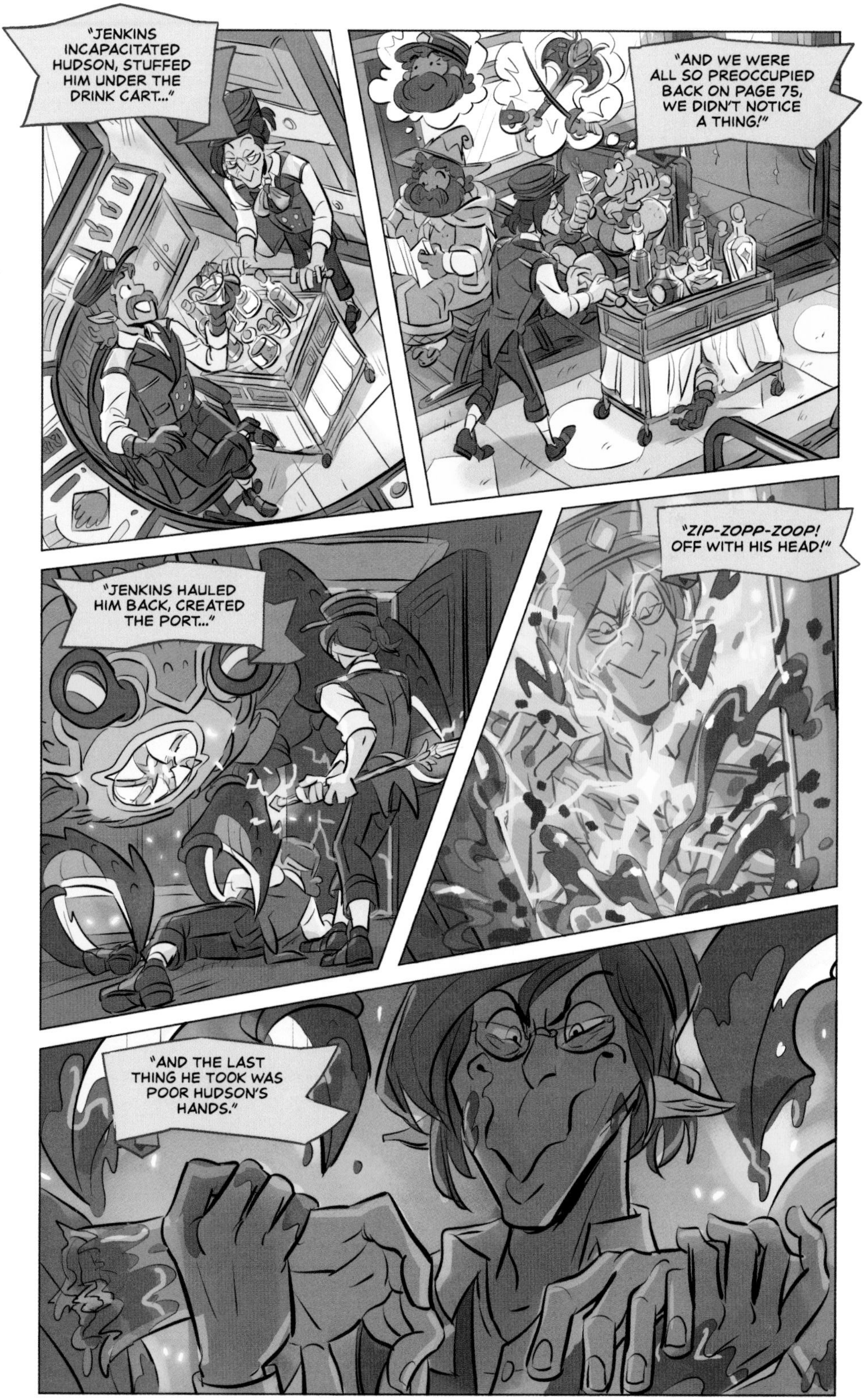
"JENKINS INCAPACITATED HUDSON, STUFFED HIM UNDER THE DRINK CART..."
"AND WE WERE ALL SO PREOCCUPIED BACK ON PAGE 75, WE DIDN'T NOTICE A THING!"
"JENKINS HAULED HIM BACK, CREATED THE PORT..."
"ZIP-ZOPP-ZOOP! OFF WITH HIS HEAD!"
"AND THE LAST THING HE TOOK WAS POOR HUDSON'S HANDS."

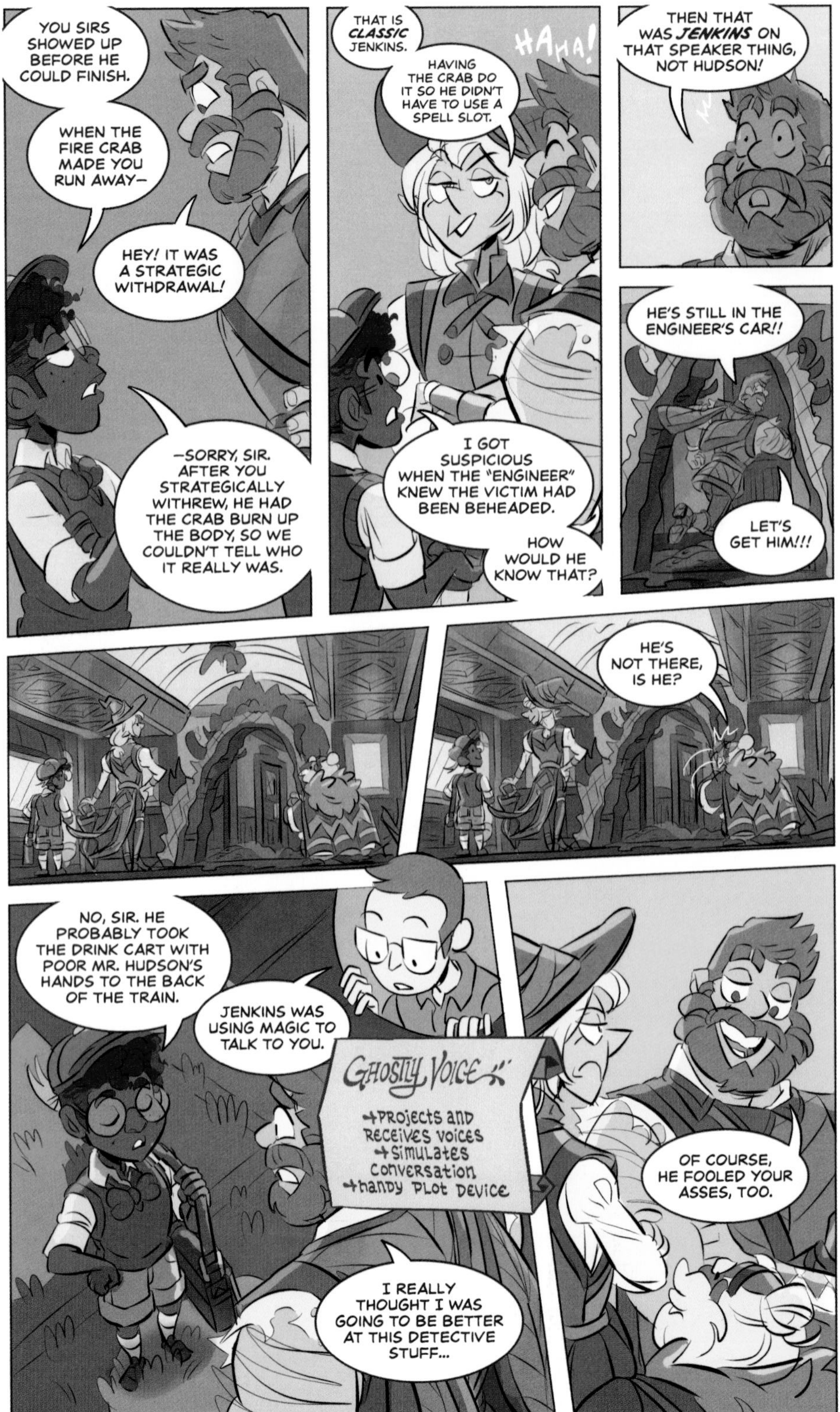
YOU SIRS SHOWED UP BEFORE HE COULD FINISH.
WHEN THE FIRE CRAB MADE YOU RUN AWAY—
HEY! IT WAS A STRATEGIC WITHDRAWAL!
—SORRY, SIR. AFTER YOU STRATEGICALLY WITHREW, HE HAD THE CRAB BURN UP THE BODY, SO WE COULDN'T TELL WHO IT REALLY WAS.
THAT IS CLASSIC JENKINS.
HAHAHA!
HAVING THE CRAB DO IT SO HE DIDN'T HAVE TO USE A SPELL SLOT.
I GOT SUSPICIOUS WHEN THE "ENGINEER" KNEW THE VICTIM HAD BEEN BEHEADED.
HOW WOULD HE KNOW THAT?
THEN THAT WAS JENKINS ON THAT SPEAKER THING, NOT HUDSON!
HE'S STILL IN THE ENGINEER'S CAR!!
LET'S GET HIM!!!
HE'S NOT THERE, IS HE?
NO, SIR. HE PROBABLY TOOK THE DRINK CART WITH POOR MR. HUDSON'S HANDS TO THE BACK OF THE TRAIN.
JENKINS WAS USING MAGIC TO TALK TO YOU.
GHOSTLY VOICE
→Projects and Receives voices
→Simulates Conversation
→handy Plot Device
OF COURSE, HE FOOLED YOUR ASSES, TOO.
I REALLY THOUGHT I WAS GOING TO BE BETTER AT THIS DETECTIVE STUFF...

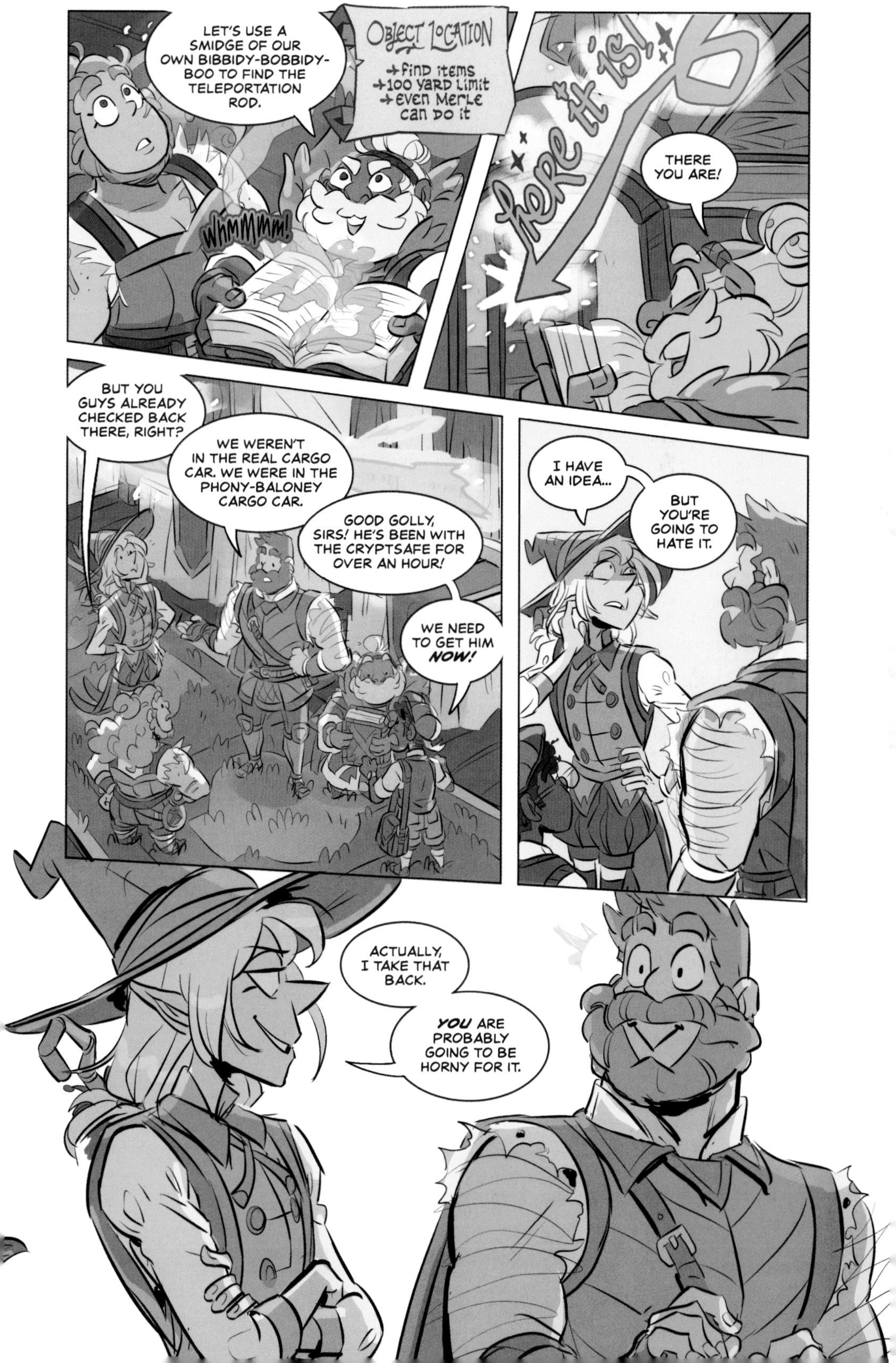
LET'S USE A SMIDGE OF OUR OWN BIBBIDY-BOBBIDY-BOO TO FIND THE TELEPORTATION ROD.
OBJECT LOCATION
→FIND ITEMS
→100 YARD LIMIT
→EVEN MERLE CAN DO IT
WHMMMM!
HERE IT IS!
THERE YOU ARE!
BUT YOU GUYS ALREADY CHECKED BACK THERE, RIGHT?
WE WEREN'T IN THE REAL CARGO CAR. WE WERE IN THE PHONY-BALONEY CARGO CAR.
GOOD GOLLY, SIRS! HE'S BEEN WITH THE CRYPTSAFE FOR OVER AN HOUR!
WE NEED TO GET HIM *NOW!*
I HAVE AN IDEA...
BUT YOU'RE GOING TO HATE IT.
ACTUALLY, I TAKE THAT BACK.
YOU ARE PROBABLY GOING TO BE HORNY FOR IT.

Chapter 6

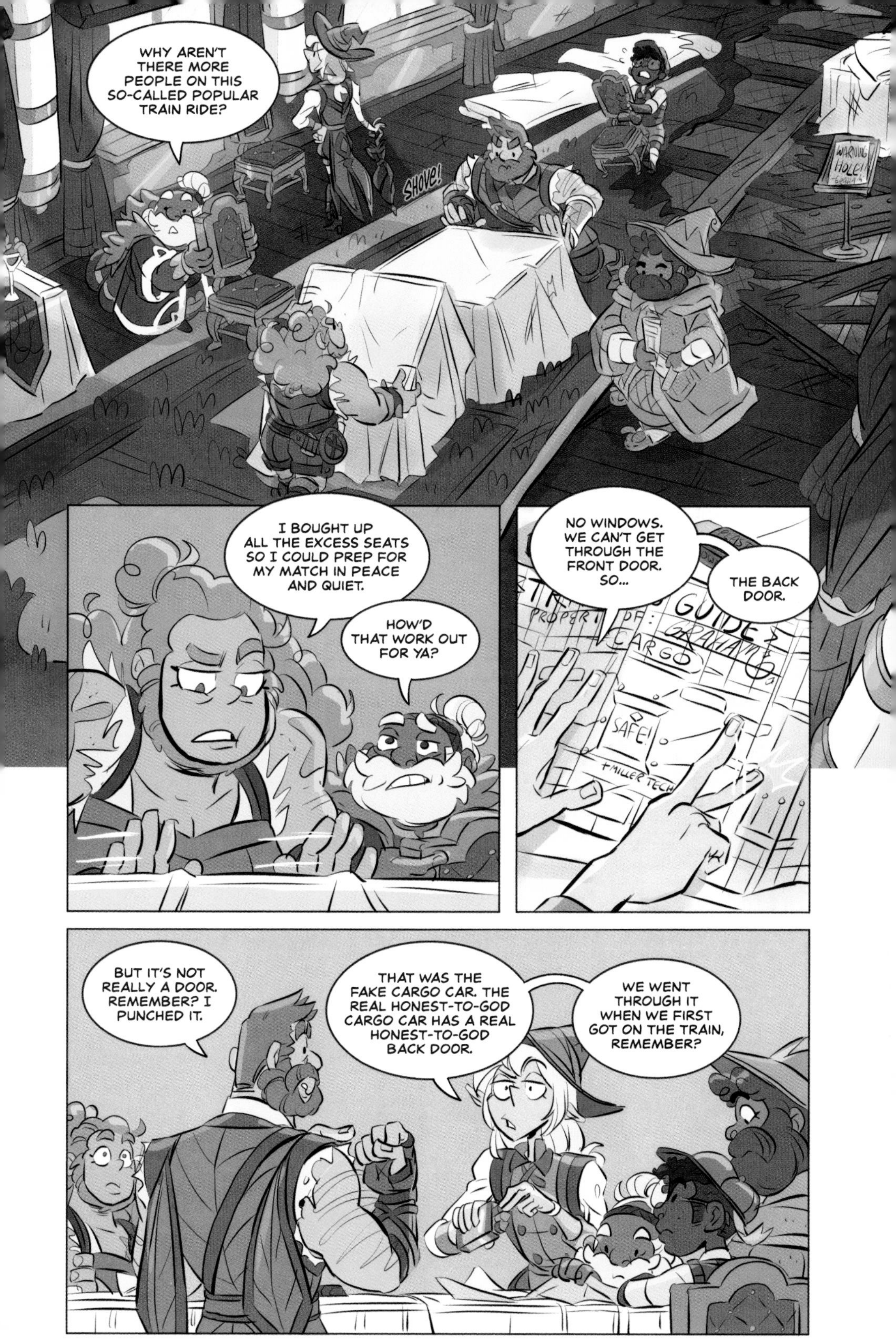
WHY AREN'T THERE MORE PEOPLE ON THIS SO-CALLED POPULAR TRAIN RIDE?
SHOVE!
WARNING HOLE!
I BOUGHT UP ALL THE EXCESS SEATS SO I COULD PREP FOR MY MATCH IN PEACE AND QUIET.
HOW'D THAT WORK OUT FOR YA?
NO WINDOWS. WE CAN'T GET THROUGH THE FRONT DOOR. SO...
THE BACK DOOR.
CARGO
SAFE!
+MILLER TECH
BUT IT'S NOT REALLY A DOOR. REMEMBER? I PUNCHED IT.
THAT WAS THE FAKE CARGO CAR. THE REAL HONEST-TO-GOD CARGO CAR HAS A REAL HONEST-TO-GOD BACK DOOR.
WE WENT THROUGH IT WHEN WE FIRST GOT ON THE TRAIN, REMEMBER?

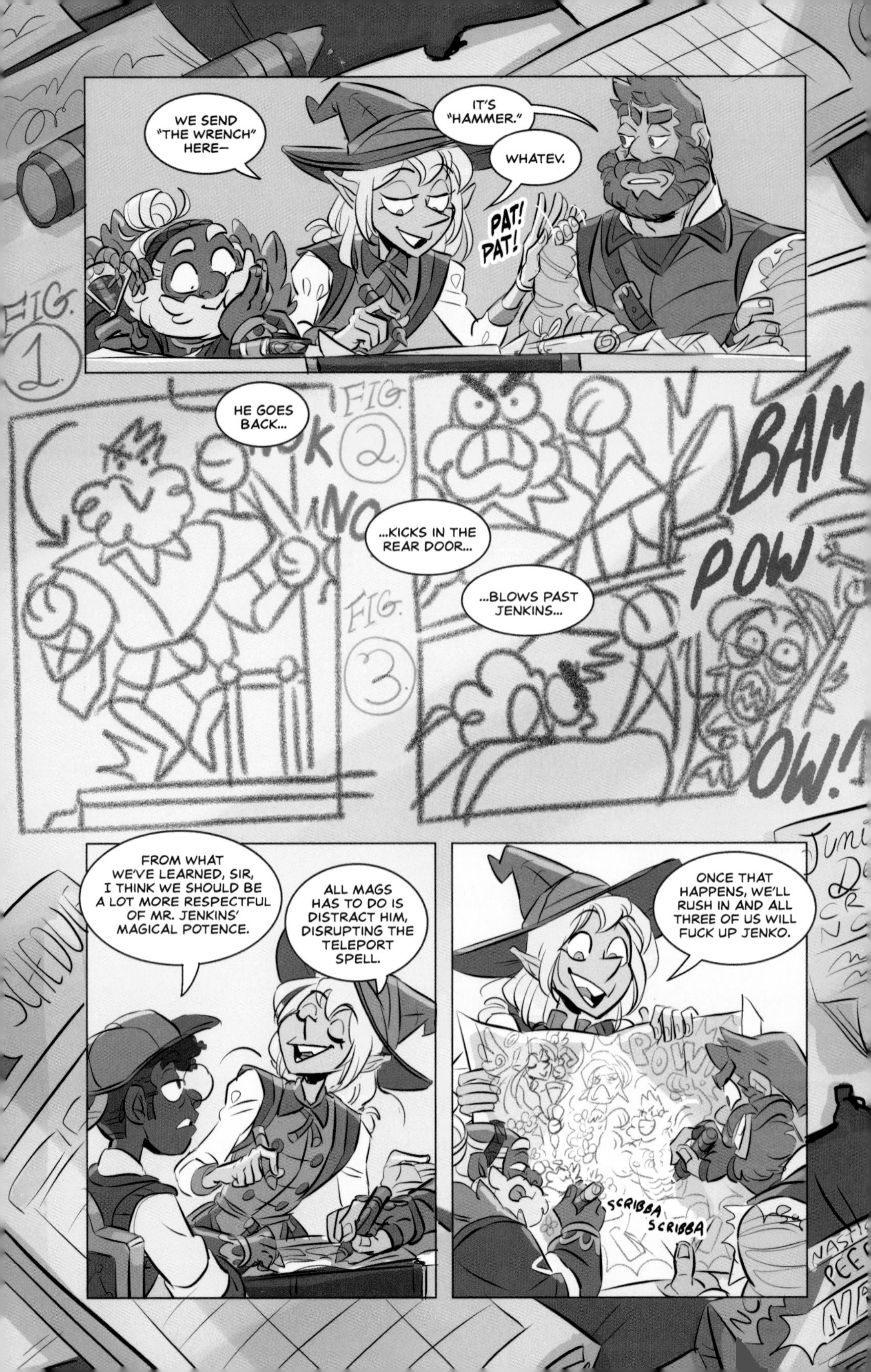

WE SEND "THE WRENCH" HERE—
IT'S "HAMMER."
WHATEV.
PAT! PAT!
FIG. 1
HE GOES BACK...
FIG. 2
NO
...KICKS IN THE REAR DOOR...
BAM
POW
...BLOWS PAST JENKINS...
FIG. 3
OW!
FROM WHAT WE'VE LEARNED, SIR, I THINK WE SHOULD BE A LOT MORE RESPECTFUL OF MR. JENKINS' MAGICAL POTENCE.
ALL MAGS HAS TO DO IS DISTRACT HIM, DISRUPTING THE TELEPORT SPELL.
ONCE THAT HAPPENS, WE'LL RUSH IN AND ALL THREE OF US WILL FUCK UP JENKO.
SCRIBBA SCRIBBA

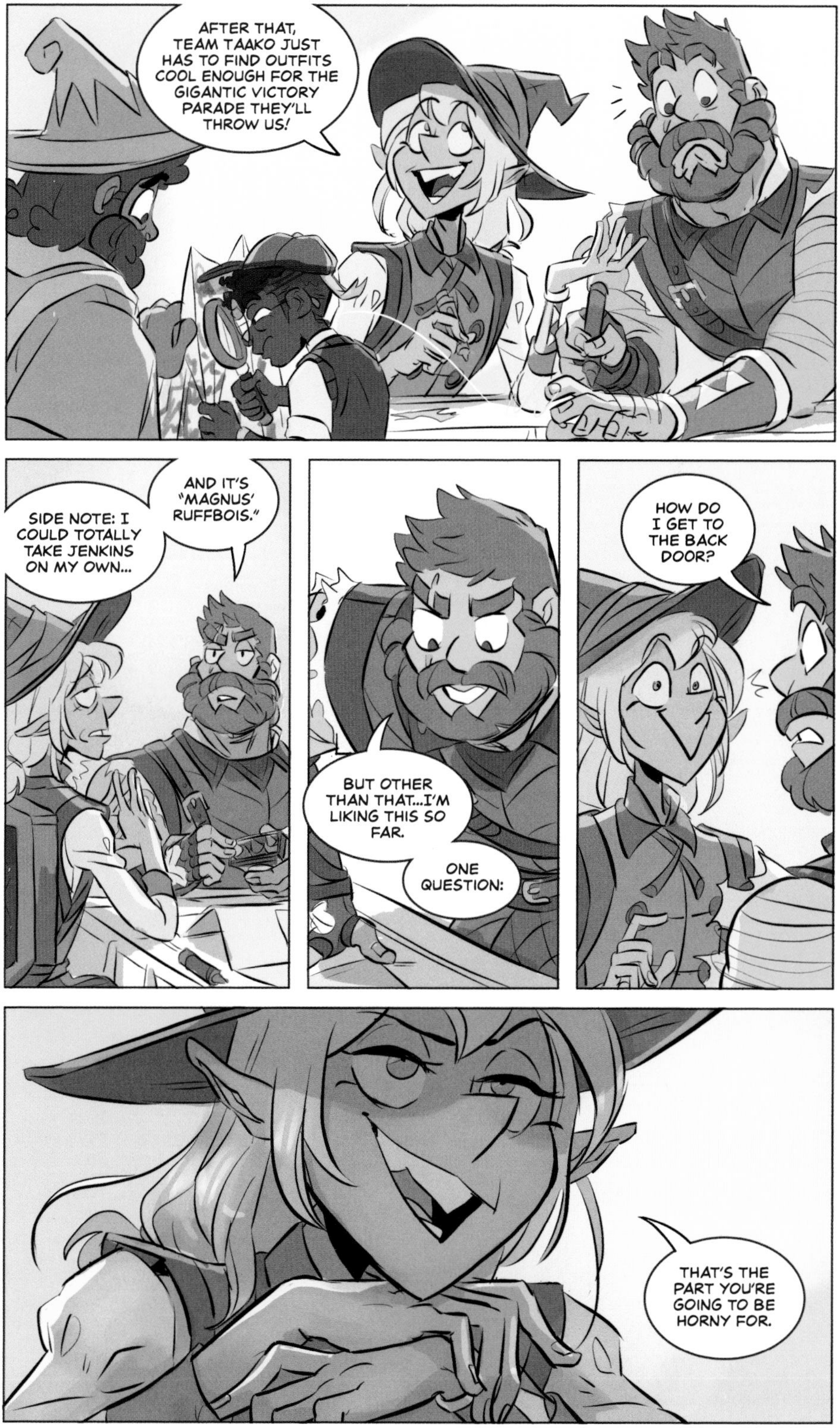
AFTER THAT, TEAM TAAKO JUST HAS TO FIND OUTFITS COOL ENOUGH FOR THE GIGANTIC VICTORY PARADE THEY'LL THROW US!
SIDE NOTE: I COULD TOTALLY TAKE JENKINS ON MY OWN...
AND IT'S "MAGNUS' RUFFBOIS."
BUT OTHER THAN THAT...I'M LIKING THIS SO FAR.
ONE QUESTION:
HOW DO I GET TO THE BACK DOOR?
THAT'S THE PART YOU'RE GOING TO BE HORNY FOR.

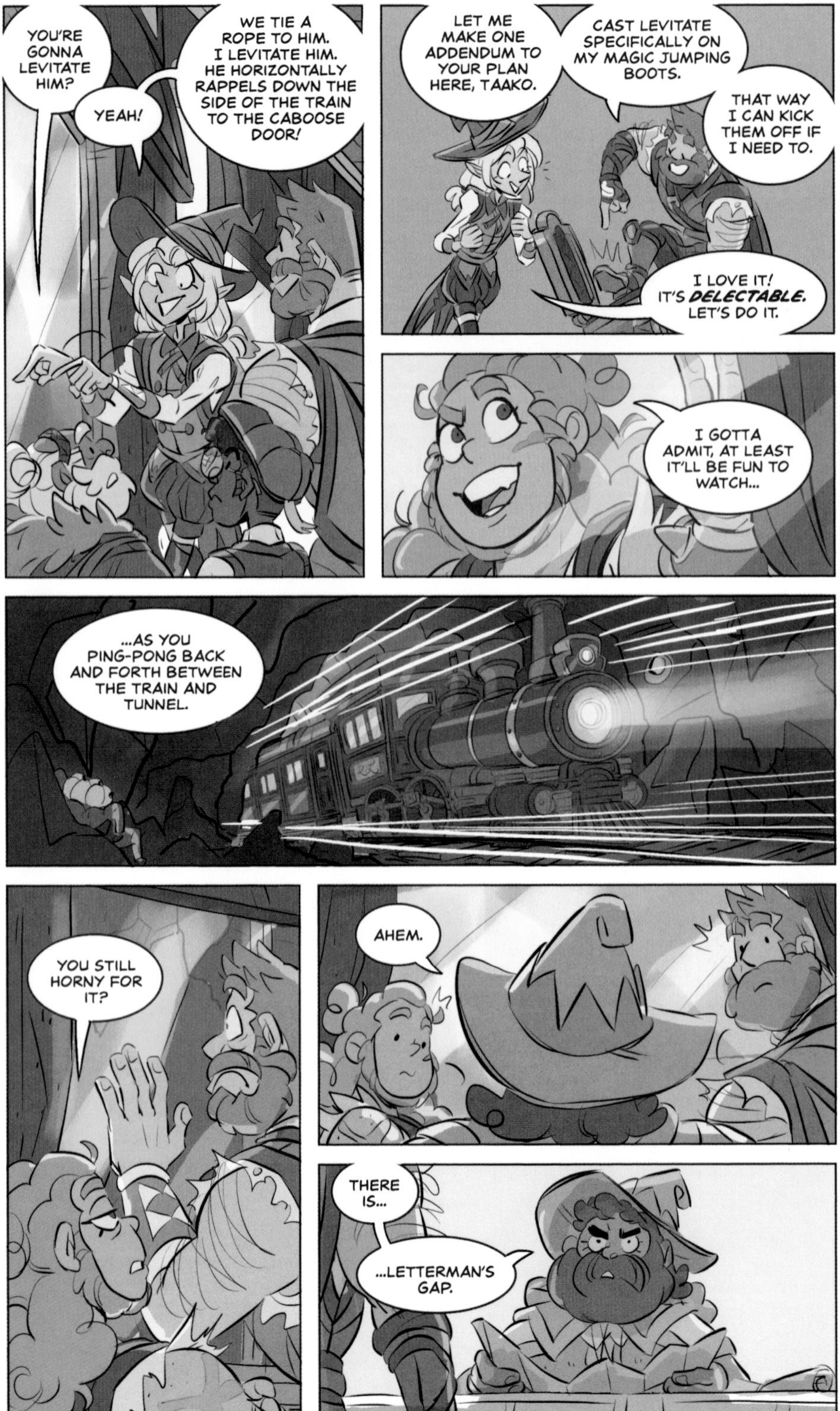
YOU'RE GONNA LEVITATE HIM?
WE TIE A ROPE TO HIM. I LEVITATE HIM. HE HORIZONTALLY RAPPELS DOWN THE SIDE OF THE TRAIN TO THE CABOOSE DOOR!
YEAH!
LET ME MAKE ONE ADDENDUM TO YOUR PLAN HERE, TAAKO.
CAST LEVITATE SPECIFICALLY ON MY MAGIC JUMPING BOOTS.
THAT WAY I CAN KICK THEM OFF IF I NEED TO.
I LOVE IT! IT'S DELECTABLE. LET'S DO IT.
I GOTTA ADMIT, AT LEAST IT'LL BE FUN TO WATCH...
...AS YOU PING-PONG BACK AND FORTH BETWEEN THE TRAIN AND TUNNEL.
YOU STILL HORNY FOR IT?
AHEM.
THERE IS...
...LETTERMAN'S GAP.

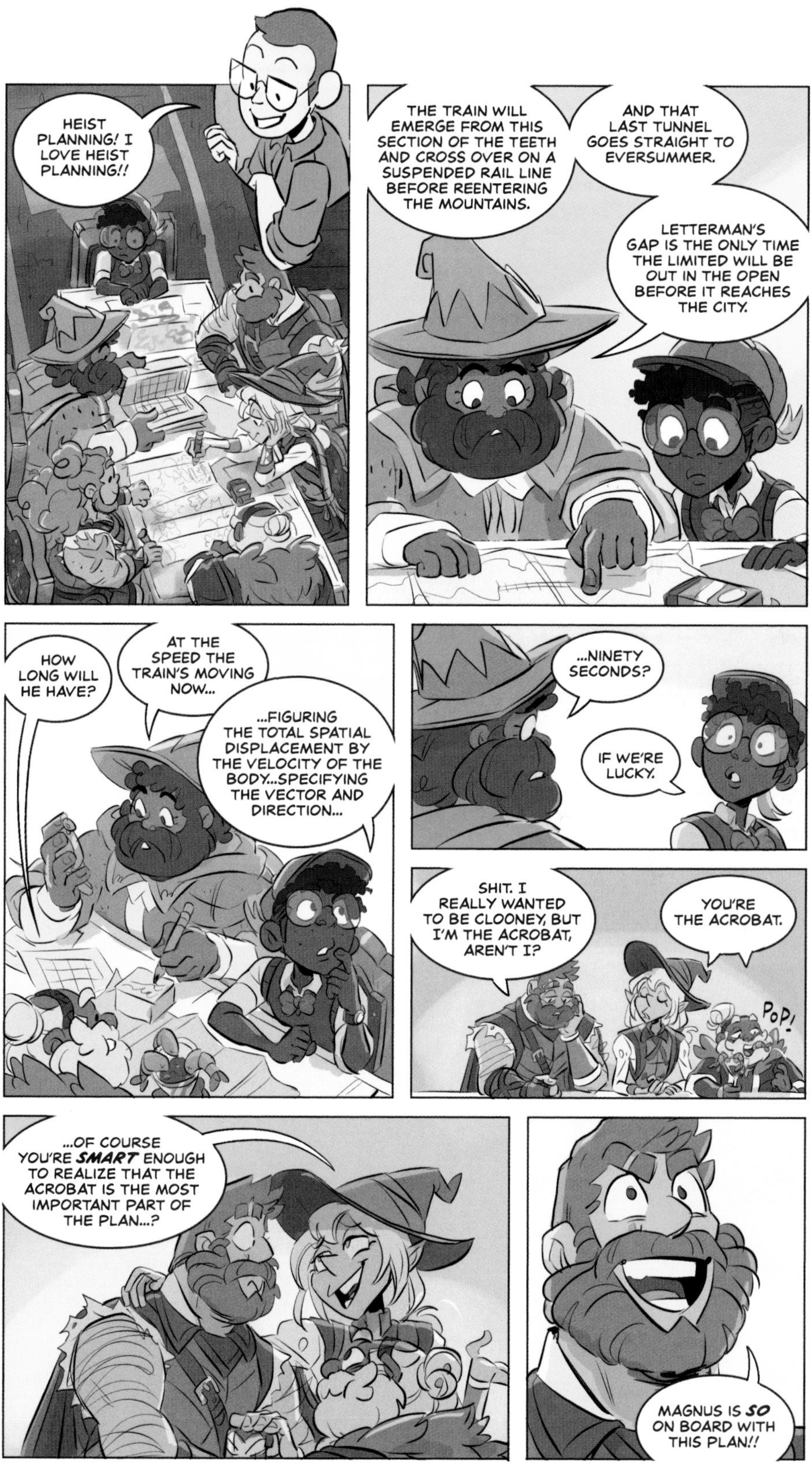
HEIST PLANNING! I LOVE HEIST PLANNING!!
THE TRAIN WILL EMERGE FROM THIS SECTION OF THE TEETH AND CROSS OVER ON A SUSPENDED RAIL LINE BEFORE REENTERING THE MOUNTAINS.
AND THAT LAST TUNNEL GOES STRAIGHT TO EVERSUMMER.
LETTERMAN'S GAP IS THE ONLY TIME THE LIMITED WILL BE OUT IN THE OPEN BEFORE IT REACHES THE CITY.
HOW LONG WILL HE HAVE?
AT THE SPEED THE TRAIN'S MOVING NOW...
...FIGURING THE TOTAL SPATIAL DISPLACEMENT BY THE VELOCITY OF THE BODY...SPECIFYING THE VECTOR AND DIRECTION...
...NINETY SECONDS?
IF WE'RE LUCKY.
SHIT. I REALLY WANTED TO BE CLOONEY, BUT I'M THE ACROBAT, AREN'T I?
YOU'RE THE ACROBAT.
POP!
...OF COURSE YOU'RE SMART ENOUGH TO REALIZE THAT THE ACROBAT IS THE MOST IMPORTANT PART OF THE PLAN...?
MAGNUS IS SO ON BOARD WITH THIS PLAN!!

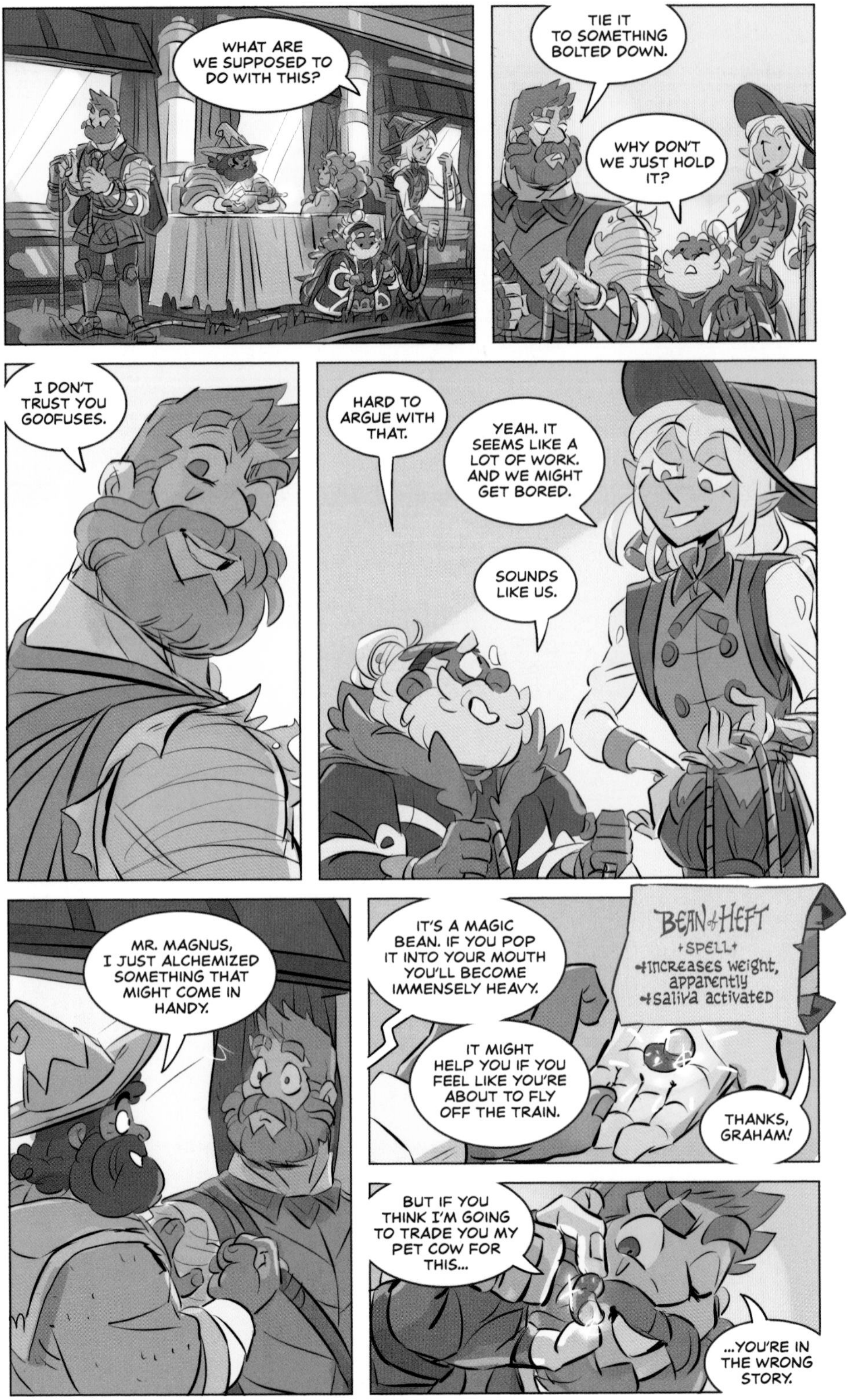
WHAT ARE WE SUPPOSED TO DO WITH THIS?
TIE IT TO SOMETHING BOLTED DOWN.
WHY DON'T WE JUST HOLD IT?
I DON'T TRUST YOU GOOFUSES.
HARD TO ARGUE WITH THAT.
YEAH. IT SEEMS LIKE A LOT OF WORK. AND WE MIGHT GET BORED.
SOUNDS LIKE US.
MR. MAGNUS, I JUST ALCHEMIZED SOMETHING THAT MIGHT COME IN HANDY.
IT'S A MAGIC BEAN. IF YOU POP IT INTO YOUR MOUTH YOU'LL BECOME IMMENSELY HEAVY.
BEAN of HEFT
+SPELL+
+increases weight, apparently
+saliva activated
IT MIGHT HELP YOU IF YOU FEEL LIKE YOU'RE ABOUT TO FLY OFF THE TRAIN.
THANKS, GRAHAM!
BUT IF YOU THINK I'M GOING TO TRADE YOU MY PET COW FOR THIS...
...YOU'RE IN THE WRONG STORY.

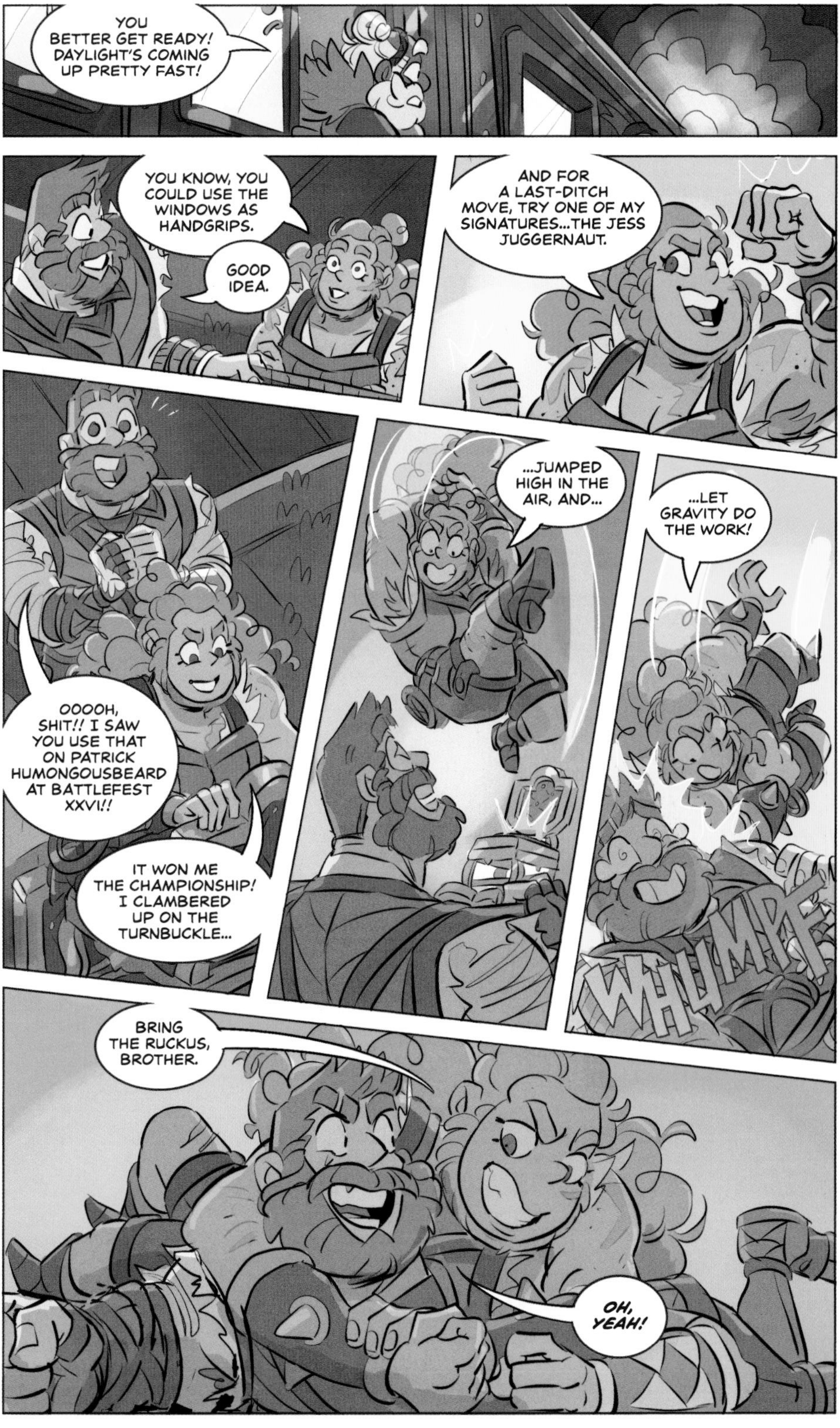
YOU BETTER GET READY! DAYLIGHT'S COMING UP PRETTY FAST!
YOU KNOW, YOU COULD USE THE WINDOWS AS HANDGRIPS.
GOOD IDEA.
AND FOR A LAST-DITCH MOVE, TRY ONE OF MY SIGNATURES...THE JESS JUGGERNAUT.
OOOOH, SHIT!! I SAW YOU USE THAT ON PATRICK HUMONGOUSBEARD AT BATTLEFEST XXVI!!
IT WON ME THE CHAMPIONSHIP! I CLAMBERED UP ON THE TURNBUCKLE...
...JUMPED HIGH IN THE AIR, AND...
...LET GRAVITY DO THE WORK!
WHUMPF
BRING THE RUCKUS, BROTHER.
OH, YEAH!

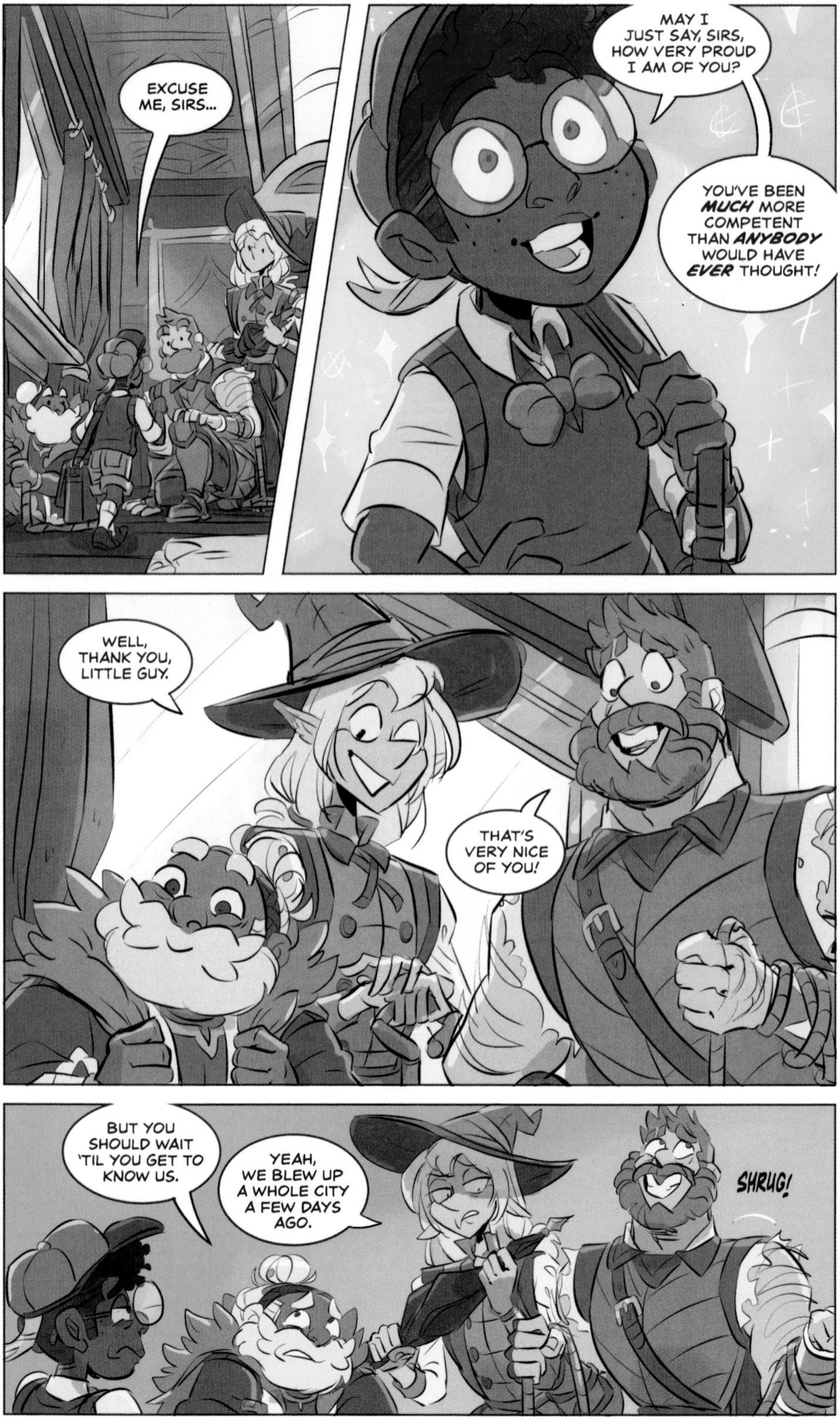
EXCUSE ME, SIRS...
MAY I JUST SAY, SIRS, HOW VERY PROUD I AM OF YOU?
YOU'VE BEEN MUCH MORE COMPETENT THAN ANYBODY WOULD HAVE EVER THOUGHT!
WELL, THANK YOU, LITTLE GUY.
THAT'S VERY NICE OF YOU!
BUT YOU SHOULD WAIT 'TIL YOU GET TO KNOW US.
YEAH, WE BLEW UP A WHOLE CITY A FEW DAYS AGO.
SHRUG!

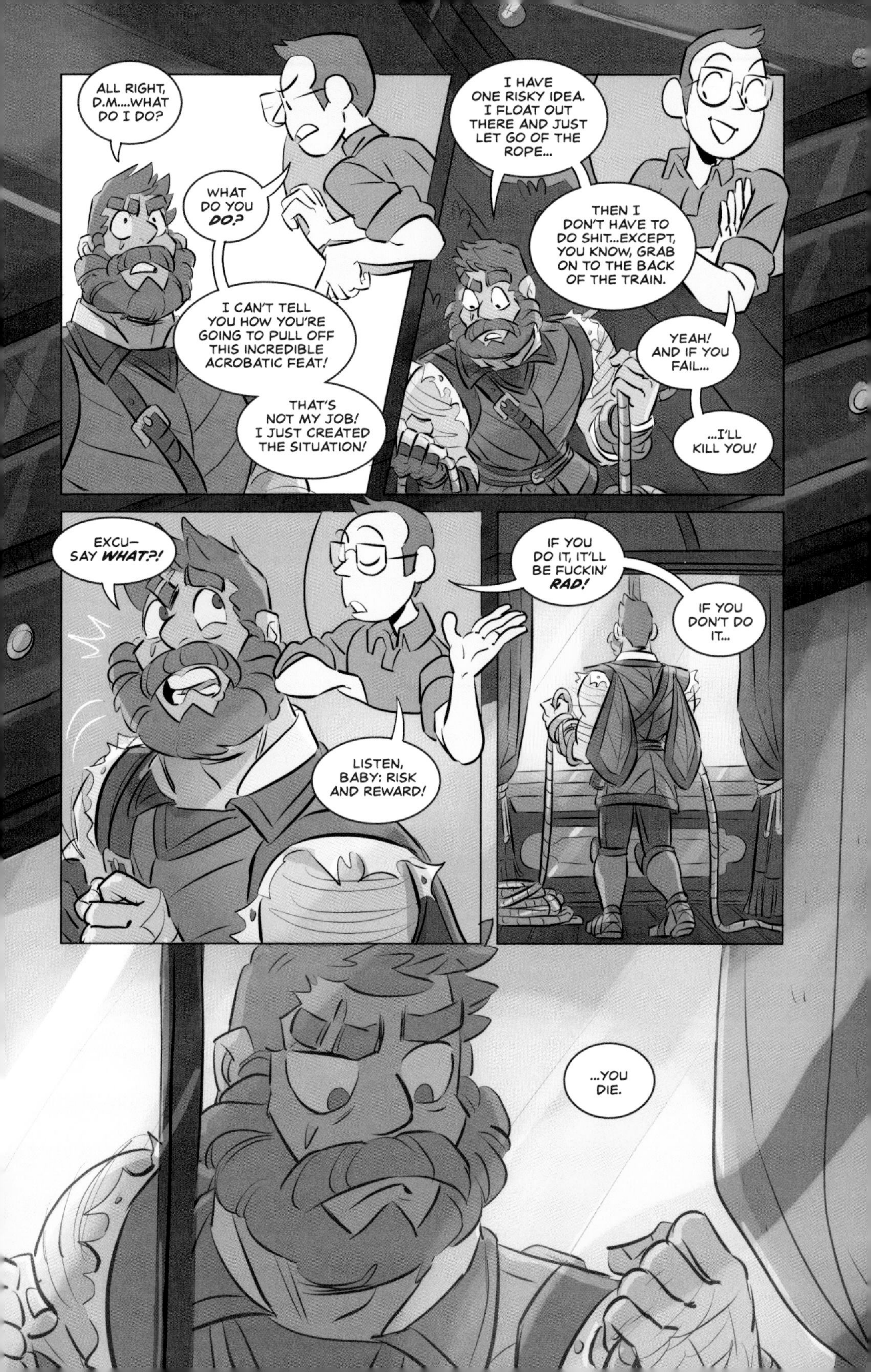
ALL RIGHT, D.M....WHAT DO I DO?
WHAT DO YOU *DO?*
I CAN'T TELL YOU HOW YOU'RE GOING TO PULL OFF THIS INCREDIBLE ACROBATIC FEAT!
THAT'S NOT MY JOB! I JUST CREATED THE SITUATION!
I HAVE ONE RISKY IDEA. I FLOAT OUT THERE AND JUST LET GO OF THE ROPE...
THEN I DON'T HAVE TO DO SHIT...EXCEPT, YOU KNOW, GRAB ON TO THE BACK OF THE TRAIN.
YEAH! AND IF YOU FAIL...
...I'LL KILL YOU!
EXCU— SAY ***WHAT?!***
LISTEN, BABY: RISK AND REWARD!
IF YOU DO IT, IT'LL BE FUCKIN' ***RAD!***
IF YOU DON'T DO IT...
...YOU DIE.

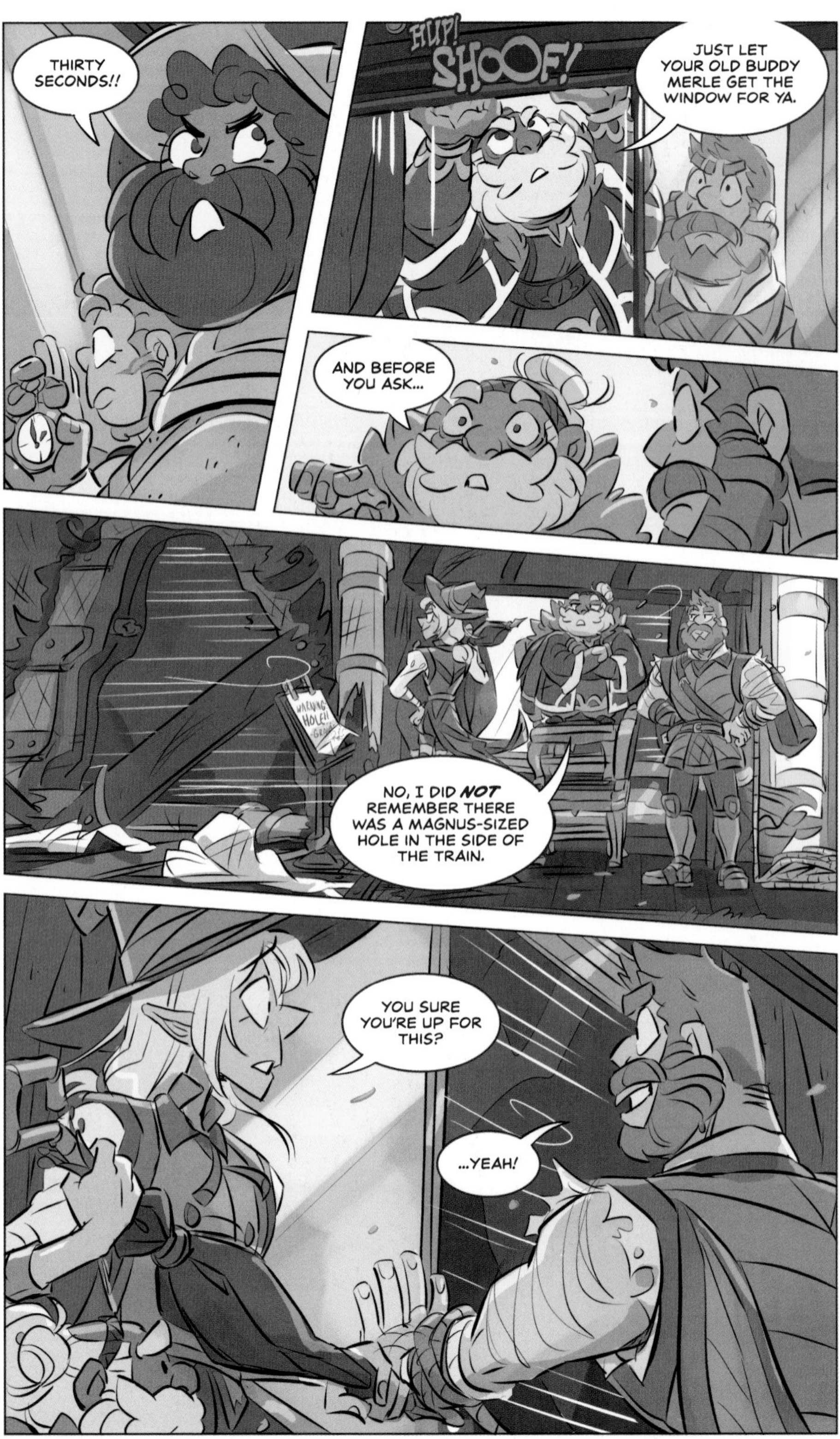
THIRTY SECONDS!!
HUP!
SHOOF!
JUST LET YOUR OLD BUDDY MERLE GET THE WINDOW FOR YA.
AND BEFORE YOU ASK...
NO, I DID NOT REMEMBER THERE WAS A MAGNUS-SIZED HOLE IN THE SIDE OF THE TRAIN.
YOU SURE YOU'RE UP FOR THIS?
...YEAH!

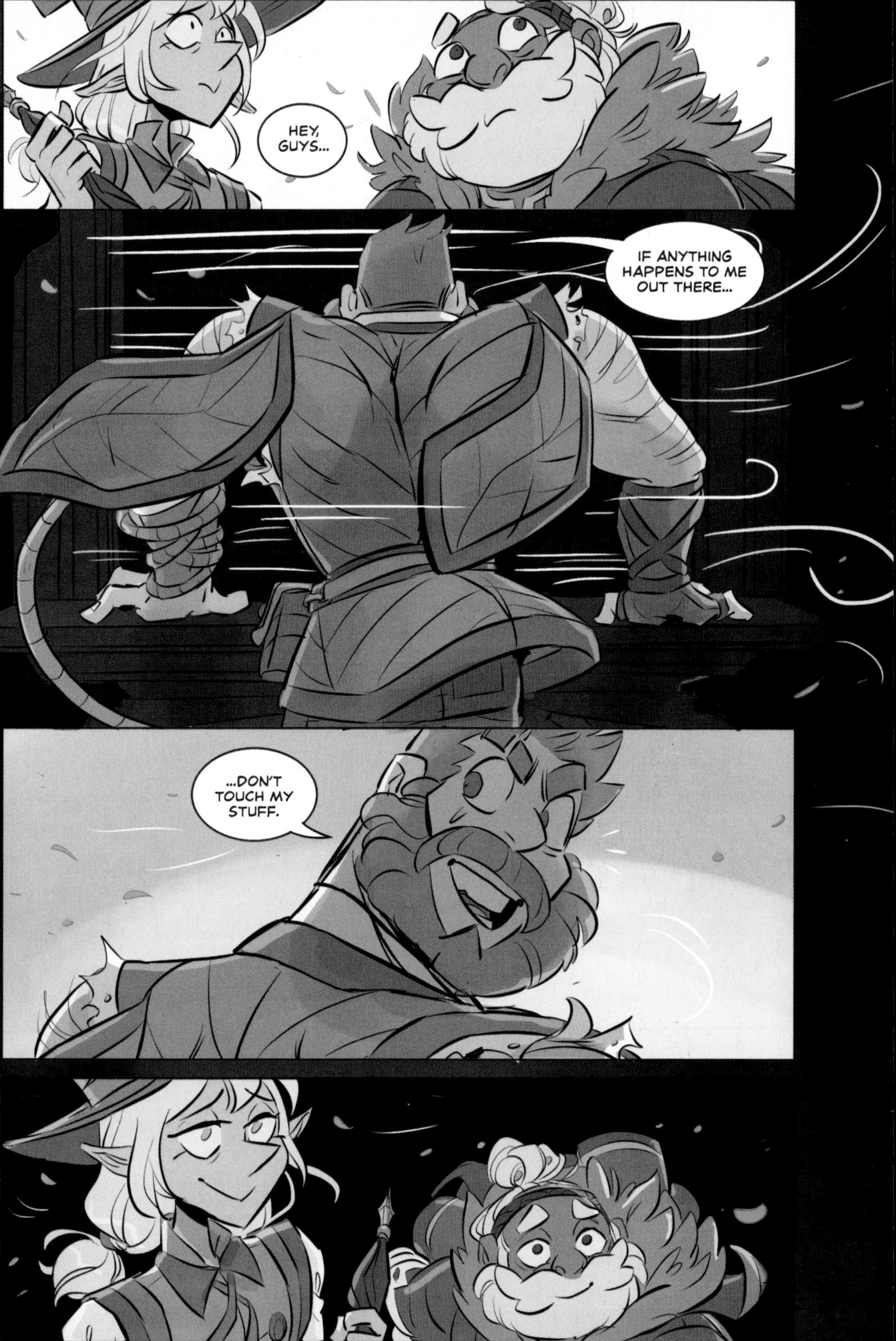
HEY, GUYS...
IF ANYTHING HAPPENS TO ME OUT THERE...
...DON'T TOUCH MY STUFF.

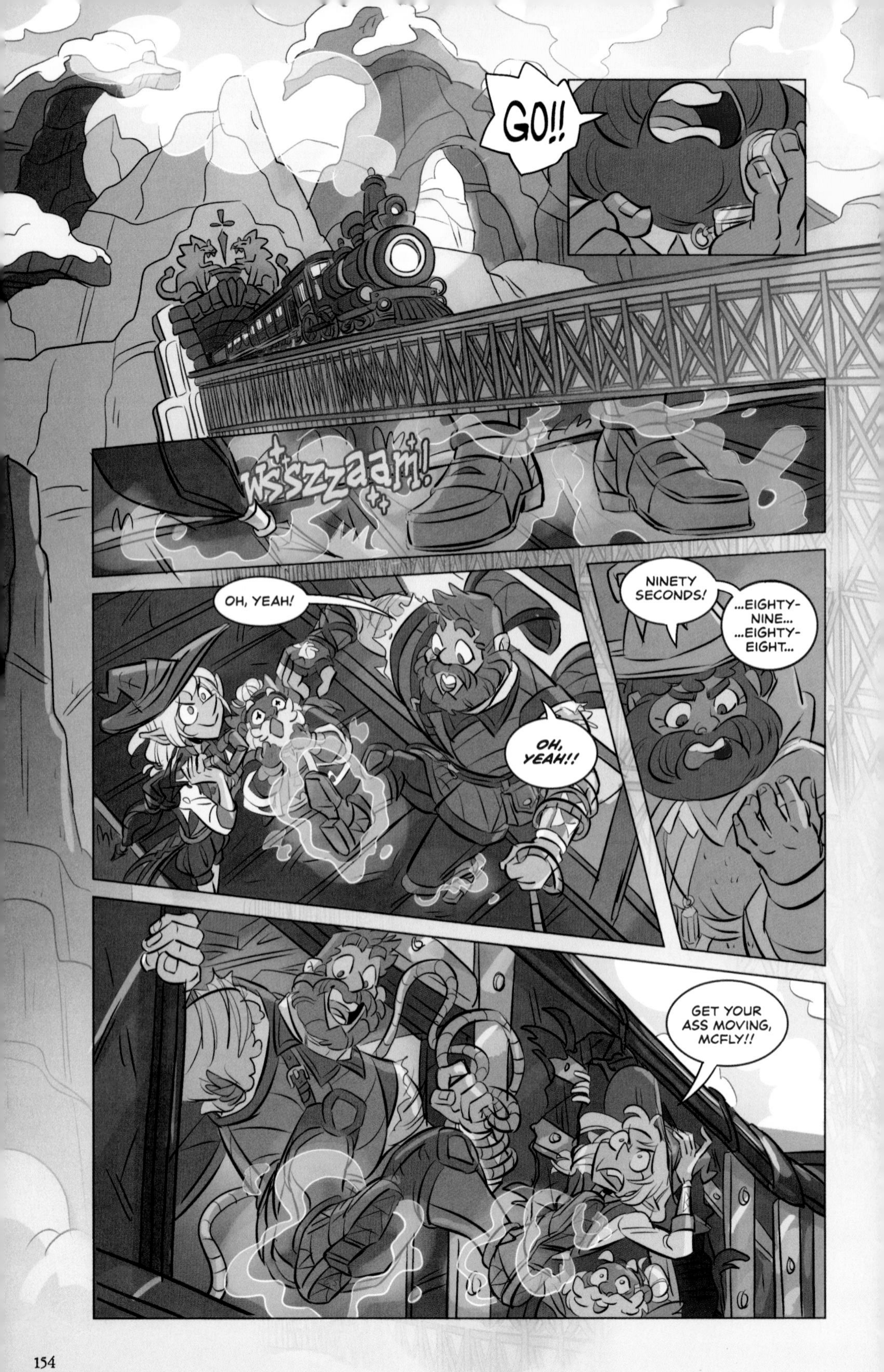
GO!!
WSSZZAAM!
OH, YEAH!
OH, YEAH!!
NINETY SECONDS!
...EIGHTY-NINE...
...EIGHTY-EIGHT...
GET YOUR ASS MOVING, MCFLY!!

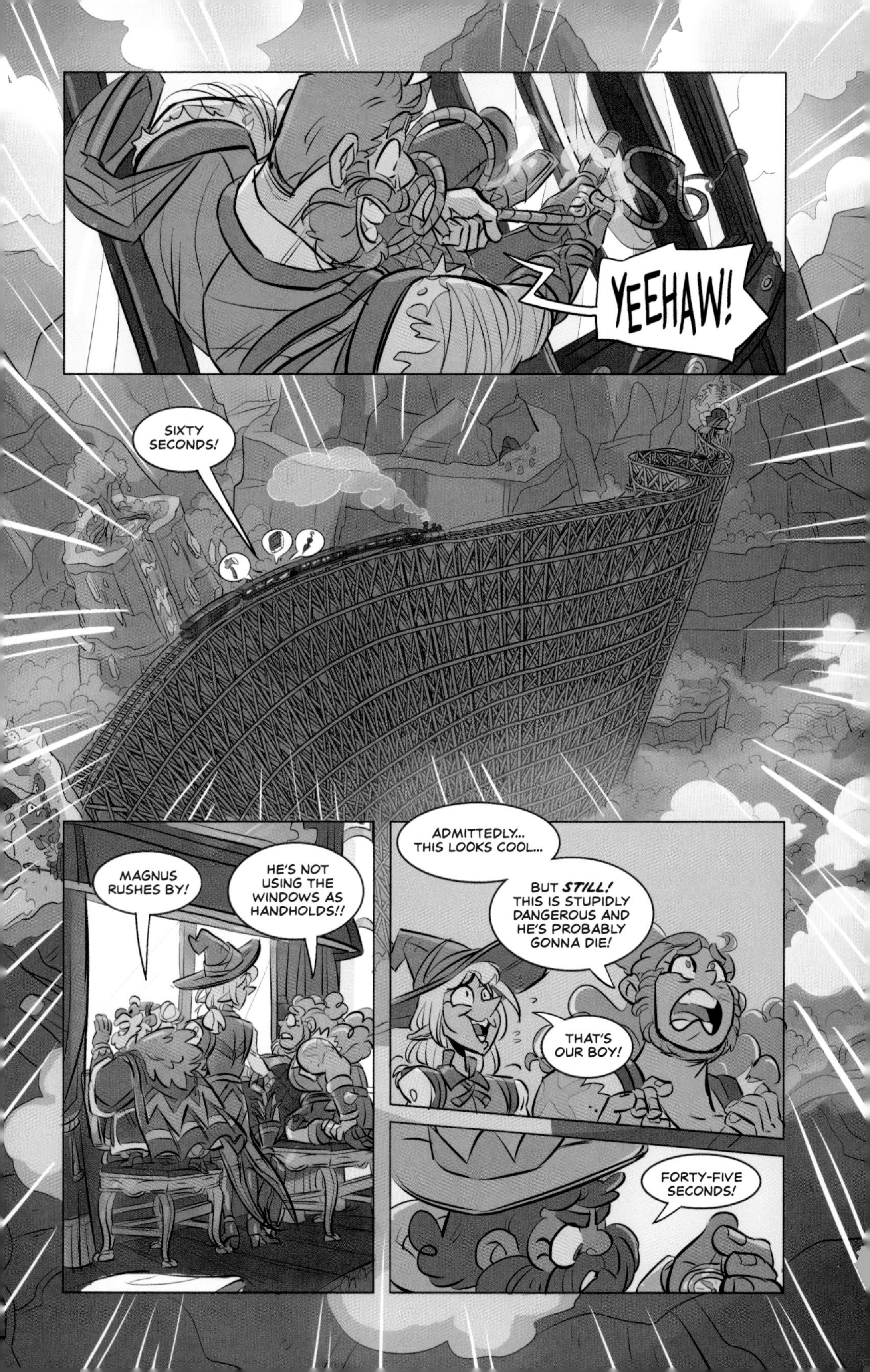
YEEHAW!
SIXTY SECONDS!
MAGNUS RUSHES BY!
HE'S NOT USING THE WINDOWS AS HANDHOLDS!!
ADMITTEDLY... THIS LOOKS COOL...
BUT *STILL!* THIS IS STUPIDLY DANGEROUS AND HE'S PROBABLY GONNA DIE!
THAT'S OUR BOY!
FORTY-FIVE SECONDS!

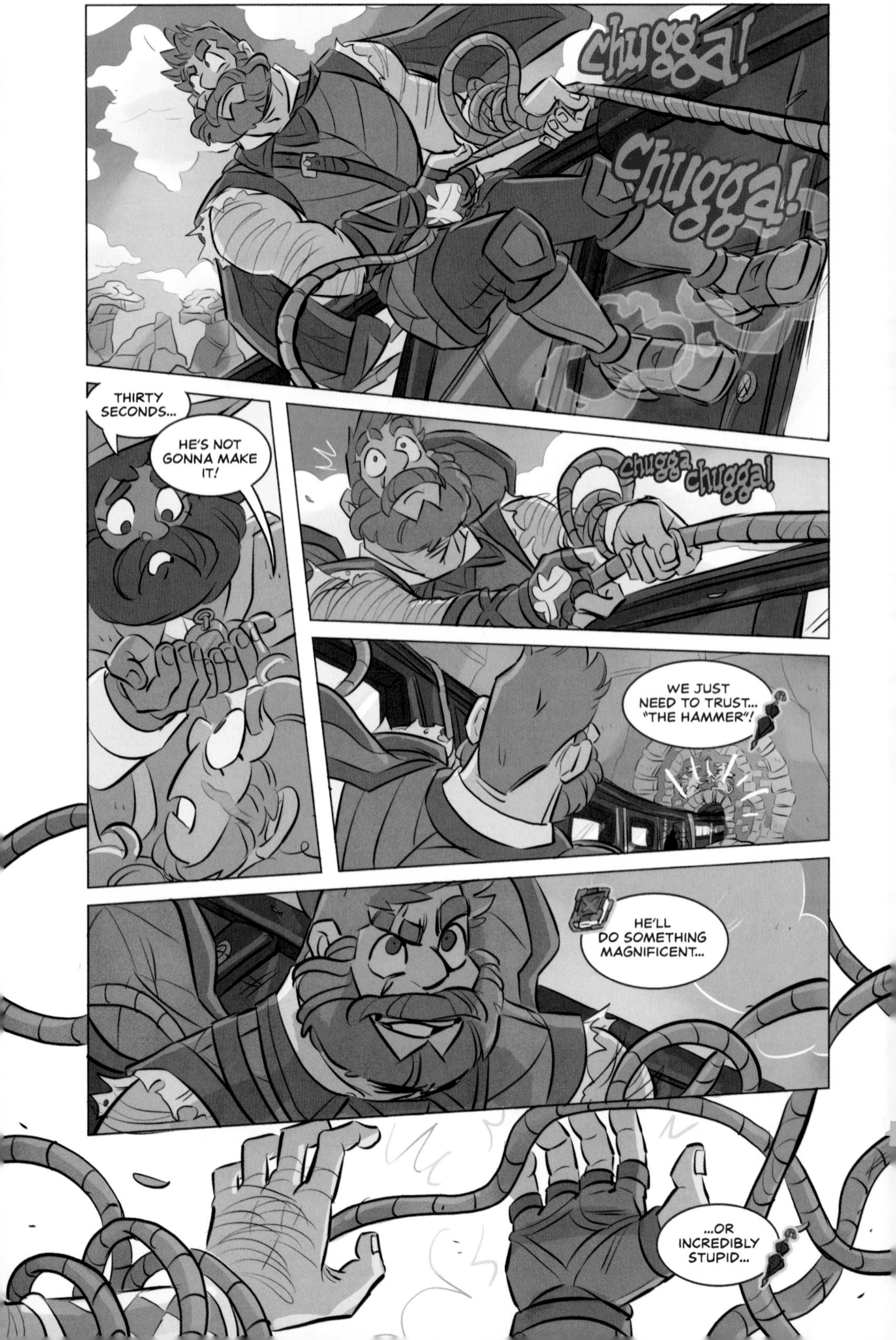
Chugga!
Chugga!
THIRTY SECONDS...
HE'S NOT GONNA MAKE IT!
Chugga chugga!
WE JUST NEED TO TRUST... "THE HAMMER"!
HE'LL DO SOMETHING MAGNIFICENT...
...OR INCREDIBLY STUPID...

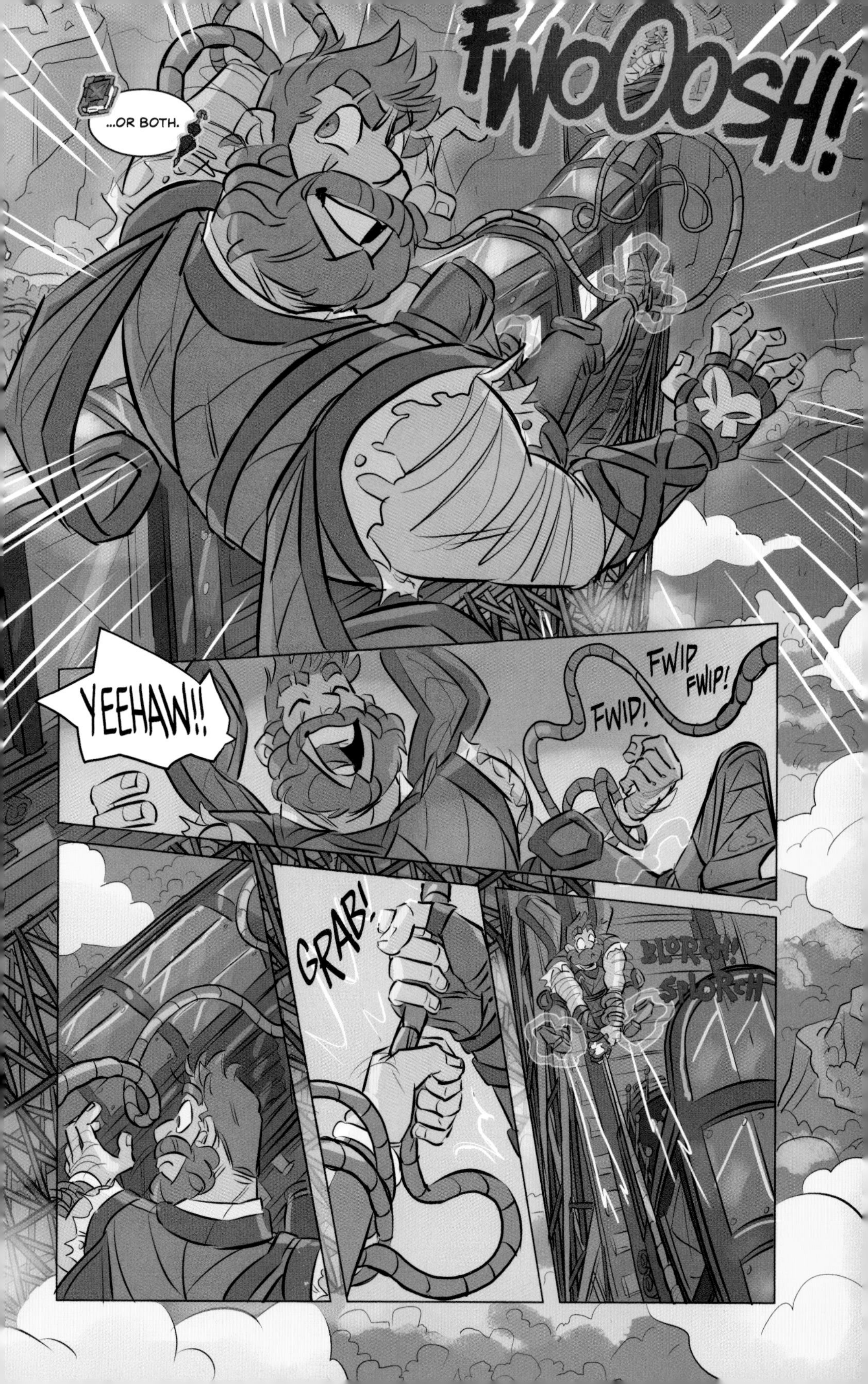
...OR BOTH.
FWOOOSH!
YEEHAW!!
FWIP
FWIP!
FWIP!
GRAB!
BLORCH!
SPLORCH

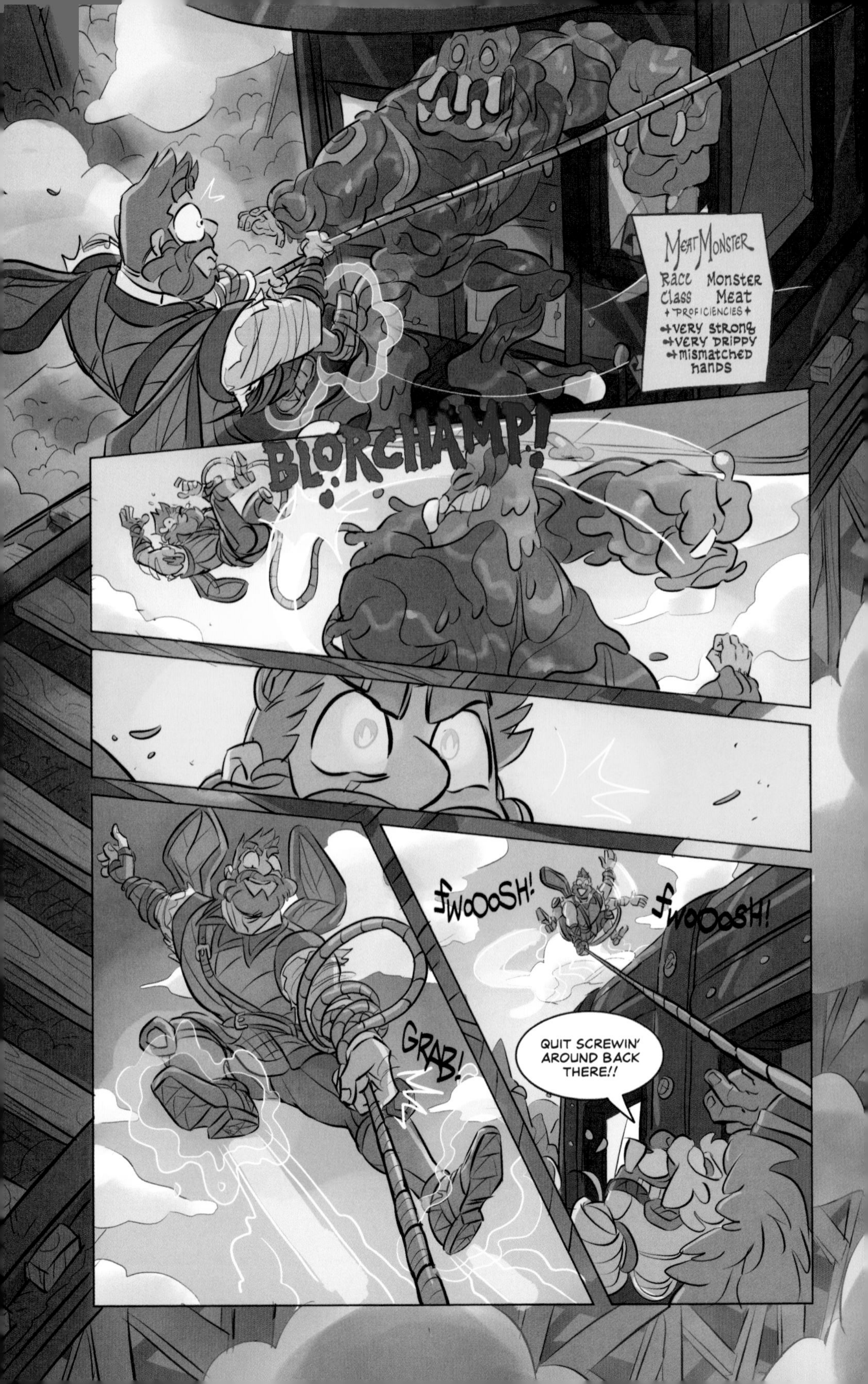
MEAT MONSTER
Race Monster
Class Meat
PROFICIENCIES
very strong
very drippy
mismatched hands
BLORCHAMP!
FWOOOSH!
FWOOOSH!
GRAB!
QUIT SCREWIN' AROUND BACK THERE!!

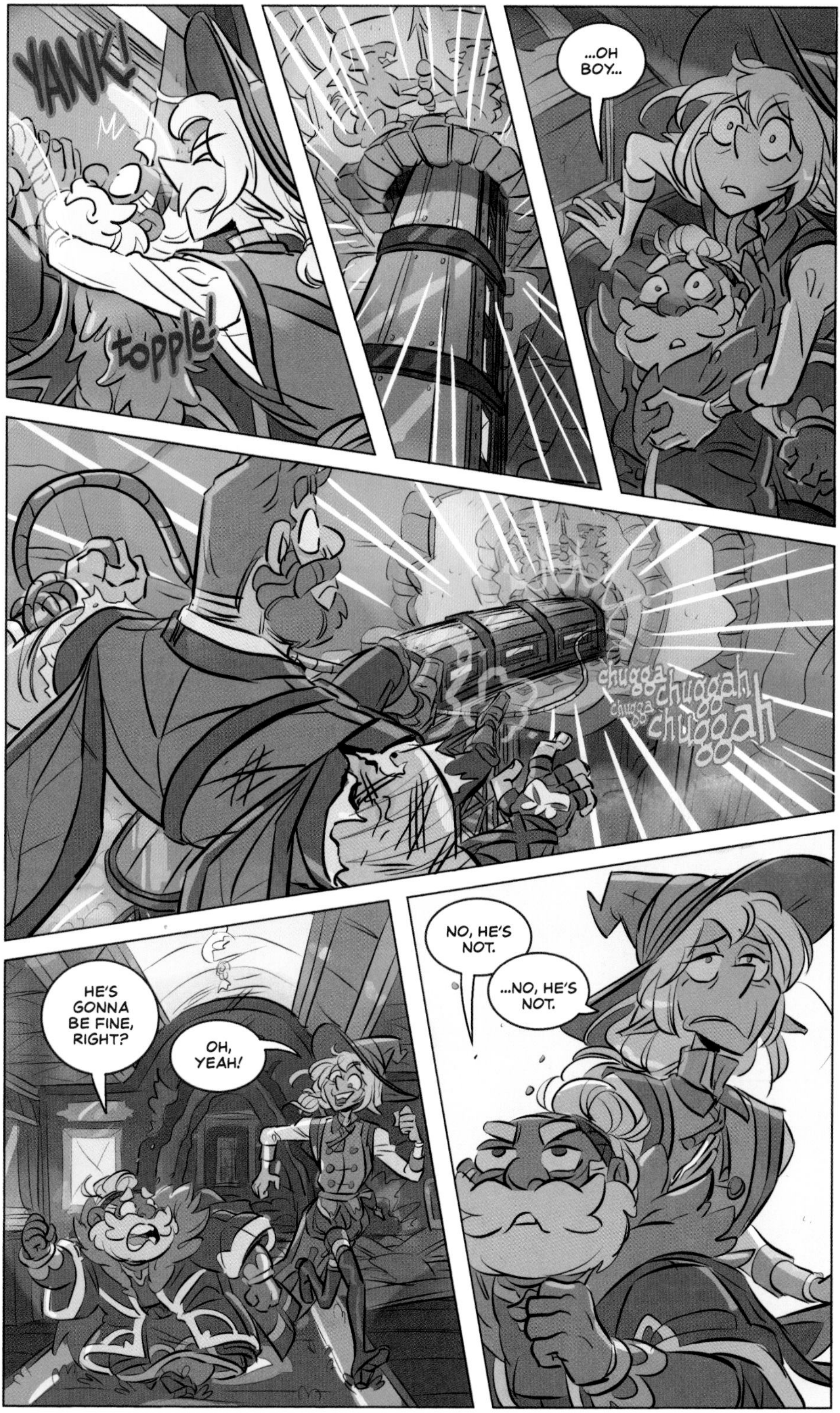
YANK!
topple!
...OH BOY...
chugga chuggah chugga chuggah
HE'S GONNA BE FINE, RIGHT?
OH, YEAH!
NO, HE'S NOT.
...NO, HE'S NOT.

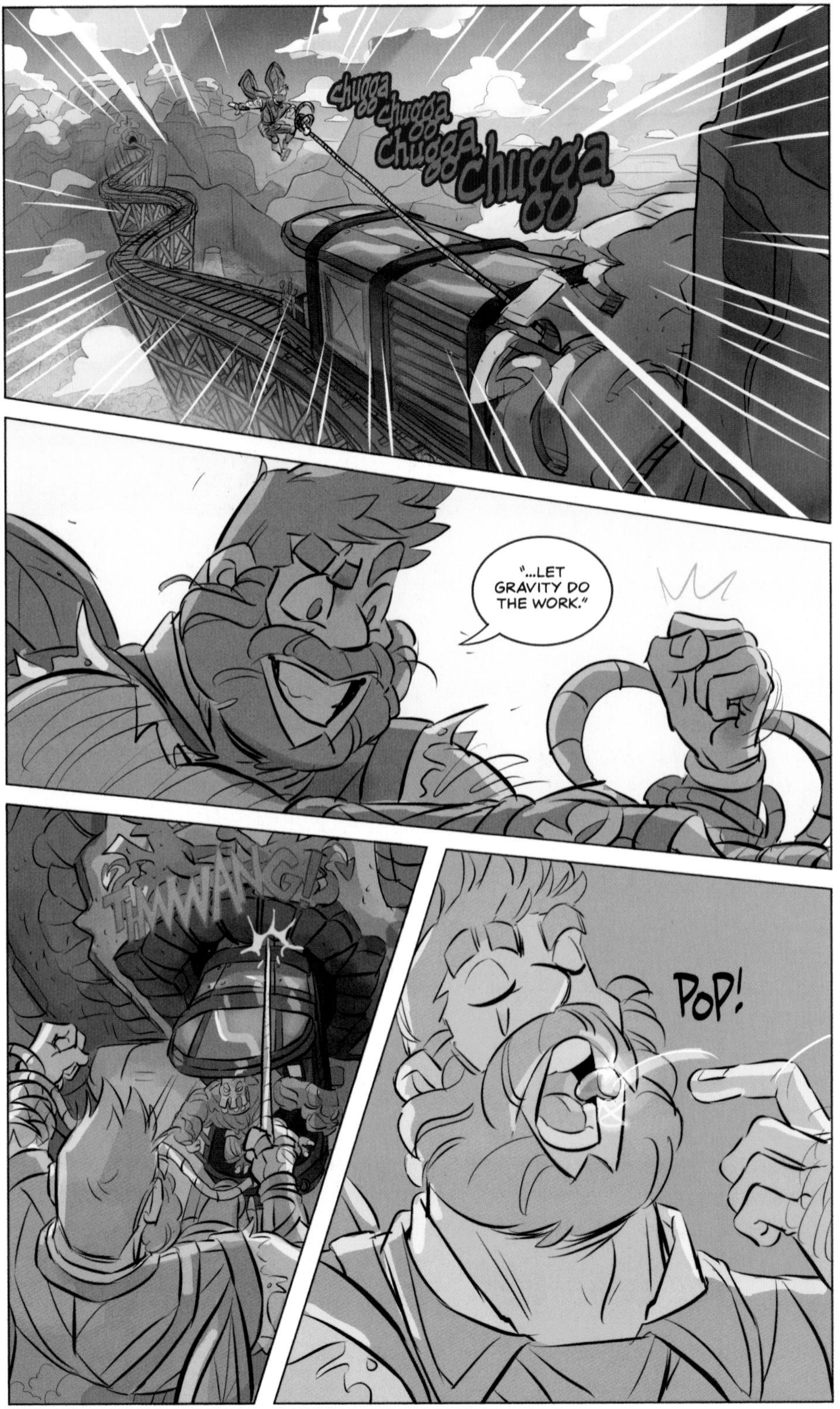
chugga chugga chugga chugga
"...LET GRAVITY DO THE WORK."
THWANG!
POP!

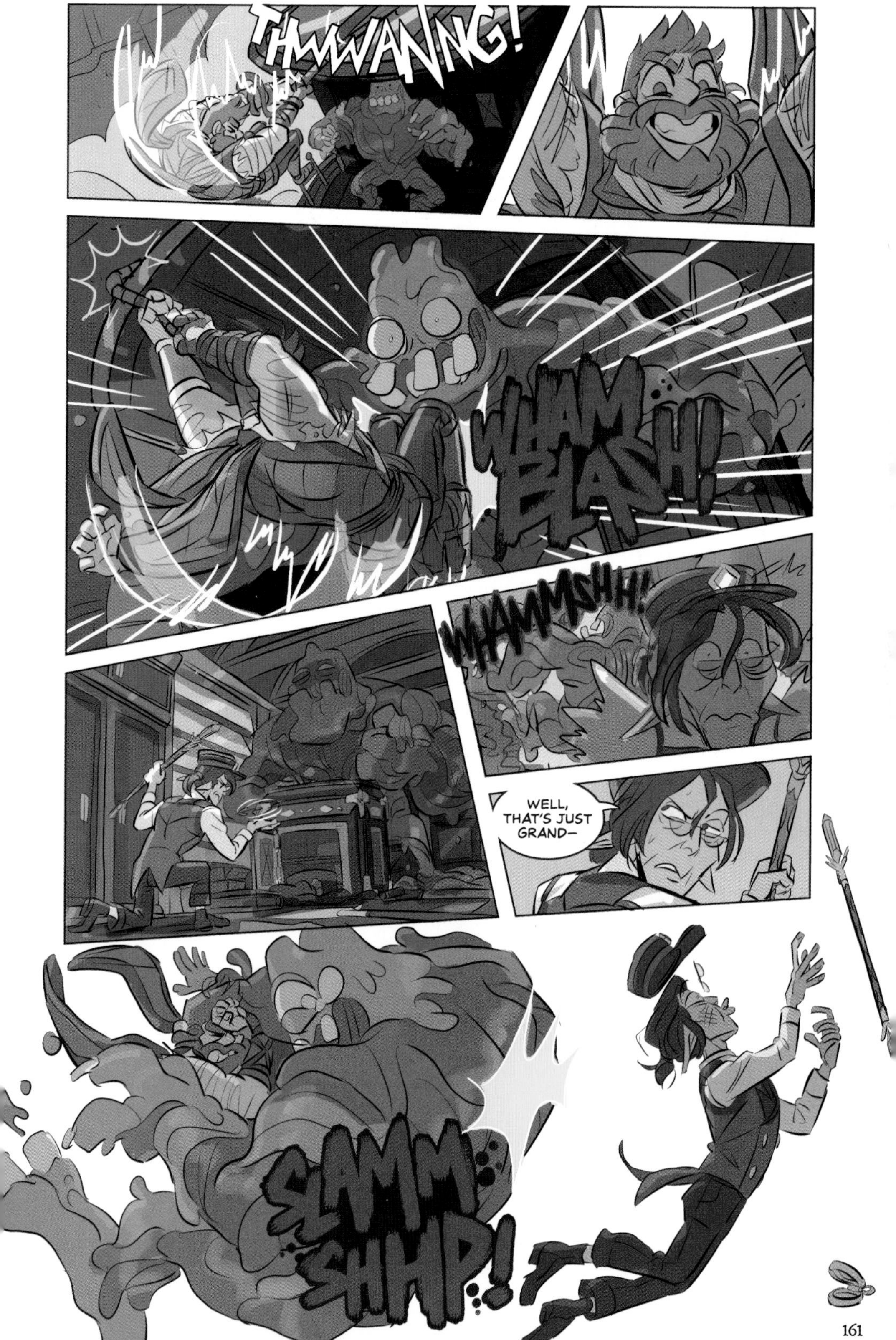
THWANNG!
WHAM BLASH!
WHAMMSHH!
WELL, THAT'S JUST GRAND—
SLAMM SHHP!

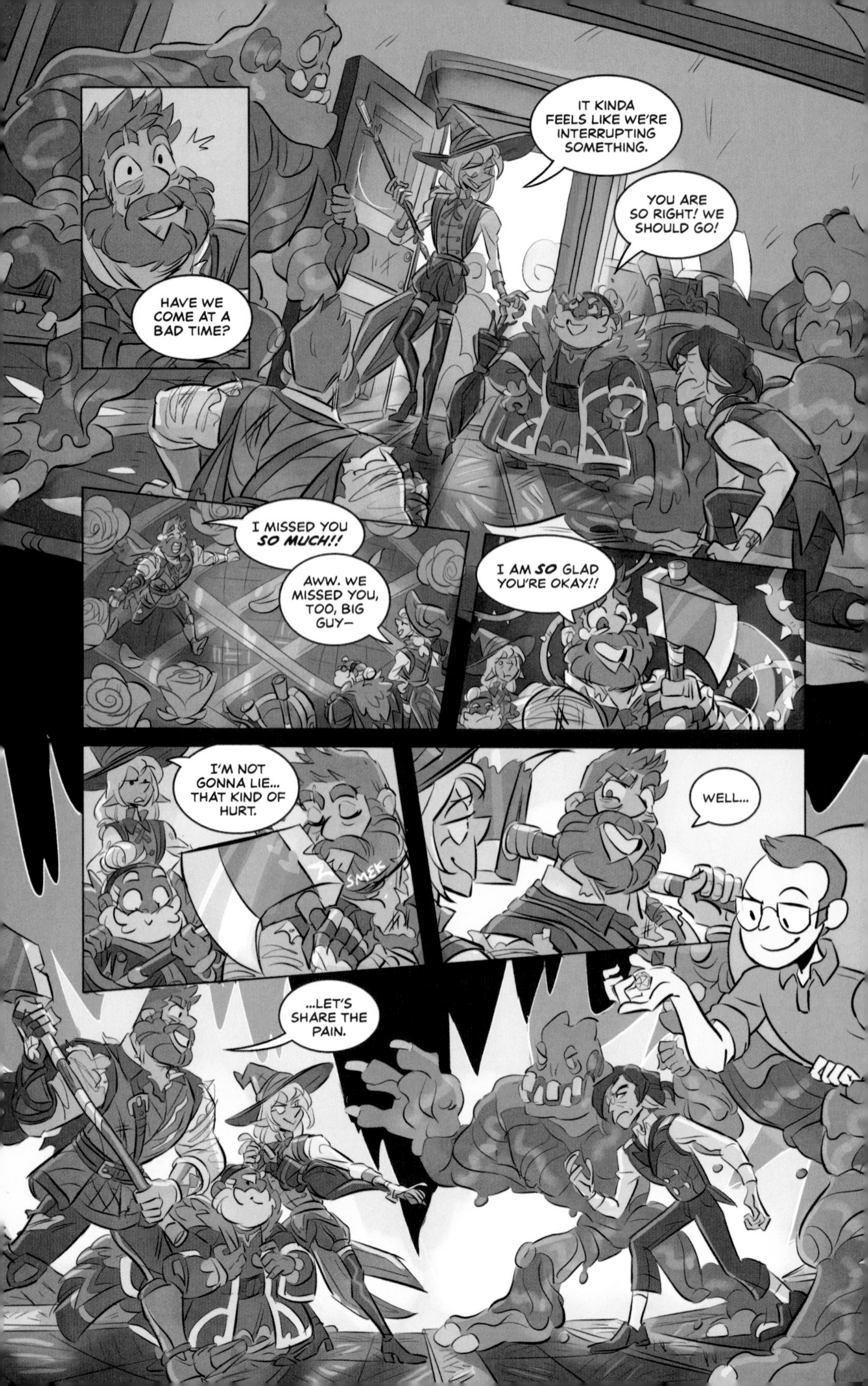
HAVE WE COME AT A BAD TIME?
IT KINDA FEELS LIKE WE'RE INTERRUPTING SOMETHING.
YOU ARE SO RIGHT! WE SHOULD GO!
I MISSED YOU **SO MUCH!!**
AWW. WE MISSED YOU, TOO, BIG GUY—
I AM **SO** GLAD YOU'RE OKAY!!
I'M NOT GONNA LIE... THAT KIND OF HURT.
SMEK
WELL...
...LET'S SHARE THE PAIN.

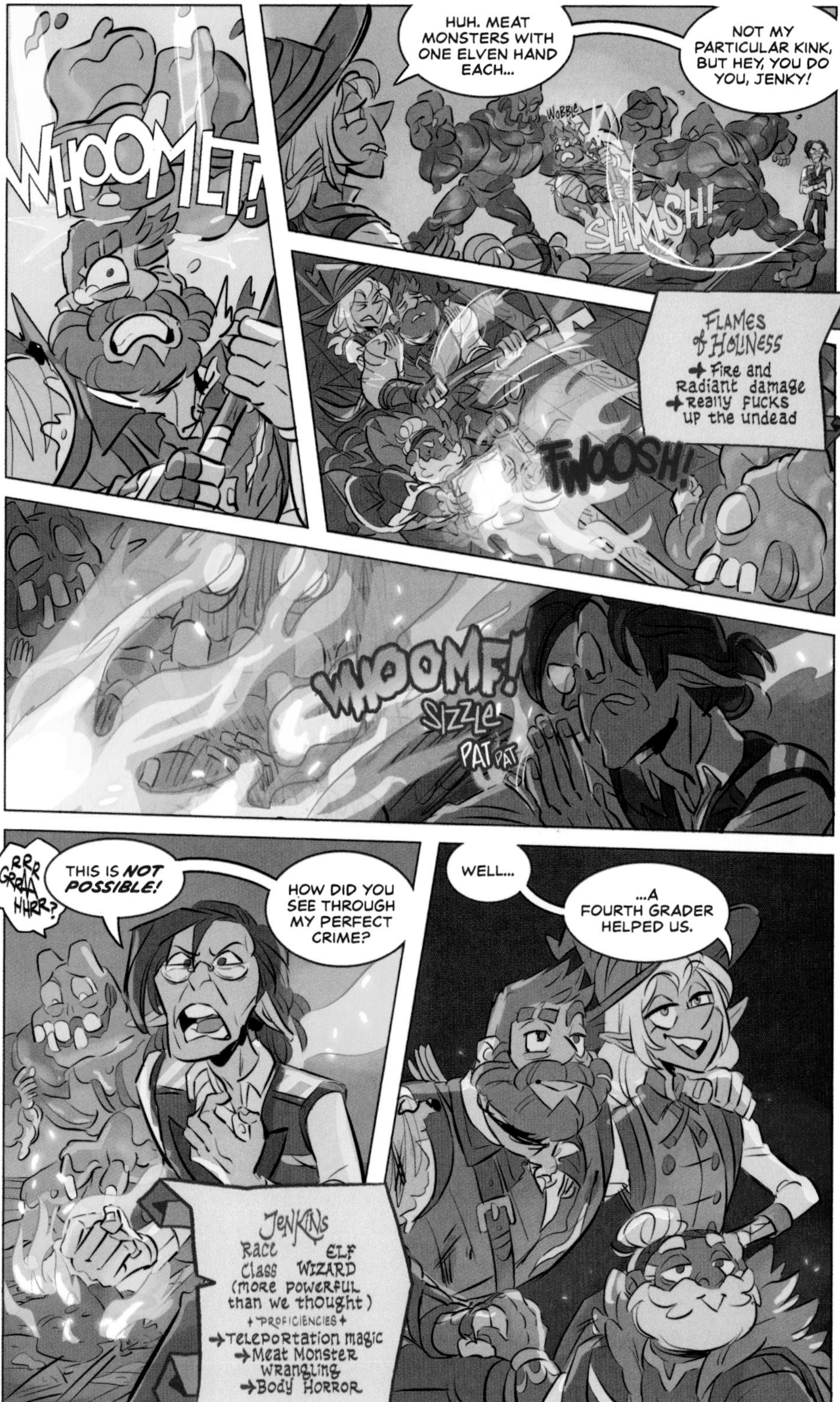
WHOOMLT!
HUH. MEAT MONSTERS WITH ONE ELVEN HAND EACH...
NOT MY PARTICULAR KINK, BUT HEY, YOU DO YOU, JENKY!
WOBBLE
SLAMSH!
FLAMES OF HOLINESS
+ Fire and Radiant damage
+ Really FUCKS up the undead
FWOOSH!
WHOOMF!
SIZZLE
PAT PAT
RRR GRRAA HHRR?
THIS IS **NOT POSSIBLE!**
HOW DID YOU SEE THROUGH MY PERFECT CRIME?
WELL...
...A FOURTH GRADER HELPED US.
JENKINS
Race ELF
Class WIZARD
(more powerful than we thought)
+ PROFICIENCIES +
→Teleportation magic
→Meat Monster wrangling
→Body Horror

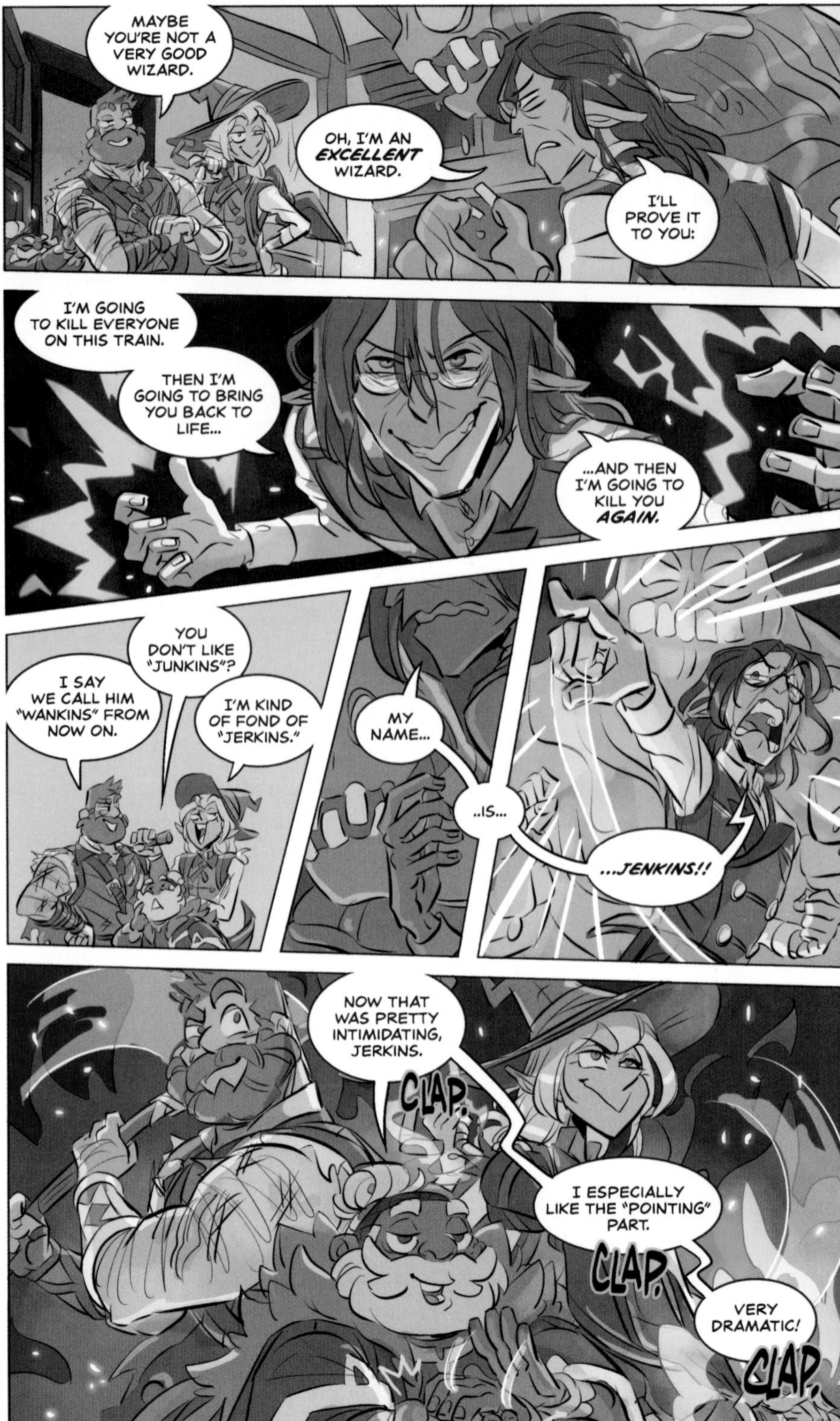
MAYBE YOU'RE NOT A VERY GOOD WIZARD.
OH, I'M AN *EXCELLENT* WIZARD.
I'LL PROVE IT TO YOU:
I'M GOING TO KILL EVERYONE ON THIS TRAIN.
THEN I'M GOING TO BRING YOU BACK TO LIFE...
...AND THEN I'M GOING TO KILL YOU ***AGAIN.***
YOU DON'T LIKE "JUNKINS"?
I SAY WE CALL HIM "WANKINS" FROM NOW ON.
I'M KIND OF FOND OF "JERKINS."
MY NAME...
..IS...
...JENKINS!!
NOW THAT WAS PRETTY INTIMIDATING, JERKINS.
CLAP.
I ESPECIALLY LIKE THE "POINTING" PART.
CLAP.
VERY DRAMATIC!
CLAP.

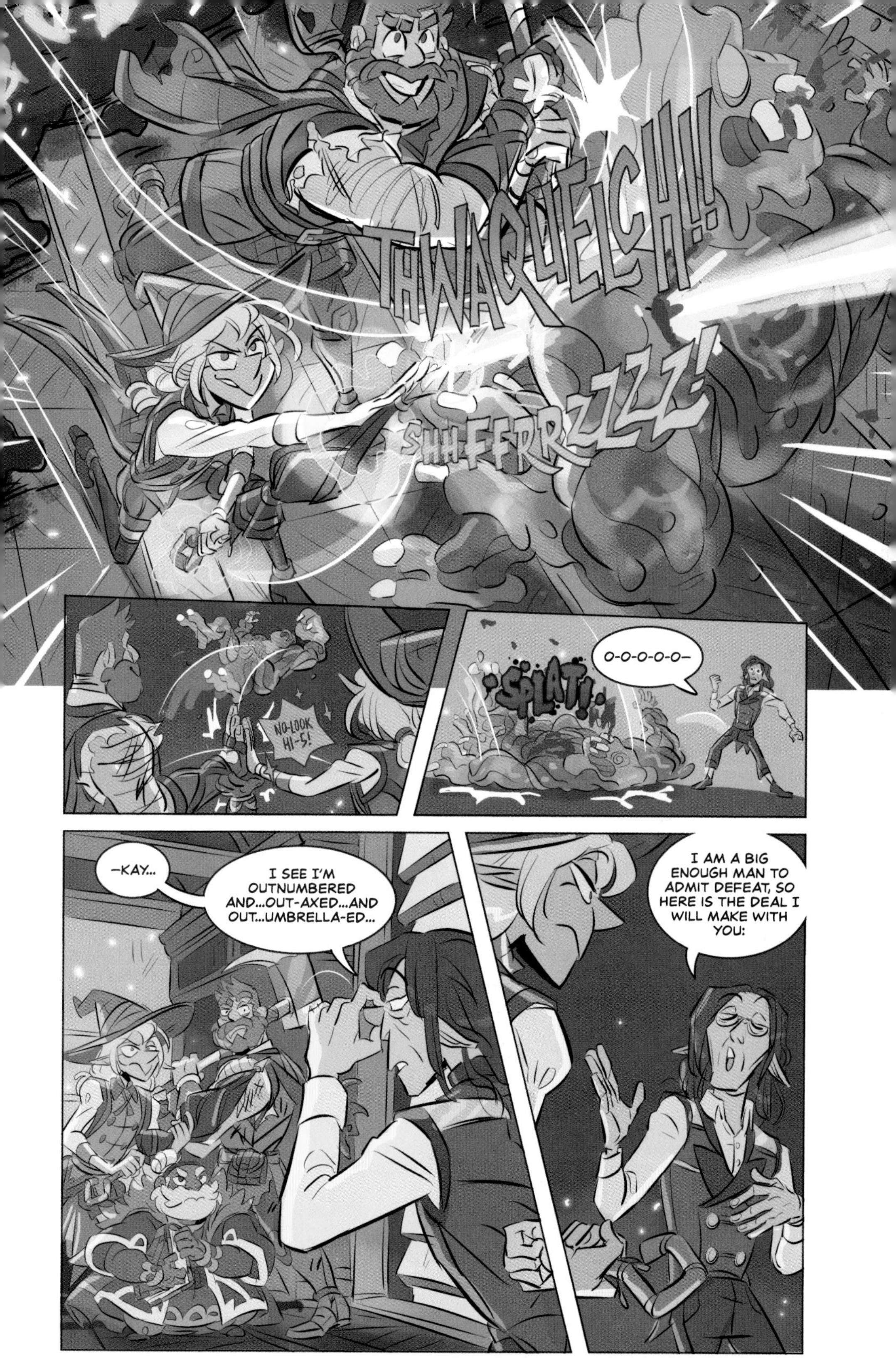
THWAQUELCH!!!
SHHFFRRZZZZZ!
NO-LOOK HI-5!
SPLAT!
O-O-O-O-O-
—KAY...
I SEE I'M OUTNUMBERED AND...OUT-AXED...AND OUT...UMBRELLA-ED...
I AM A BIG ENOUGH MAN TO ADMIT DEFEAT, SO HERE IS THE DEAL I WILL MAKE WITH YOU:

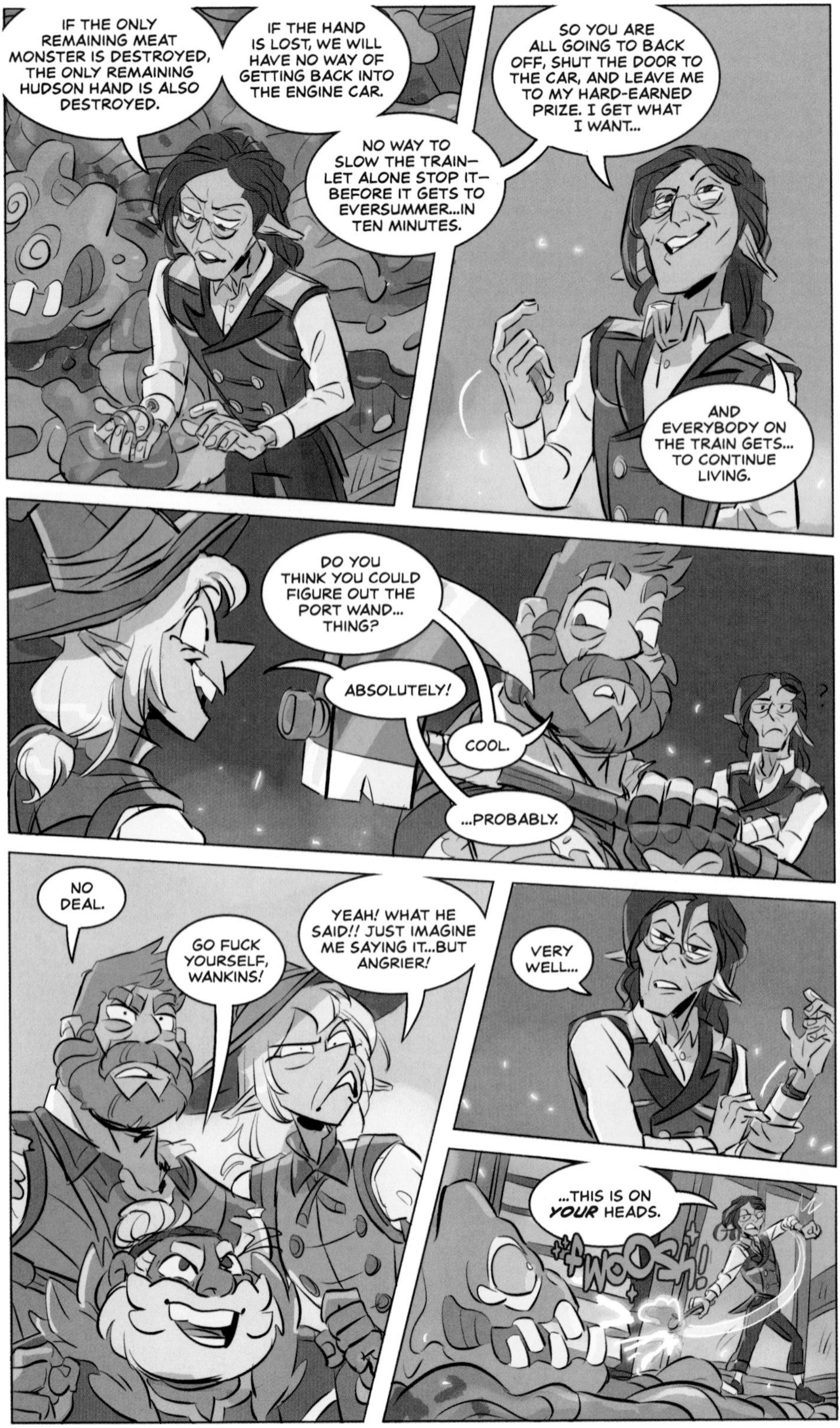
IF THE ONLY REMAINING MEAT MONSTER IS DESTROYED, THE ONLY REMAINING HUDSON HAND IS ALSO DESTROYED.
IF THE HAND IS LOST, WE WILL HAVE NO WAY OF GETTING BACK INTO THE ENGINE CAR.
NO WAY TO SLOW THE TRAIN—LET ALONE STOP IT—BEFORE IT GETS TO EVERSUMMER...IN TEN MINUTES.
SO YOU ARE ALL GOING TO BACK OFF, SHUT THE DOOR TO THE CAR, AND LEAVE ME TO MY HARD-EARNED PRIZE. I GET WHAT I WANT...
AND EVERYBODY ON THE TRAIN GETS... TO CONTINUE LIVING.
DO YOU THINK YOU COULD FIGURE OUT THE PORT WAND... THING?
ABSOLUTELY!
COOL.
...PROBABLY.
?
NO DEAL.
GO FUCK YOURSELF, WANKINS!
YEAH! WHAT HE SAID!! JUST IMAGINE ME SAYING IT...BUT ANGRIER!
VERY WELL...
...THIS IS ON *YOUR* HEADS.
WOOSH!

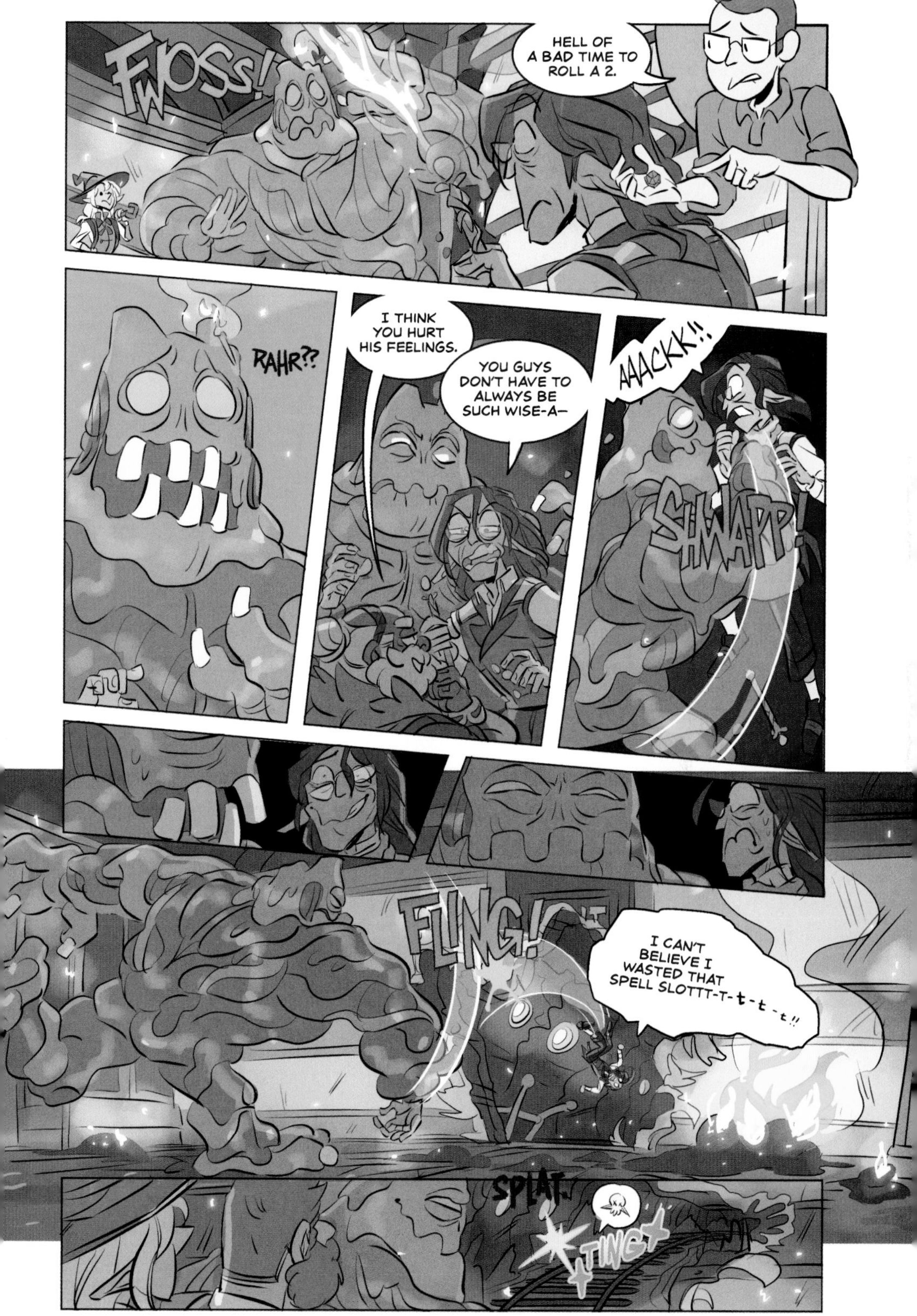
FWOSS!
HELL OF A BAD TIME TO ROLL A 2.
RAHR??
I THINK YOU HURT HIS FEELINGS.
YOU GUYS DON'T HAVE TO ALWAYS BE SUCH WISE-A—
AAACKK!!
SHWAPP!
FLING!
I CAN'T BELIEVE I WASTED THAT SPELL SLOTTT-T-t-t-t!!
SPLAT.
TING

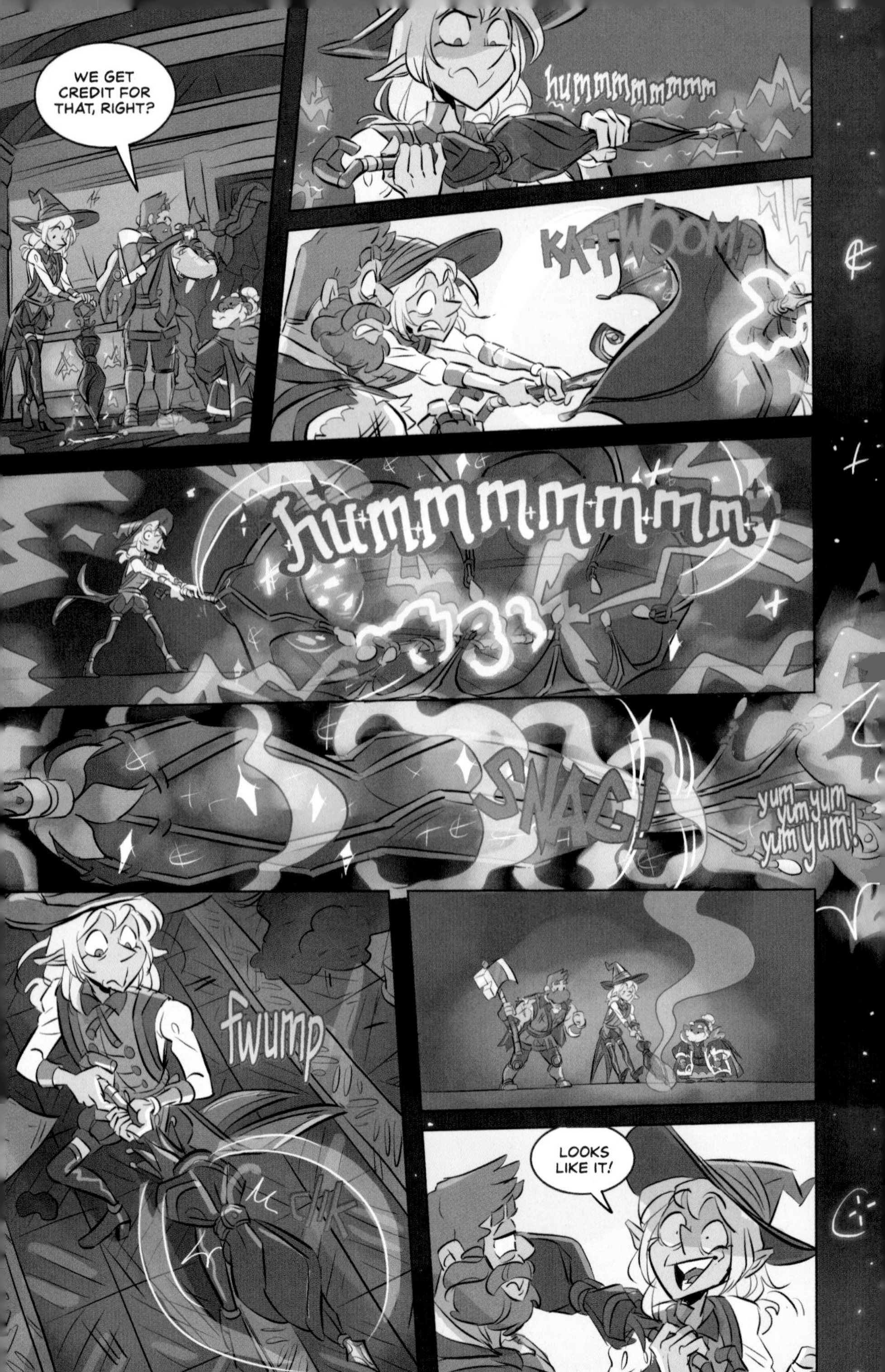

WE GET CREDIT FOR THAT, RIGHT?
hummmmmmmm
KA-FWOOMP
hummmmmmmm
SNAG!
yum yum yum yum yum!
fwump
clik
LOOKS LIKE IT!

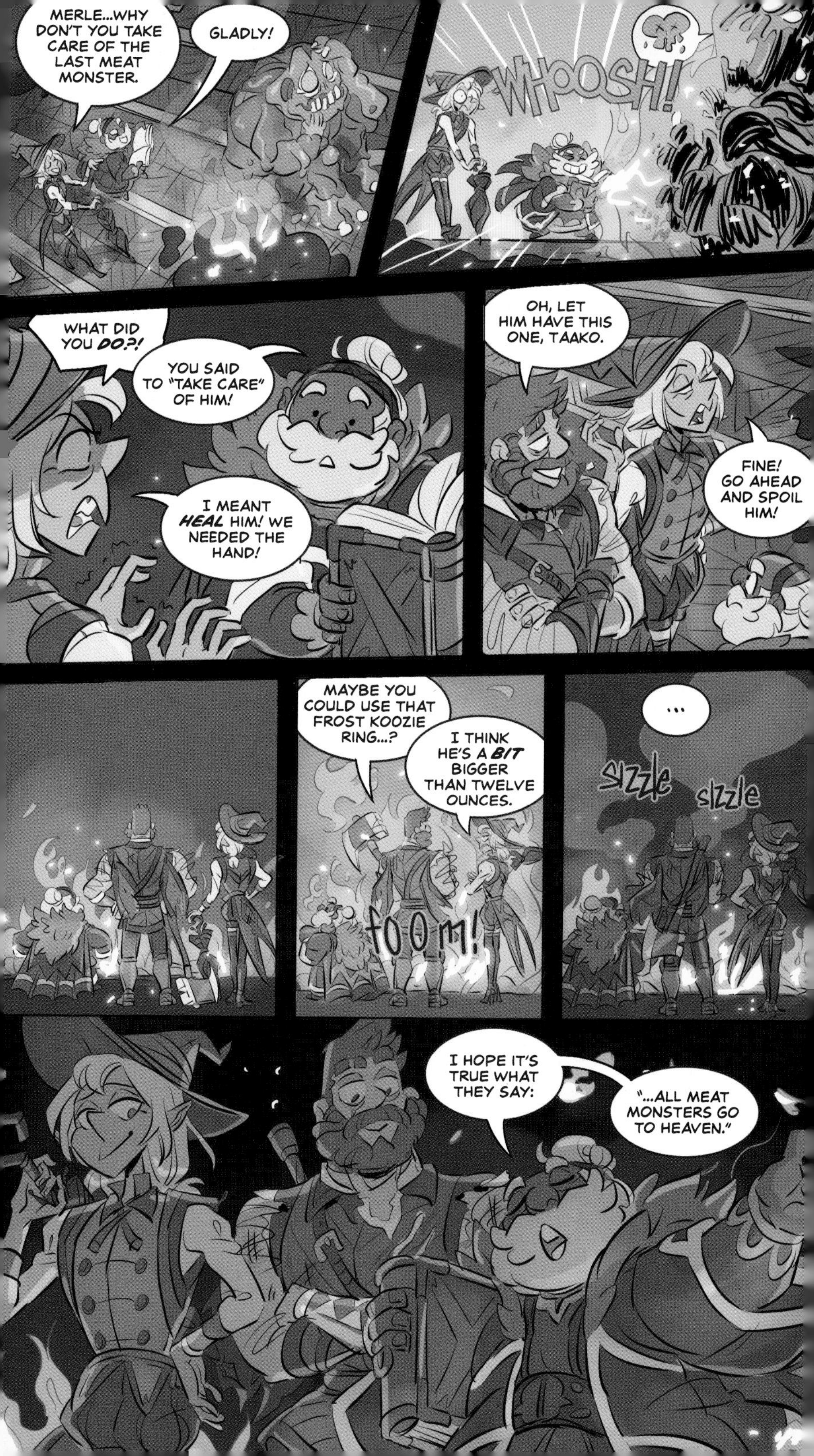
MERLE...WHY DON'T YOU TAKE CARE OF THE LAST MEAT MONSTER.
GLADLY!
WHOOSH!
WHAT DID YOU *DO?!*
YOU SAID TO "TAKE CARE" OF HIM!
I MEANT ***HEAL*** HIM! WE NEEDED THE HAND!
OH, LET HIM HAVE THIS ONE, TAAKO.
FINE! GO AHEAD AND SPOIL HIM!
MAYBE YOU COULD USE THAT FROST KOOZIE RING...?
I THINK HE'S A ***BIT*** BIGGER THAN TWELVE OUNCES.
fOOm!
...
sizzle
sizzle
I HOPE IT'S TRUE WHAT THEY SAY:
"...ALL MEAT MONSTERS GO TO HEAVEN."

Chapter 7

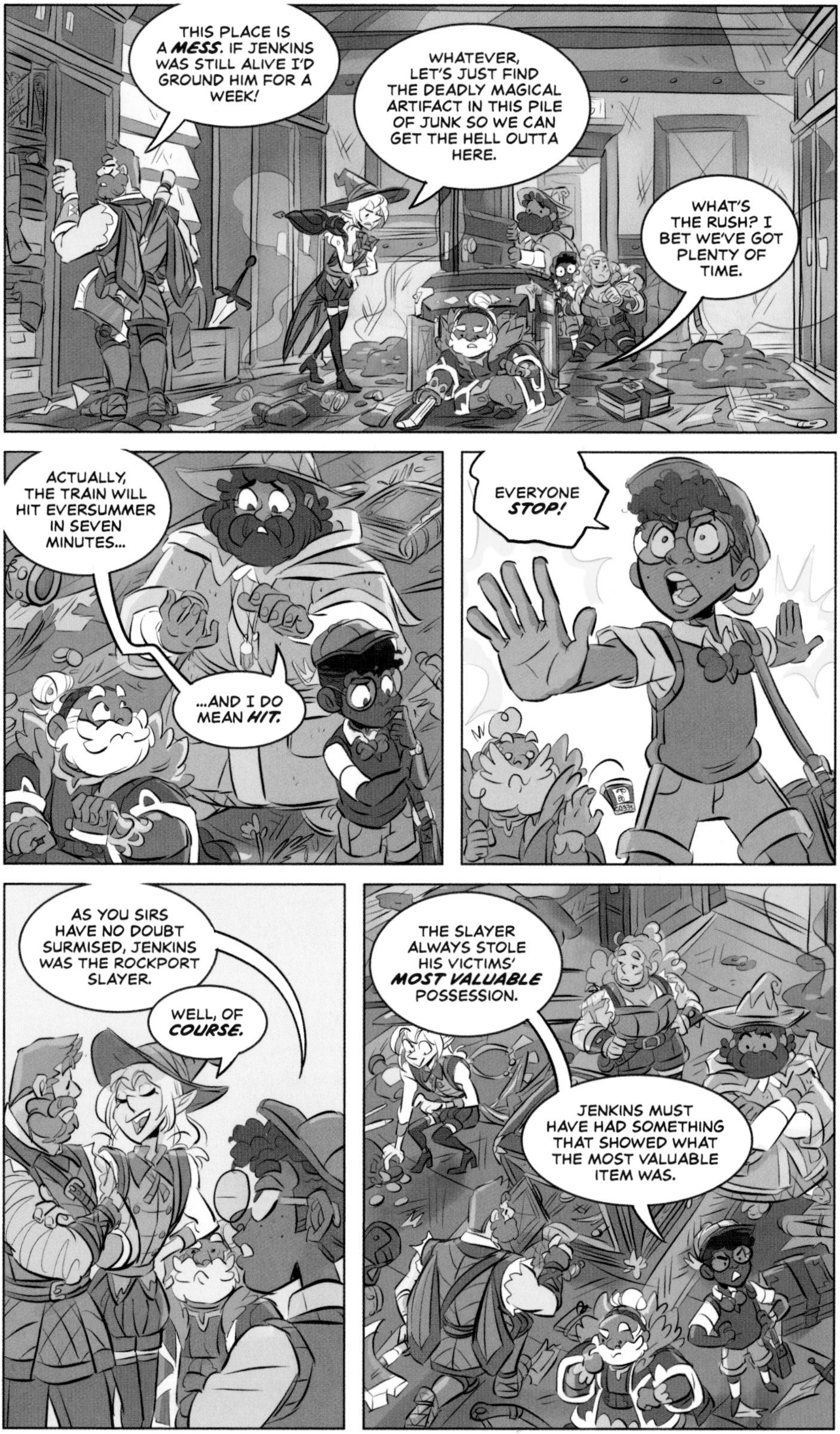

THIS PLACE IS A **MESS**. IF JENKINS WAS STILL ALIVE I'D GROUND HIM FOR A WEEK!
WHATEVER, LET'S JUST FIND THE DEADLY MAGICAL ARTIFACT IN THIS PILE OF JUNK SO WE CAN GET THE HELL OUTTA HERE.
WHAT'S THE RUSH? I BET WE'VE GOT PLENTY OF TIME.
ACTUALLY, THE TRAIN WILL HIT EVERSUMMER IN SEVEN MINUTES...
...AND I DO MEAN ***HIT.***
EVERYONE ***STOP!***
AS YOU SIRS HAVE NO DOUBT SURMISED, JENKINS WAS THE ROCKPORT SLAYER.
WELL, OF ***COURSE.***
THE SLAYER ALWAYS STOLE HIS VICTIMS' ***MOST VALUABLE*** POSSESSION.
JENKINS MUST HAVE HAD SOMETHING THAT SHOWED WHAT THE MOST VALUABLE ITEM WAS.

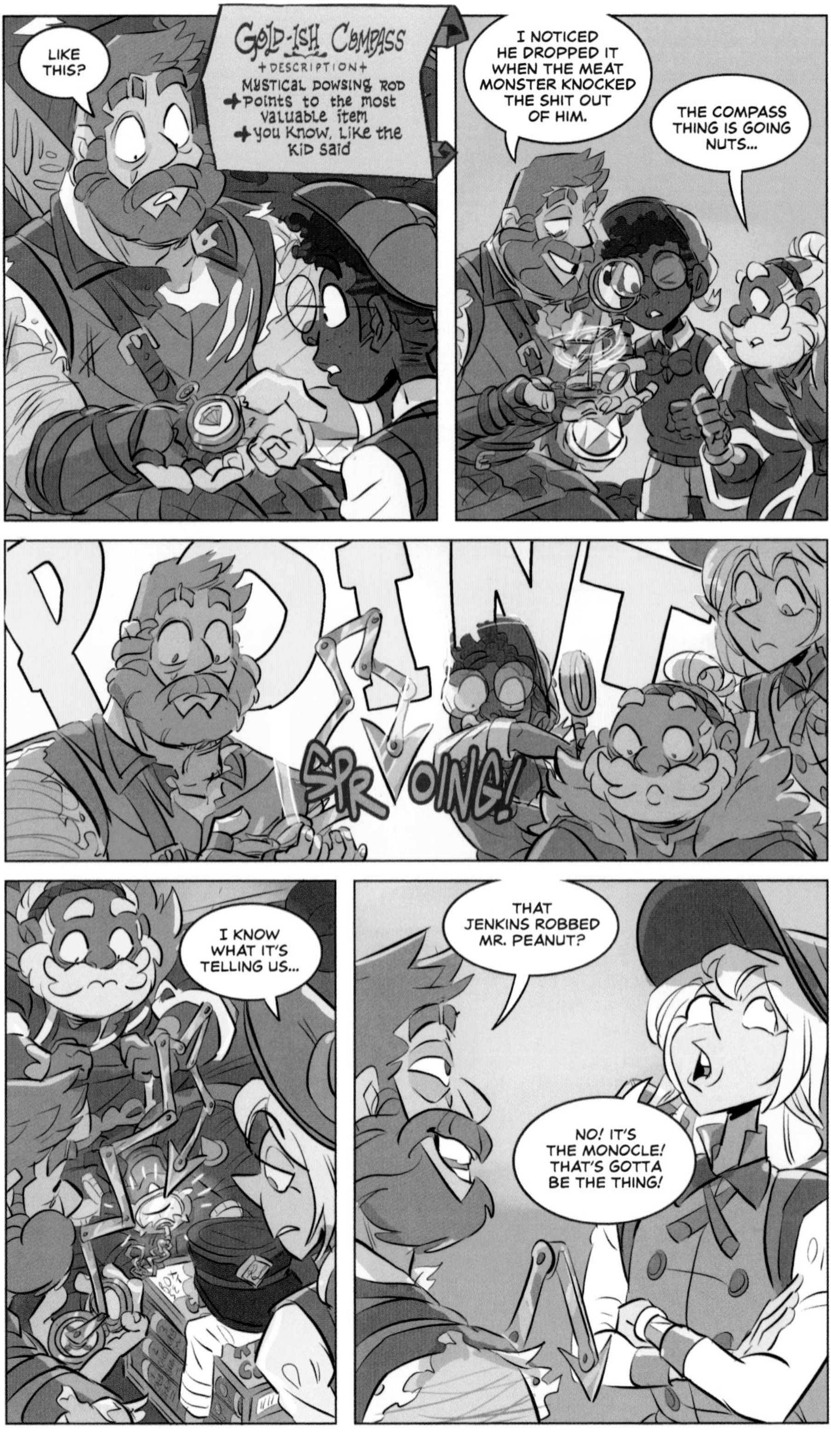
LIKE THIS?
GOLD-ISH COMPASS
+DESCRIPTION+
MYSTICAL DOWSING ROD
+Points to the most valuable item
+you know, like the kid said
I NOTICED HE DROPPED IT WHEN THE MEAT MONSTER KNOCKED THE SHIT OUT OF HIM.
THE COMPASS THING IS GOING NUTS...
POINT
SPROING!
I KNOW WHAT IT'S TELLING US...
THAT JENKINS ROBBED MR. PEANUT?
NO! IT'S THE MONOCLE! THAT'S GOTTA BE THE THING!

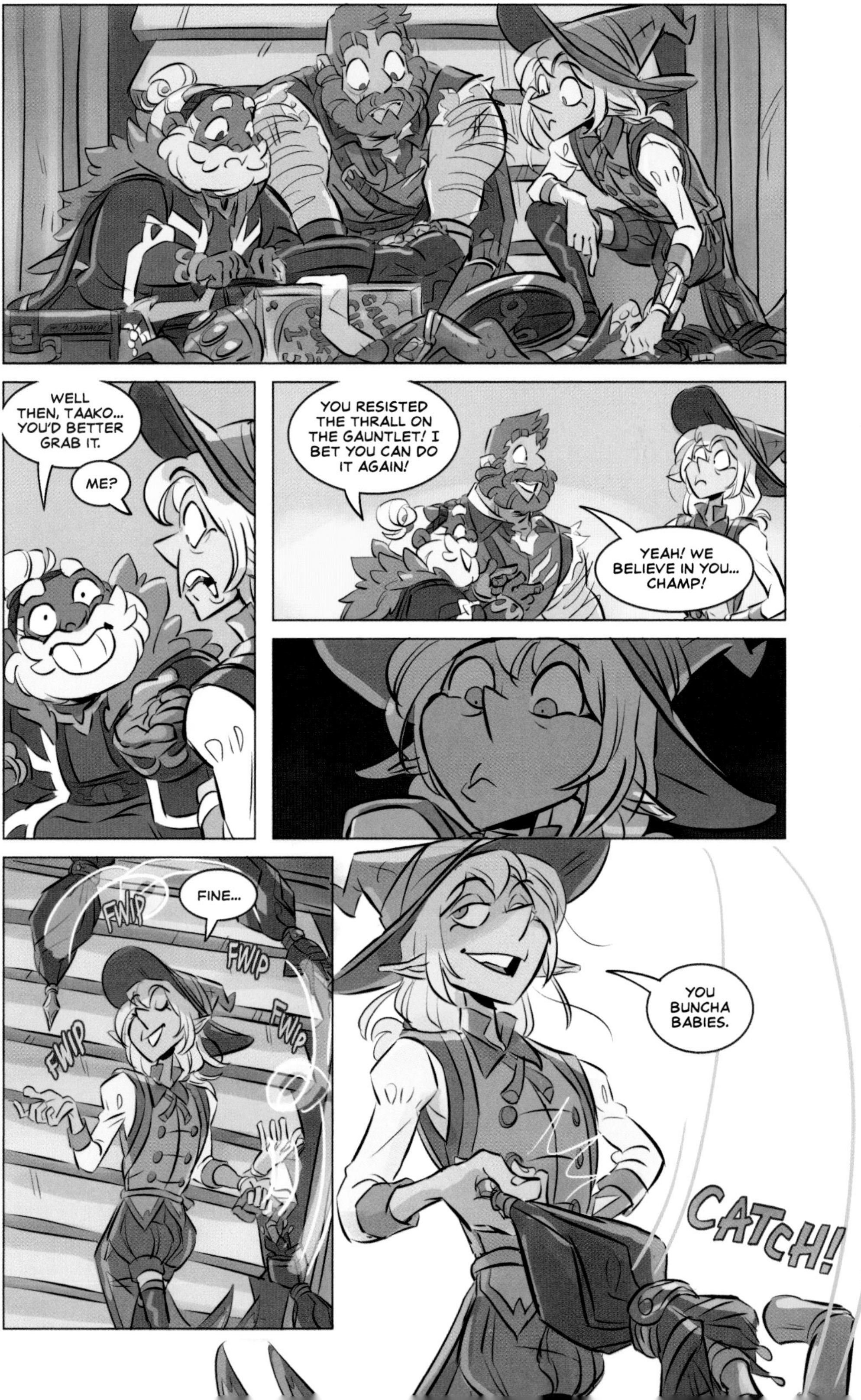
WELL THEN, TAAKO... YOU'D BETTER GRAB IT.
ME?
YOU RESISTED THE THRALL ON THE GAUNTLET! I BET YOU CAN DO IT AGAIN!
YEAH! WE BELIEVE IN YOU... CHAMP!
FINE...
FWIP
FWIP
FWIP
FWIP
YOU BUNCHA BABIES.
CATCH!

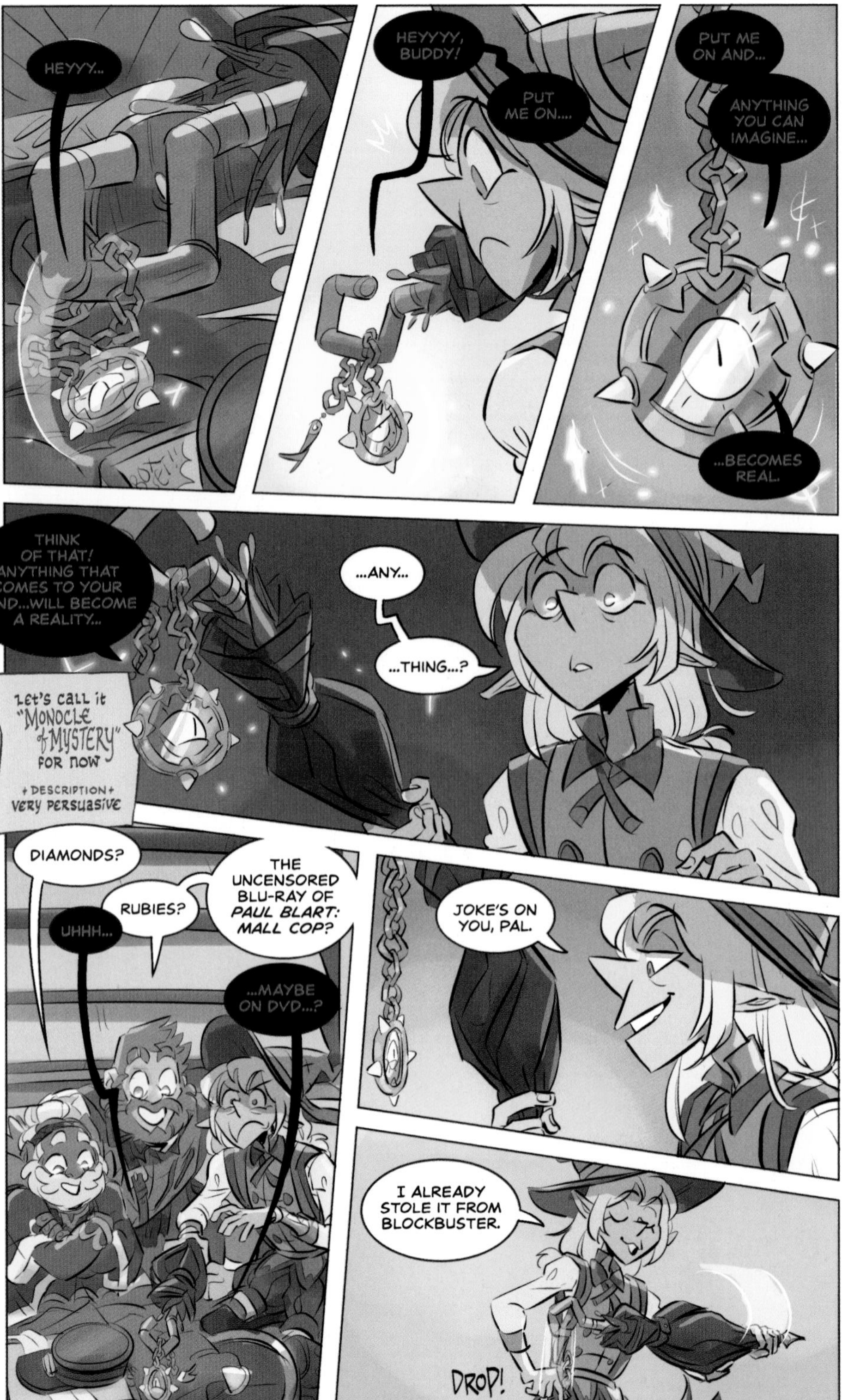
HEYYY...
HEYYYY, BUDDY!
PUT ME ON....
PUT ME ON AND...
ANYTHING YOU CAN IMAGINE...
...BECOMES REAL.
THINK OF THAT! ANYTHING THAT COMES TO YOUR MIND...WILL BECOME A REALITY...
...ANY...
...THING...?
Let's call it "MONOCLE of MYSTERY" for now
DESCRIPTION
very persuasive
DIAMONDS?
RUBIES?
THE UNCENSORED BLU-RAY OF PAUL BLART: MALL COP?
UHHH...
...MAYBE ON DVD...?
JOKE'S ON YOU, PAL.
I ALREADY STOLE IT FROM BLOCKBUSTER.
DROP!

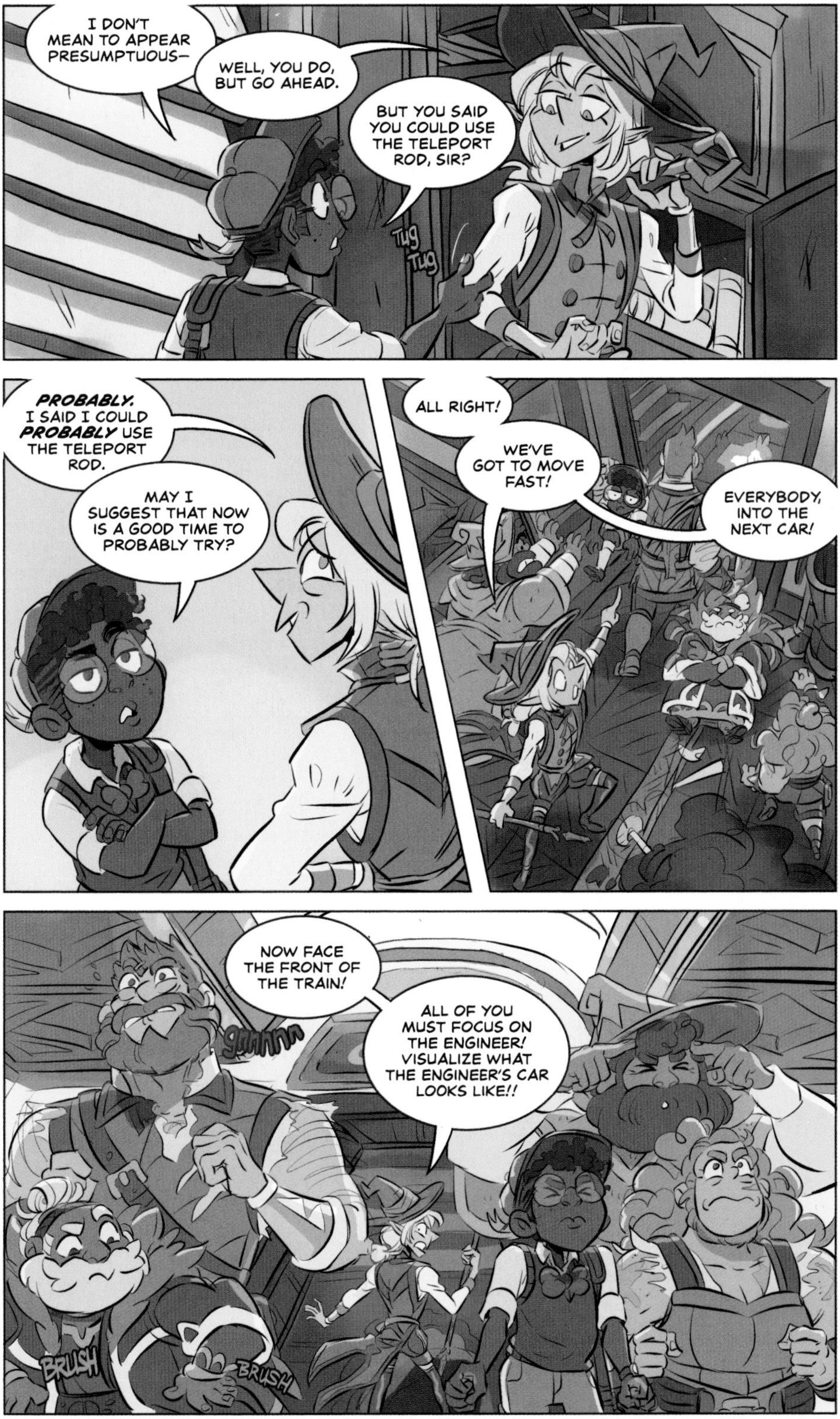
I DON'T MEAN TO APPEAR PRESUMPTUOUS—
WELL, YOU DO, BUT GO AHEAD.
BUT YOU SAID YOU COULD USE THE TELEPORT ROD, SIR?
TUG TUG
PROBABLY. I SAID I COULD PROBABLY USE THE TELEPORT ROD.
MAY I SUGGEST THAT NOW IS A GOOD TIME TO PROBABLY TRY?
ALL RIGHT!
WE'VE GOT TO MOVE FAST!
EVERYBODY, INTO THE NEXT CAR!
NOW FACE THE FRONT OF THE TRAIN!
ALL OF YOU MUST FOCUS ON THE ENGINEER! VISUALIZE WHAT THE ENGINEER'S CAR LOOKS LIKE!!
GRRHHNN
BRUSH
BRUSH

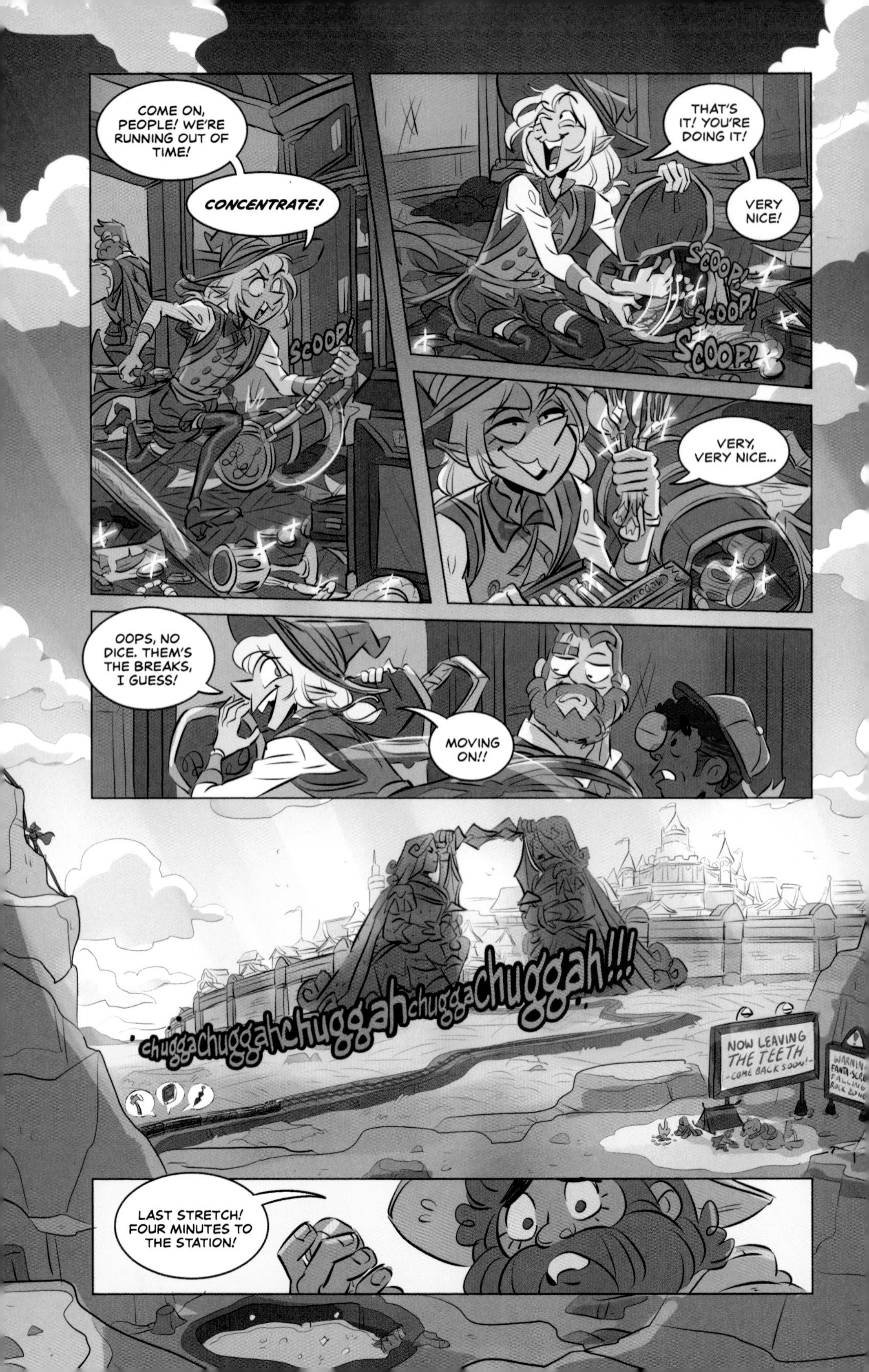
COME ON, PEOPLE! WE'RE RUNNING OUT OF TIME!
CONCENTRATE!
SCOOP!
THAT'S IT! YOU'RE DOING IT!
VERY NICE!
SCOOP! SCOOP! SCOOP!
VERY, VERY NICE...
OOPS, NO DICE. THEM'S THE BREAKS, I GUESS!
MOVING ON!!
chuggachuggahchuggahchuggachuggah!!!
NOW LEAVING THE TEETH -COME BACK SOON!-
LAST STRETCH! FOUR MINUTES TO THE STATION!

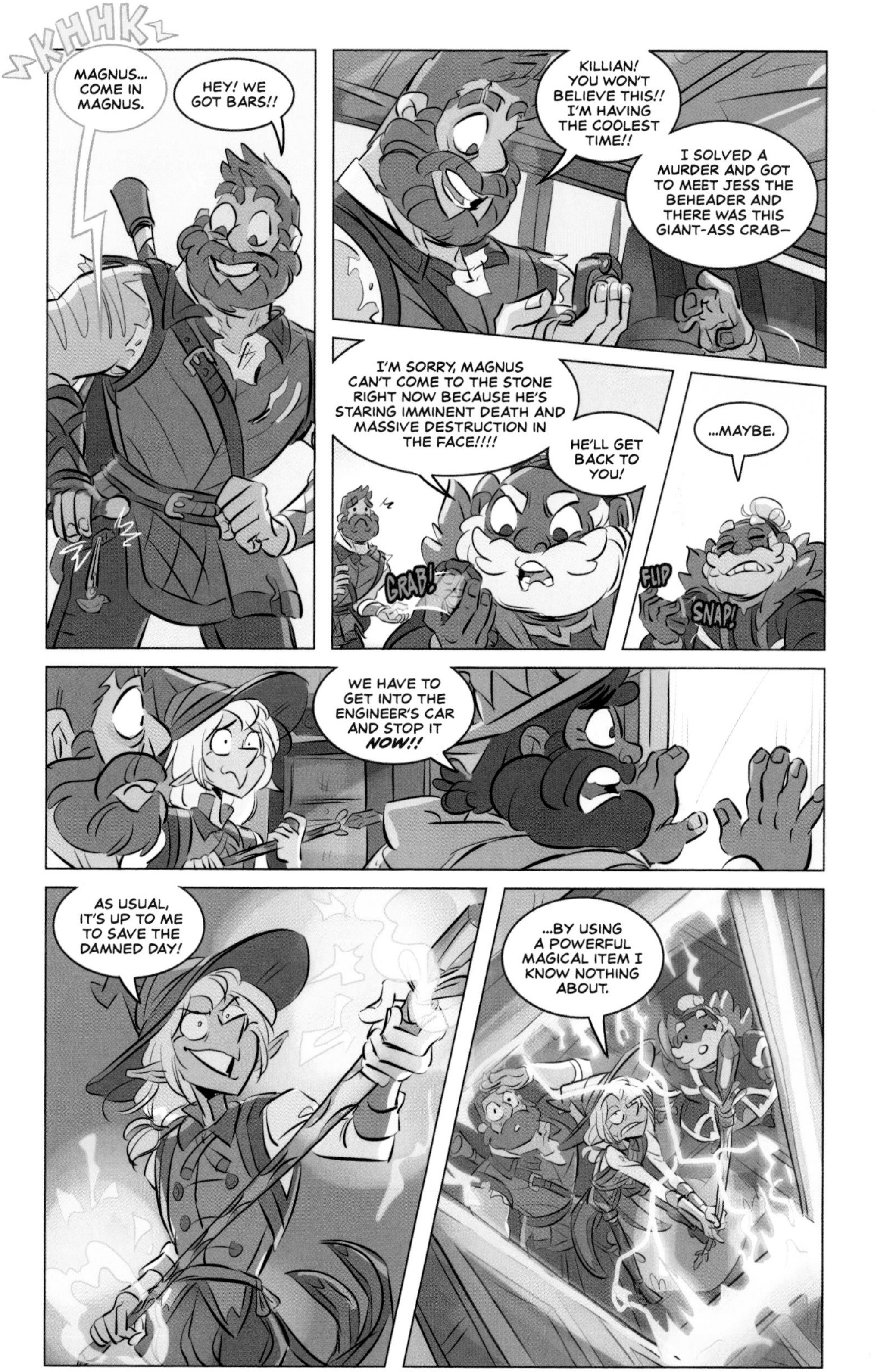
KHHK
MAGNUS... COME IN MAGNUS.
HEY! WE GOT BARS!!
KILLIAN! YOU WON'T BELIEVE THIS!! I'M HAVING THE COOLEST TIME!!
I SOLVED A MURDER AND GOT TO MEET JESS THE BEHEADER AND THERE WAS THIS GIANT-ASS CRAB—
I'M SORRY, MAGNUS CAN'T COME TO THE STONE RIGHT NOW BECAUSE HE'S STARING IMMINENT DEATH AND MASSIVE DESTRUCTION IN THE FACE!!!!
HE'LL GET BACK TO YOU!
GRAB!
...MAYBE.
FLIP
SNAP!
WE HAVE TO GET INTO THE ENGINEER'S CAR AND STOP IT NOW!!
AS USUAL, IT'S UP TO ME TO SAVE THE DAMNED DAY!
...BY USING A POWERFUL MAGICAL ITEM I KNOW NOTHING ABOUT.

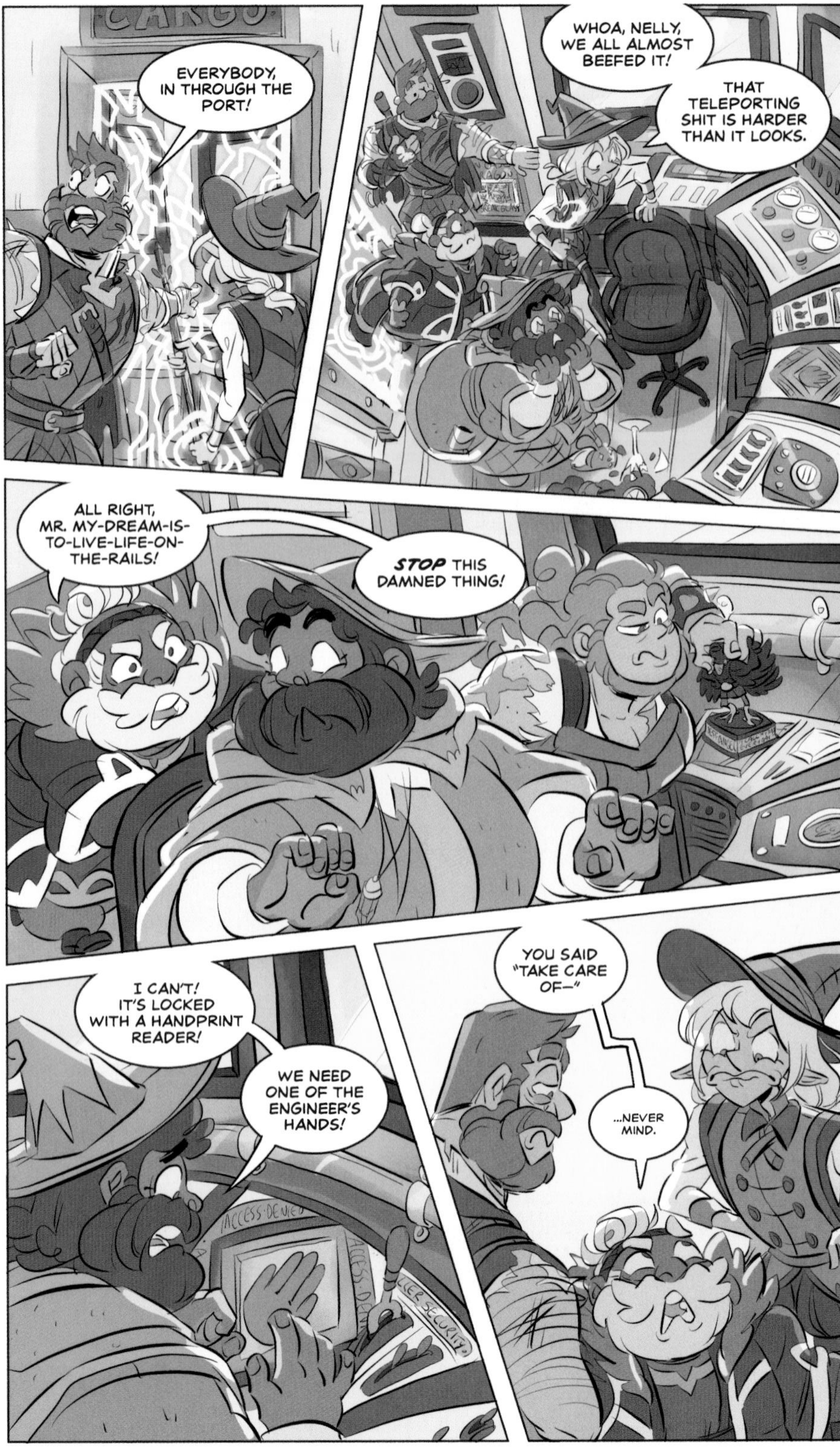
CARGO
EVERYBODY, IN THROUGH THE PORT!
WHOA, NELLY, WE ALL ALMOST BEEFED IT!
THAT TELEPORTING SHIT IS HARDER THAN IT LOOKS.
ALL RIGHT, MR. MY-DREAM-IS-TO-LIVE-LIFE-ON-THE-RAILS!
STOP THIS DAMNED THING!
I CAN'T! IT'S LOCKED WITH A HANDPRINT READER!
WE NEED ONE OF THE ENGINEER'S HANDS!
ACCESS DENIED
YOU SAID "TAKE CARE OF—"
...NEVER MIND.

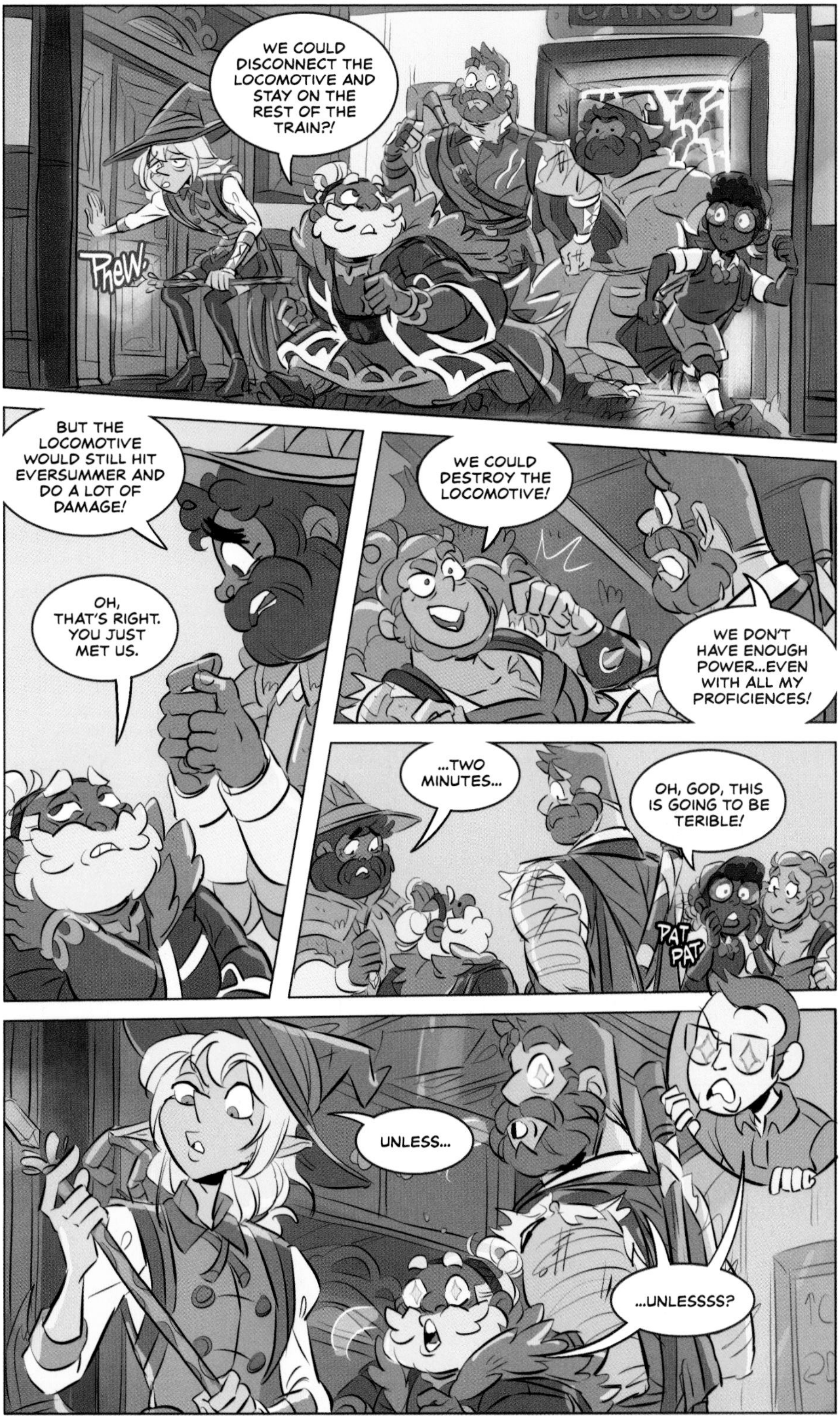
WE COULD DISCONNECT THE LOCOMOTIVE AND STAY ON THE REST OF THE TRAIN?!
PHEW!
BUT THE LOCOMOTIVE WOULD STILL HIT EVERSUMMER AND DO A LOT OF DAMAGE!
OH, THAT'S RIGHT. YOU JUST MET US.
WE COULD DESTROY THE LOCOMOTIVE!
WE DON'T HAVE ENOUGH POWER...EVEN WITH ALL MY PROFICIENCES!
...TWO MINUTES...
OH, GOD, THIS IS GOING TO BE TERIBLE!
PAT PAT
UNLESS...
...UNLESSSS?

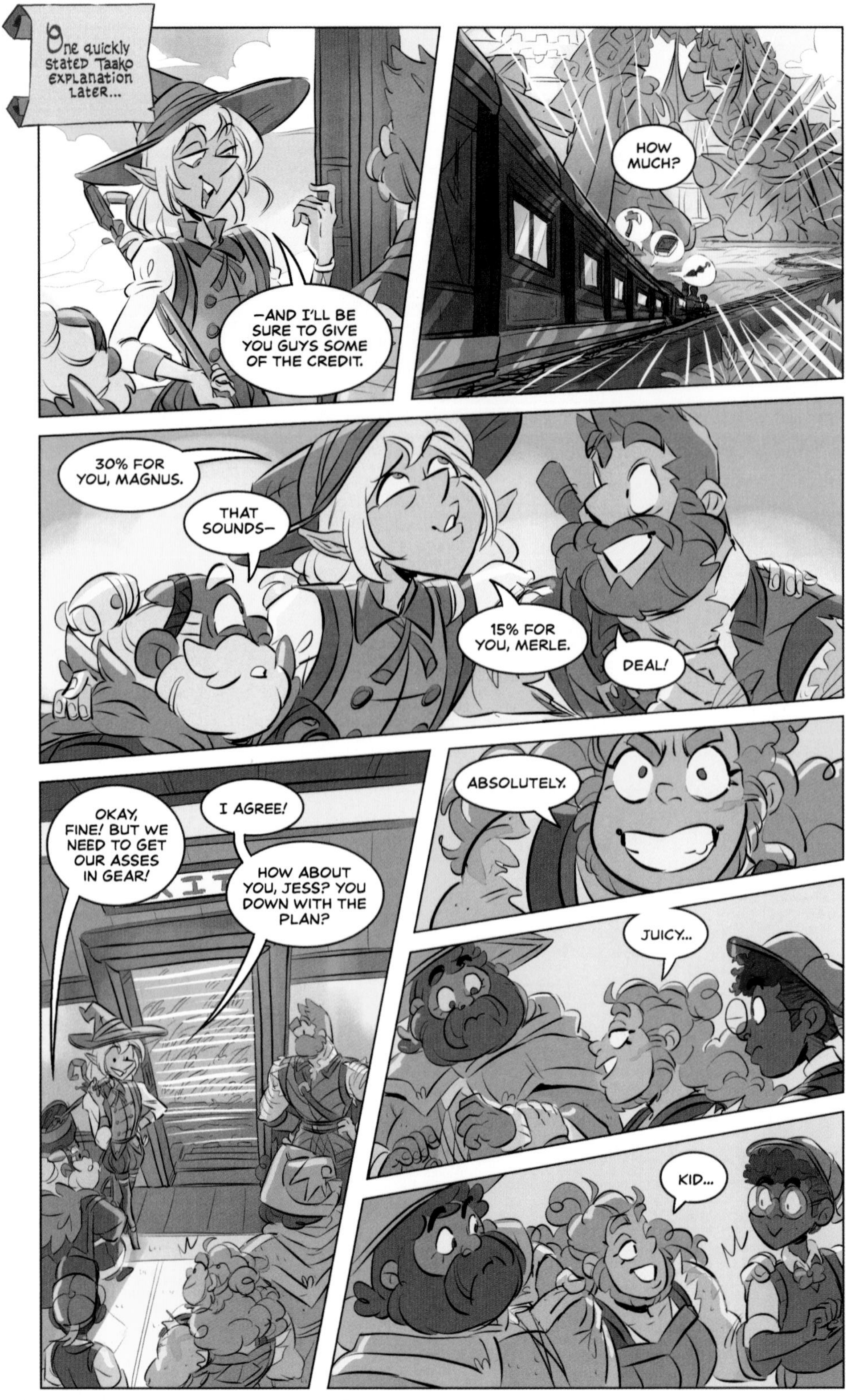
One quickly stated Taako explanation later...
—AND I'LL BE SURE TO GIVE YOU GUYS SOME OF THE CREDIT.
HOW MUCH?
30% FOR YOU, MAGNUS.
THAT SOUNDS—
15% FOR YOU, MERLE.
DEAL!
OKAY, FINE! BUT WE NEED TO GET OUR ASSES IN GEAR!
I AGREE!
HOW ABOUT YOU, JESS? YOU DOWN WITH THE PLAN?
ABSOLUTELY.
JUICY...
KID...

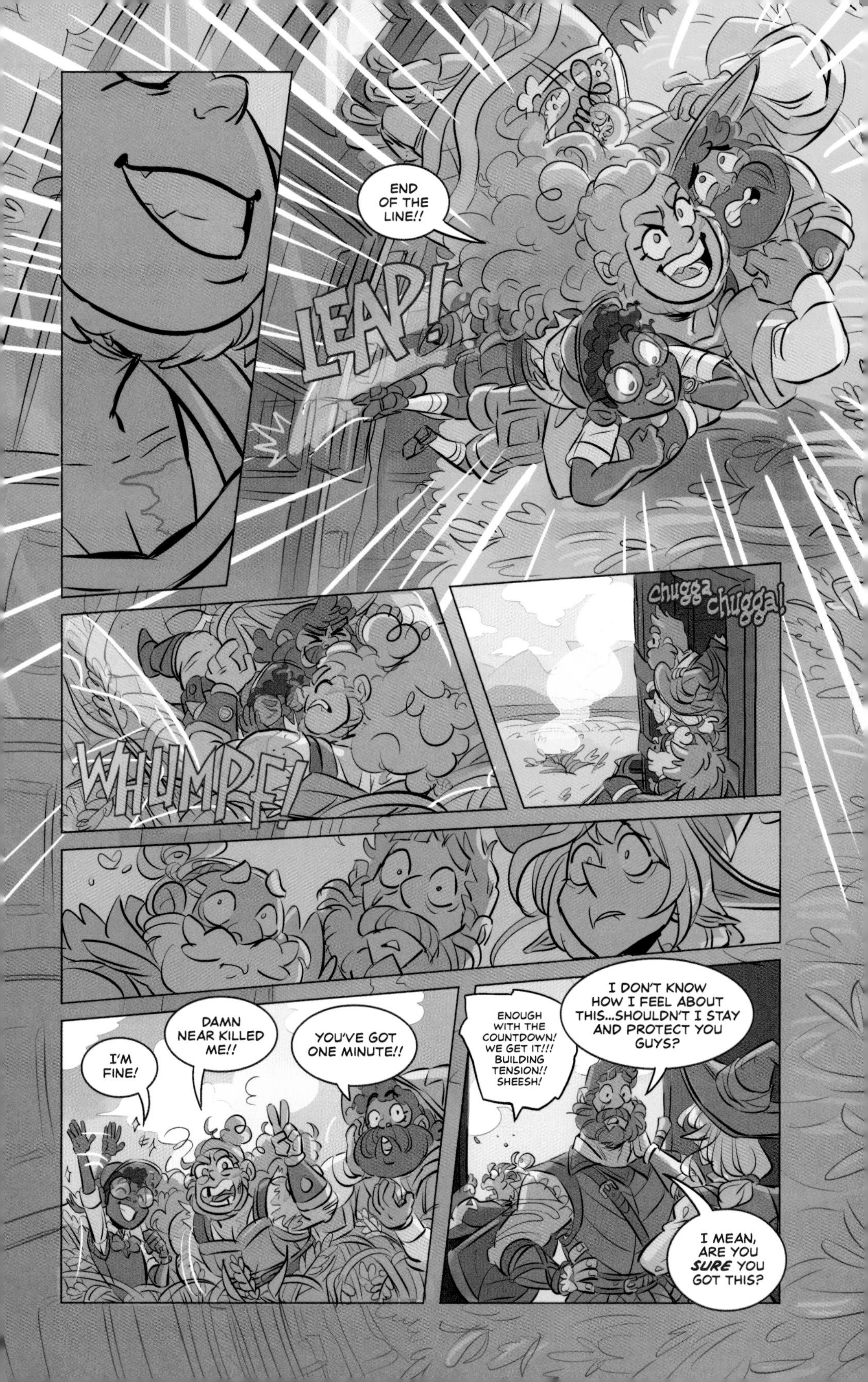

END OF THE LINE!!
LEAP!
WHUMPF!
chugga chugga!
I'M FINE!
DAMN NEAR KILLED ME!!
YOU'VE GOT ONE MINUTE!!
ENOUGH WITH THE COUNTDOWN! WE GET IT!!! BUILDING TENSION!! SHEESH!
I DON'T KNOW HOW I FEEL ABOUT THIS...SHOULDN'T I STAY AND PROTECT YOU GUYS?
I MEAN, ARE YOU *SURE* YOU GOT THIS?

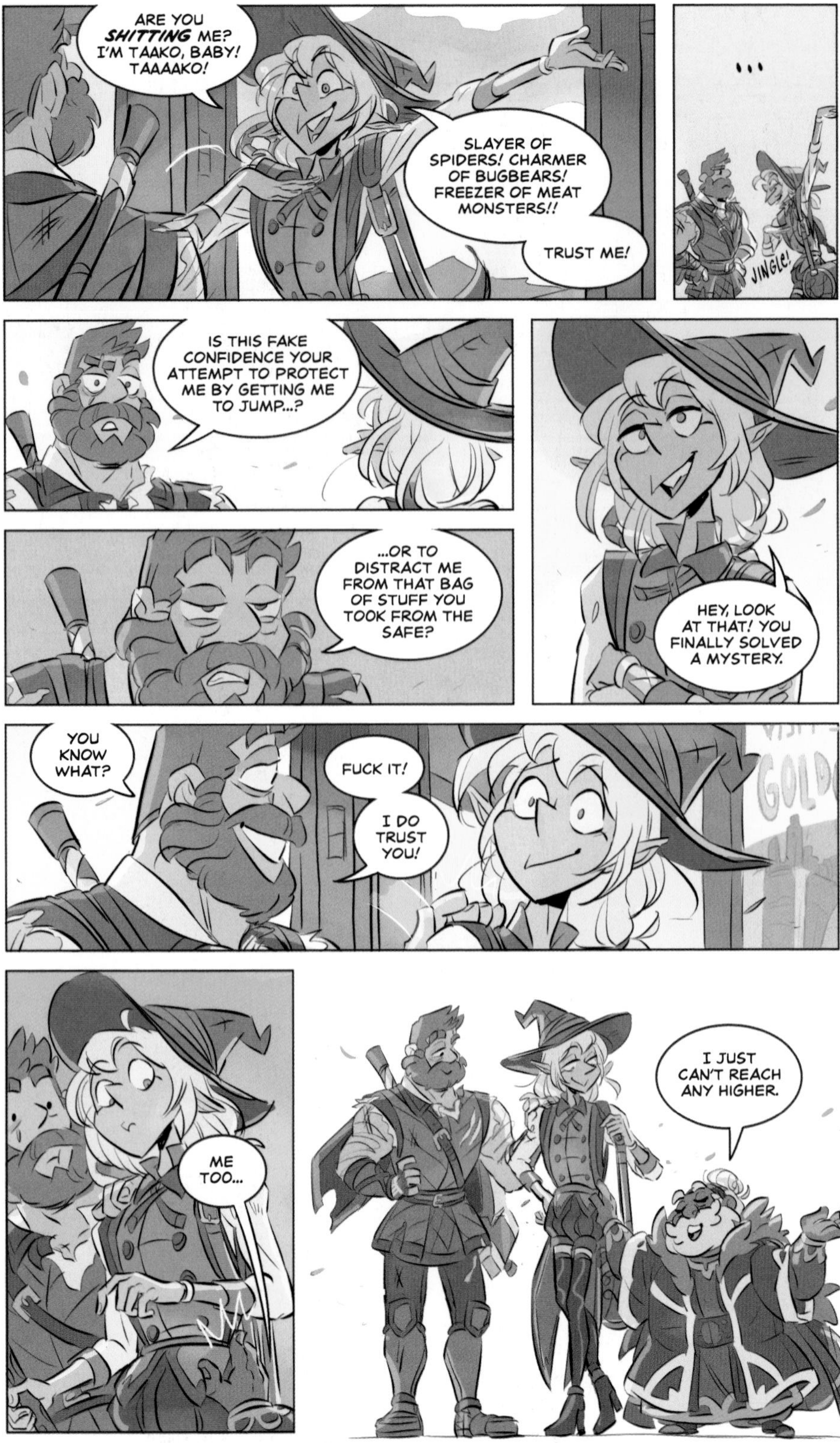
ARE YOU *SHITTING* ME? I'M TAAKO, BABY! TAAAAKO!
SLAYER OF SPIDERS! CHARMER OF BUGBEARS! FREEZER OF MEAT MONSTERS!!
TRUST ME!
...
JINGLE!
IS THIS FAKE CONFIDENCE YOUR ATTEMPT TO PROTECT ME BY GETTING ME TO JUMP...?
...OR TO DISTRACT ME FROM THAT BAG OF STUFF YOU TOOK FROM THE SAFE?
HEY, LOOK AT THAT! YOU FINALLY SOLVED A MYSTERY.
YOU KNOW WHAT?
FUCK IT!
I DO TRUST YOU!
ME TOO...
I JUST CAN'T REACH ANY HIGHER.

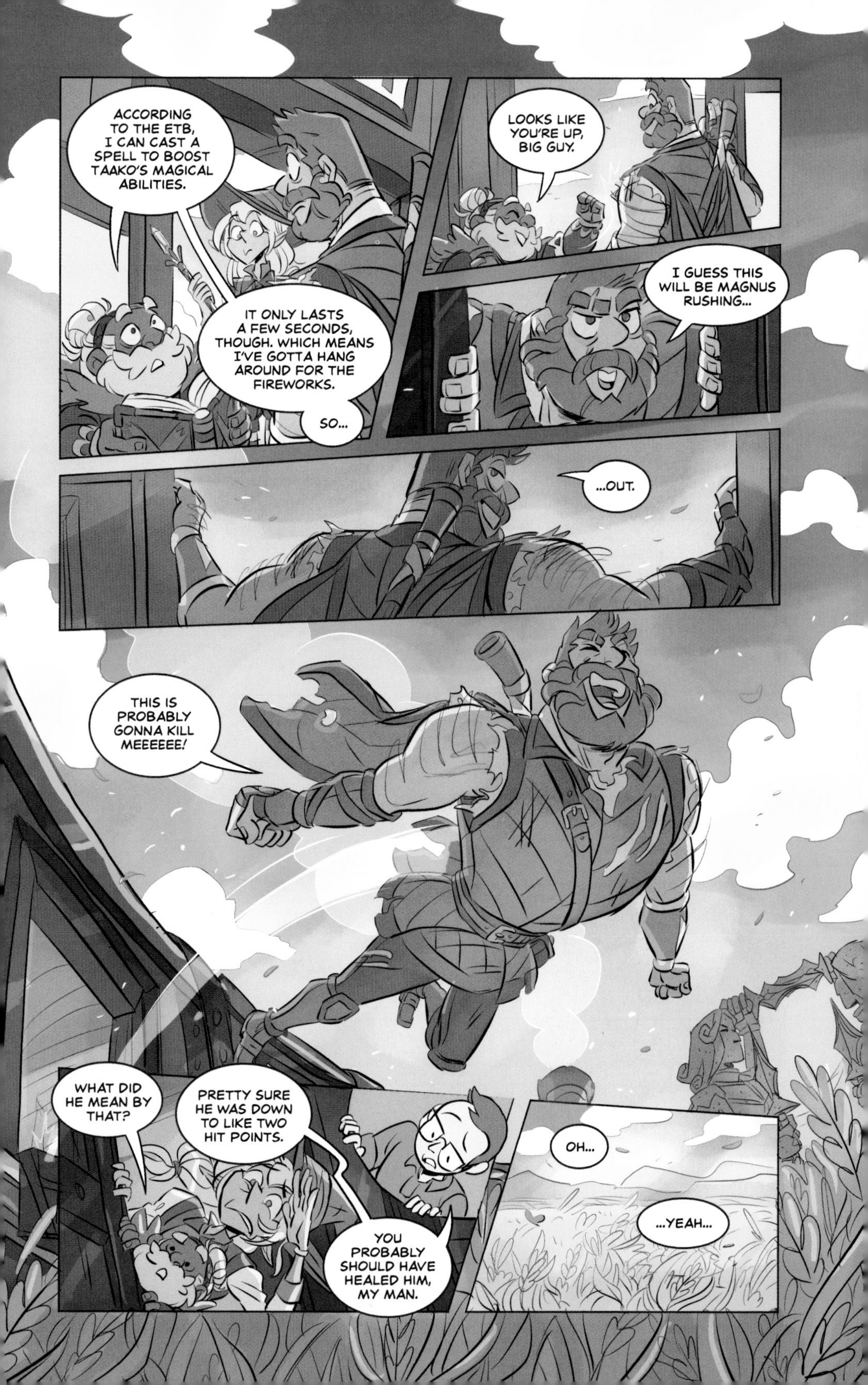
ACCORDING TO THE ETB, I CAN CAST A SPELL TO BOOST TAAKO'S MAGICAL ABILITIES.
IT ONLY LASTS A FEW SECONDS, THOUGH. WHICH MEANS I'VE GOTTA HANG AROUND FOR THE FIREWORKS.
SO...
LOOKS LIKE YOU'RE UP, BIG GUY.
I GUESS THIS WILL BE MAGNUS RUSHING...
...OUT.
THIS IS PROBABLY GONNA KILL MEEEEEE!
WHAT DID HE MEAN BY THAT?
PRETTY SURE HE WAS DOWN TO LIKE TWO HIT POINTS.
YOU PROBABLY SHOULD HAVE HEALED HIM, MY MAN.
OH...
...YEAH...

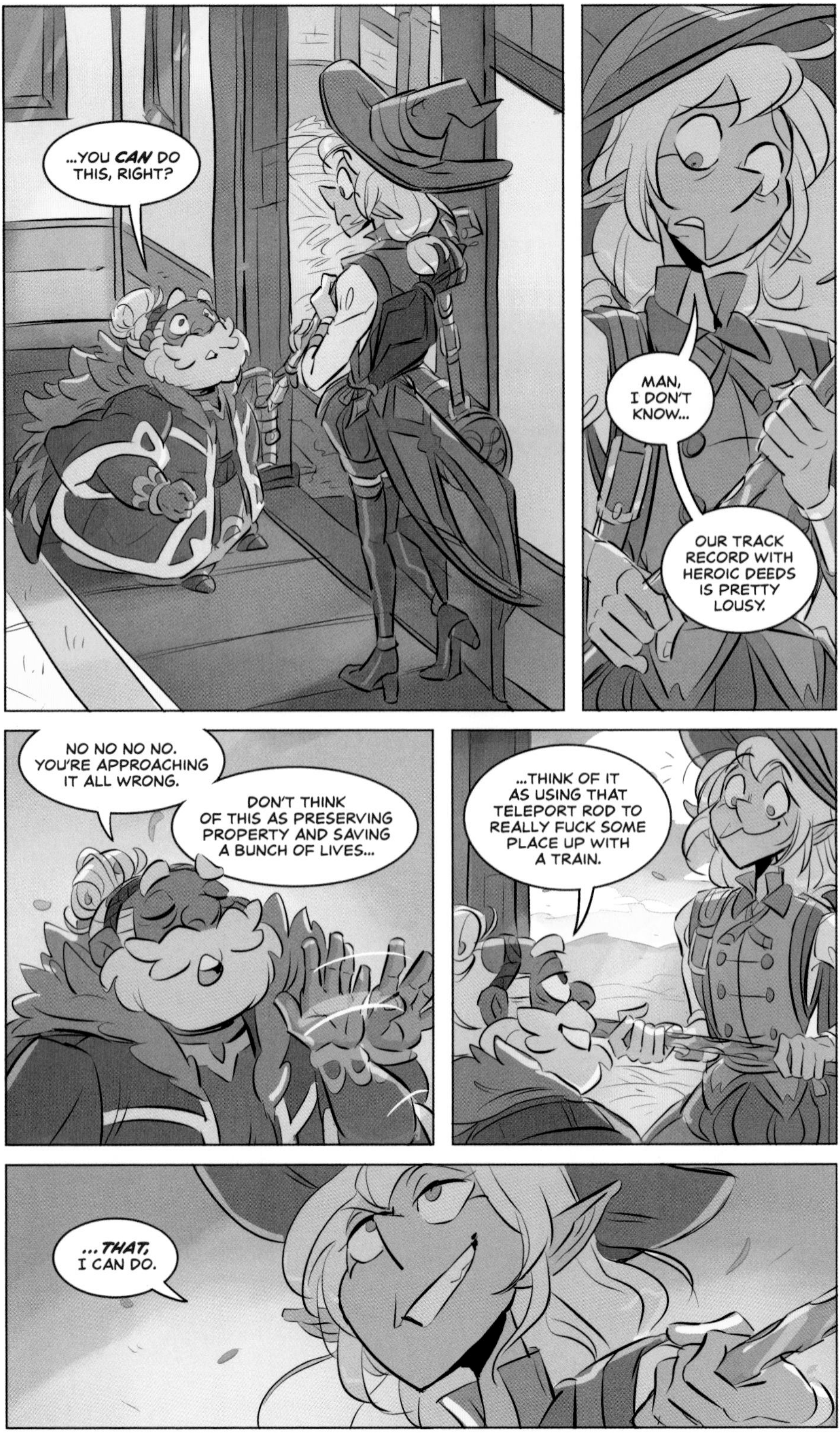
...YOU CAN DO THIS, RIGHT?
MAN, I DON'T KNOW...
OUR TRACK RECORD WITH HEROIC DEEDS IS PRETTY LOUSY.
NO NO NO NO. YOU'RE APPROACHING IT ALL WRONG.
DON'T THINK OF THIS AS PRESERVING PROPERTY AND SAVING A BUNCH OF LIVES...
...THINK OF IT AS USING THAT TELEPORT ROD TO REALLY FUCK SOME PLACE UP WITH A TRAIN.
...THAT, I CAN DO.

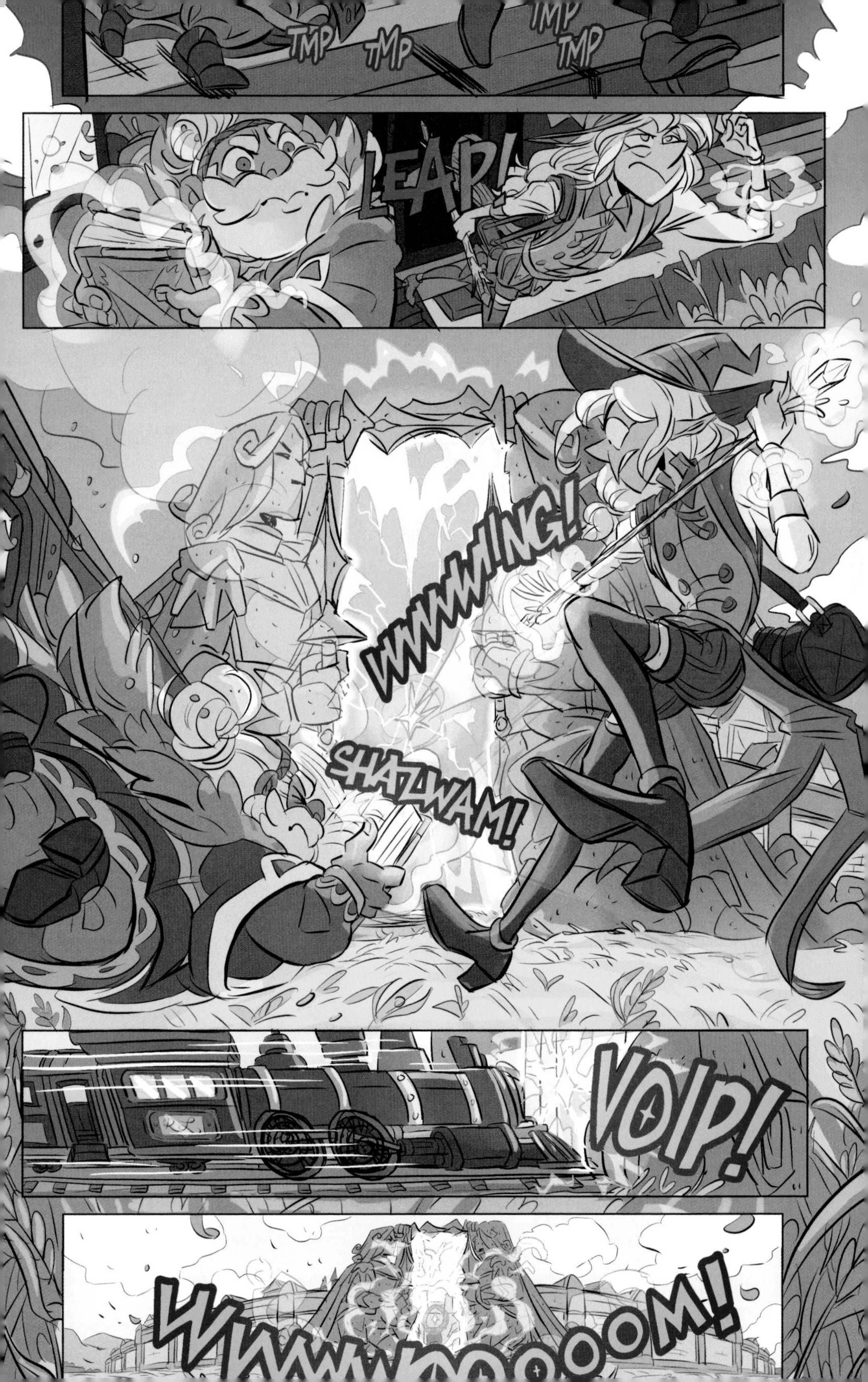
TMP
TMP
TMP
TMP
LEAP!
WWWWWING!
SHAZWAM!
VOIP!
WWWWOOOOOM!

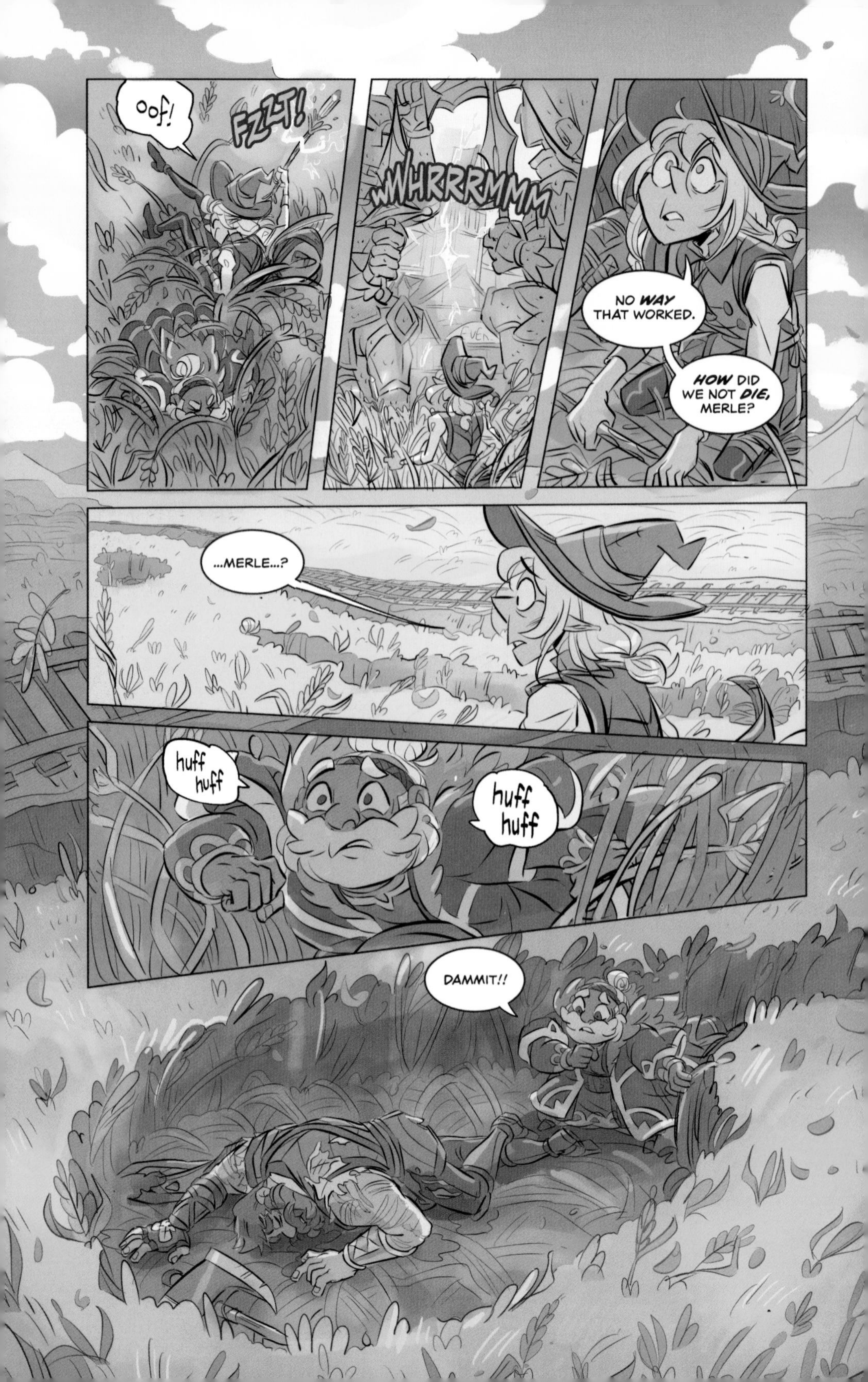
oof!
FZZZT!
wWHRRRMMM
NO WAY THAT WORKED.
HOW DID WE NOT DIE, MERLE?
...MERLE...?
huff huff
huff huff
DAMMIT!!

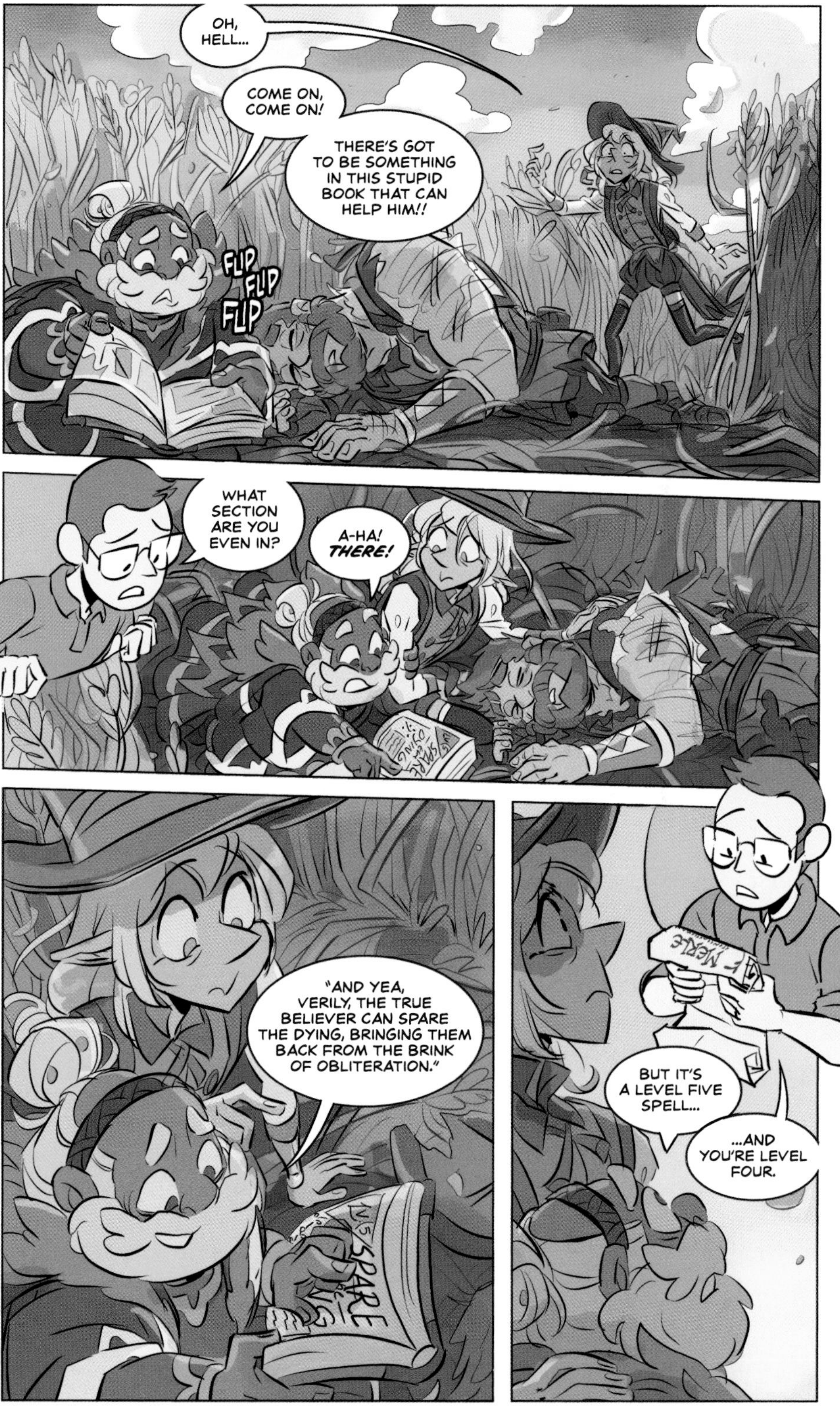
OH, HELL...
COME ON, COME ON!
THERE'S GOT TO BE SOMETHING IN THIS STUPID BOOK THAT CAN HELP HIM!!
FLIP FLIP FLIP
WHAT SECTION ARE YOU EVEN IN?
A-HA! THERE!
"AND YEA, VERILY, THE TRUE BELIEVER CAN SPARE THE DYING, BRINGING THEM BACK FROM THE BRINK OF OBLITERATION."
BUT IT'S A LEVEL FIVE SPELL...
...AND YOU'RE LEVEL FOUR.

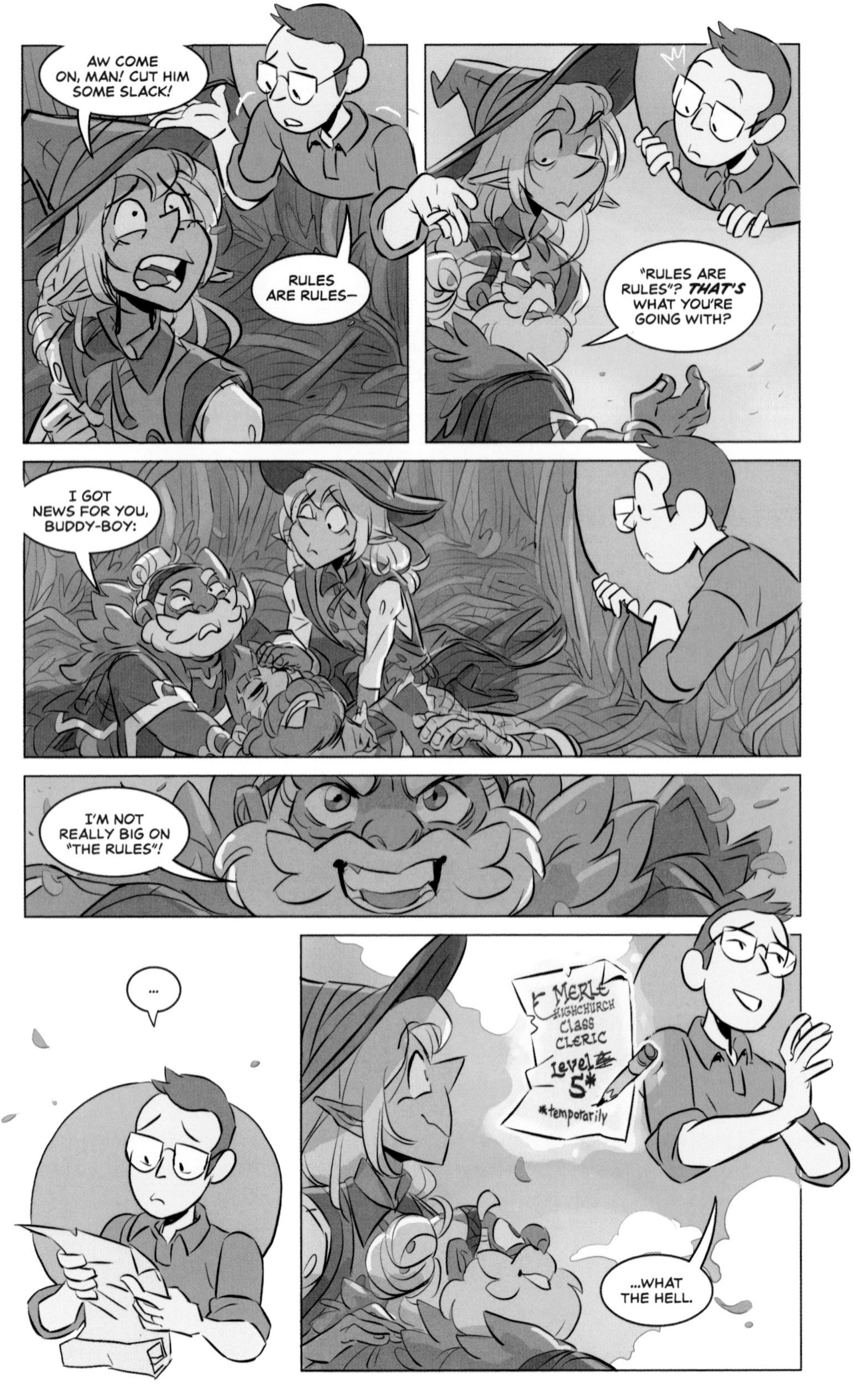
AW COME ON, MAN! CUT HIM SOME SLACK!
RULES ARE RULES—
"RULES ARE RULES"? THAT'S WHAT YOU'RE GOING WITH?
I GOT NEWS FOR YOU, BUDDY-BOY:
I'M NOT REALLY BIG ON "THE RULES"!
...
MERLE HIGHCHURCH
Class CLERIC
Level 5*
*temporarily
...WHAT THE HELL.

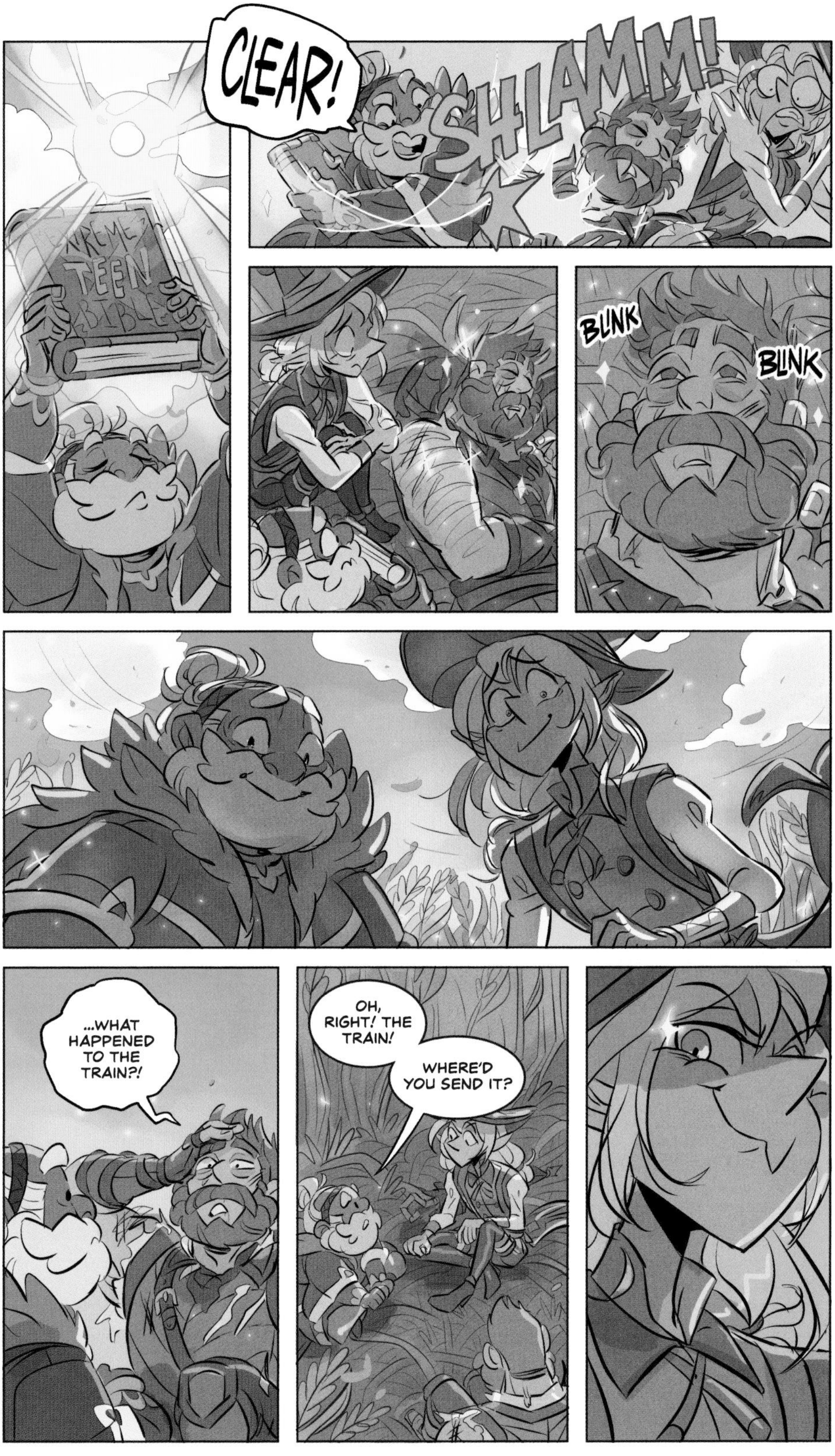
CLEAR!
SHLAMM!
SUPREME TEEN BIBLE
BLINK
BLINK
...WHAT HAPPENED TO THE TRAIN?!
OH, RIGHT! THE TRAIN!
WHERE'D YOU SEND IT?

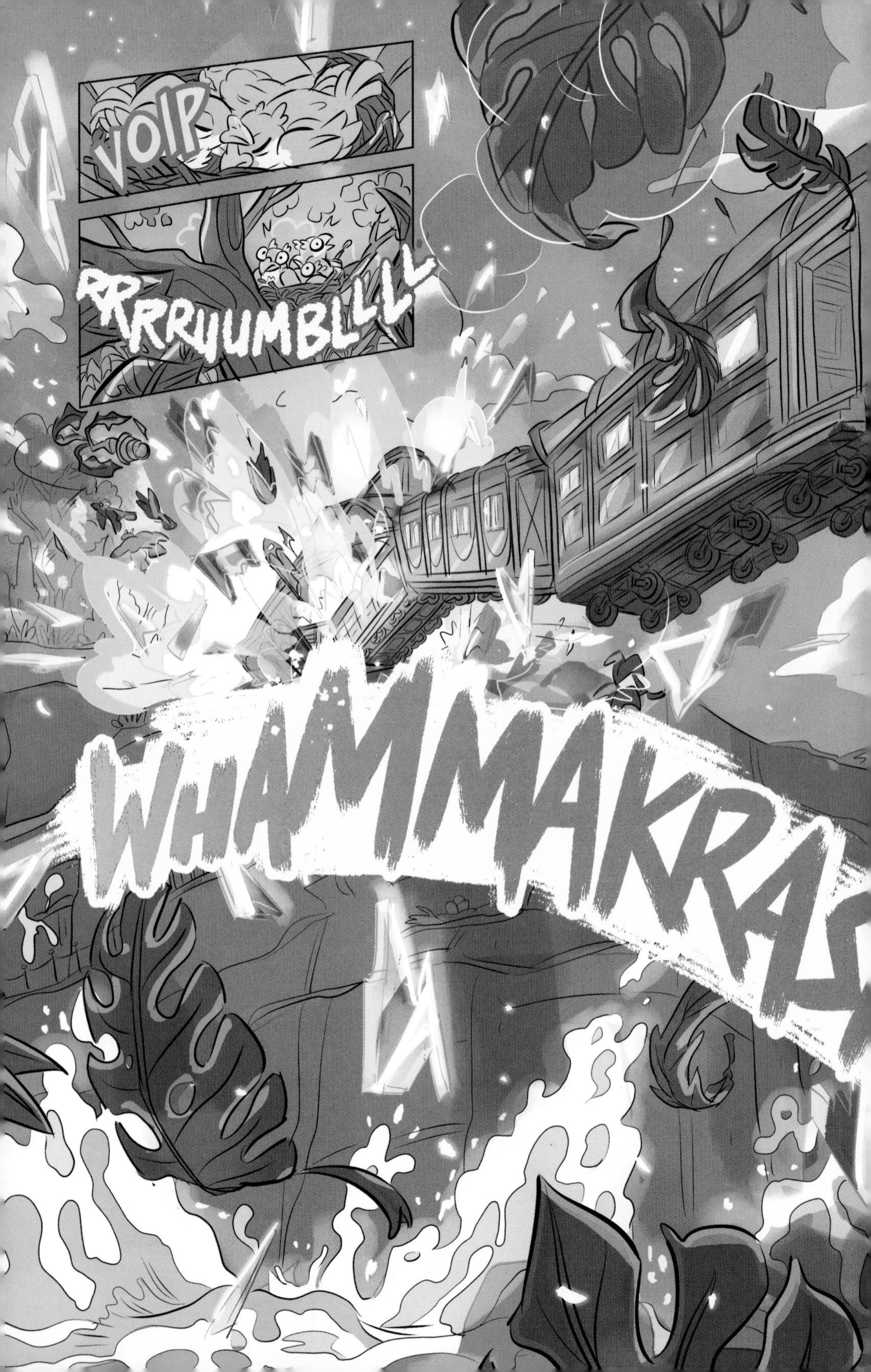
VOIP
RRRRUUMBLLLLL
WHAMMAKRAS

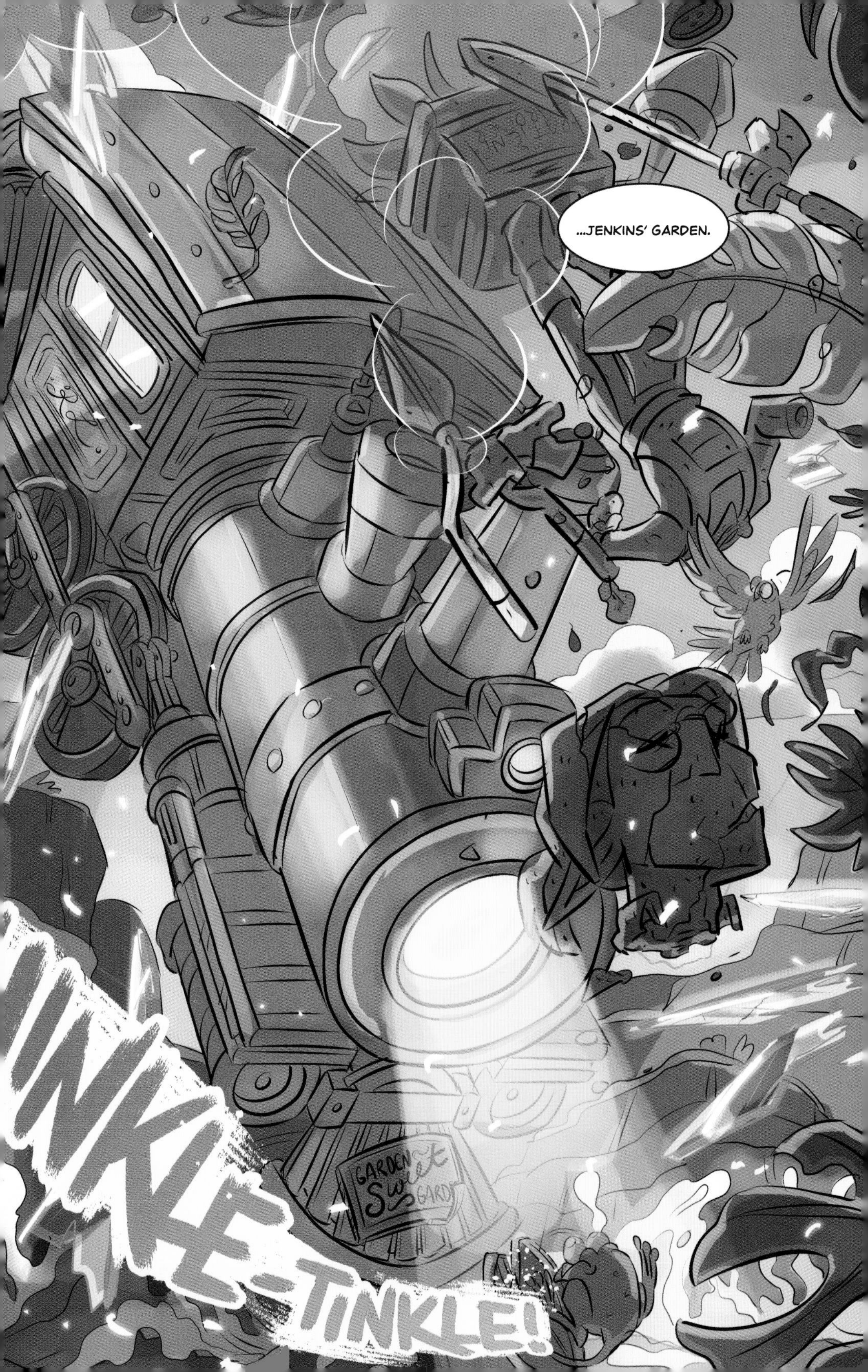
...JENKINS' GARDEN.
INKLE-TINKLE!

Chapter 8

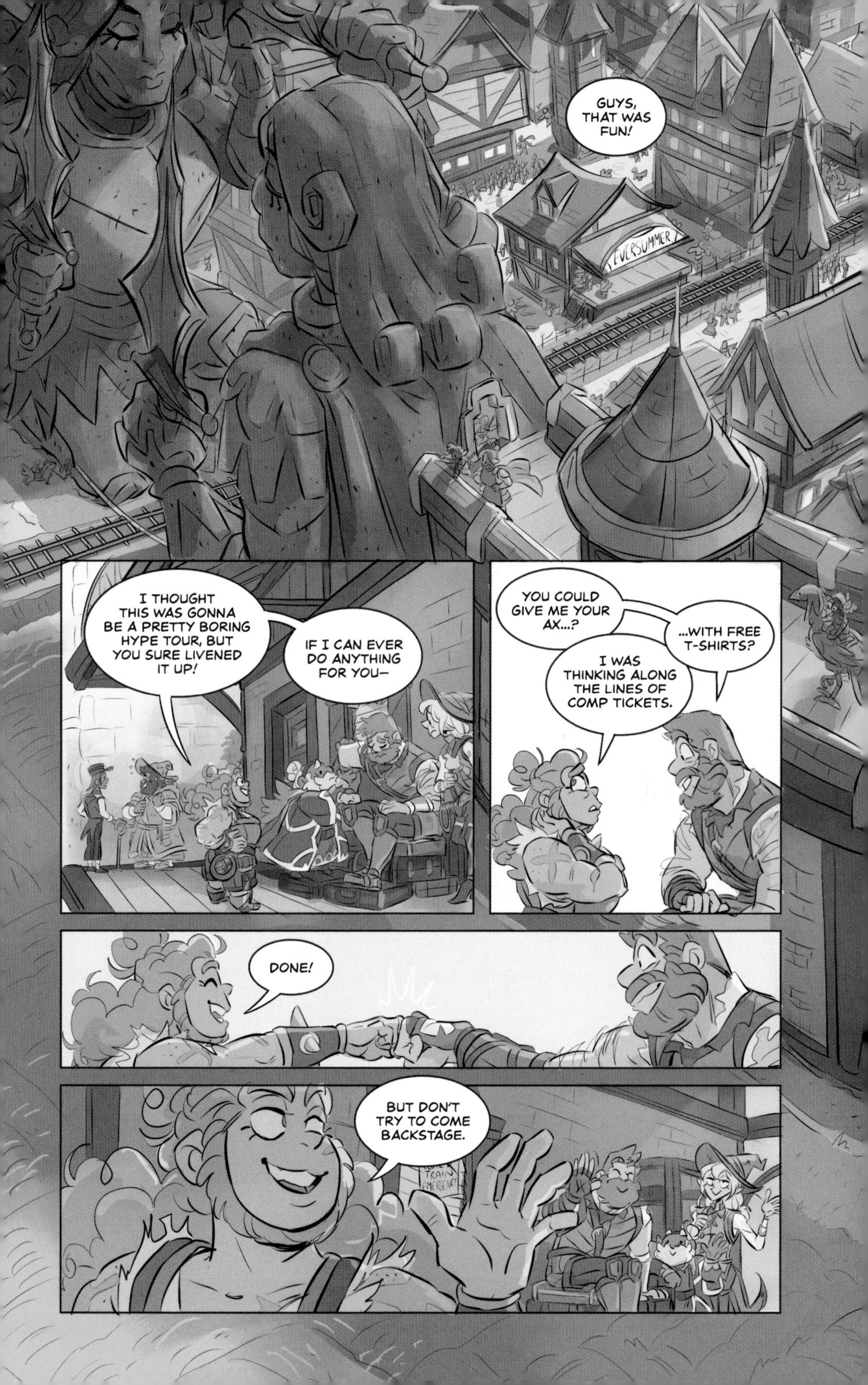
GUYS, THAT WAS FUN!
EVERSUMMER
I THOUGHT THIS WAS GONNA BE A PRETTY BORING HYPE TOUR, BUT YOU SURE LIVENED IT UP!
IF I CAN EVER DO ANYTHING FOR YOU—
YOU COULD GIVE ME YOUR AX...?
...WITH FREE T-SHIRTS?
I WAS THINKING ALONG THE LINES OF COMP TICKETS.
DONE!
BUT DON'T TRY TO COME BACKSTAGE.

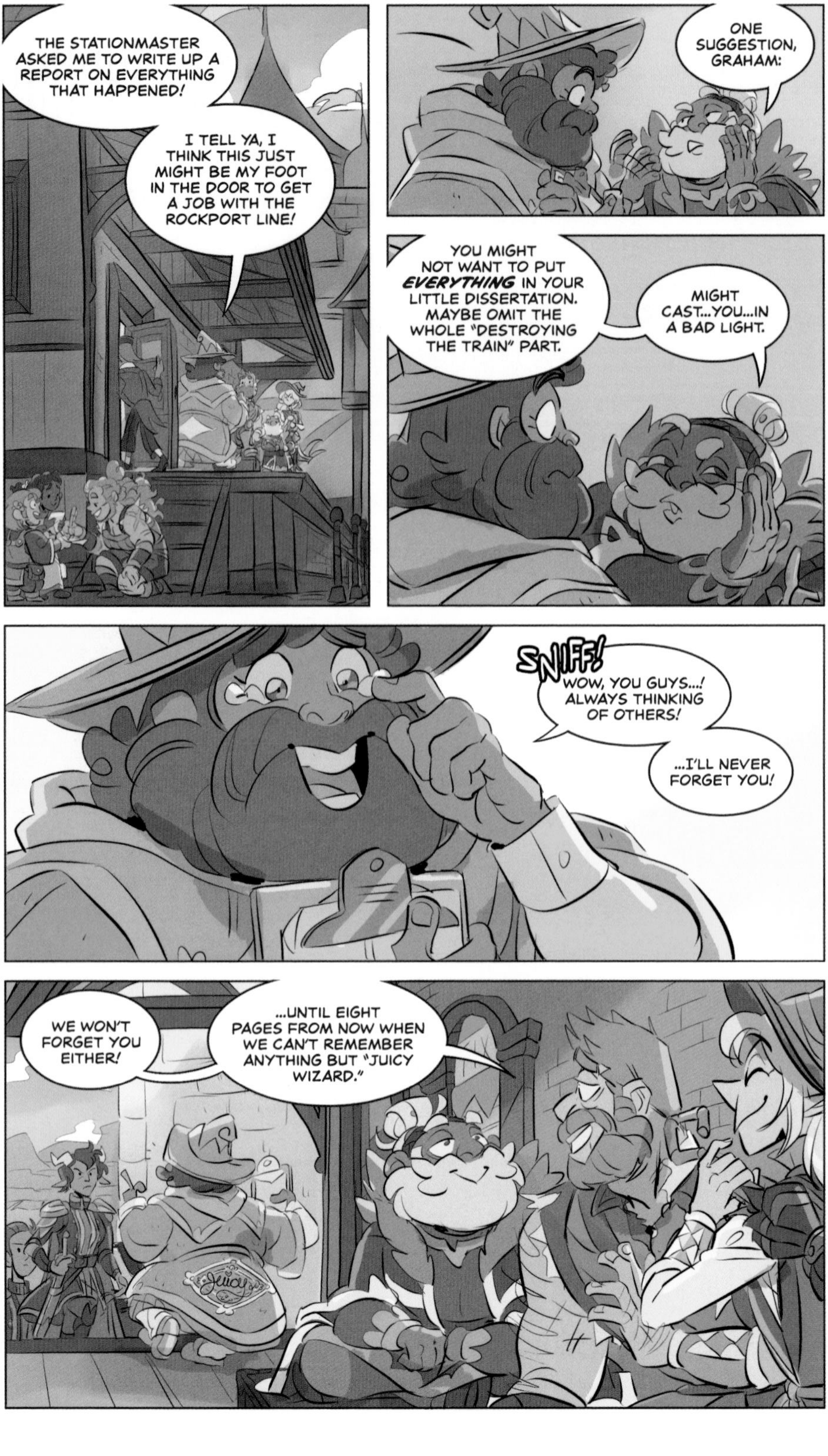
THE STATIONMASTER ASKED ME TO WRITE UP A REPORT ON EVERYTHING THAT HAPPENED!
I TELL YA, I THINK THIS JUST MIGHT BE MY FOOT IN THE DOOR TO GET A JOB WITH THE ROCKPORT LINE!
ONE SUGGESTION, GRAHAM:
YOU MIGHT NOT WANT TO PUT EVERYTHING IN YOUR LITTLE DISSERTATION. MAYBE OMIT THE WHOLE "DESTROYING THE TRAIN" PART.
MIGHT CAST...YOU...IN A BAD LIGHT.
SNIFF!
WOW, YOU GUYS...! ALWAYS THINKING OF OTHERS!
...I'LL NEVER FORGET YOU!
WE WON'T FORGET YOU EITHER!
...UNTIL EIGHT PAGES FROM NOW WHEN WE CAN'T REMEMBER ANYTHING BUT "JUICY WIZARD."
JUICY

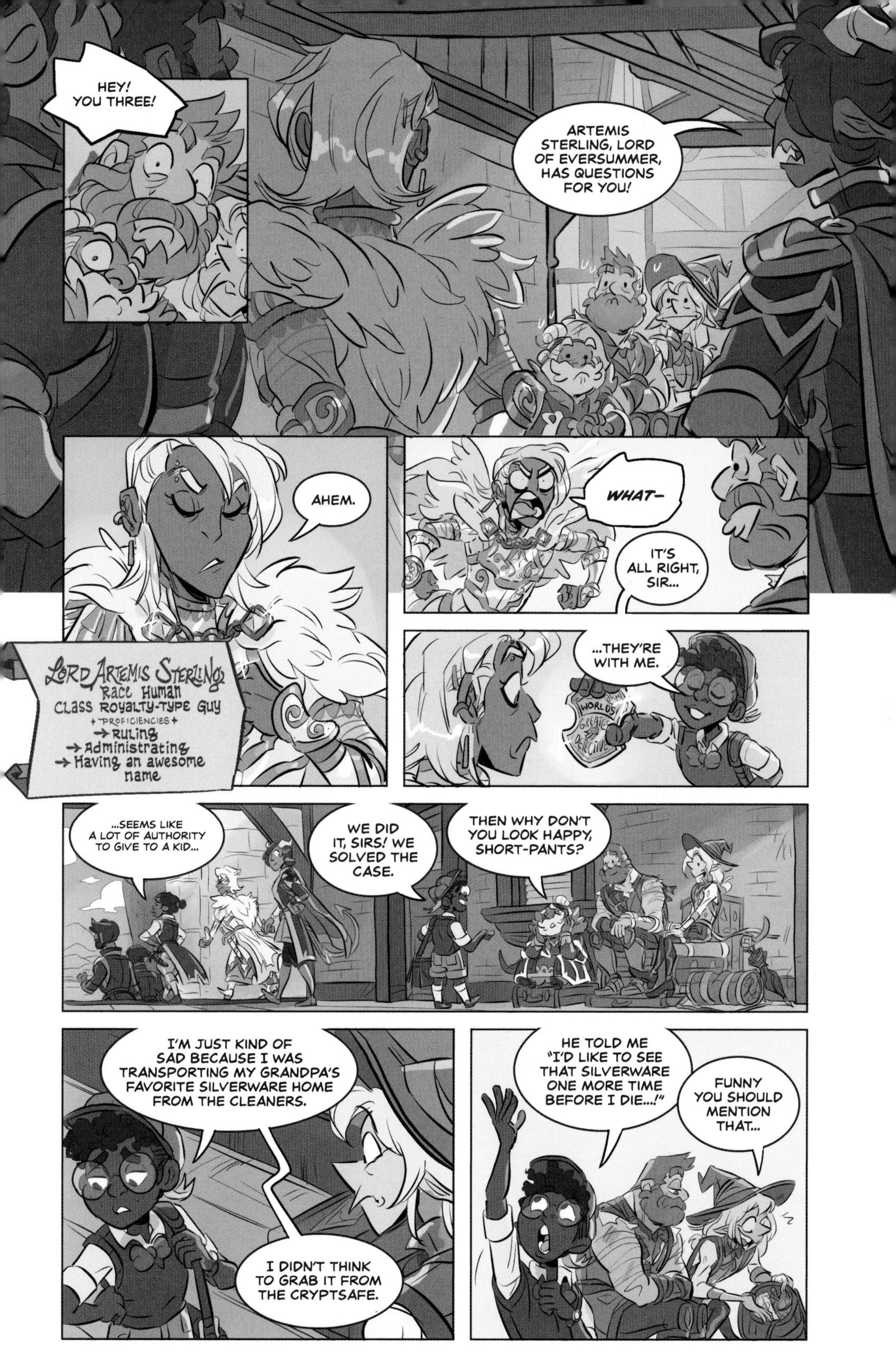

HEY! YOU THREE!
ARTEMIS STERLING, LORD OF EVERSUMMER, HAS QUESTIONS FOR YOU!
AHEM.
WHAT–
IT'S ALL RIGHT, SIR...
LORD ARTEMIS STERLING
Race Human
Class Royalty-type Guy
+ PROFICIENCIES +
→ Ruling
→ Administrating
→ Having an awesome name
...THEY'RE WITH ME.
...SEEMS LIKE A LOT OF AUTHORITY TO GIVE TO A KID...
WE DID IT, SIRS! WE SOLVED THE CASE.
THEN WHY DON'T YOU LOOK HAPPY, SHORT-PANTS?
I'M JUST KIND OF SAD BECAUSE I WAS TRANSPORTING MY GRANDPA'S FAVORITE SILVERWARE HOME FROM THE CLEANERS.
I DIDN'T THINK TO GRAB IT FROM THE CRYPTSAFE.
HE TOLD ME "I'D LIKE TO SEE THAT SILVERWARE ONE MORE TIME BEFORE I DIE...!"
FUNNY YOU SHOULD MENTION THAT...

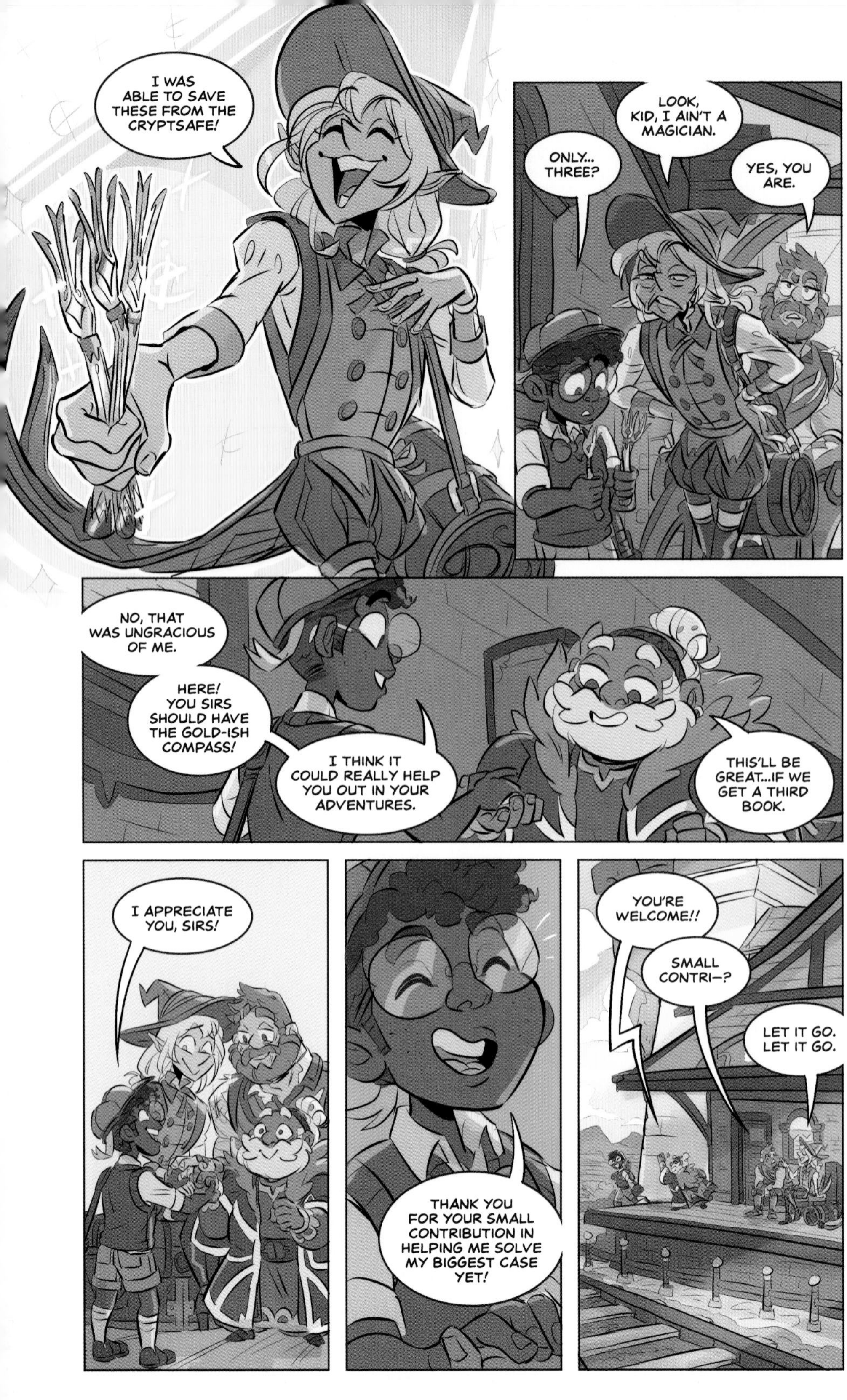
I WAS ABLE TO SAVE THESE FROM THE CRYPTSAFE!
ONLY... THREE?
LOOK, KID, I AIN'T A MAGICIAN.
YES, YOU ARE.
NO, THAT WAS UNGRACIOUS OF ME.
HERE! YOU SIRS SHOULD HAVE THE GOLD-ISH COMPASS!
I THINK IT COULD REALLY HELP YOU OUT IN YOUR ADVENTURES.
THIS'LL BE GREAT...IF WE GET A THIRD BOOK.
I APPRECIATE YOU, SIRS!
THANK YOU FOR YOUR SMALL CONTRIBUTION IN HELPING ME SOLVE MY BIGGEST CASE YET!
YOU'RE WELCOME!!
SMALL CONTRI—?
LET IT GO. LET IT GO.

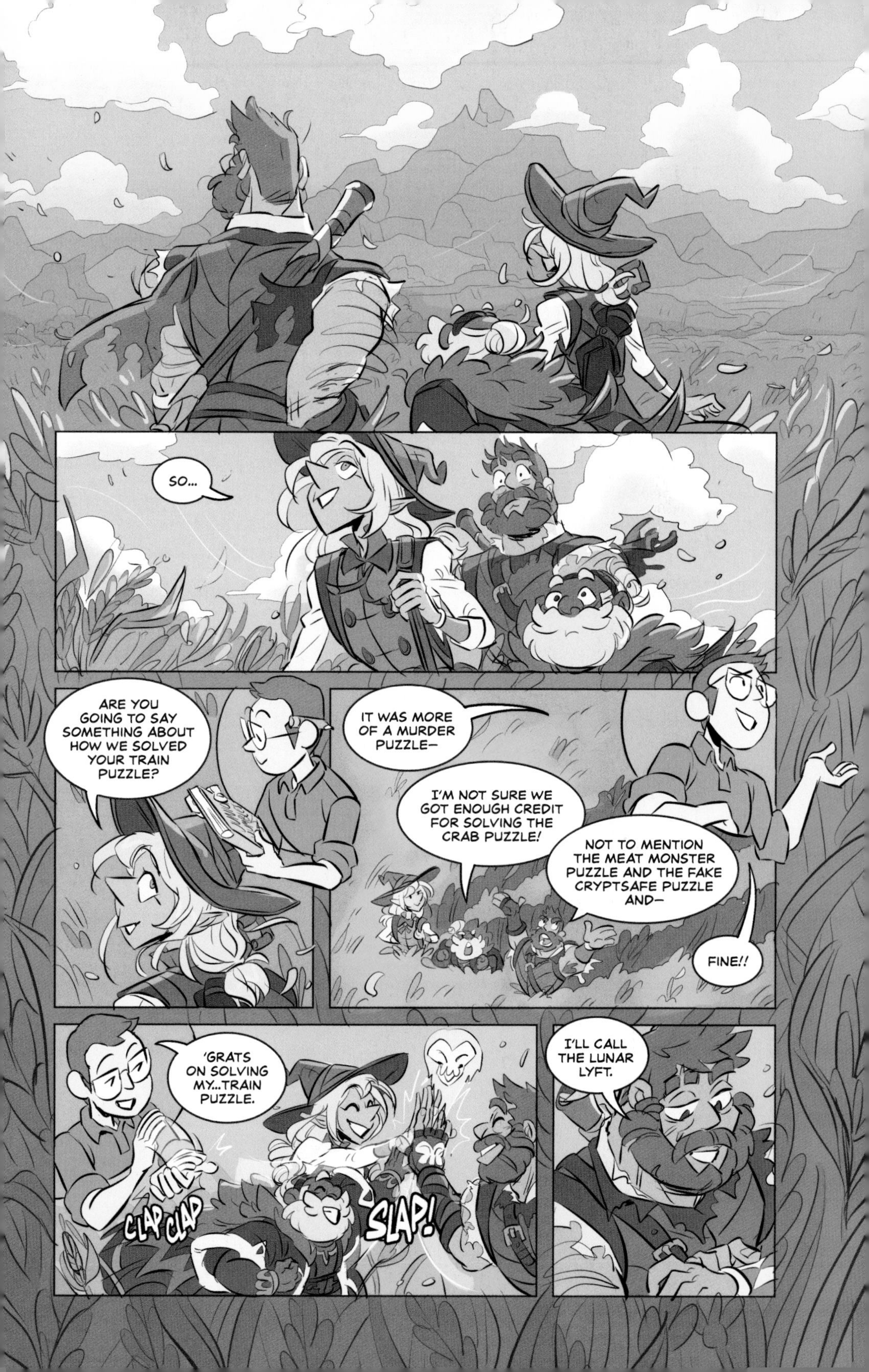
SO...
ARE YOU GOING TO SAY SOMETHING ABOUT HOW WE SOLVED YOUR TRAIN PUZZLE?
IT WAS MORE OF A MURDER PUZZLE—
I'M NOT SURE WE GOT ENOUGH CREDIT FOR SOLVING THE CRAB PUZZLE!
NOT TO MENTION THE MEAT MONSTER PUZZLE AND THE FAKE CRYPTSAFE PUZZLE AND—
FINE!!
'GRATS ON SOLVING MY...TRAIN PUZZLE.
CLAP CLAP
SLAP!
I'LL CALL THE LUNAR LYFT.

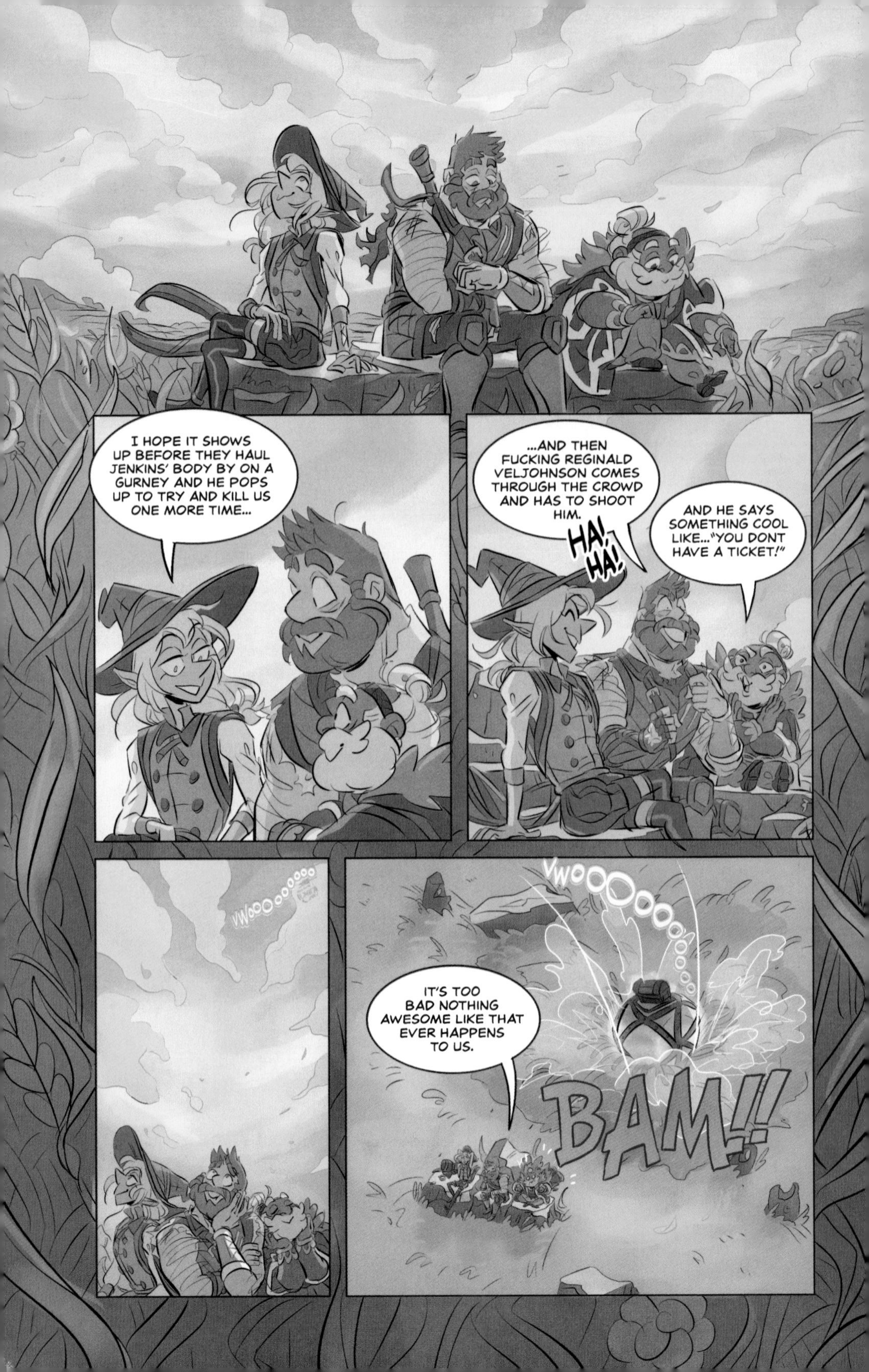
I HOPE IT SHOWS UP BEFORE THEY HAUL JENKINS' BODY BY ON A GURNEY AND HE POPS UP TO TRY AND KILL US ONE MORE TIME...
...AND THEN FUCKING REGINALD VELJOHNSON COMES THROUGH THE CROWD AND HAS TO SHOOT HIM.
HA! HA!
AND HE SAYS SOMETHING COOL LIKE..."YOU DONT HAVE A TICKET!"
VWOOOOOOOOO
VWOOOOOOOOOOO
IT'S TOO BAD NOTHING AWESOME LIKE THAT EVER HAPPENS TO US.
BAM!!

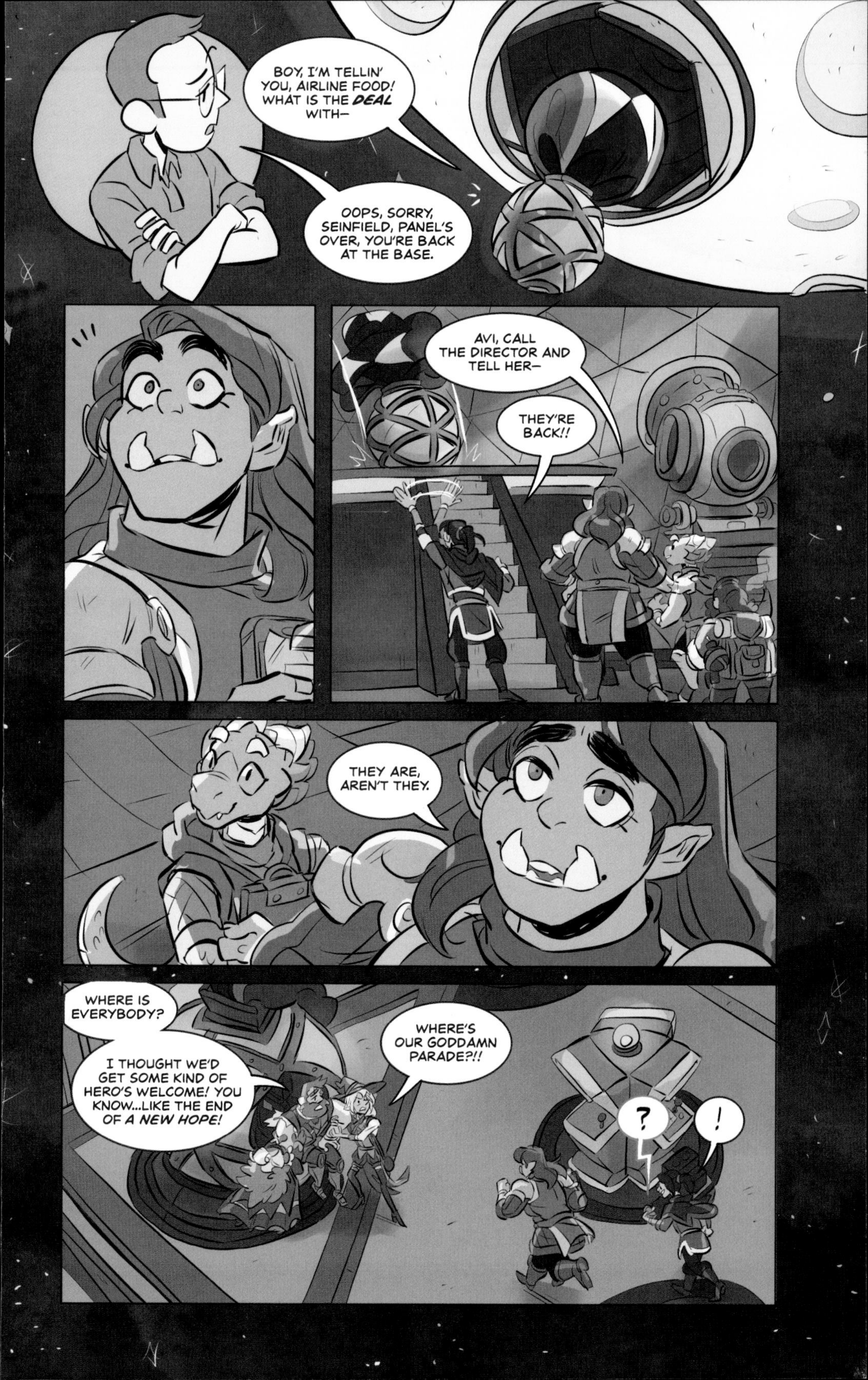
BOY, I'M TELLIN' YOU, AIRLINE FOOD! WHAT IS THE *DEAL* WITH—
OOPS, SORRY, SEINFIELD, PANEL'S OVER, YOU'RE BACK AT THE BASE.
AVI, CALL THE DIRECTOR AND TELL HER—
THEY'RE BACK!!
THEY ARE, AREN'T THEY.
WHERE IS EVERYBODY?
I THOUGHT WE'D GET SOME KIND OF HERO'S WELCOME! YOU KNOW...LIKE THE END OF *A NEW HOPE!*
WHERE'S OUR GODDAMN PARADE?!!
?
!

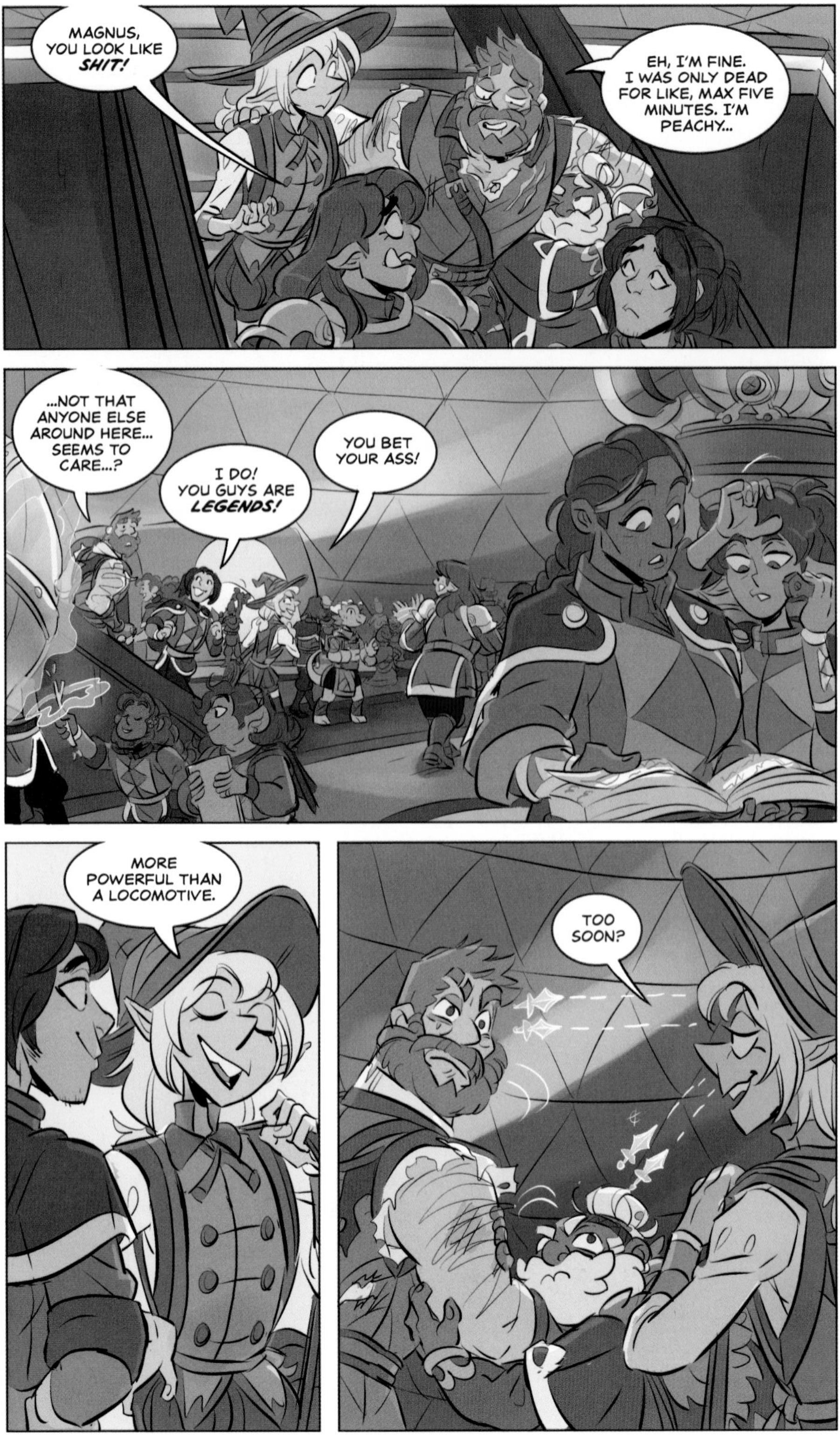
MAGNUS, YOU LOOK LIKE SHIT!
EH, I'M FINE. I WAS ONLY DEAD FOR LIKE, MAX FIVE MINUTES. I'M PEACHY...
...NOT THAT ANYONE ELSE AROUND HERE... SEEMS TO CARE...?
I DO! YOU GUYS ARE LEGENDS!
YOU BET YOUR ASS!
MORE POWERFUL THAN A LOCOMOTIVE.
TOO SOON?

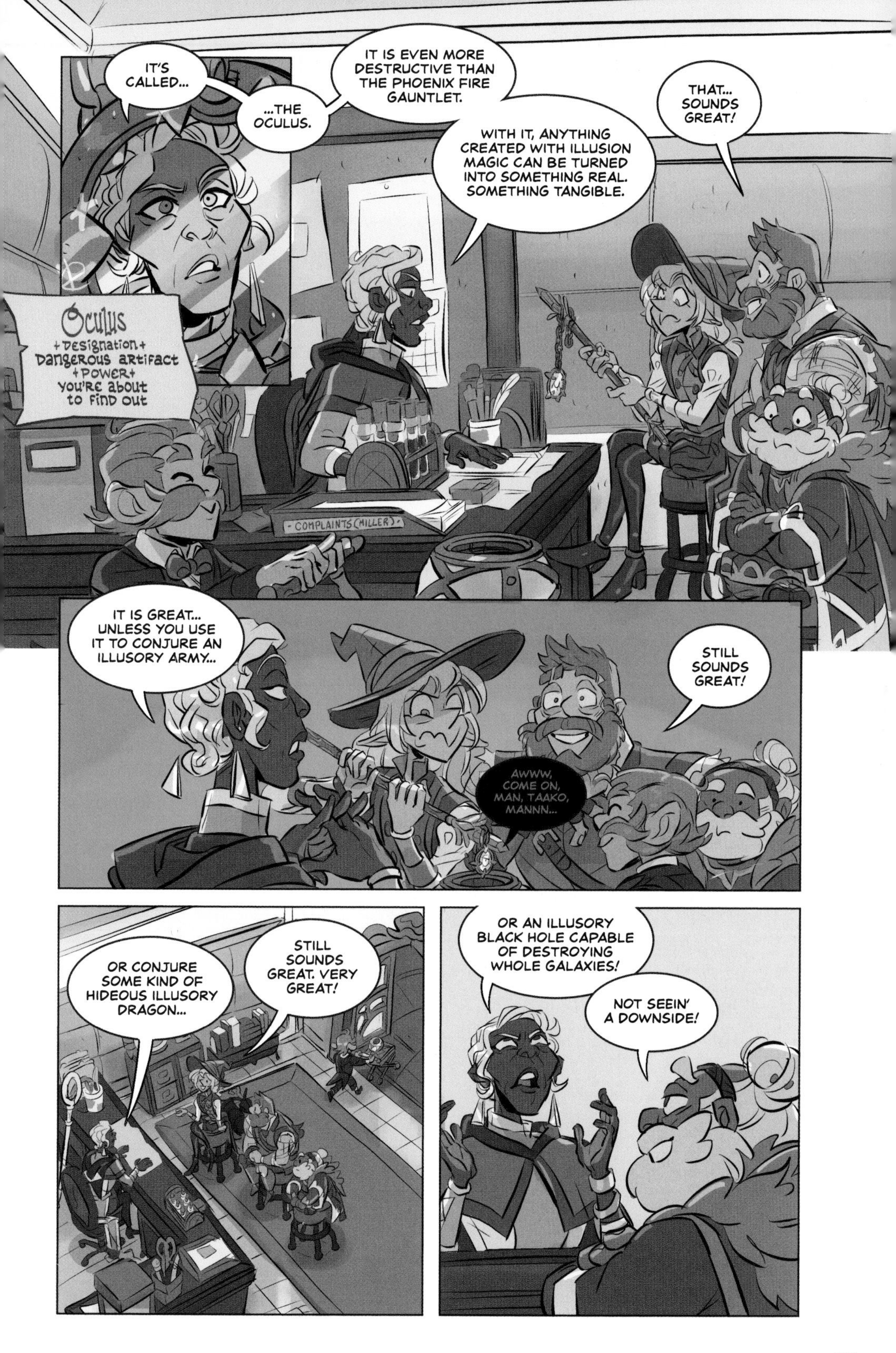

IT'S CALLED...
...THE OCULUS.
IT IS EVEN MORE DESTRUCTIVE THAN THE PHOENIX FIRE GAUNTLET.
WITH IT, ANYTHING CREATED WITH ILLUSION MAGIC CAN BE TURNED INTO SOMETHING REAL. SOMETHING TANGIBLE.
THAT... SOUNDS GREAT!
Oculus
+Designation+
Dangerous artifact
+POWER+
You're about to find out
COMPLAINTS (MILLER)
IT IS GREAT... UNLESS YOU USE IT TO CONJURE AN ILLUSORY ARMY...
STILL SOUNDS GREAT!
AWWW, COME ON, MAN, TAAKO, MANNN...
OR CONJURE SOME KIND OF HIDEOUS ILLUSORY DRAGON...
STILL SOUNDS GREAT. VERY GREAT!
OR AN ILLUSORY BLACK HOLE CAPABLE OF DESTROYING WHOLE GALAXIES!
NOT SEEIN' A DOWNSIDE!

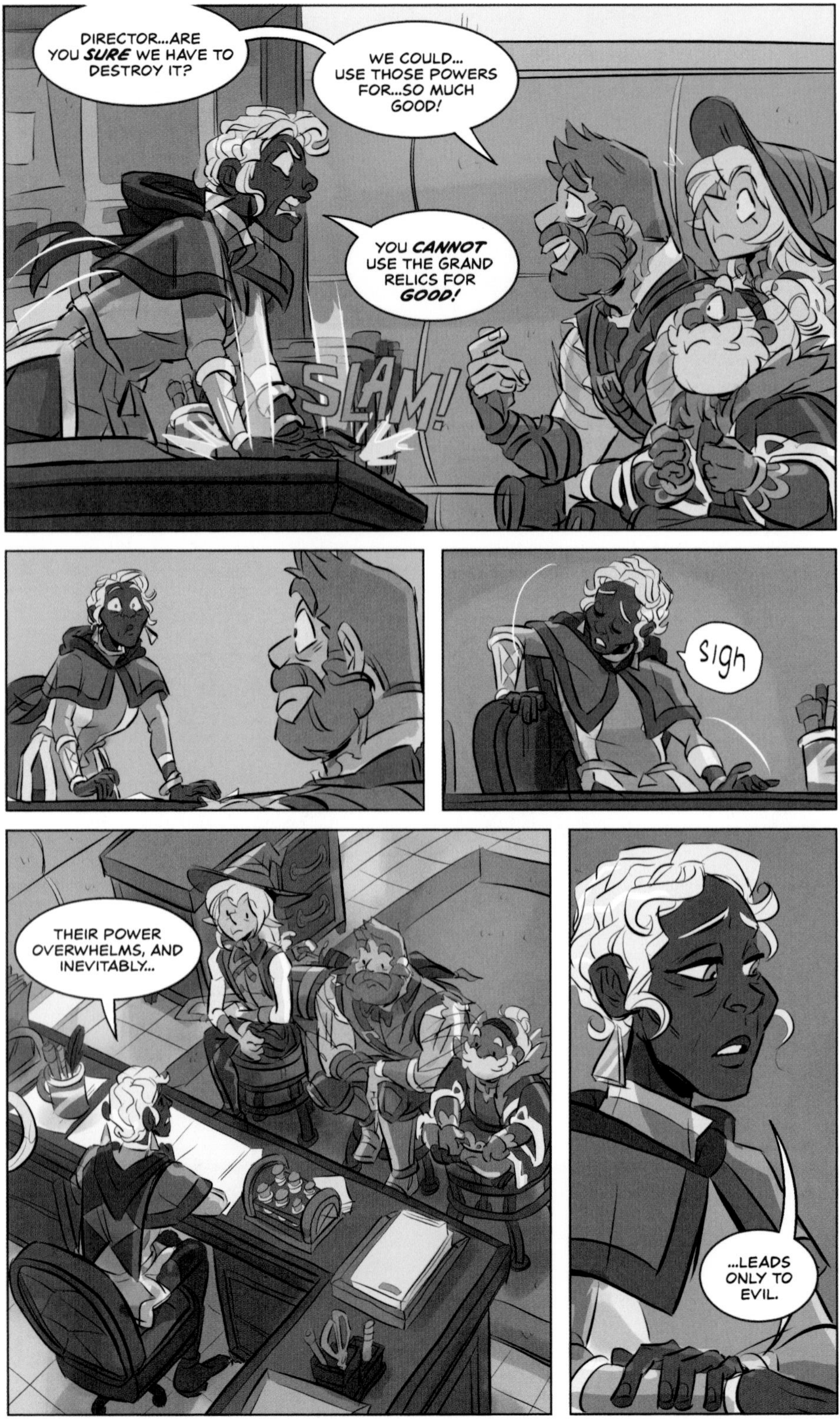
DIRECTOR...ARE YOU *SURE* WE HAVE TO DESTROY IT?
WE COULD... USE THOSE POWERS FOR...SO MUCH GOOD!
YOU *CANNOT* USE THE GRAND RELICS FOR *GOOD!*
SLAM!
sigh
THEIR POWER OVERWHELMS, AND INEVITABLY...
...LEADS ONLY TO EVIL.

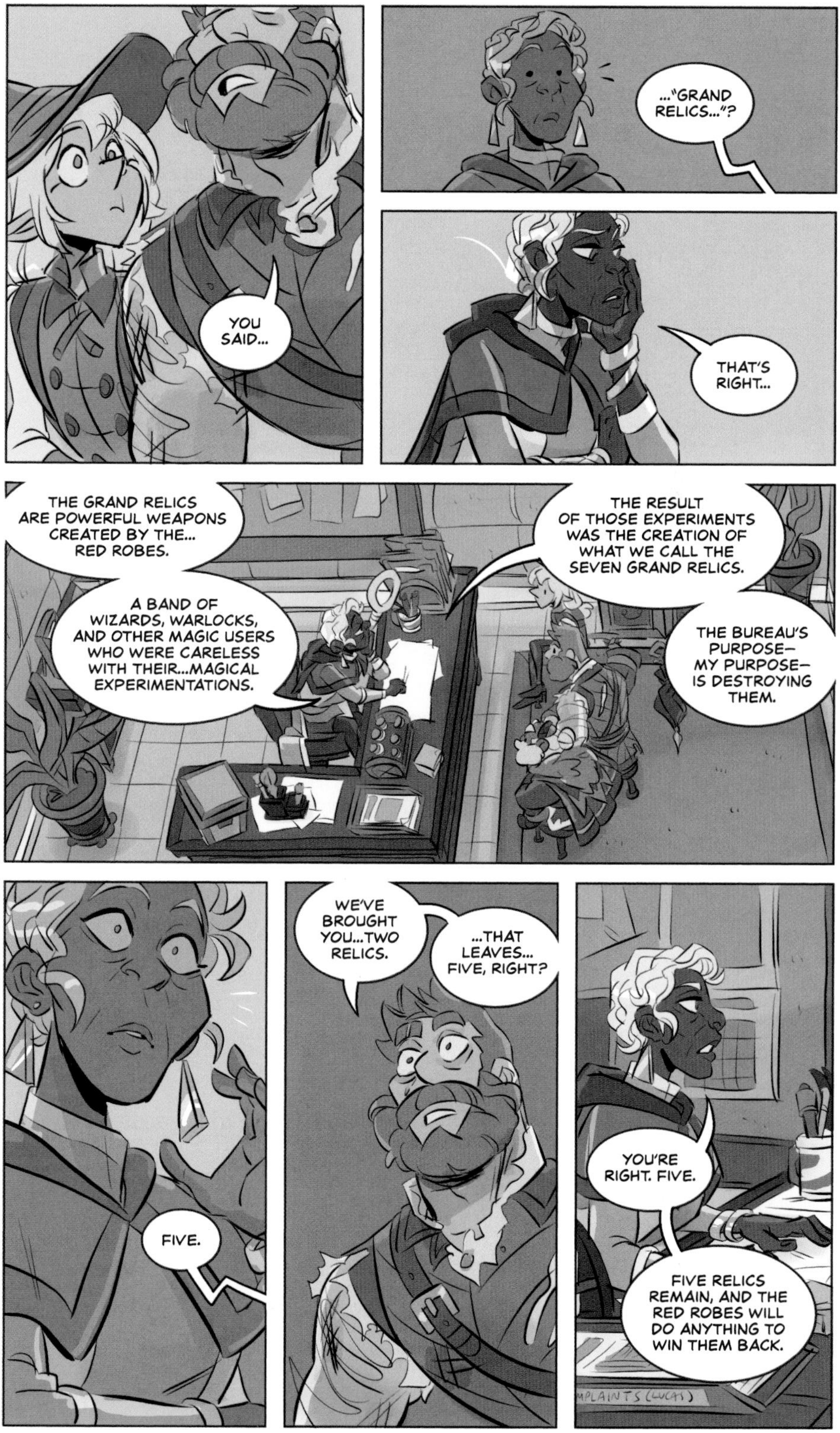
YOU SAID...
..."GRAND RELICS..."?
THAT'S RIGHT...
THE GRAND RELICS ARE POWERFUL WEAPONS CREATED BY THE... RED ROBES.
A BAND OF WIZARDS, WARLOCKS, AND OTHER MAGIC USERS WHO WERE CARELESS WITH THEIR...MAGICAL EXPERIMENTATIONS.
THE RESULT OF THOSE EXPERIMENTS WAS THE CREATION OF WHAT WE CALL THE SEVEN GRAND RELICS.
THE BUREAU'S PURPOSE— MY PURPOSE— IS DESTROYING THEM.
FIVE.
WE'VE BROUGHT YOU...TWO RELICS.
...THAT LEAVES... FIVE, RIGHT?
YOU'RE RIGHT. FIVE.
FIVE RELICS REMAIN, AND THE RED ROBES WILL DO ANYTHING TO WIN THEM BACK.

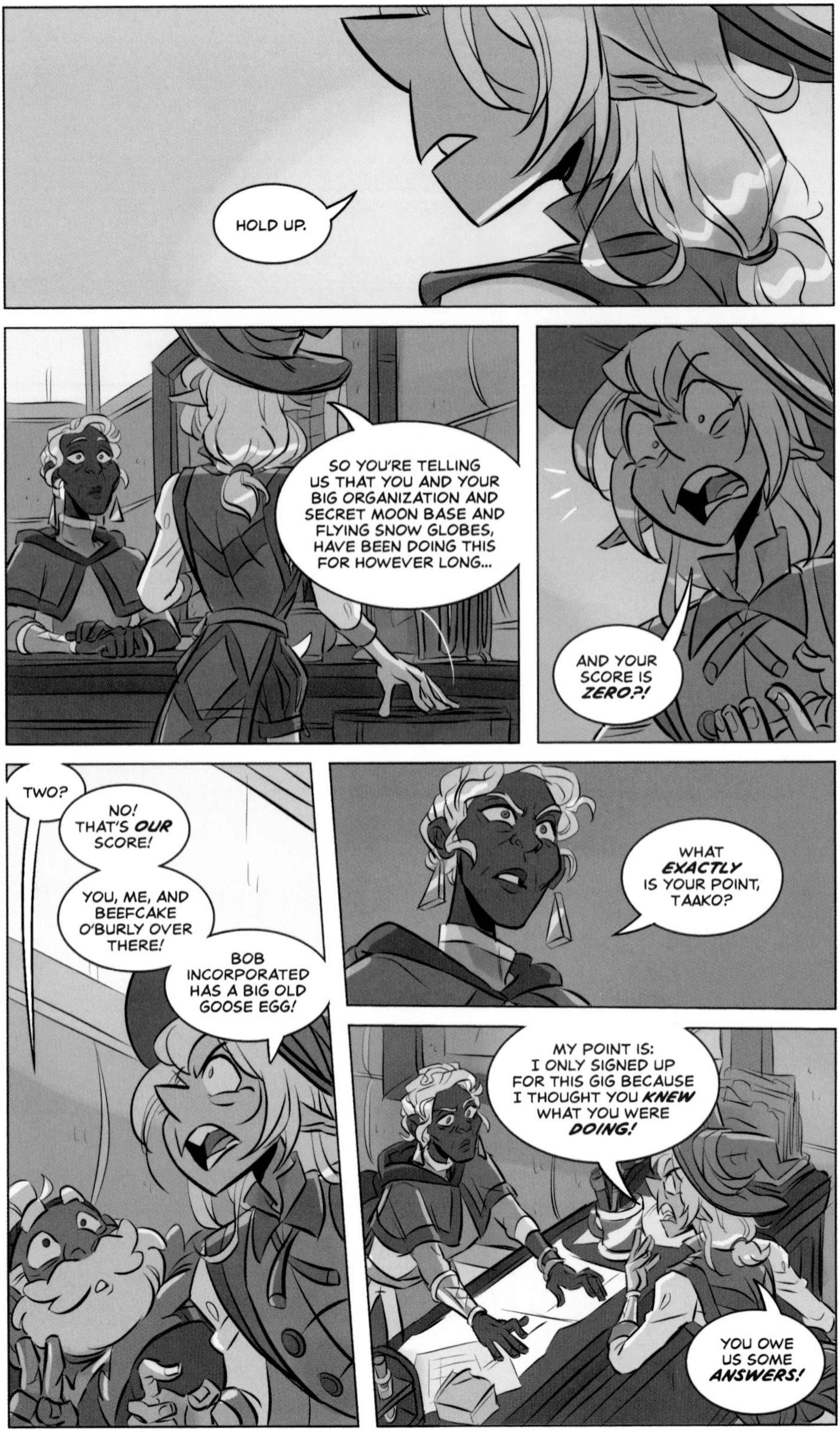
HOLD UP.
SO YOU'RE TELLING US THAT YOU AND YOUR BIG ORGANIZATION AND SECRET MOON BASE AND FLYING SNOW GLOBES, HAVE BEEN DOING THIS FOR HOWEVER LONG...
AND YOUR SCORE IS ZERO?!
TWO?
NO! THAT'S OUR SCORE!
YOU, ME, AND BEEFCAKE O'BURLY OVER THERE!
BOB INCORPORATED HAS A BIG OLD GOOSE EGG!
WHAT EXACTLY IS YOUR POINT, TAAKO?
MY POINT IS: I ONLY SIGNED UP FOR THIS GIG BECAUSE I THOUGHT YOU KNEW WHAT YOU WERE DOING!
YOU OWE US SOME ANSWERS!

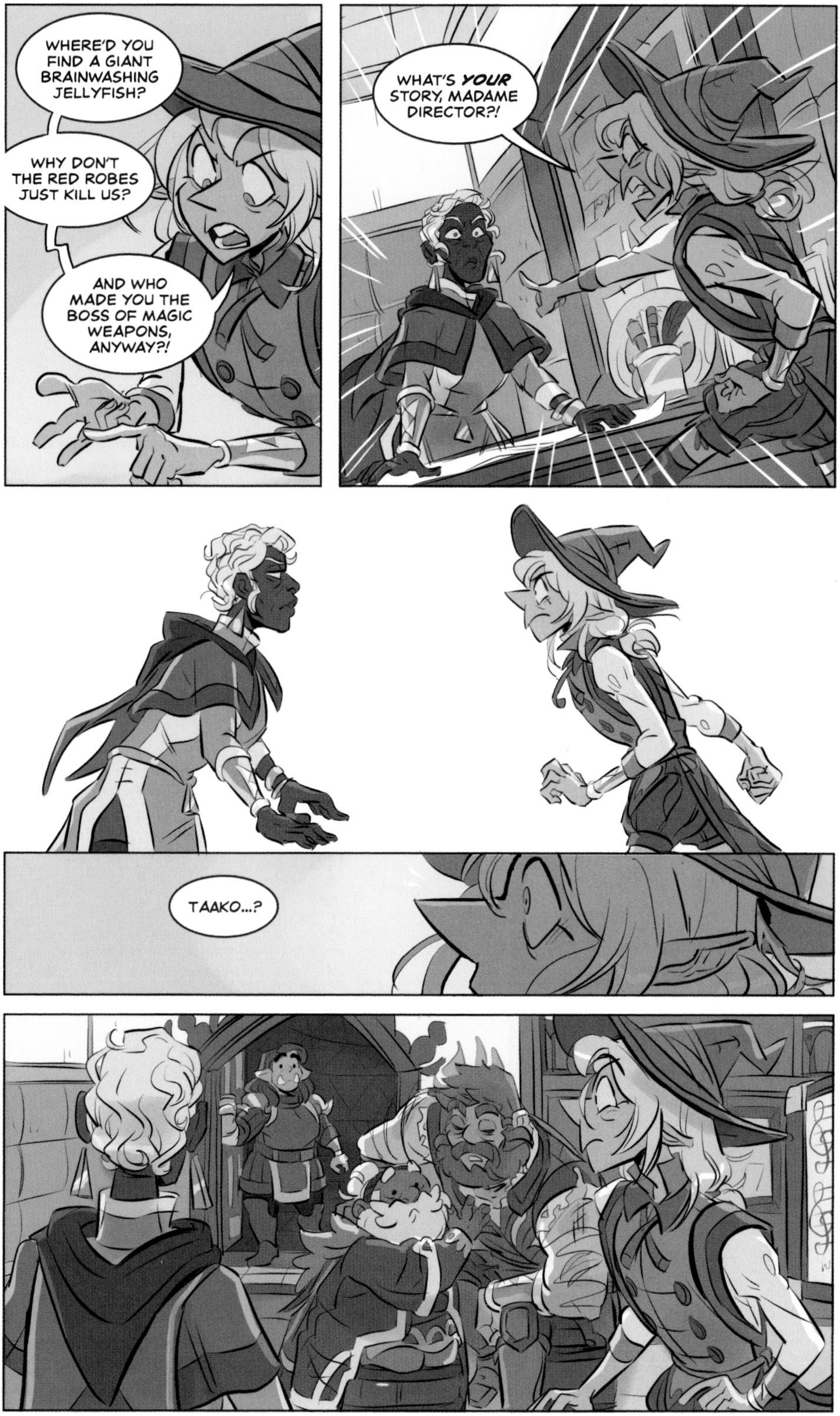
WHERE'D YOU FIND A GIANT BRAINWASHING JELLYFISH?
WHY DON'T THE RED ROBES JUST KILL US?
AND WHO MADE YOU THE BOSS OF MAGIC WEAPONS, ANYWAY?!
WHAT'S *YOUR* STORY, MADAME DIRECTOR?!
TAAKO...?

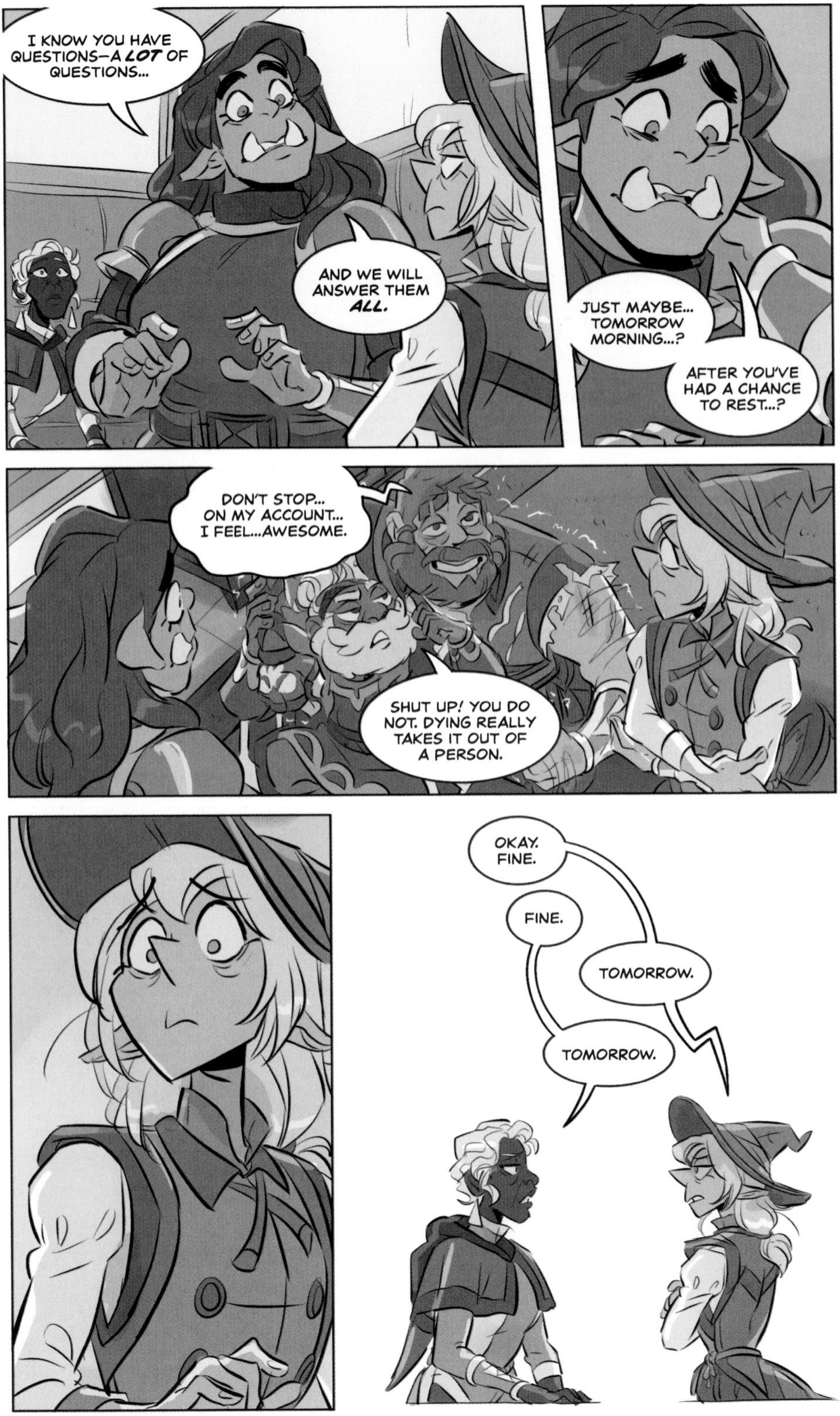
I KNOW YOU HAVE QUESTIONS—A *LOT* OF QUESTIONS...
AND WE WILL ANSWER THEM *ALL.*
JUST MAYBE... TOMORROW MORNING...?
AFTER YOU'VE HAD A CHANCE TO REST...?
DON'T STOP... ON MY ACCOUNT... I FEEL...AWESOME.
SHUT UP! YOU DO NOT. DYING REALLY TAKES IT OUT OF A PERSON.
OKAY. FINE.
FINE.
TOMORROW.
TOMORROW.

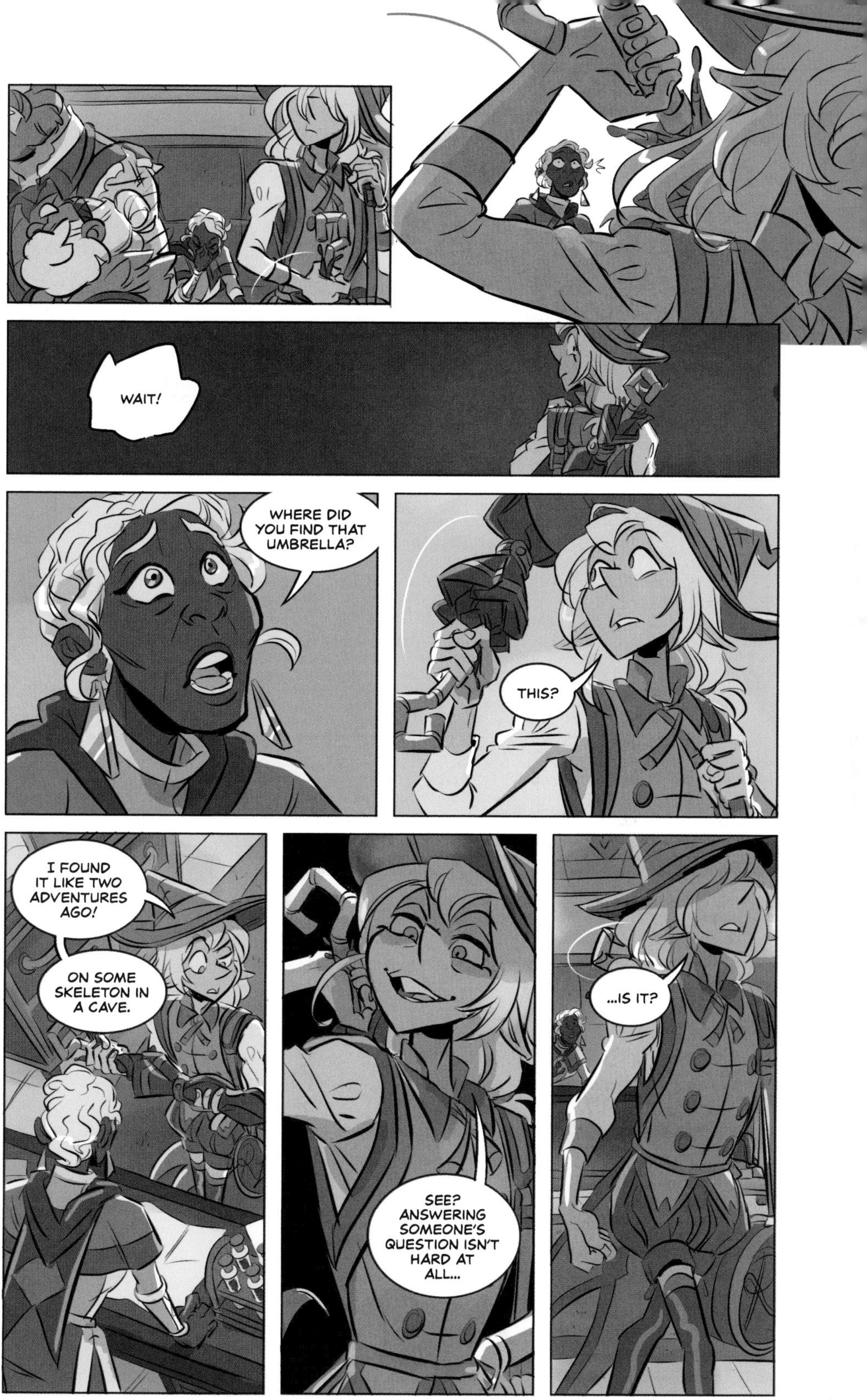
WAIT!
WHERE DID YOU FIND THAT UMBRELLA?
THIS?
I FOUND IT LIKE TWO ADVENTURES AGO!
ON SOME SKELETON IN A CAVE.
SEE? ANSWERING SOMEONE'S QUESTION ISN'T HARD AT ALL...
...IS IT?

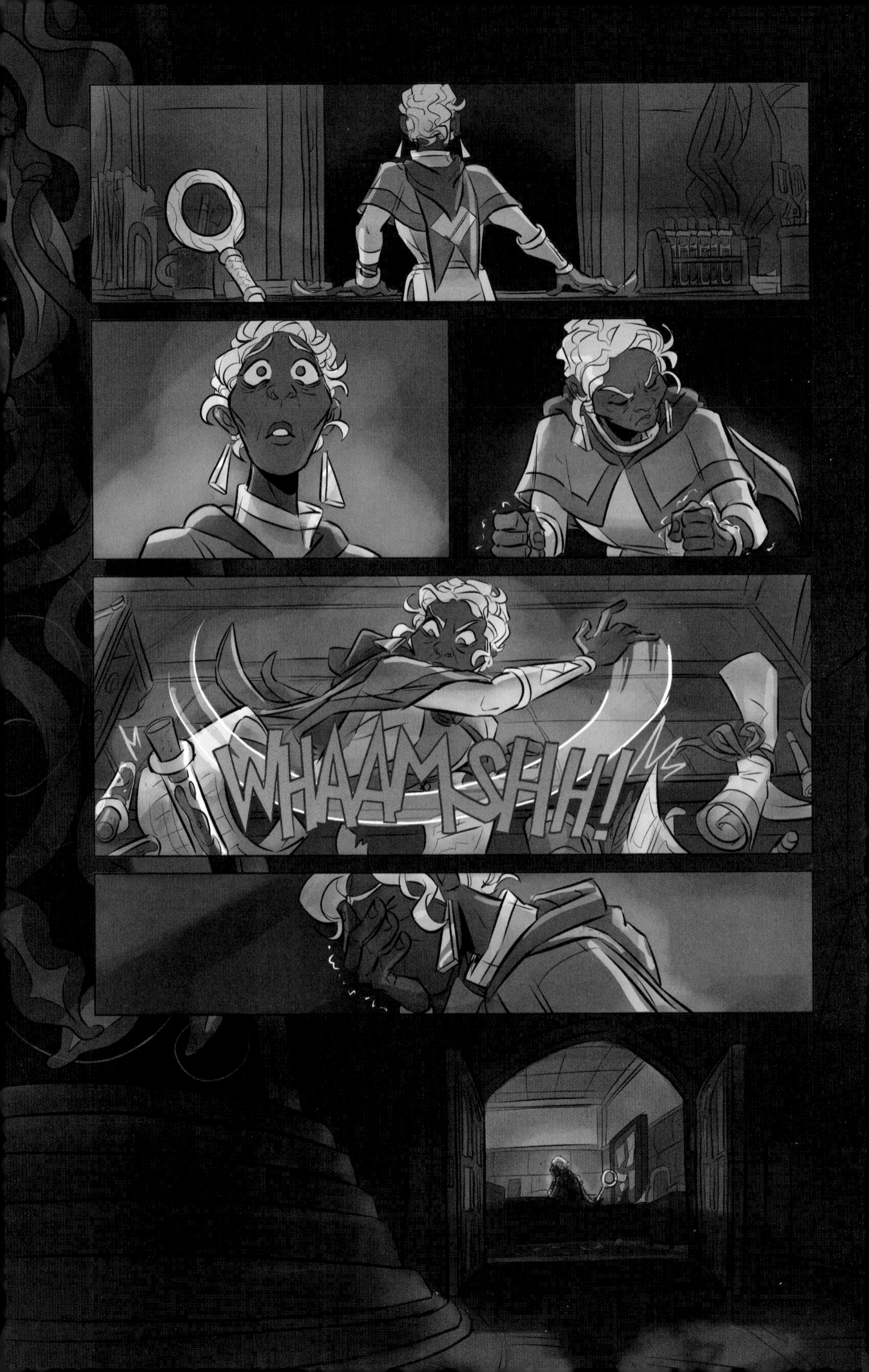
WHAAMSHH!

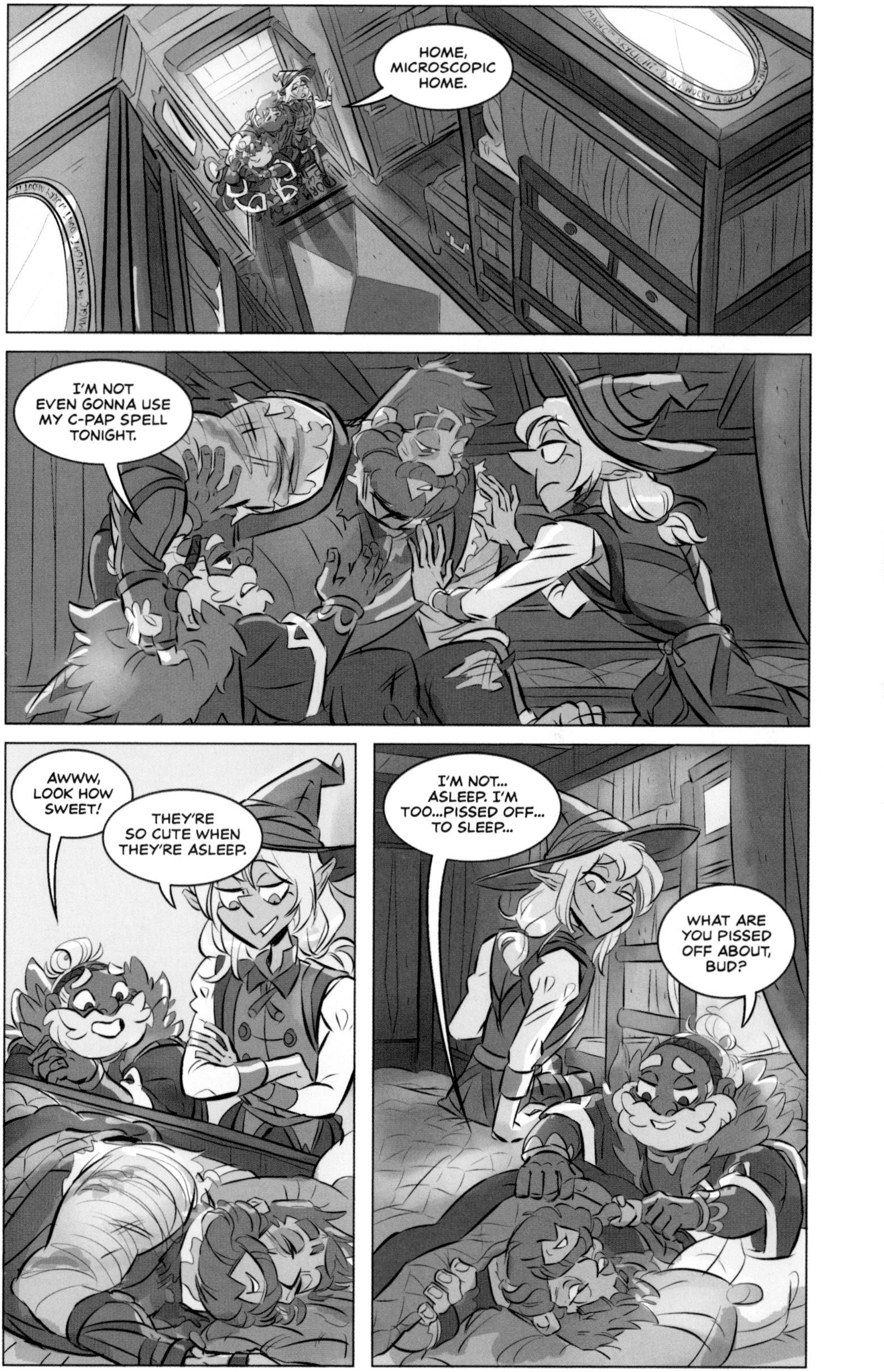
HOME, MICROSCOPIC HOME.
I'M NOT EVEN GONNA USE MY C-PAP SPELL TONIGHT.
AWWW, LOOK HOW SWEET!
THEY'RE SO CUTE WHEN THEY'RE ASLEEP.
I'M NOT... ASLEEP. I'M TOO...PISSED OFF... TO SLEEP...
WHAT ARE YOU PISSED OFF ABOUT, BUD?

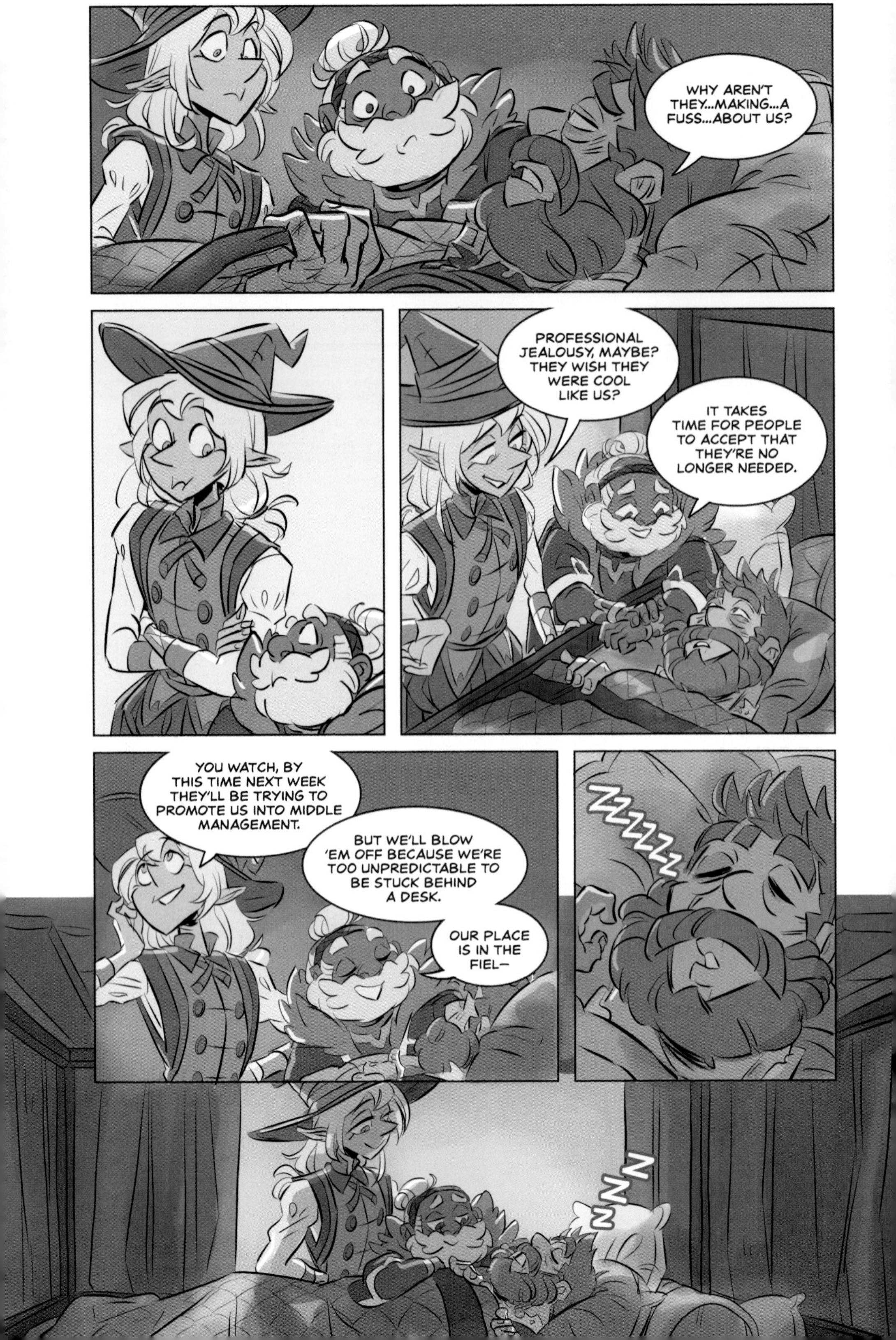
WHY AREN'T THEY...MAKING...A FUSS...ABOUT US?
PROFESSIONAL JEALOUSY, MAYBE? THEY WISH THEY WERE COOL LIKE US?
IT TAKES TIME FOR PEOPLE TO ACCEPT THAT THEY'RE NO LONGER NEEDED.
YOU WATCH, BY THIS TIME NEXT WEEK THEY'LL BE TRYING TO PROMOTE US INTO MIDDLE MANAGEMENT.
BUT WE'LL BLOW 'EM OFF BECAUSE WE'RE TOO UNPREDICTABLE TO BE STUCK BEHIND A DESK.
OUR PLACE IS IN THE FIEL—
ZZZZZZ
ZZZ

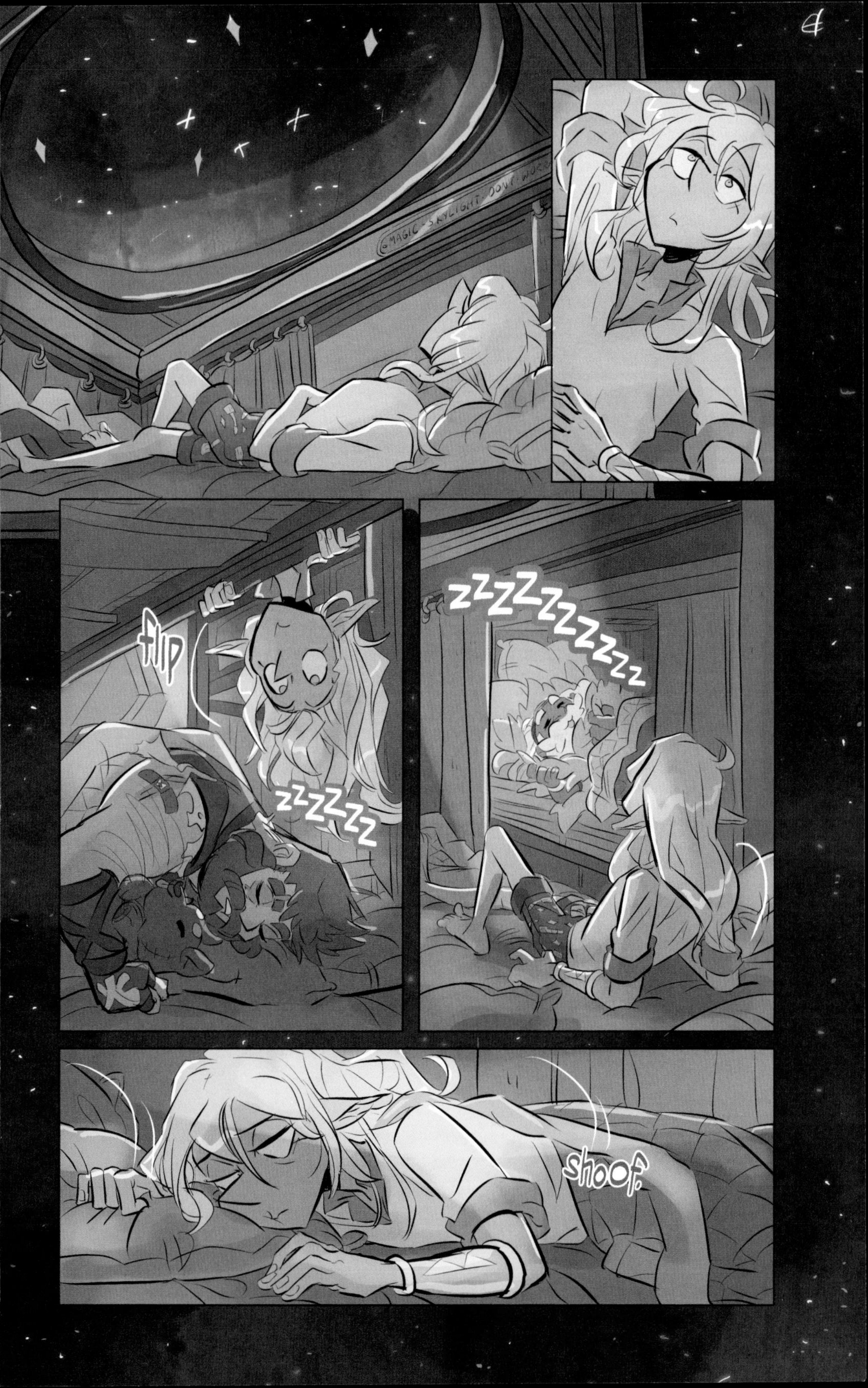
MAGIC · SKYLIGHT · DON'T
flip
zzzzzz
zzzzzzzzzzzzz
shoof.

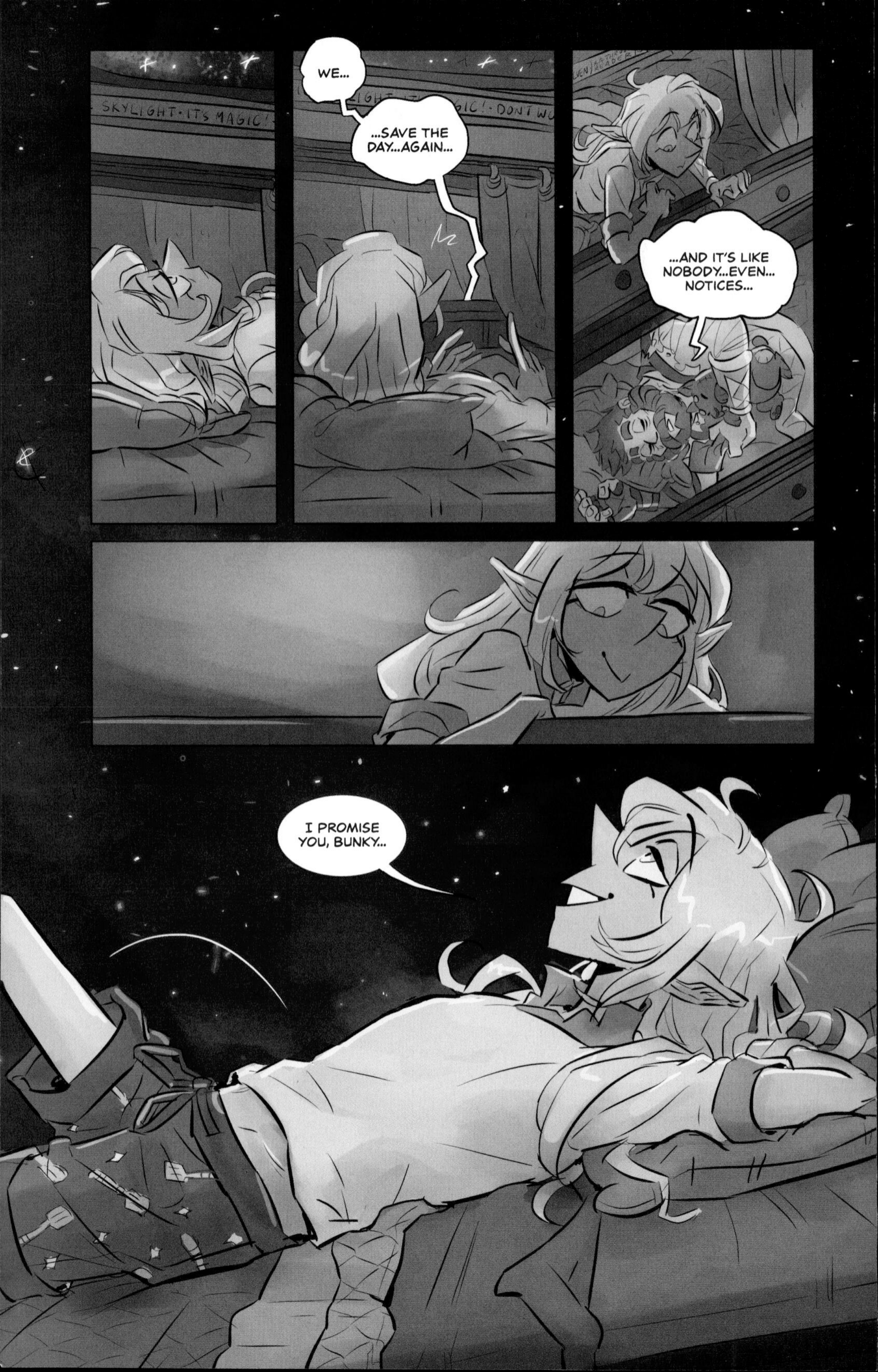
SKYLIGHT • IT'S MAGIC!
WE...
...SAVE THE DAY...AGAIN...
...AND IT'S LIKE NOBODY...EVEN... NOTICES...
I PROMISE YOU, BUNKY...

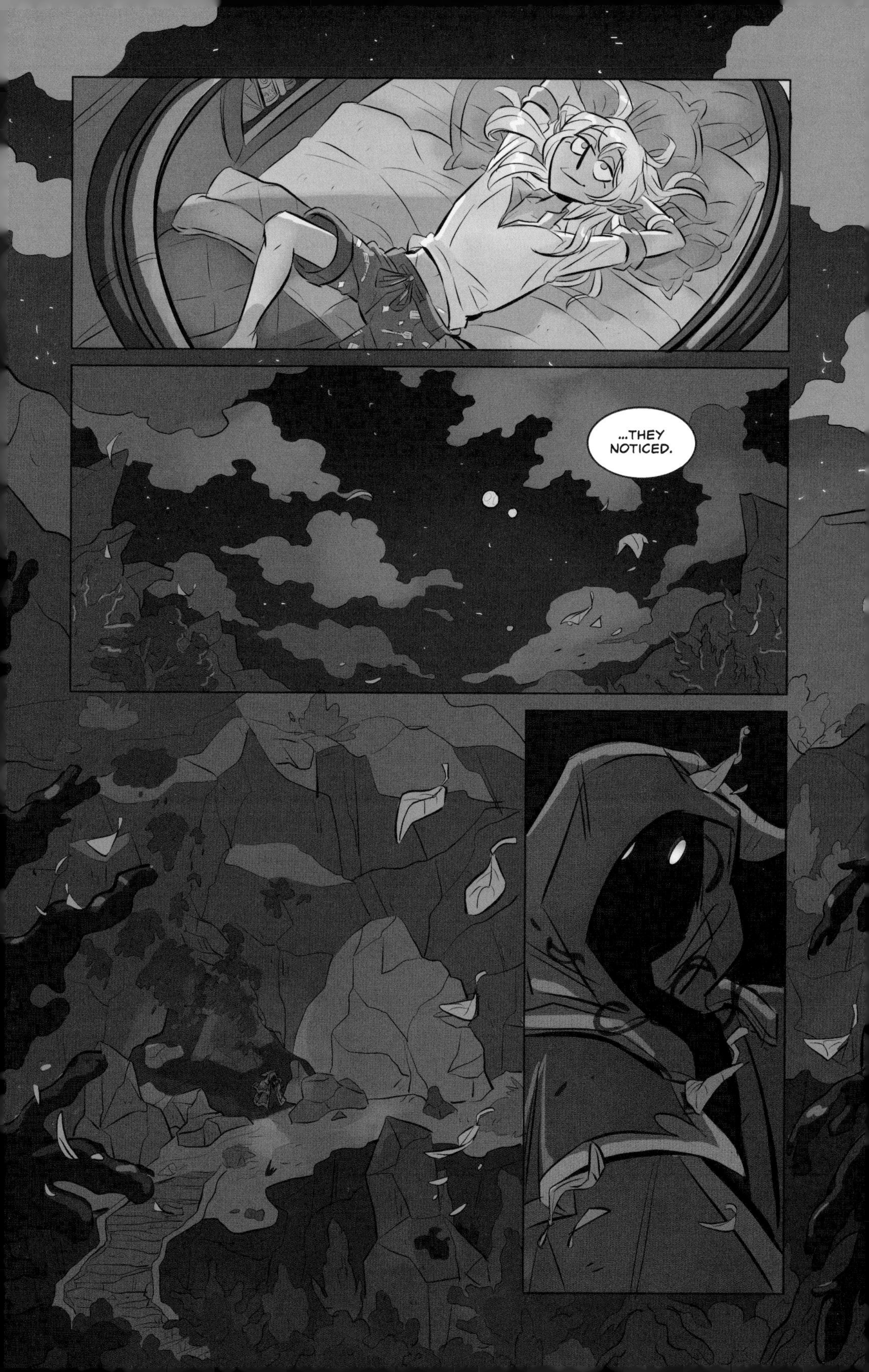
...THEY NOTICED.

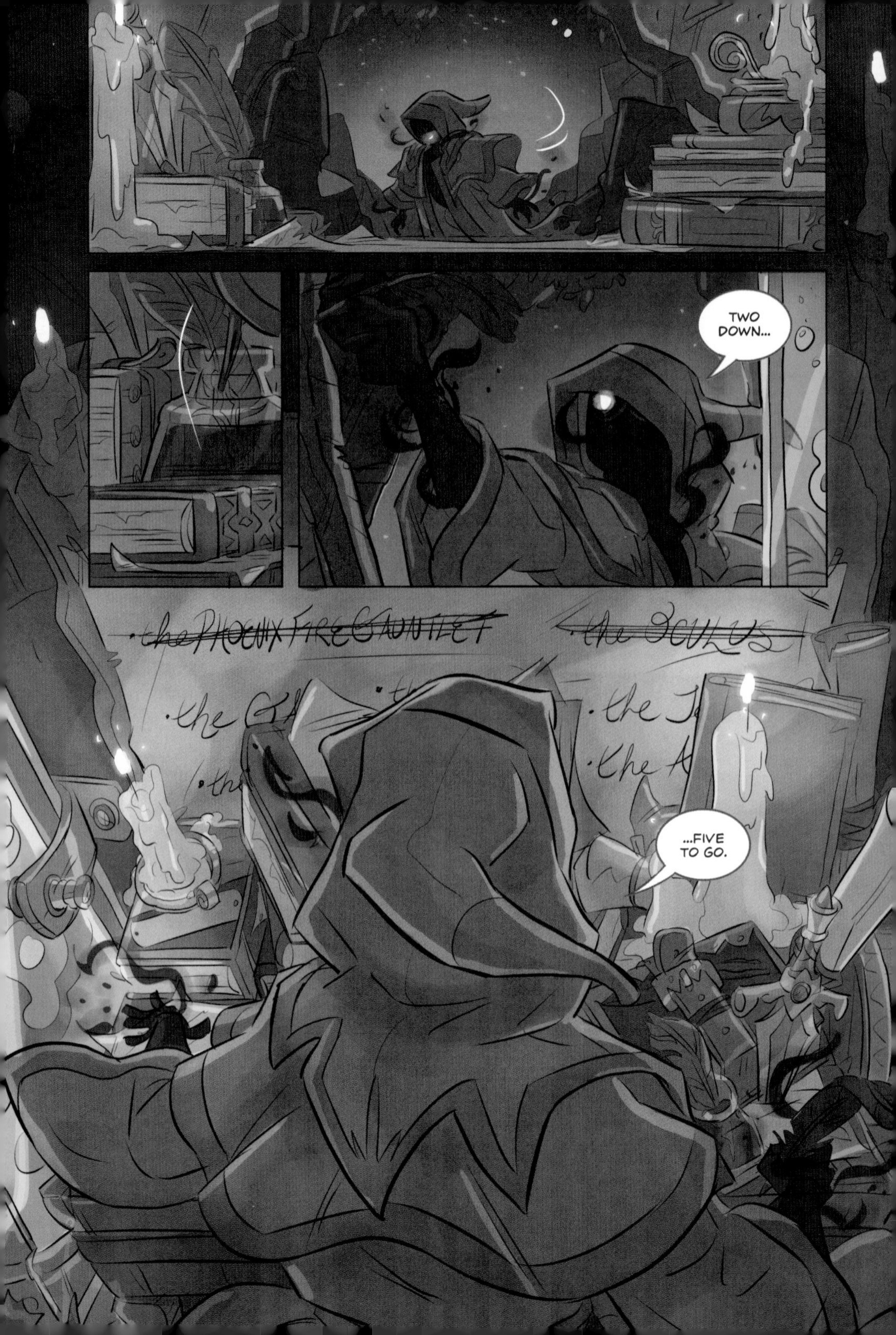
TWO DOWN...
the PHOENIX FIRE GAUNTLET
the OCULUS
...FIVE TO GO.

Fan Art Gallery

The *Adventure Zone* has been lucky enough to garner a passionate and deeply creative fandom. Many thanks to the fan artists who contributed pieces to this gallery—and to all the writers, artists, creators, and fans of all stripes who have made *The Adventure Zone* what it is.

The ADVENTURE CONTINUES in

Coming Soon!

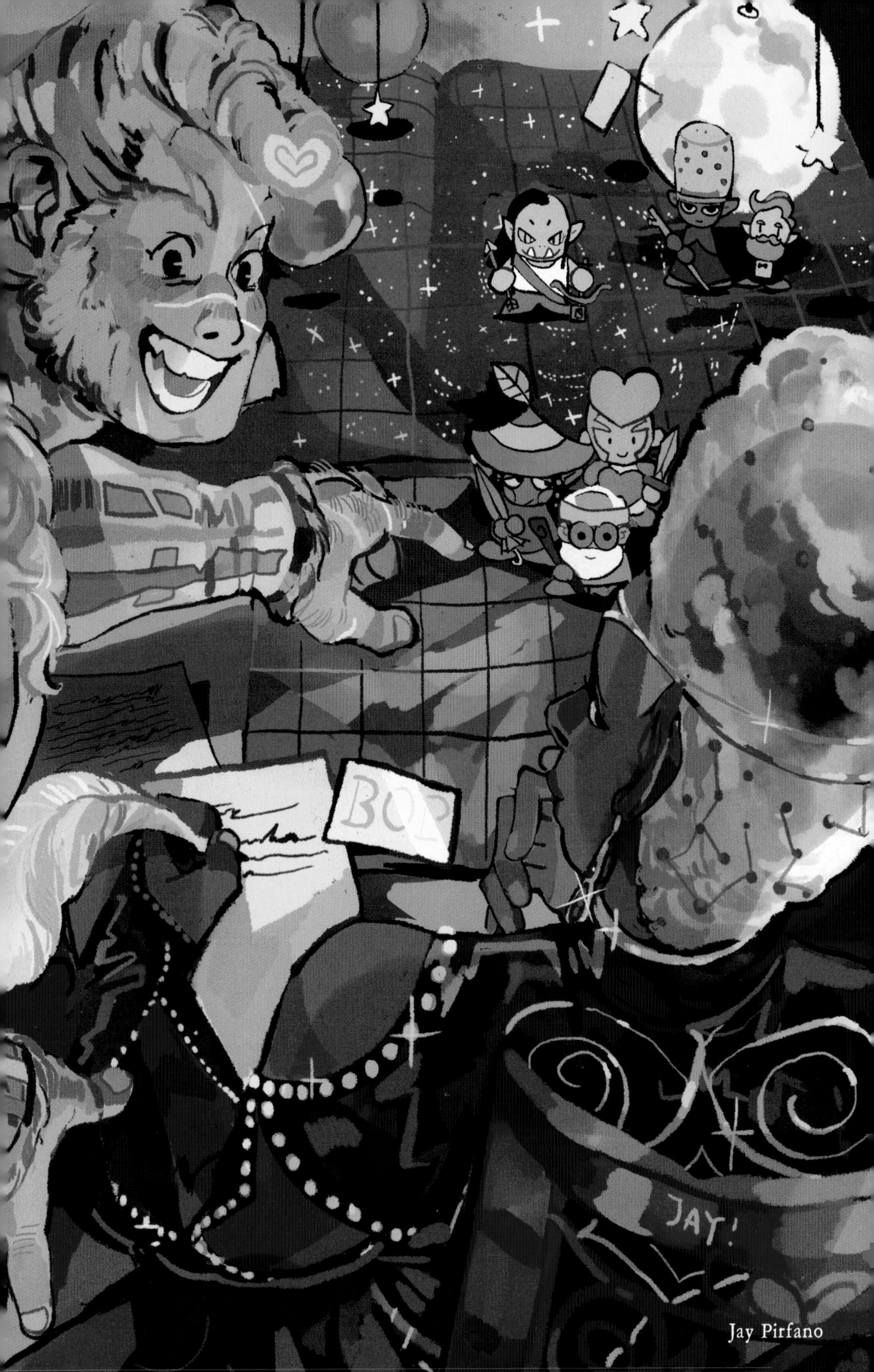
BOP
JAY!
Jay Pirfano

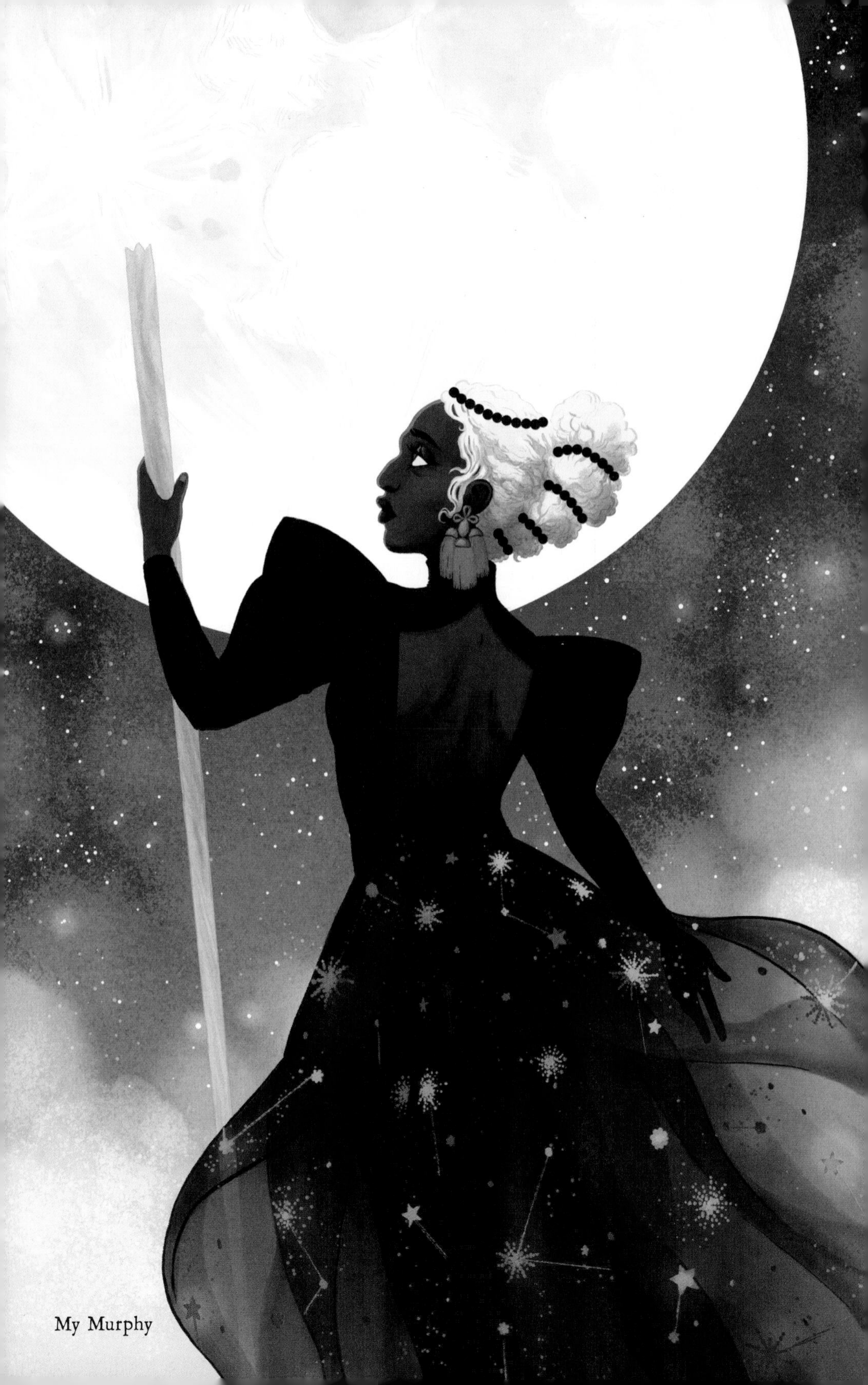

My Murphy

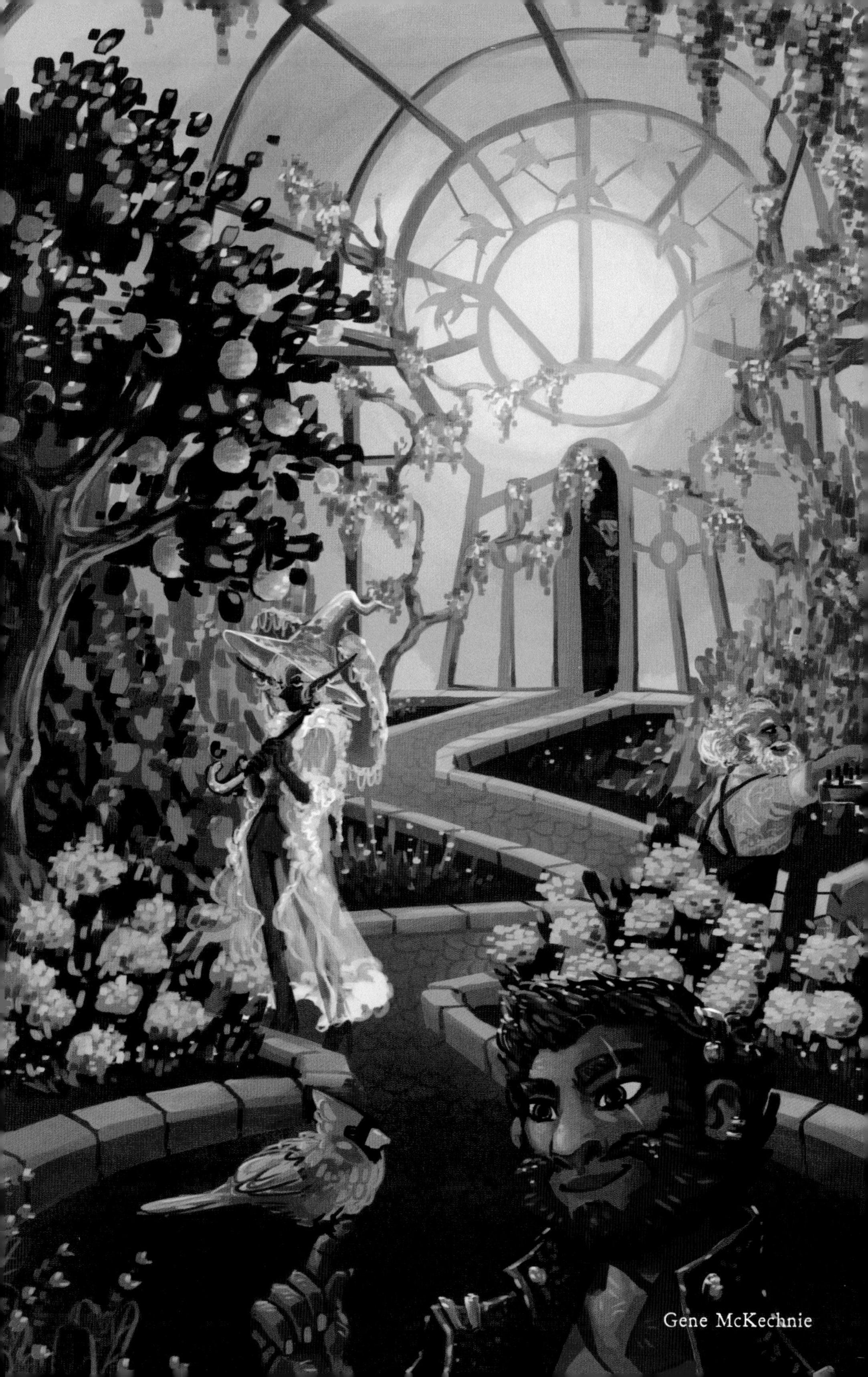

Gene McKechnie

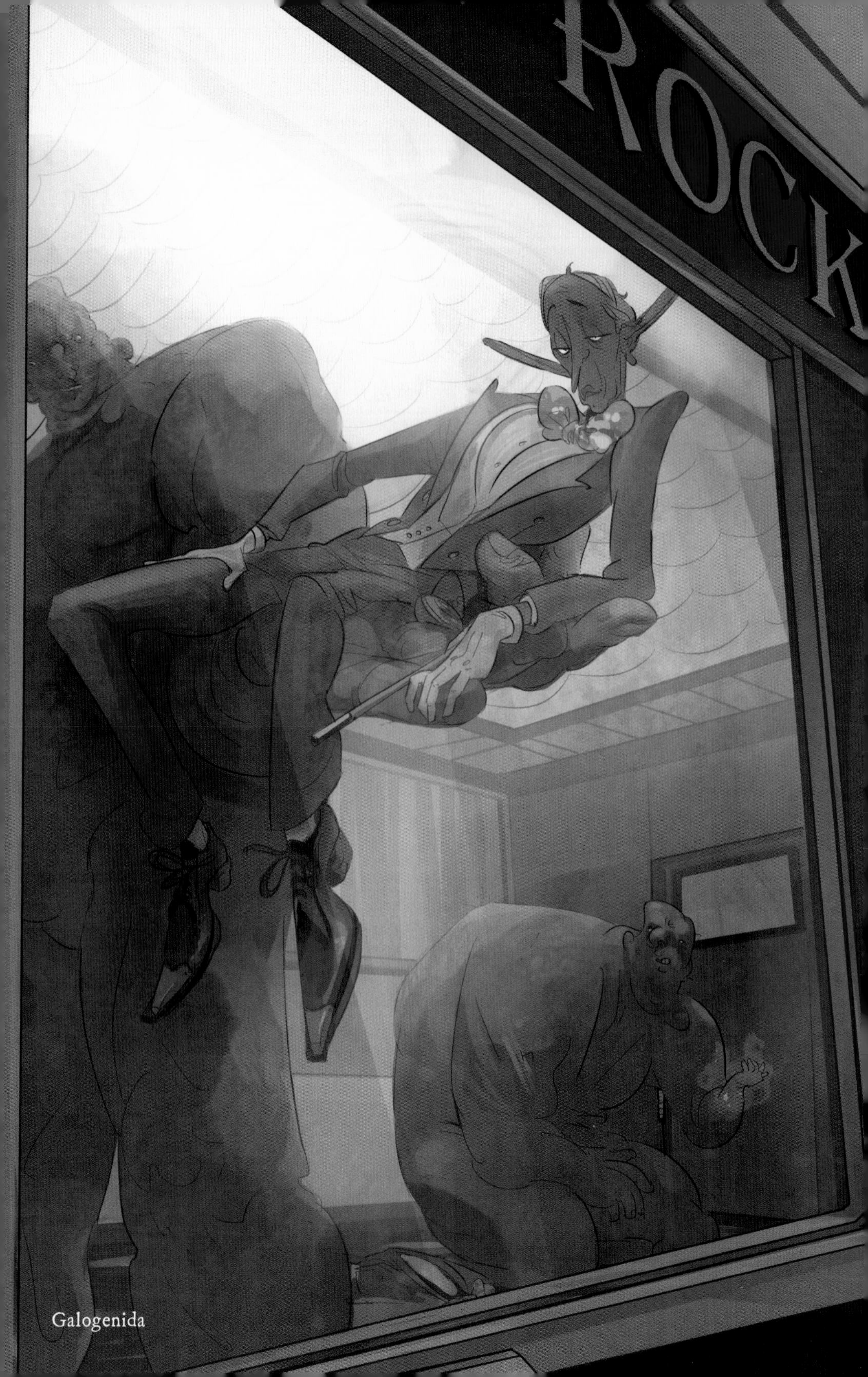
ROCK

Galogenida

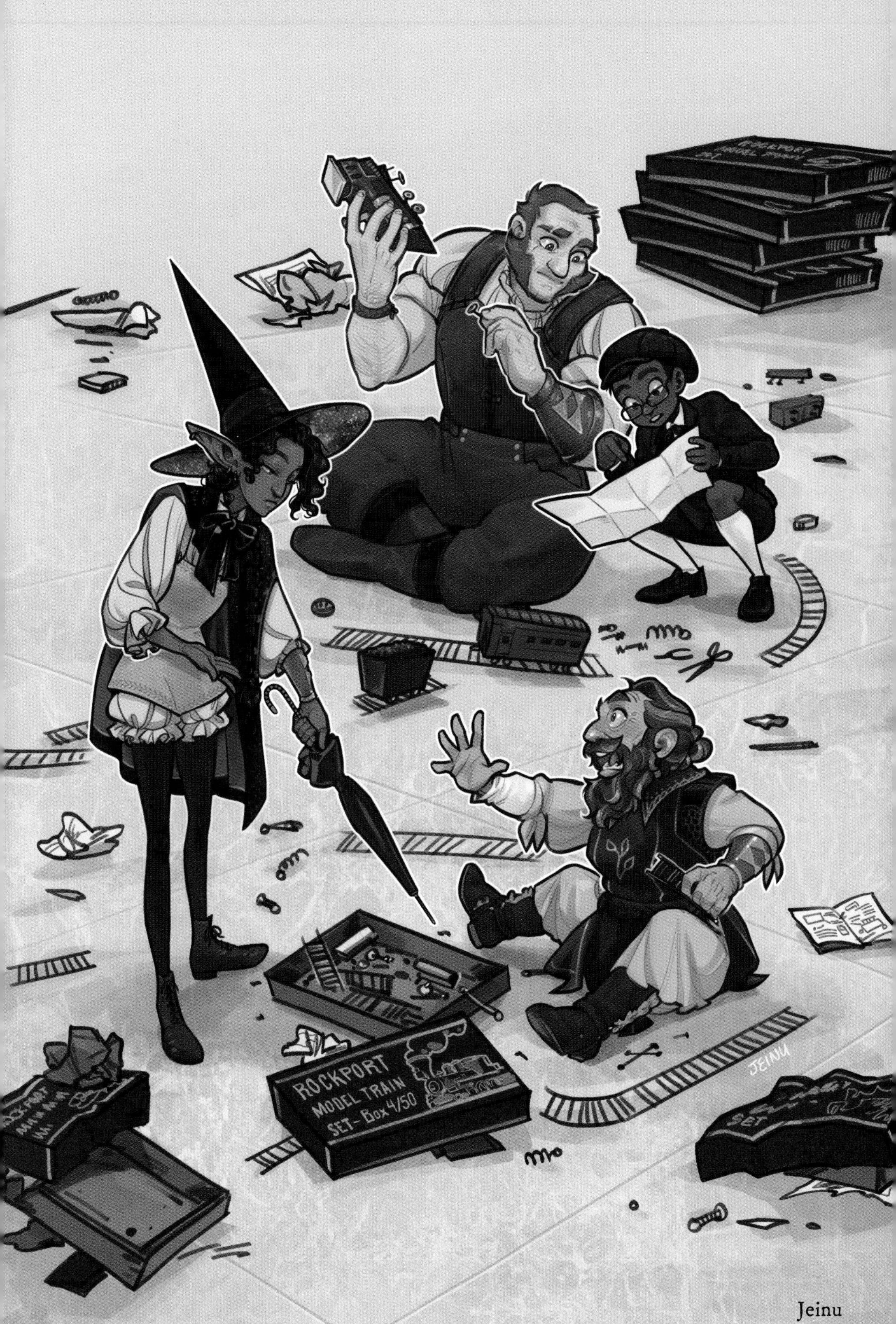
ROCKPORT
MODEL TRAIN
SET- Box 4/50
JEINU

Jeinu

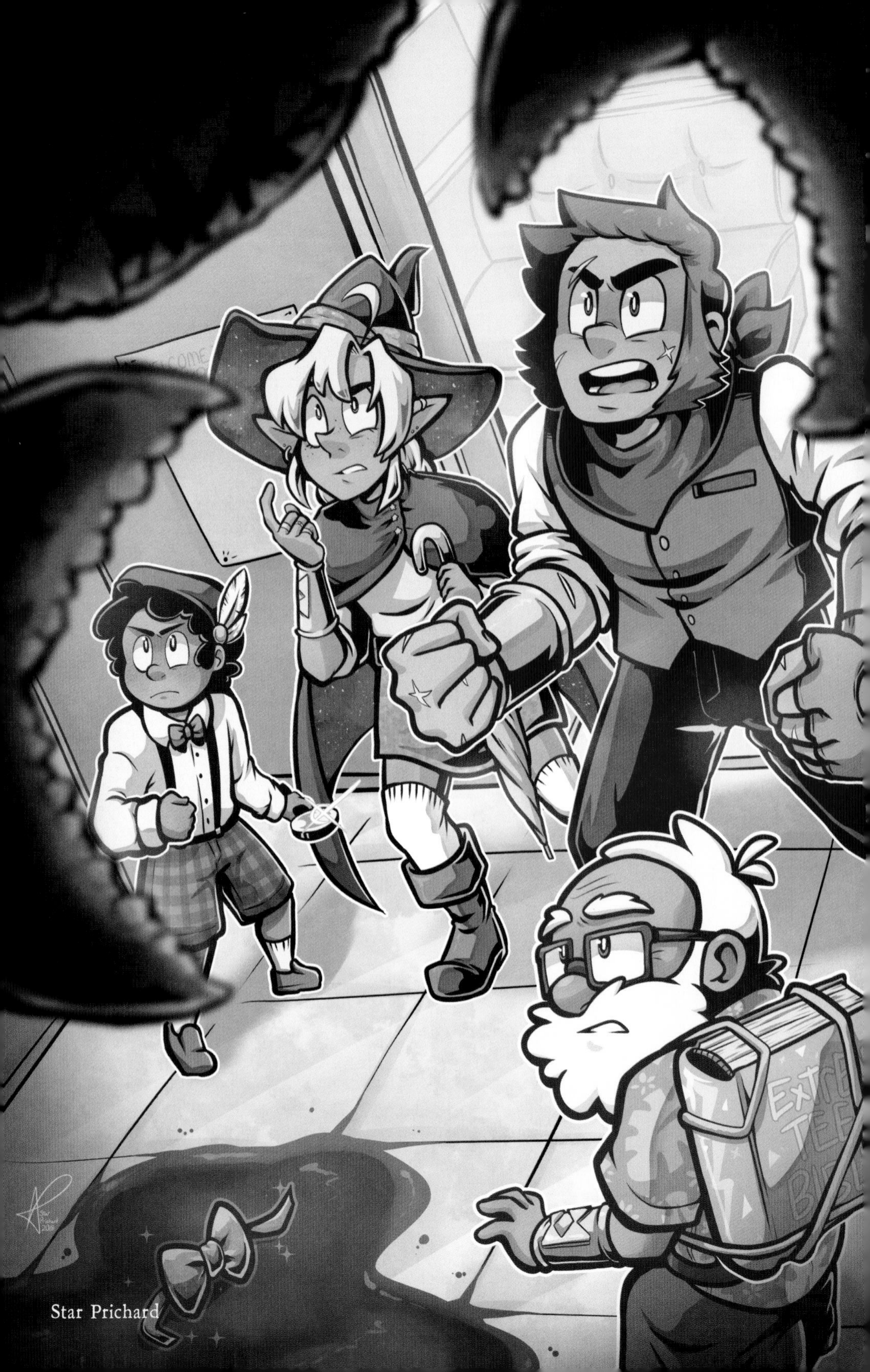

Star Prichard

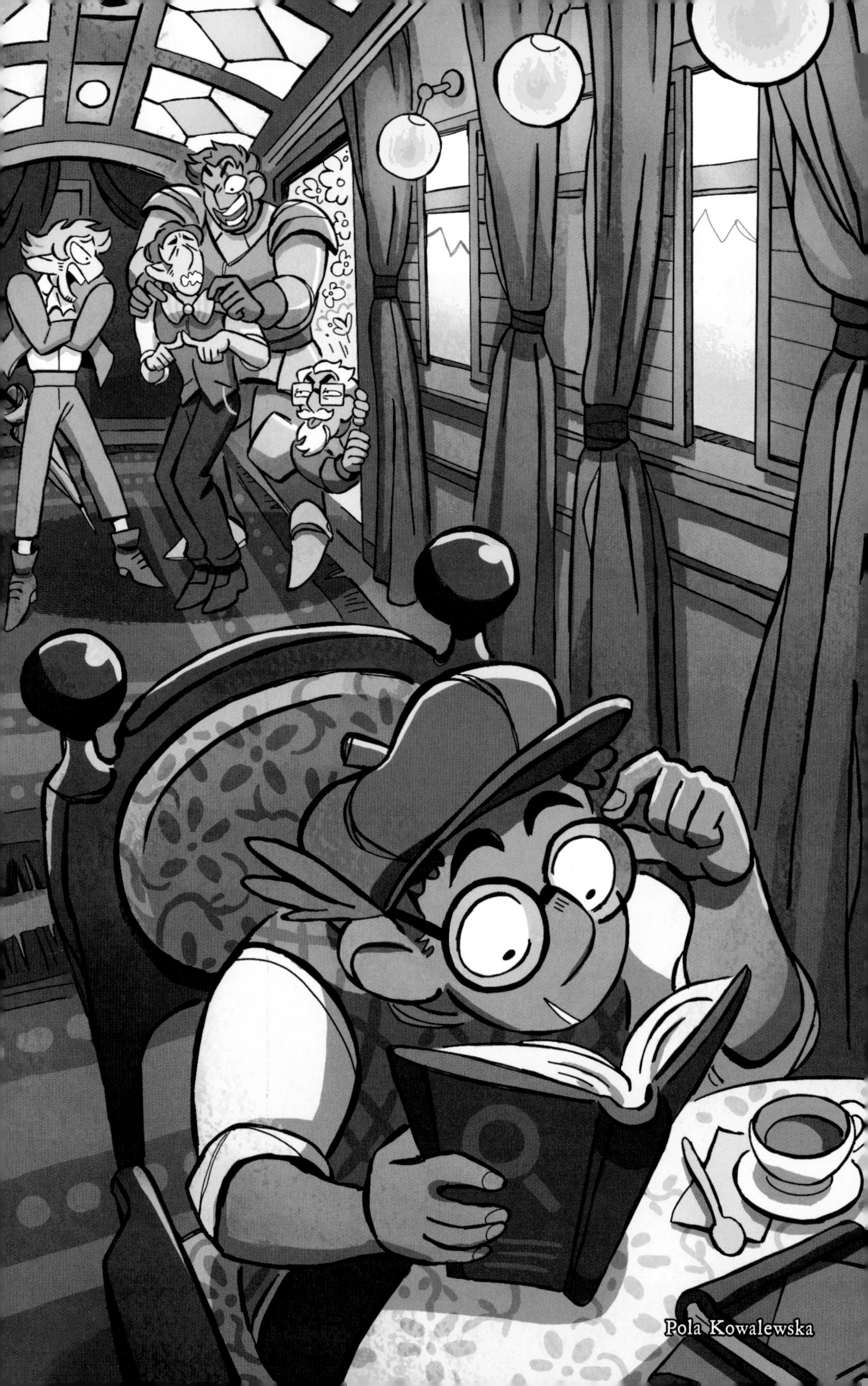
Pola Kowalewska

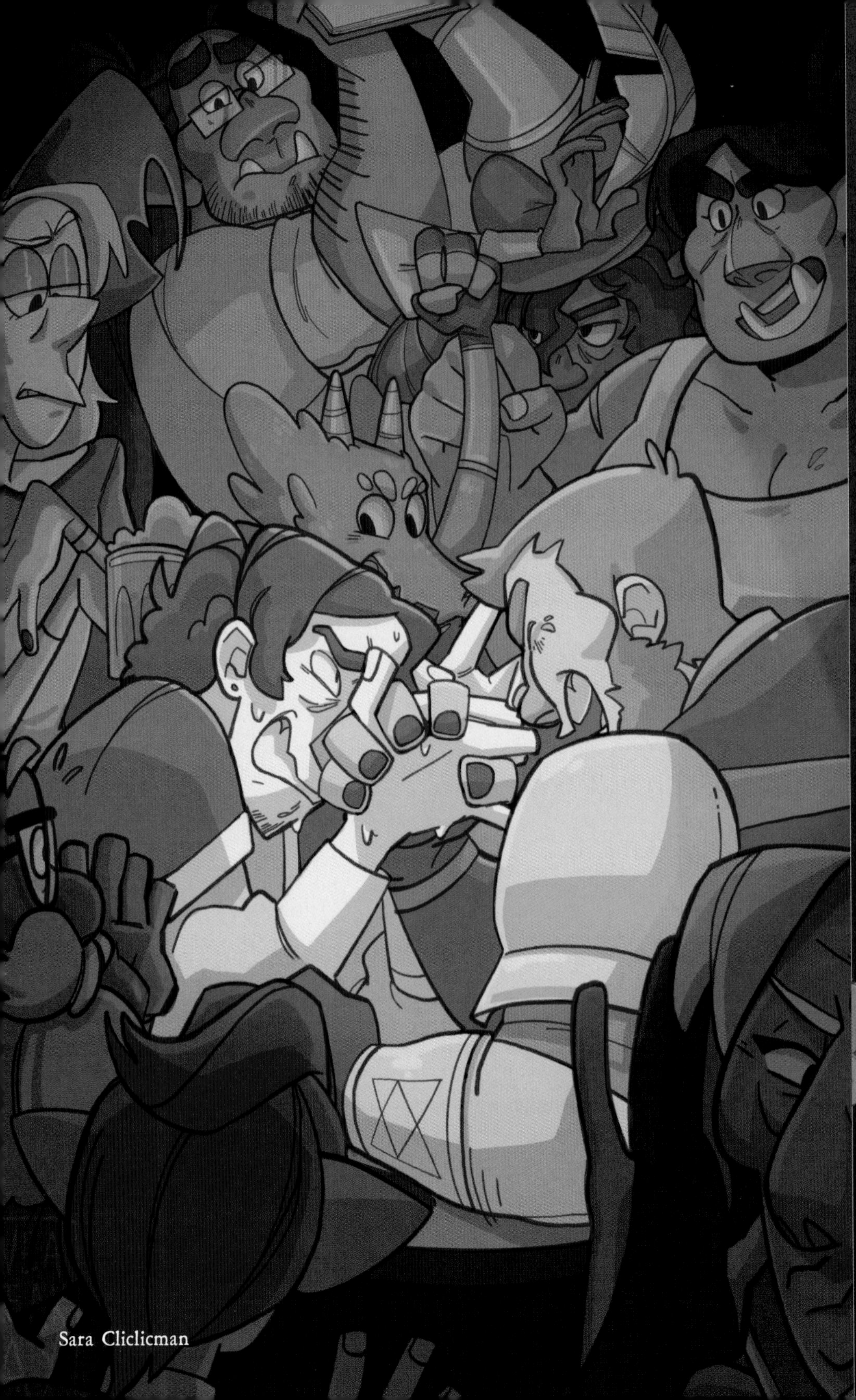

Sara Cliclicman

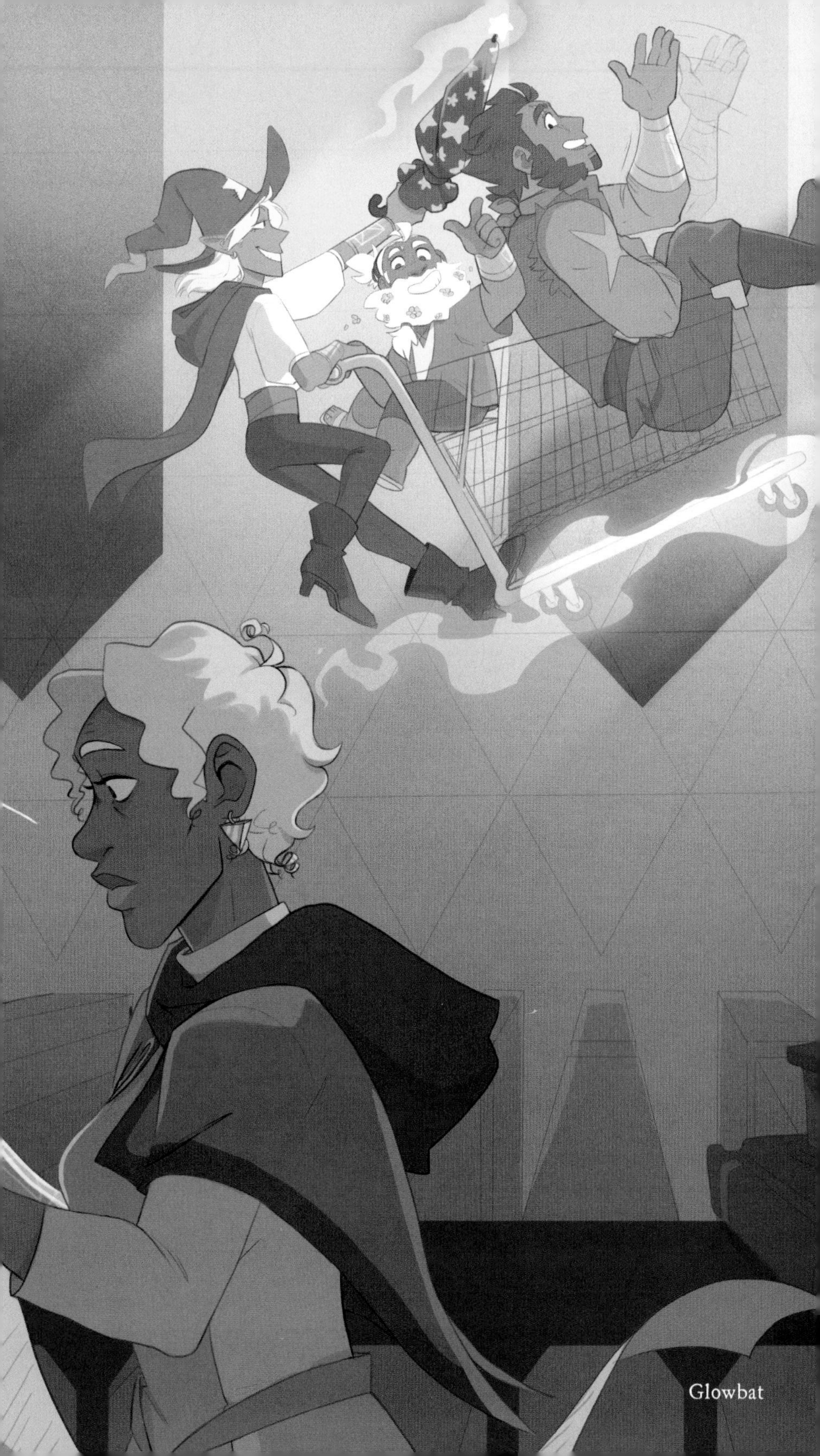
Glowbat

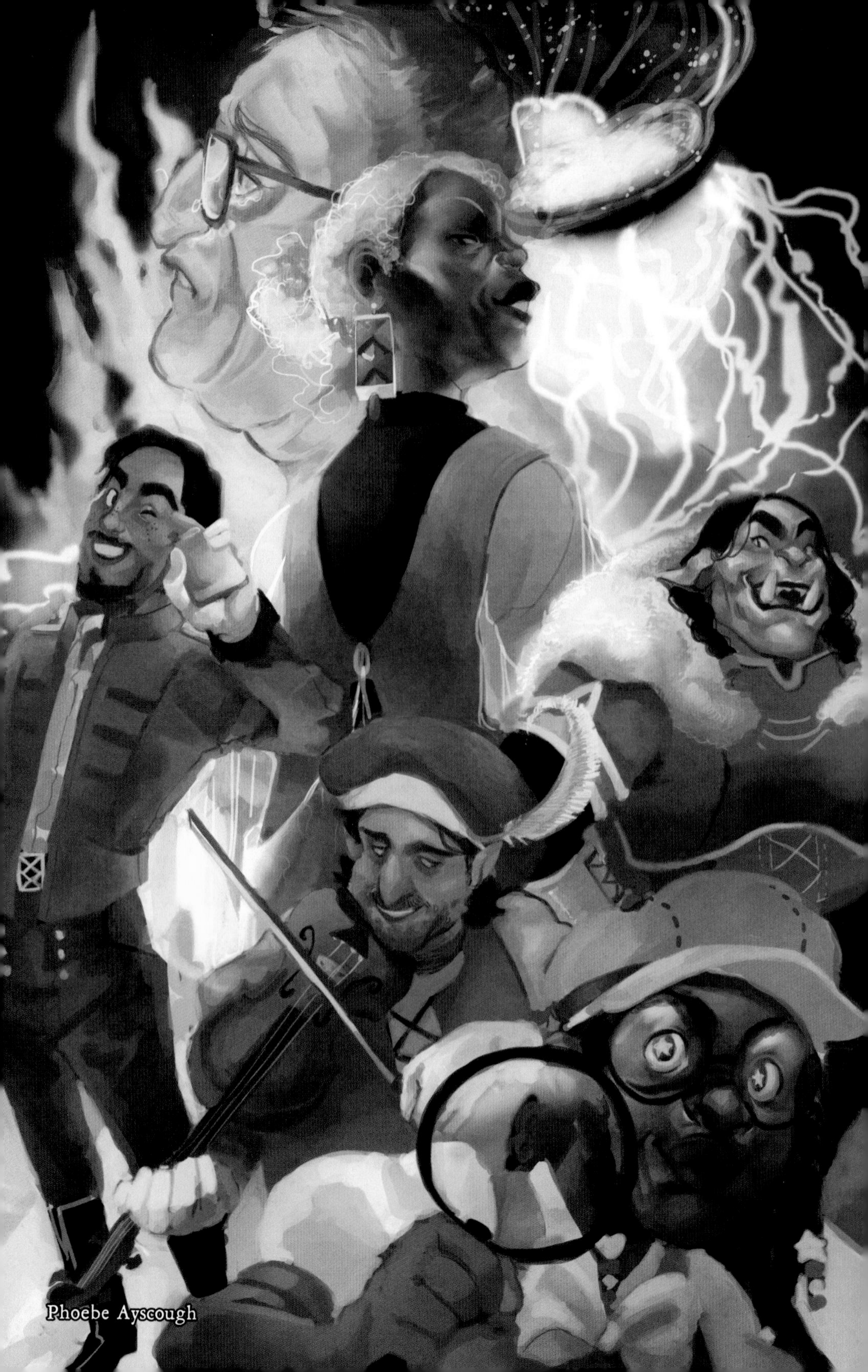
Phoebe Ayscough

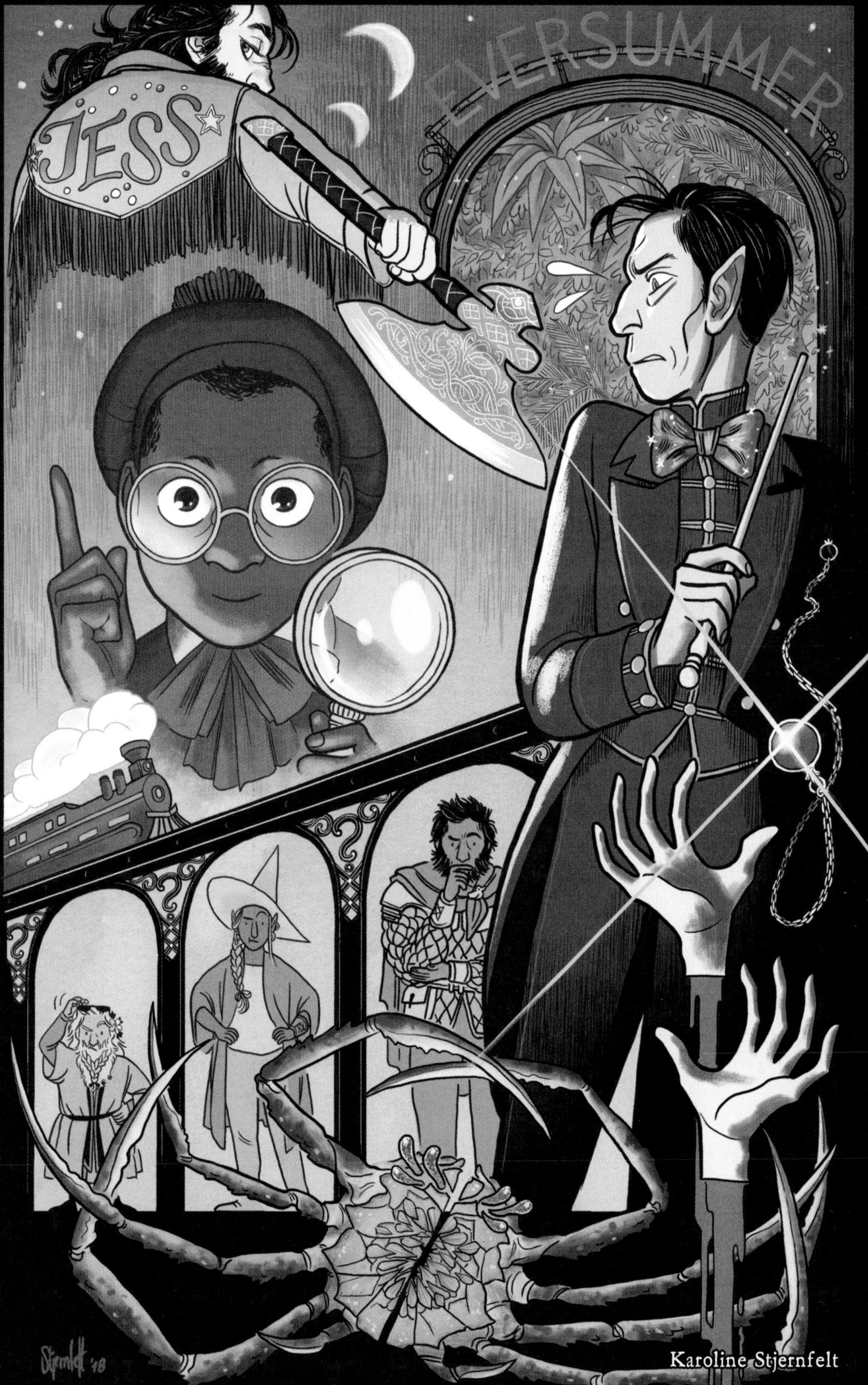
JESS
EVERSUMMER

Karoline Stjernfelt

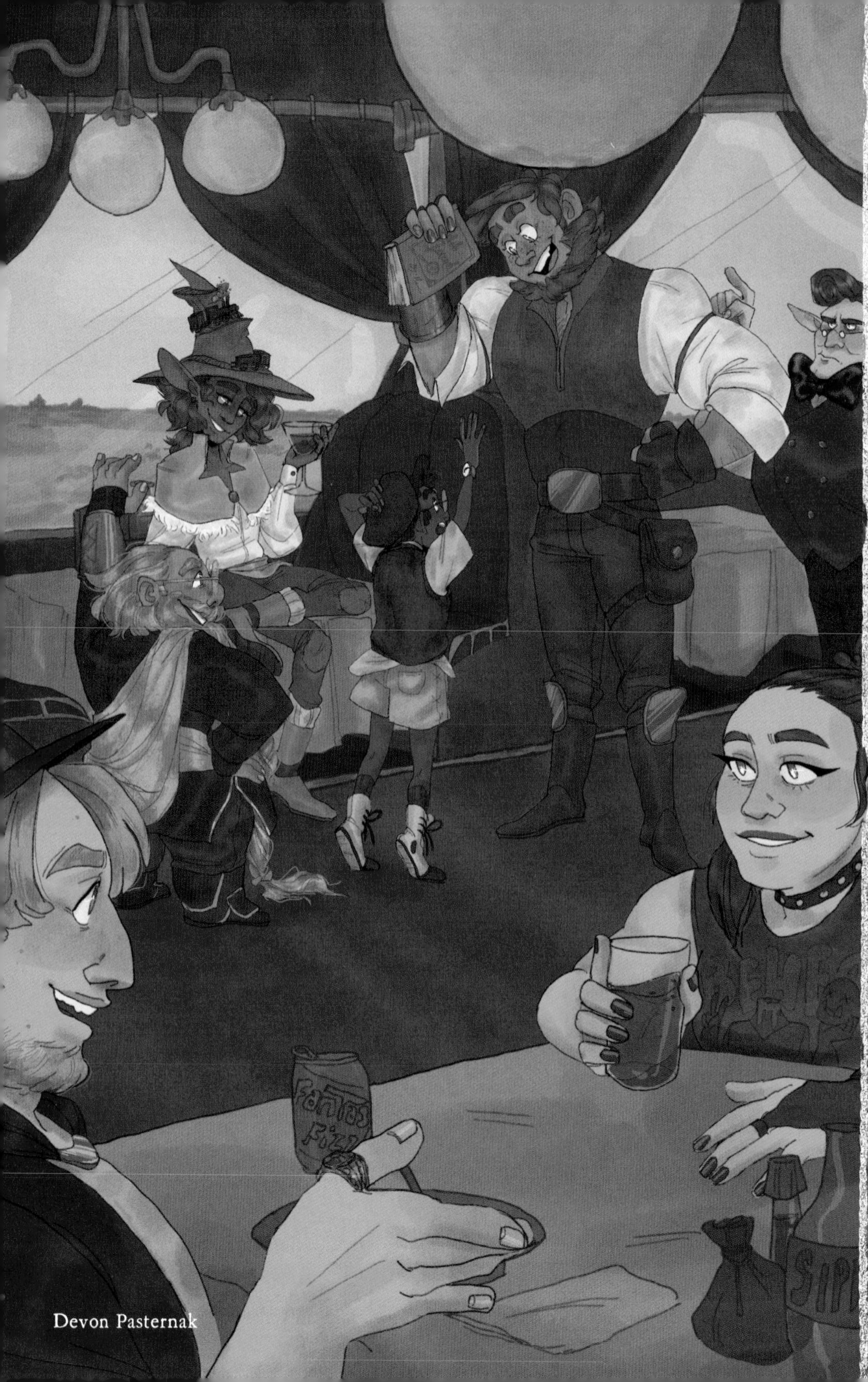
Fantas

Devon Pasternak

SEP 2019